HEAD**LIGHT**

1

Cornelsen

English G · Headlight · Band 1

Im Auftrag des Verlages herausgegeben von
Wolfgang Biederstädt, Köln

Konzepterarbeitung von
Susan Abbey, Nenagh, Irland
Wolfgang Biederstädt, Köln
Frank Donoghue, Nenagh, Irland

Erarbeitet von
Marc Proulx, Berlin
Susan Abbey, Nenagh, Irland
Frank Donoghue, Nenagh, Irland

unter Mitarbeit von
Joachim Blombach, Herford
Joachim Sauer, Rerik
Jennifer Seidl, München
Udo Wagner, Voerde

in Zusammenarbeit mit der Englischredaktion
Klaus Unger (Projektleitung); Jutta Seuren
(koordinierende Redakteurin); Britta Bensmann
(Bildredaktion); Doreen Arnold; Kirsten Bleck;
Cornelia Frisse; Irja Fröhling; Dr. Eva Grabowski;
Undine Griebel; Olivia Gruver; Solveig Heinrich;
Mara Leibowitz; Kathrin Spiegelberg; Uwe Tröger
sowie Eva Baumgart und Christine Maxwell

Anhang
Ingrid Raspe, Düsseldorf

Beratende Mitwirkung
Simone Beattie, Aalen; Eugen Blumenstock, Loßburg;
Peer Brändel, Gütersloh; Uwe Chormann, Einselthum;
Matthew George, Frankfurt a. M.; Bernhard Hunger,
Dettingen; Anke Husmann-Niemann, Osnabrück;
Ulrike Rath, Aachen; Mirjam Schrade, Stuttgart;
Udo Wagner, Voerde

Illustrationen
Steffen Wolff, Brohl-Lützing sowie Carlos Borrell,
Berlin; Christian Görke, Berlin; Jeongsook Lee,
Heidelberg; David Norman, Meerbusch; Elwood H.
Smith, Rhinebeck, USA

Fotos
Trevor Burrows Photography, Plymouth

Layoutkonzept und technische Umsetzung
Klein & Halm Grafikdesign, Berlin

Umschlaggestaltung
Cornelsen Schulverlage Design unter Verwendung
der Entwürfe von Klein & Halm Grafikdesign, Berlin
und kleiner & bold, Berlin

Für die freundliche Unterstützung danken wir dem
Eggbuckland Community College, Plymouth.

www.cornelsen.de

Druck: Livonia Print, Riga

1. Auflage, 6. Druck 2024
ISBN 978-3-06-032600-6 – broschiert

1. Auflage, 8. Druck 2024
ISBN 978-3-06-032601-3 – gebunden

ISBN 978-3-06-033599-2 – E-Book

PEFC zertifiziert
Dieses Produkt stammt aus nachhaltig
bewirtschafteten Wäldern und kontrollierten
Quellen.

PEFC
PEFC/12-31-006

www.pefc.de

Dein Englischbuch enthält folgende Teile:

Unit 1 bis 6	Die sechs Kapitel des Buches
Diff-Bank	Weitere Aufgaben – unterschiedlich schwer
Wordbank	Zusätzliche Wörter zu bestimmten Themen
Text file TF	Interessante Texte, passend zu den Units
Skills file SF	Beschreibung wichtiger Lern- und Arbeitstechniken
Language file LF	Zusammenfassung wichtiger Sprachregeln
Vocabulary	Wörterverzeichnis zum Lernen der neuen Wörter
Dictionary	Alphabetisches Wörterverzeichnis zum Nachschlagen (*English-German* und *German-English*)

Die Units bestehen aus diesen Teilen:

Lead-in	Einstieg in die neue Unit
Theme 1 / Theme 2	Neue Themen mit vielen Aktivitäten und Übungen
Focus on language	Texte und Aufgaben zum Entdecken von Regeln und Üben wichtiger Strukturen
Story	Eine Geschichte zum Lesen
Skills training	Hören – Lesen – Sprechen – Schreiben – Sprachmittlung – Viewing
STOP! CHECK! GO!	Üben, Vertiefen, Lernfortschritt feststellen

In den Units findest du diese Symbole:

👥 👥👥	Partnerarbeit / Gruppenarbeit
🎧 🎧	nur auf CD / auf CD und im Schülerbuch
🎥	Filme auf der DVD
MK	Aufgaben zur Schulung von Medienkompetenz
○ ●	leichtere Übungen/schwierigere Übungen
○ //●	Bei dieser Aufgabe gibt es eine leichte Variante in der Unit und eine schwierigere in der Diff-Bank.
More help p.125	Hilfen zu einer Aufgabe in der Diff-Bank
More practice 1 p.123	Weitere Übungen in der Diff-Bank

INHALT

Nice to meet you!

Unit 1 · Welcome to our school

Unit 2 · At home with Ellie

Unit 3 · My Plymouth

INHALT

Unit 4 · Berry's world

Unit 5 · All about Adam

Unit 6 · School is out – for summer

Anhang

L	Listening
R	Reading
S	Speaking
W	Writing
M	Mediation
I	Intercultural competence
V	Viewing
ST	Study skill
*	Fakultativ

Die Angebote des Schüler-
buches sind nicht obliga-
torisch abzuarbeiten.
Die Auswahl der Übungen
und Übungsteile richtet sich
nach den Schwerpunkten
des schulinternen Curriculums.

Nice to meet you!

(Speech bubbles in the illustration:)

Hi, nice to meet you! I'm Cyril the crab. What's your name?

I'm four. How old are you?

I'm from Plymouth in England. Where are you from?

1 Meet Cyril

🎧 **a)** Listen.

🎧 **b)** Repeat.

🎧 **c)** Listen and answer Cyril's questions.

Hi, I'm Sabina.

I'm ten.

I'm from Leimen in Germany.

2 👥 Meet your class

Walk around: Talk to different partners.

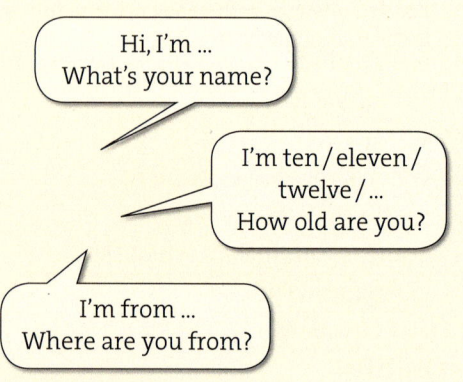

Hi, I'm … What's your name?

I'm ten / eleven / twelve / … How old are you?

I'm from … Where are you from?

3 GAME I can see …

a) Say what you can see in the picture. Find eight things.

b) 👥 Play the game.

I can see Cyril.

I can see Cyril and a beach.

I can see Cyril and a beach and …

🎧 **4 Cyril's song**

Listen to Cyril's song. Sing and act the chorus.

CYRIL'S SONG

I'm Cyril the crab
And I like the sea.
I love water
All around me.

Chorus:
I run and I hide,
I dive in the sand.
Don't pick me up
Or I'll pinch your hand.

I love the beach
And sandcastles too.
I like playing football.
What about you?

Chorus

Ice cream and orange juice,
Picnics in the sun.
Boats and surfboards,
The beach is great fun.

Chorus

I'm going to Plymouth,
You can come too.
We can be friends,
Nice to meet you!

Chorus

My favourite colours

1 Places and colours
Match Ellie's words (A–C) with pictures 2–4.

A I love the aquarium … and I love fish. •
B Hoe Park is great! • C Look at all the sweets!

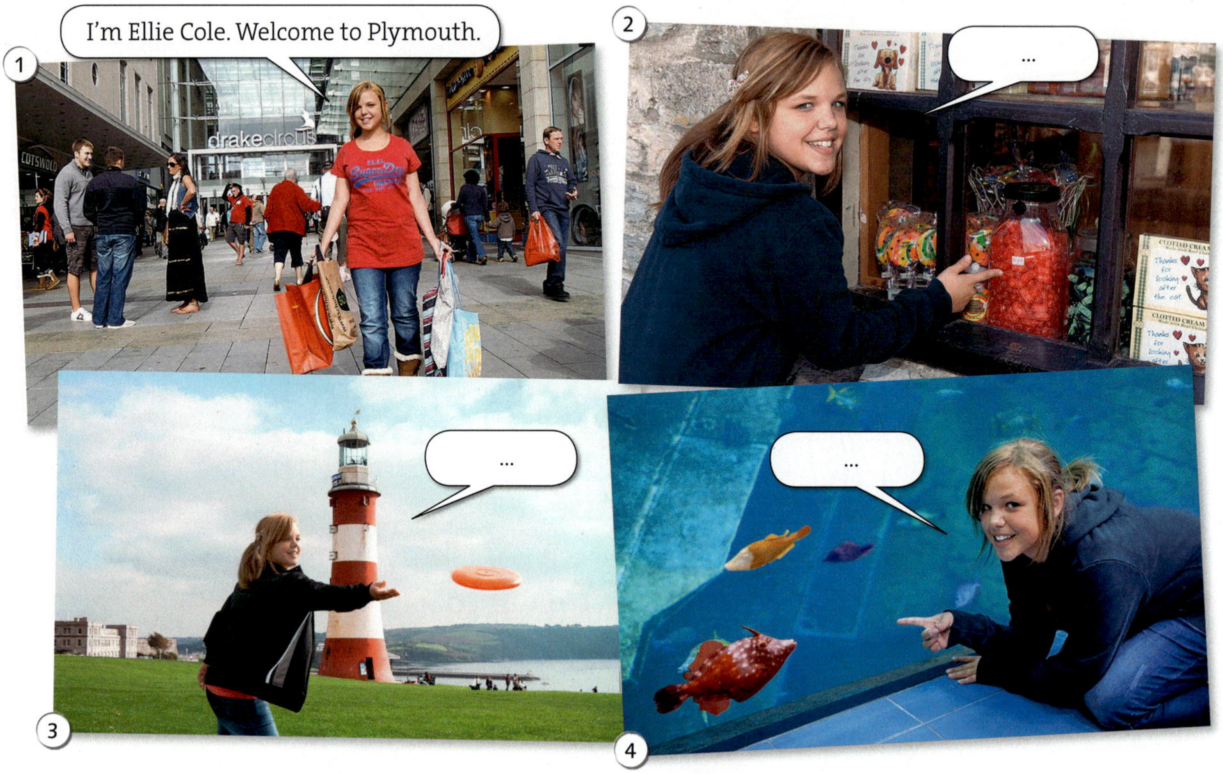

I'm Ellie Cole. Welcome to Plymouth.

…

…

…

2 Colours in Plymouth
a) What colours can you see in the photos?

green red yellow brown

black blue purple grey

white pink orange

b) Make colour cards.

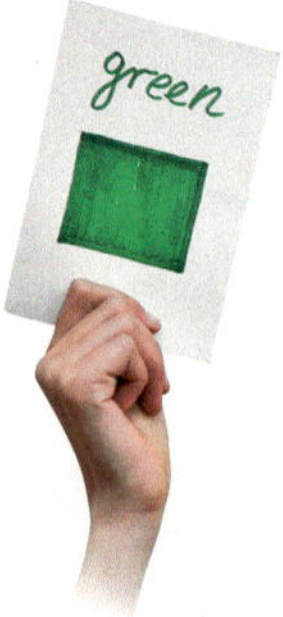

🎧 **c)** Listen to Ellie.
What colours can you hear?

green

d) Listen again. Ellie says:
– I like …
– I don't like …
– My favourite colour is …

3 Your favourite colour
a) 👥 Walk around:
Talk to three
different partners.
Make notes.

Name	Favourite colour
Anna	blue
Ben	…
…	…

Hi, Anna. What's your
favourite colour?

I like blue. What
about you?

b) 👥 Tell a new partner.
– Anna's favourite colour is blue.
– Ben's favourite colour is red.

My favourite sports and hobbies

I'm Adam Osmanovic. I like football and music. And I like watching TV too.

dancing • football •
playing games •
reading books • riding •
skateboarding •
swimming •
watching TV

1 What are the sports and hobbies?

a) Write the names of the eight sports and hobbies: *1 football, 2 ..., ...*

b) 👥 Now check with your partner.
Photo number 1 is ...

2 What about you?

a) Find the names of your favourite sports and hobbies. ▸ *Wordbank 1, p. 184*

b) 👥 Walk around: Talk to three different partners.

I like ... What about you?

I like ... too.

My favourite hobby is ...

I don't like ..., but I like ...

My favourite sport is ...

3 A sports and hobbies poster

Make a big class poster. Write labels.

Favourite sports and hobbies in our class

Cycling is cool.

I love chess.

Drawing is fun.

▸ *Workbook 3–4, pp. 3–4*

My favourite animals

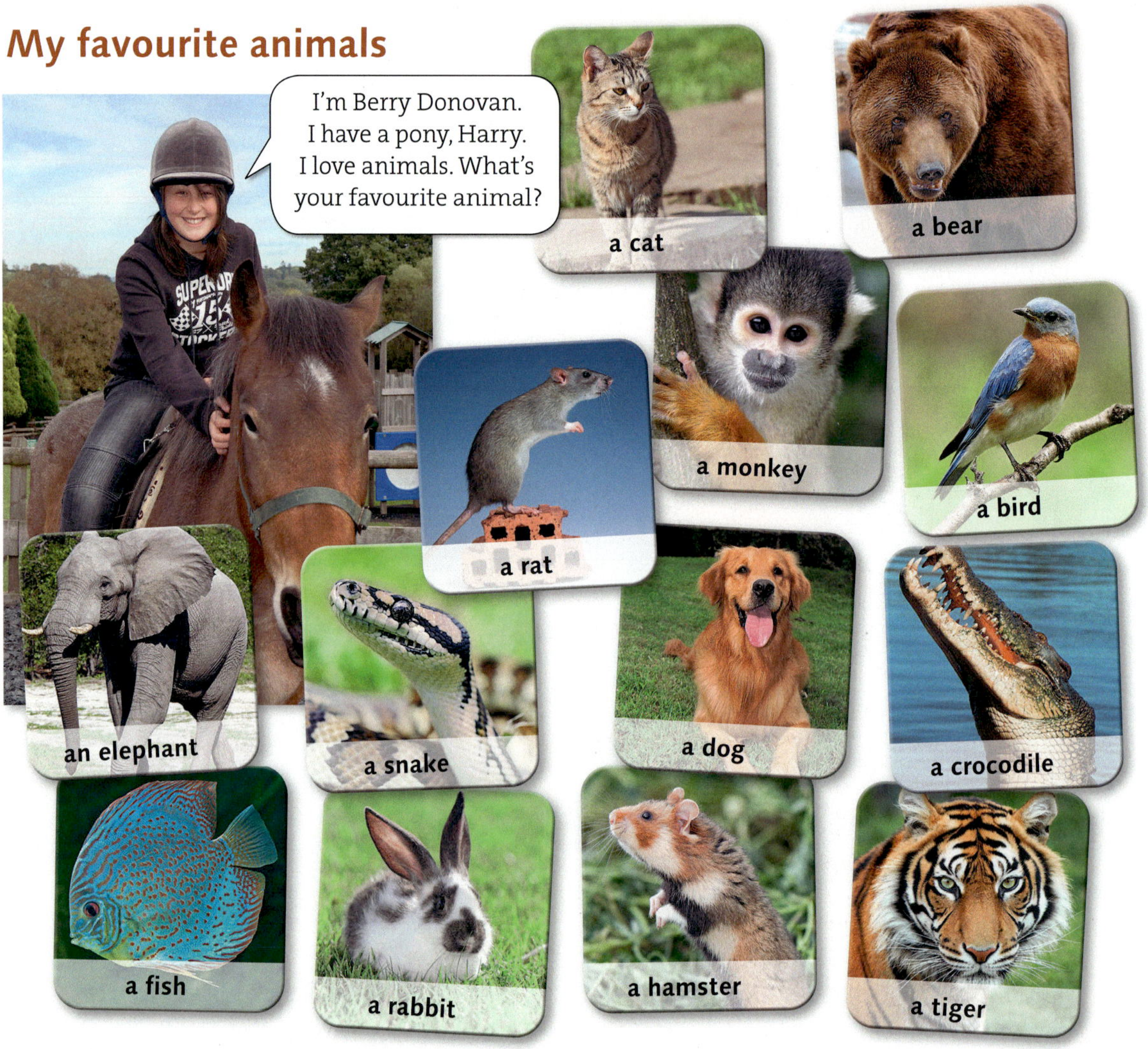
a cat
a bear
I'm Berry Donovan. I have a pony, Harry. I love animals. What's your favourite animal?
a monkey
a bird
a rat
an elephant
a snake
a dog
a crocodile
a fish
a rabbit
a hamster
a tiger

1 Can you remember?

a) Look at the animals for one minute. Then close your book. How many animals can you and your partner remember?

b) Pets or wild animals? Make a table. Add more animals.

pets	wild animals
pony	...

2 Favourite animals

Talk to a partner about your favourite animals.

A: What's your favourite pet / wild animal?

B: My favourite pet / wild animal is a(n) ...

3 The animal quiz

Listen to the school class and play the animal quiz. Write your answers.

1. t
2.
3.

► Workbook 5, p. 4

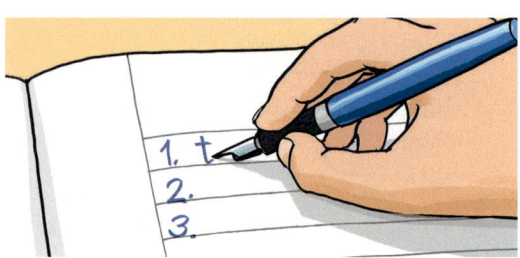

My favourite thing

1 Luca's favourite thing

a) What's Luca's favourite thing?

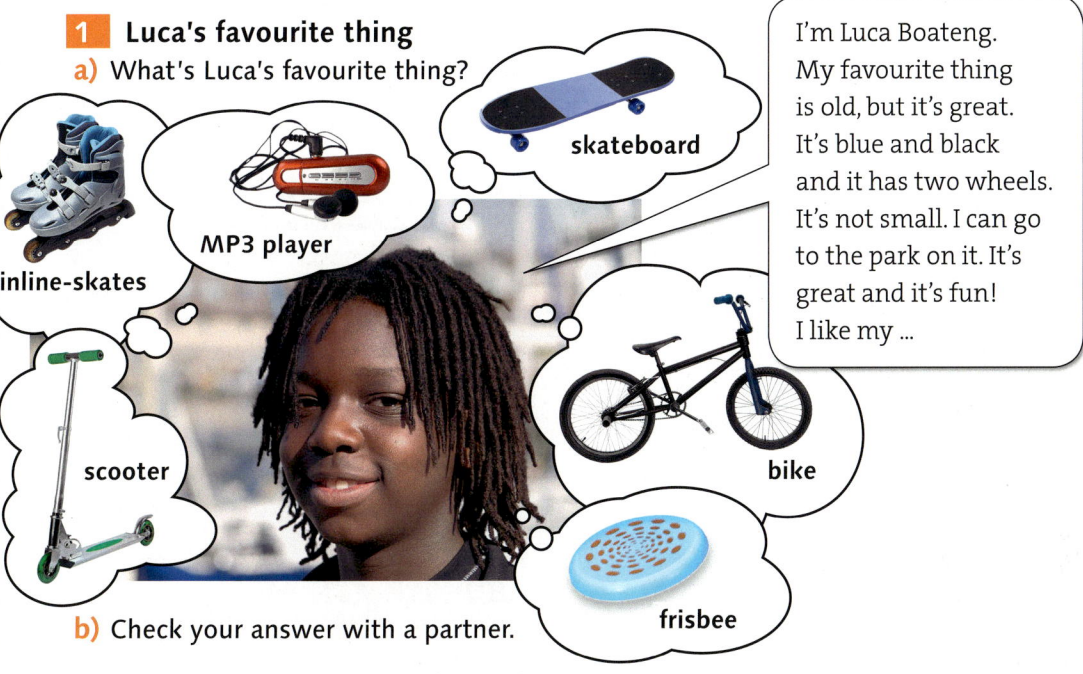

skateboard

inline-skates

MP3 player

scooter

bike

frisbee

I'm Luca Boateng. My favourite thing is old, but it's great. It's blue and black and it has two wheels. It's not small. I can go to the park on it. It's great and it's fun! I like my ...

b) Check your answer with a partner.

2 Your favourite thing

a) What's your favourite thing?

b) Write about your favourite thing.

> It's old / new / ...
> It's red / green / black / ...
> It's big / small / ...
> It has a camera / ...
> I can go to ... on / with it.
> I can listen to music / play games / talk on it.
> It's great / cool / nice / fun / ...

c) Practise your text. Ask the class about your favourite thing.

It's ...
It has ...
I can ...
What's my favourite thing?

▶ *Wordbank 2, p. 185*

The last day of the holidays

1 **A story**

a) Look at the pictures on this page. Who can you see?

b) Listen to part one of the story. Put the pictures in the right order. Check with a partner.

c) Listen to part two of the story. Put the pictures in the right order. Then check with a partner.

The last day of the holidays – yippee!

2   A chant
Listen and repeat.

Holidays are great,
Holidays are fun!
No more work or school for me,
Just sitting in the sun.

The holidays are over,
The holidays are done.
No more sitting on the beach,
No more summer fun!

Welcome to our school

A

B

1 School sights

What can you see in pictures A–D?

In picture ... I can see ... / One student has a ... in picture ...

🎧 2 School sounds

Listen. What can you hear? Point at the right pictures.

 a bike

boys and girls

 a teacher

 a bird

 a car

 a mobile phone

 a dog

 a football

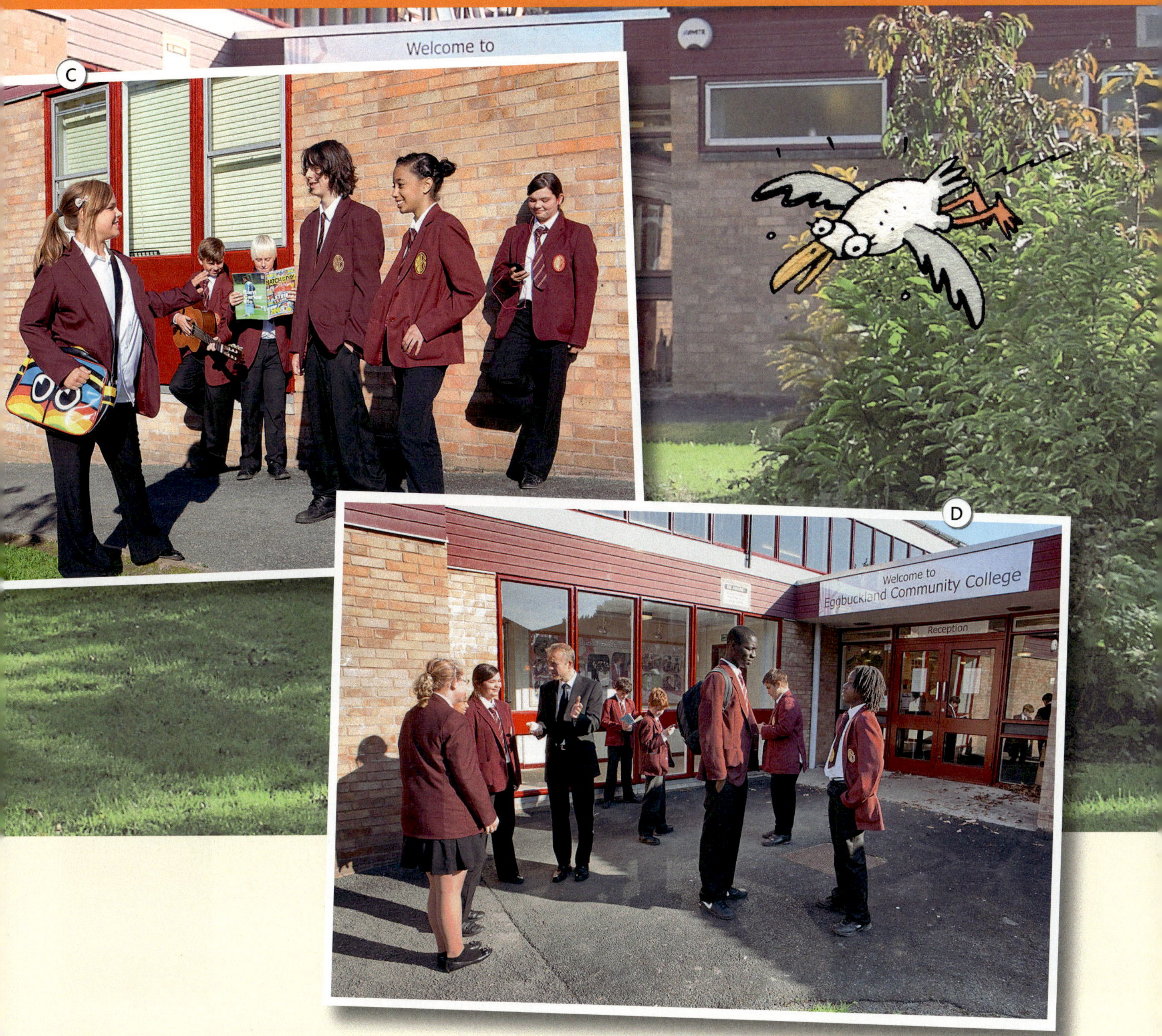
Welcome to
C
D
Welcome to
Eggbuckland Community College
Reception

3 The first morning

a) Listen. Put the pictures (A–D) in the right order.

b) Listen to the people and repeat.

c) Practise the dialogue with a partner. Practise both roles A and B.

A: Hello, I'm ...
What's your name?
B: Hi, I'm ...
A: Nice to meet you, ...
B: Nice to meet you too.
A: This is my first day here.
B: I'm new too.
A: Well, have a good day.
B: Thanks, you too.
A: Goodbye.
B: Bye, ...

More practice 1 p. 129

▸ Workbook 1–2, p. 7

Me and my class

1   Good morning, class 7Y

a) Who's in class 7Y? Who's the English teacher?

Good morning, class 7Y.
I'm Ms Lee – your
English teacher.
And who are you?

Hi, I'm Berry.
I'm eleven.
I'm not from Plymouth.
I'm from Woolwell,
a village near Plymouth.
I have no brothers and
sisters.
I have a pony – Harry.
He's twelve.
My hobby is riding.

I'm Ellie. I'm twelve.
I have two brothers and one sister.
We're from Plymouth.
My hobby is tae kwon do.
My best friends are Ruby and
Charlie. They're at this school.
They aren't in class 7Y. They're in
class 7X. Oh, and I have two cats.

Hi, I'm Luca.
I'm from Plymouth too.
I'm not twelve, I'm ten.
I have one brother – Jack. He's
fourteen and he's at this school.
And I have one sister – Grace.
She's six. She isn't at this school.
We have no pets. My hobby is
riding my BMX.

b) Copy and complete the table.

Name	Age	From	Brothers	Sisters	Hobbies	Pets
Berry						
Luca						
Ellie						

c) ☐ Listen to Adam.
Which is the right picture?

1

2

d) Listen again.
Complete the table for Adam.

e) 👥 Check your table with a partner.

2 NOW YOU

a) Copy the table and make notes about yourself.

Name:	Brothers:
Age:	Sisters:
From:	Pet:
School:	Best friends:
Class:	Hobby / Sport:
Class teacher:	Favourite colour:

b) 👥 Make groups of four. Use your notes. Talk to your group.

🔘 Start like this: ⚫ Say more:

> My name is ...
> I'm ... (age)
> I'm from ...
> I'm at ... school.
> I'm in class ...
> My class teacher is ...

> I have one brother. He's ...
> I have one sister. She's ...
> I have no pets / a pet / ...
> My best friends are ...
> My favourite hobby / sport is ...
> My favourite colour is ...

| More practice 2 | p. 129 |

c) ⚫ Who's like you? Write sentences. Report to your class.

– Anna is eleven. I'm eleven too.
– Hendrik has one sister. I have one sister too. | More practice 3 | p. 129 |

3 About me and my class

Write a short text about yourself. You can put your text on the class notice board. Then put it in your DOSSIER.

> Das Dossier ist eine Mappe, in der du deine wichtigen und schönen Arbeiten sammeln kannst. Es gehört zum Portfolio.

Me and my class

🔘
> Hi, I'm Vanessa.
> I'm eleven.
> I'm at Erich-Kästner-School. I'm in class 5a. My class teacher is Mrs Schmidt.
> My hobby is reading.
> I like animals too.

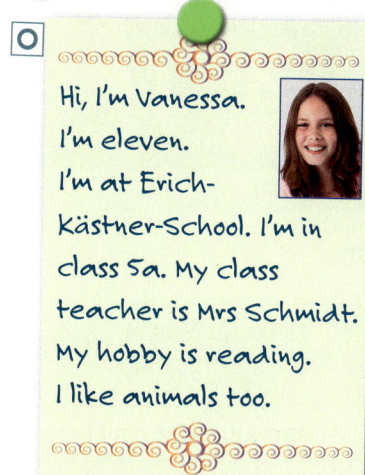

⚫
> Hello, I'm Tim. I'm from Düsseldorf in Germany. I'm at Erich-Kästner-School. My favourite teacher is Mr Jahn. He's great!
>
> I have two sisters  and one dog 😃.
>
> My best friends are Samir and Patrick. They're cool.
>
> My favourite sport is football and my favourite colours are red and white.

The first day at school

🎧 **1** **A tour of the school**

a) Class 7Y is on a tour of the school with Ms Lee. Listen and put the pictures in the right order.

C   in the computer room

A   in the canteen

D   in the art room

B   in the science lab

E   in the sports hall

b) Listen again. Match the speech bubbles 1–7 with the rooms. Two speech bubbles are not in the text.

1 is in the sports hall, 2 …, 3 …

1 We aren't in a PE lesson now.

2 Welcome to Eggy!

3 Hello, Mr Martin.

4 I'm your ICT teacher.

5 I'm not lost. I'm here.

6 Where's Ellie? She isn't here.

7 Ms Lee, I don't like this room!

2 School rap

a) Listen to the rap song and sing along.

Chorus All my teachers say,
Work hard every day!

Every day I go to class,
I have English, I have maths,
I have French, I have German,
I do lots and lots of learnin'.

Chorus All my teachers say, ...

Science, French and ICT,
Art, history and PE,
Drama and technology,
Music and geography.

Chorus All my teachers say, ...

b) What lessons in the rap do you know?

3 The new timetable

Eggbuckland Community College
Class 7Y timetable

Lesson	Time	Monday	Tuesday	Wednesday	Thursday	Friday
	8.40 – 9.00	ASSEMBLY / REGISTRATION				
1	9.00 – 10.00	English	music	technology	geography	PE
2	10.00 – 11.00	maths	English	history	French	PE
	11.00 – 11.25	BREAK				
3	11.25 – 12.25	art	history	English	science	geography
4	12.25 – 1.25	art	science	maths	science	English
	1.25 – 2.05	LUNCH				
5	2.05 – 3.05	French	drama	science	ICT	technology

a) Look at the Eggy timetable.
What's right? What's wrong?
1 Class 7Y has lunch at school every day.
2 Class 7Y has six lessons every day.
3 Lesson one on Monday is French.
4 Lesson two on Tuesday is music.

b) ● Write your own right and wrong sentences (8–10) about the timetable.
c) 👥 Read your sentences to a partner. He or she says 'right' or 'wrong'.

Lesson one on Monday is English.

Right.

Wrong. It's history.

Lesson two on Wednesday is PE.

1 👥 **The unit quiz**

How many questions can you answer?
Work with a partner. Write your answers in your exercise book. Check your answers on page 157.

1 It's in England. It's a city. It starts with 'P'. What is it?

2 We're two girls in class 7Y. We aren't sisters. Who are we?

3 He's a student at Eggy. He's ten. Who is he?

4 They're brothers. They aren't Adam and Zack. Who are they?

8 You aren't brothers or sisters. You're quiz partners. Who are you?

7 She isn't from Plymouth. She's from Woolwell. Who is she?

6 I'm at Eggy too. I'm not a student, I'm an English teacher. Who am I?

5 He isn't a student. He's a pony. Who is he?

9 She's a girl. She's six. She isn't at Eggy. Who is she?

10 I'm a girl. I'm not eleven – I'm twelve. Who am I?

11 It's a lesson. It isn't in a classroom. It's in the sports hall. What is it?

12 You're a student. You aren't at Eggy. Who are you?

2 **Positive** Yes

a) Complete the sentences from the quiz.
1 I... at Eggy too.
2 You... a student.
3 He... ten.
4 She... from Woolwell.
5 It... in England.
6 We... two girls in Class 7Y.
7 You... quiz partners.
8 They... brothers.

b) Now make the rule.

FOCUS	Yes
I + ...	we + ...
you + ...	you + ...
he, she, it + ...	they + ...

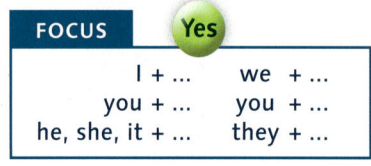

Look at the quiz cards!

3 **Negative** No

a) Complete the sentences from the quiz.
1 I... eleven – I'm twelve.
2 You ... at Eggy.
3 He ... a student.
4 She ... from Plymouth.
5 It ... in a classroom.
6 We ... sisters.
7 You ... brothers or sisters.
8 They ... Adam and Zack.

b) Now make the rule.

FOCUS	No
I + ...	we + ...
you + ...	you + ...
he, she, it + ...	they + ...

▶ *Language file 2, pp. 176–177*

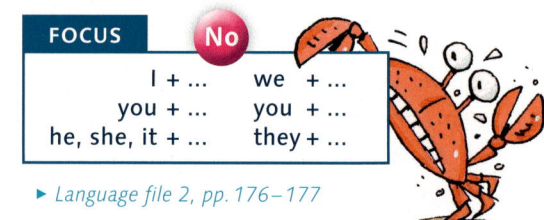

4 ◯ **At Eggy** // ● p.129

Put in: *I • You • He • She • It • We • You • They*

1 Eggy is my new school. ...'s big.
2 Luca is a new student at Eggy. ...'s cool.
3 "My name is Berry. ...'m from Woolwell."
4 "Thanks, Ms Lee. ...'re a great teacher."
5 "Can we have lunch now, Ms Lee? ...'re hungry!"
6 Adam and Berry aren't in class 7X. ...'re in class 7Y.
7 "I like you, Ruby and Charlie. ...'re my best friends!"
8 Mrs Ford is at Eggy too. ...'s the art teacher.

he   she

EGGBUCKLAND COMMUNITY COLLEGE

it   they

▶ *Language file 1, p. 176*

5 **Pets and friends**

a) Fill in the gaps.

Hi, I... (1) Berry. Remember Harry? He... (2) my pony.
Connie and William are our ponies too. They... (3) fun.
Connie is old. She... (4) seventeen. William is five. He... (5)
small. Harry is twelve. He... (6) big. I like talking to Harry.
I say, "Harry, you ... (7) great!". He... (8) my favourite pony.
But we... (9) all friends.

b) Write about your friend(s) or pet(s). More help p.130

– Lucy is my friend. She's ten. She isn't in my class. ...
– Daisy and Bob are my pets. Daisy is a dog and Bob is a hamster. They're ...

Bei Tieren, zu denen man eine persönliche Beziehung hat (z.B. Haustiere), sagt man *he* oder *she*, also merke:

dog → it
Charlie → he

6 **People and places in Plymouth**

a) Write about the people and places in Plymouth – as many sentences as you can.

Plymouth		students.
Eggy		a seagull.
Cyril		teachers.
Sandy	isn't	in Germany.
Mr Brown	aren't	girls.
Ellie and Berry		a crab.
Luca and Adam		a maths teacher.
Ms Lee and Mrs Ford		in London.

b) Write more sentences: *Plymouth isn't in Germany. It's in England.* More help p.130

7 **Make a quiz for the class**

a) ● 👥 Write quiz cards – as many as you can. More help p.131

b) Read a card for the class. Who / What is it?

It's a lesson.
It isn't English.
It's lesson three on Friday. What is it?

She's in our class.
She isn't from Halle.
She's from Berlin.
Who is she?

They're best friends.
They're in our class.
They aren't girls.
Who are they?

1 Before you read

a) What can you see?

I can see a green … / black …

> blazer • pullover • shirt • shoes • skirt •
> socks • sweatshirt • tie • tights • trousers

b) Who is in every picture?

🎧 In trouble at Eggy

It's assembly at Eggy.

Miss Borowski — Good morning, boys and
girls. I'm Miss Borowski, the school
principal. I hope you're happy at
your new school. It's nice to see you
in your uniforms. Please remember
– the uniform is important!

Ellie — Oh no! My tie!

Assembly is over.

Miss B — Hello. What's your name?

Ellie — Hello, Miss Borowski. I'm Ellie Cole.

Miss B — Where's your tie, Ellie?

Ellie — Sorry. It's at home.

Miss B — That isn't good, Ellie. Remember
– the uniform is important!

Ellie — OK, Miss Borowski.

In the English lesson …

Luca — Where's your tie, Ellie?

Ellie — It's at home.

Luca — Oh, but you know the uniform is
important!

Ellie — I know, I know.

In the science lesson …

Berry — Where's your tie, Ellie?

Ellie — It's at home.

Berry — Oh, but you know the uniform is …

Ellie — … important! Yes, I know, I know.

5

In the art lesson ...

Ellie ___ Look, Adam – I have no tie.
Adam ___ That's bad, Ellie.
Ellie ___ I know, I know. The uniform is important!
Luca ___ Hey, I have an idea.
Berry ___ What's your idea, Luca?
Luca ___ We need paper, scissors, colours, ...
Adam ___ I like it.

6

In the canteen ...

Berry ___ I like your tie, Ellie.
Adam ___ Yes, it's a cool tie.
Luca ___ The colours are nice.
Ellie ___ Thanks, guys.
Miss B ___ It's a very nice tie, Ellie.
Ellie ___ Thanks, Miss Borowski.
Miss B ___ But it isn't the school tie. You know what I say, ...
All ___ The uniform is important!
Miss B ___ Yes, that's right.

2 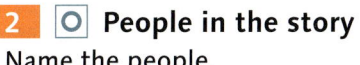 **People in the story**

Name the people.

1 Who has no tie?
2 Who says, "Where's your tie?"
3 Who is in trouble?
4 Who has a good idea?
5 Who likes Ellie's new tie?
6 Who says, "The uniform is important!"?

> More practice 4 p. 131

3 Eggy uniform words

a) Finish the lists in your exercise book.

> *Uniforms*
>
> | for boys and girls | for girls |
> | --- | --- |
> | blazer | ... |

b) Write right/wrong sentences.
Girls at Eggy have red blazers. Boys have ...

c)  Practise your sentences with a partner.
A: Girls at Eggy have red blazers.
B: Right.

> More practice 5 p. 131

4 What do you think?

Start with "I think ..." and make sentences.

the Eggy uniform ties Ellie Miss Borowski Luca's idea art lessons	is / isn't are / aren't	good. bad. cool. nice. ugly. fun. boring.

– I think the Eggy uniform is ...

5 **THEATRE TIME**

a) Make groups of six students: Ellie, Luca, Adam, Berry, Miss Borowski and a narrator. Read the scenes.

b) 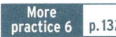 Act the scenes for the class.
What's the best group?

> More practice 6 p. 132

1 A brochure

Before you read: What's Martins? (A) a brochure? (B) a school? (C) a shop? (D) a book?

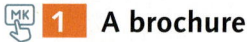

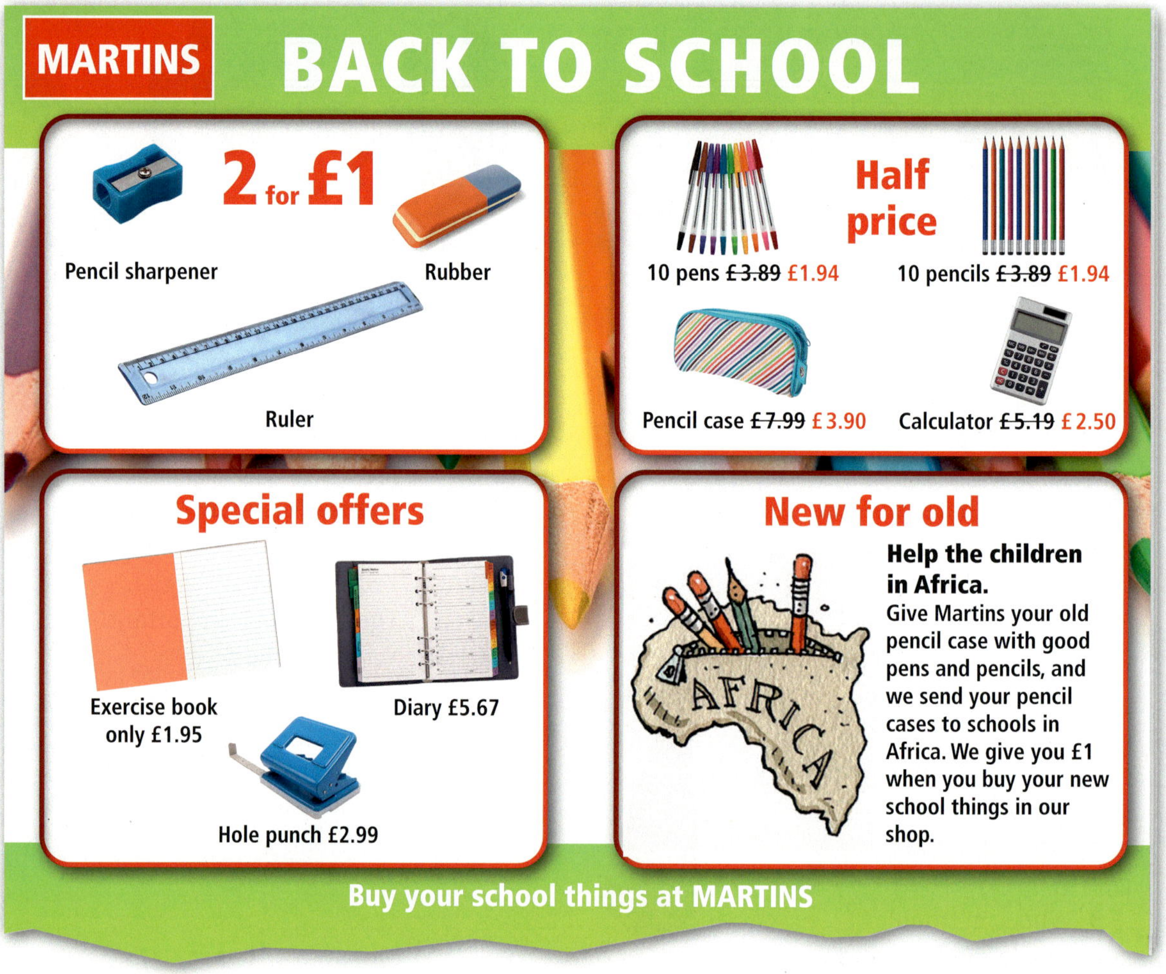
MARTINS
BACK TO SCHOOL
2 for £1
Pencil sharpener
Rubber
Ruler
Half price
10 pens ~~£3.89~~ £1.94
10 pencils ~~£3.89~~ £1.94
Pencil case ~~£7.99~~ £3.90
Calculator ~~£5.19~~ £2.50
Special offers
Exercise book only £1.95
Diary £5.67
Hole punch £2.99
New for old
Help the children in Africa.
Give Martins your old pencil case with good pens and pencils, and we send your pencil cases to schools in Africa. We give you £1 when you buy your new school things in our shop.
AFRICA
Buy your school things at MARTINS

2 ○ School things at Martins

Look at the brochure.

What can you buy …

1 for half price? → *I can buy ten pens, …*

2 on special offer?

3 for £1?

3 Your school things

a) Make a list of the things in your pencil case: *I have a red ruler, two brown pencils, …*

b) You can buy some things at Martins. You have £10. Write a shopping list.

c) Compare with a partner. Who can buy more? I can buy … What about you?

4 ● MEDIATION Help children in Africa

Wie kannst du Mädchen und Jungen aus Afrika mit der Aktion *New for old* helfen? Wähle (A), (B) oder (C).

(A) Schicke dein Federmäppchen an eine Schule in Afrika.

(B) Kaufe bei Martins so viele neue Dinge wie möglich.

(C) Martins schickt dein altes Federmäppchen an eine Schule in Afrika.

► *Text file 1, pp. 158–159* ► *Workbook 16, p. 13*

1   Make networks

a) ⭕ Copy the network. `// ● p.133`
Complete it with words from the box.

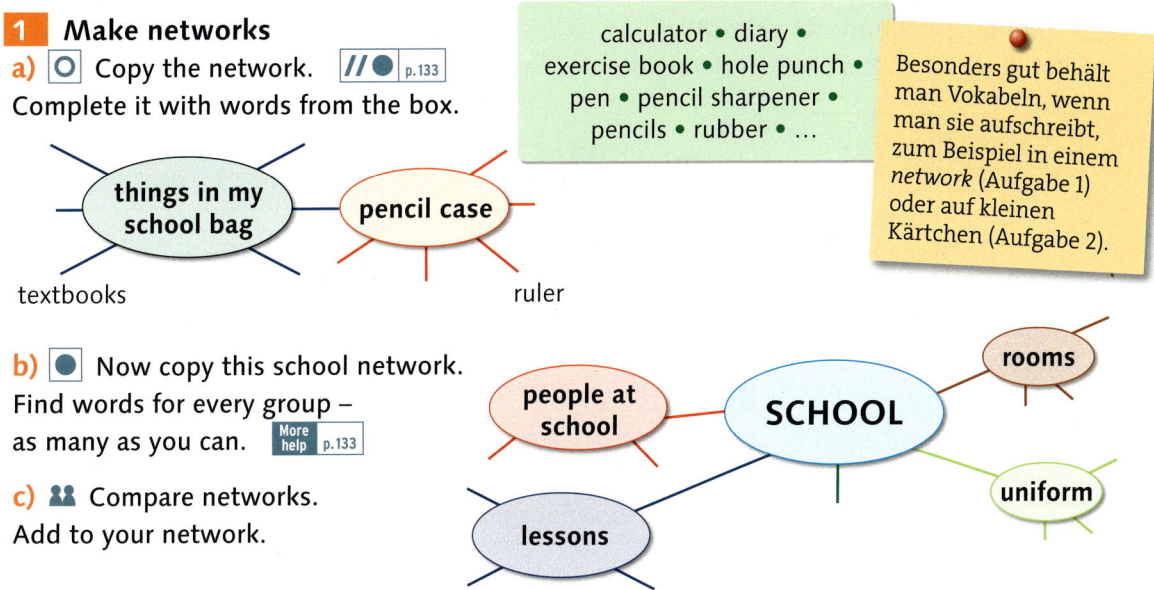

calculator • diary •
exercise book • hole punch •
pen • pencil sharpener •
pencils • rubber • …

Besonders gut behält man Vokabeln, wenn man sie aufschreibt, zum Beispiel in einem *network* (Aufgabe 1) oder auf kleinen Kärtchen (Aufgabe 2).

things in my school bag

pencil case

textbooks

ruler

b) ● Now copy this school network.
Find words for every group –
as many as you can. `More help p.133`

c) 👥 Compare networks.
Add to your network.

people at school

SCHOOL

rooms

uniform

lessons

2   Make word and phrase cards

a) Pick words and phrases from the green box and make cards.

Welcome to our school.

Nice to meet you.
Have a good day.
How are you?
Fine, thanks.
See you later.
Good morning.
Hello.
I'm in class 5.
Sorry.
Welcome to our school.
Thanks.
I'm from Germany.
We're best friends.
What's your name?
That's right.
I have an idea.
I know.
It's at home.

b) Write the German phrase on the back of the card.

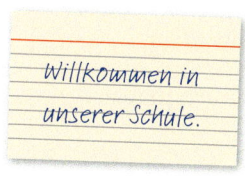

Willkommen in unserer Schule.

Word and phrase box

c) Put the cards in a box.

d) 👥 Swap cards with your partner. Ask your partner to check you. Then check your partner.

What's 'Willkommen in unserer Schule' in English?

Welcome to our school.

Right.

Lerne Vokabeln regelmäßig – lieber jeden Tag 5–10 Minuten als einmal die Woche zwei Stunden.

Mehr Tipps zum Wörterlernen findest du im *Skills file*.

▶ *Skills file 1, p. 170*

1 Talking to friends at school

a) Put Berry's answers (A–E) in the right order.

1 Hi, Berry. How are you?

2 I'm fine too, thanks. Can I borrow a pen, please?

3 Thanks. What's the next lesson?

4 It's science. And who's your favourite teacher?

5 I like Luca. What about you?

A I like Luca too.

B Hi, Ellie. I'm fine, thanks. How are you?

C Mr Brown. He's nice. And who's your favourite boy in our class?

D Sure, here you are.

E It's PE. What's your favourite lesson?

b) Listen to the dialogue and check. Then write the dialogue in your exercise book.

c) Compare your answers. Then practise the dialogue. Swap partners.

2 NOW YOU p. 133

Practise the dialogue. Use words and phrases from 1.

Partner A	Partner B
Begrüße B. Frage, wie es ihm / ihr geht.	Grüße zurück. Sage, wie es dir geht, und frage A, wie es ihm / ihr geht.
Sage, wie es dir geht. Frage B nach seinem / ihrem Lieblingsfach.	Nenne dein Lieblingsfach. Frage A, ob du etwas ausleihen darfst.
Stimme zu und gib es B.	Bedanke dich. Frage A nach dem Mädchen / Jungen, den sie / er in der Klasse am liebsten mag.
Sage, wen du in deiner Klasse am liebsten magst.	Sage, ob du ihn / sie auch magst oder nicht.

3 Interviews

a) Copy the table and answer the four questions.

Questions	ME	NAME: ...	NAME: ...	NAME: ...
1 Who's your favourite teacher?				
2 What's your favourite lesson?				
3 What's your favourite hobby?				
4 Who's your best friend in our class?				

Who's ...? = Wer ist ...?
What's ...? = Was ist ...?

b) Walk around: Ask different partners. Write the names and the answers in the table.

c) Now tell the class.

My favourite ...   Tina's best ...   Karim's favourite ...

Sarah Paul Anna

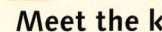

1 **The kids from Harbour Road¹:**
Meet the kids!

a) Watch the film. Where are the kids first? And then?
First they're in ... And then² they're in ...

assembly

the canteen

Harbour Road

a maths lesson

the sports hall

b) Who says what? Match the sentences (1–6) with the kids.

Anna says ...
Paul says ...
Sarah says ...

> 1 It's assembly now.

> 2 The uniform is important!

> 3 Maths is my favourite lesson.

> 4 I like lunch.

> 5 I love sport.

> 6 We can go to my house and listen to music.

Then watch again and check.

c) What do you think about the kids? Tell your partner.
Example: Anna is nice / fun / great / cool / ...   Sarah is ...   I like Sarah.   Paul is ....

2 **People and places:** **Eggbuckland Community College**

a) Watch the film. What do you think? Talk to a partner.
– I think the school is big / new / nice / terrible³ / ... –
– I think the film is cool / great / OK / boring /...
– I like / don't like the music.

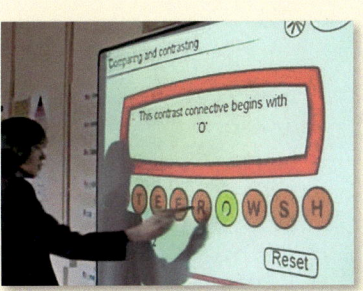

b) Watch the film again. Then work in groups. Write a list of things, people, places, lessons, sports that you see in the film – as many as you can. Which group has the best list?

---

¹ Harbour Road [hɑːbə ˈrəʊd] *Hafenstraße*   ² then [ðen] *dann, danach*   ³ terrible [ˈterəbl] *schrecklich*

STOP! CHECK! GO!

Ein Lösungsblatt für die Aufgaben 1 bis 8 kannst du von deiner Lehrerin / deinem Lehrer erhalten.
Die Audio-Datei (S.32) findest du online bei den Audio-Dateien zum Workbook.

1 ○ WORDS School things

Example: *1 blazer, 2 ..., 3 ...*

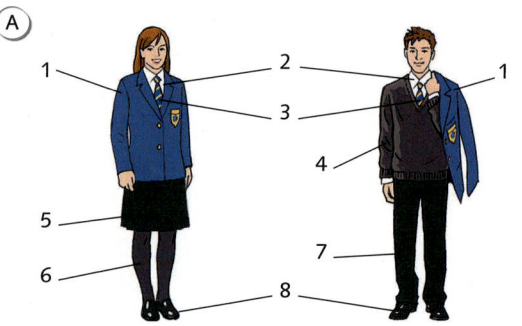

2 WORDS School words

a) Which is the wrong word?
1 pen, pencil, shirt, rubber → *shirt*
2 maths, Monday, French, science → ...
3 lunch, badminton, football, tae kwon do
4 science lab, school, classroom, art room
5 assembly, break, lesson, calculator
6 brother, student, teacher, principal

b) Find more right words for 1–6 in a).
Example: *1 ruler, ...*

c) ● Write one sentence each for 1–6.
1 My favourite pen is green.
2 ...

3 READING Remember Cyril?

a) ○ Read the text. Put the pictures (A–D) in the right order.

> Hi. I'm Cyril. I'm from Kingsand.
> It's nice. It's a beach near Plymouth.
> Benny and Babe are my friends.
> They're from Kingsand too.
> We're crabs – we love the beach!
> Look. This is Sandy. She isn't a crab.
> She's a seagull. Oh no! Mr Johnson
> is here. We're in trouble. He isn't
> nice. He likes crabs!

b) Right or wrong? Correct the wrong sentences.
1 Cyril isn't from London.
2 Kingsand is near Plymouth.
3 Benny and Babe are students.
4 They're crabs.
5 Sandy is a crab too.
6 Mr Johnson is OK.
7 Mr Johnson and Cyril aren't friends.

4 ◯ LANGUAGE   Remember Ellie? //● p.134

Ellie is with her dad. She has some pictures on her mobile. Which is the right word?

1 Look, this is / am my new school.
2 It's / 're very big.
3 The students in my class is / are OK.
4 The teachers is / are OK too.
5 This are / is my new friend, Berry.
6 She's / 're great.
7 My friends Ruby and Charlie am / are at my school too.
8 But they aren't / isn't in my class.
9 This is / are my new uniform.
10 It aren't / isn't very nice.

5 LANGUAGE   Remember Sandy?

Put in the right words.

Hi, I... (1) Sandy.

This ... (2) Cyril. He... (3) my friend.

Benny and Babe ... (4) my friends too. They... (5) fun.

We... (6) from Kingsand.

Kingsand ... (7) near Plymouth. It... (8) great!

You can look in the Language file on p. 176.

6 LANGUAGE   That's wrong, Sandy!

Sandy is wrong. Cyril is right. Finish Cyril's sentences.

1 Plymouth is in Germany.
2 Eggy is in London.
3 Cyril, you're a seagull.
4 I'm a crab.
5 Berry and Ellie are teachers.
6 Ms Lee and Mr Brown are students.
7 We're students at Eggy.

1 Plymouth isn't in Germany. It's in ...
2 Eggy isn't ... It's in ...
3 I'm not ... I'm ...
4 You ... You're ...
5 They ...
6 ...
7 ...

STOP! CHECK! GO!

🎧 **7** **LISTENING** **Adam and Luca**

a) 🔘 Name pictures 1–10.

b) Listen. Which things are Adam and Luca talking about? Write the numbers in the right order.

①  FRENCH

②  Kaiser Chiefs Ruby

③

④ 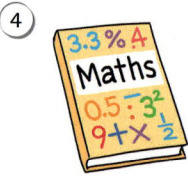 3.3 % 4 Maths 0.5 : 3² 9+X ½

⑤

⑥

⑦  Ms Lee

⑧

⑨  12345

⑩  SCIENCE

c) Match Adam's and Luca's questions and answers. Then listen and check.

1 How are you?
2 I like the Kaiser Chiefs. What about you?
3 What's your hobby?
4 Who's your favourite teacher?
5 What's the next lesson?
6 Can I borrow your calculator, please?

A I like football.
B Sorry, it's at home.
C French.
D I'm fine, thanks.
E They're OK.
F Ms Lee. She's great.

8 **WORDS** **Talking to friends**

Complete the mini-dialogues.

1 Hi. How are ...? – I'm fine, thanks.
2 Welcome ... our school. – Thanks.
3 I'm in ... 7B. – Me too.
4 See ... later. – OK, see you.

5 I like ... sweatshirt. – Oh, thanks.
6 I'm Emma. – ... to meet you, Emma.
7 What's the next ...? – It's maths.
8 Have a ... day. – You too.

9 🔘 **WRITING** **An email**

Read Anna's email to a new e-pal in England. Then write an email to your new e-pal, Jack, in Ireland. Write about your school, your class, your best friend, ...

Hi Lucy,

My name is Anna. I'm your new e-pal!
I'm 11 and I'm from Hannover.
My school is Sophie-Charlotte-Schule. It's very big. I like it!
My favourite lesson is science. The teacher is Mr Ullmann.
He's nice. I like English too.
My best friend is Lena. She's in my class. We like dancing. It's fun!
That's all for now. Have a good day!
Anna

10 ● WRITING Your timetable

Write your timetable in English. ▶ Wordbank 3, p. 185

11 ♟♟ SPEAKING A timetable

Partner B: Look at page 126.
Partner A: Copy this timetable into your exercise book. Some lessons are missing.
Ask Partner B and complete the timetable. Then answer Partner B's questions.

Our class timetable

Lesson	Monday	Tuesday	Wednesday	Thursday	Friday
1	English	....	technology	geography	....
2	....	English	history	....	PE
3	science	history	....	music	....
4	....	....	maths	....	German
5	German	German	maths	science	technology

What's lesson two on Monday?

It's maths. What's lesson five on Monday?

It's German.

Check your answers with your partner's timetable.

12 My learner log

Write your learner log. You can put it in your DOSSIER.

Im *learner log* schreibst du auf, was du gelernt hast, was du jetzt gut kannst und was noch nicht so gut geht.
Führe dein *learner log* regelmäßig.
Wichtig: Versuche immer ehrlich zu antworten!

My learner log

I THINK ENGLISH IS:
– OK.

MY FAVOURITE CHARACTER:
– Berry

MY FAVOURITE PHRASES:
– That's cool!
– See you later.
– Have a good day!
– How are you?

I REMEMBER:
Lessons: French, German, English, history, ...
School things: pens, pencils, books, ...
Uniform words: pullover, shirt, shoes, ...
Animals: dog, cat, snake, ...
Colours: red, black, green, ...

MY FAVOURITE WORDS:
– timetable
– lunch
– Eggy
– pony

DIFFICULT WORDS:
– scissors
– trousers
– remember
– science

I'M GOOD AT:
– Listening, reading

I'M NOT GOOD AT:
– Speaking, writing

I'M OK AT:
– Words, language

Unit 2

At home with Ellie

Hill Road

Greatfield Street

16.67/30

1 Homes

a) 👥 **Partner A:** Talk about one of the photos (1–9).
Partner B: Guess the right photo. Swap roles.

In this photo I can see a ...   – It's photo number ...   – Right!

In this photo	I can see a there's a	big small modern nice white ...	house / flat / block of flats. kitchen / bedroom / living room / garden / balcony / hall / ... table / chair / bed / sofa / ...

b) Listen to Ellie and Berry. Which photos (1–9) show Ellie's house? Write the numbers.

c) Listen again. What's right? What's wrong? Correct the wrong sentences.

1 Ellie likes the city.
2 Ellie lives in Hill Road.
3 Ellie lives with her father.
4 Ellie's mother has a partner.

5 Ellie's brother and sister aren't nice.
6 Ellie's house is big.
7 Ellie's bedroom isn't big.
8 Ellie is happy with her bedroom.

2 A new flat

a) Listen to Ellie and her dad. Choose the right photos (1–9).

b) Make a sentence for each photo with words from the box.

Photo number ... is Ellie's / her dad's / the ...

> balcony • bedroom • flat •
> hall • kitchen • living room

c) Listen again. Complete the sentences with the right endings.

1 The new flat is ...	big and yellow.
2 They have a kitchen and living room ...	at the end of the hall.
3 The bathroom is ...	in Greatfield Street.
4 There are two ...	a balcony.
5 They have a big bedroom with ...	in one room.
6 Ellie's bedroom is ...	toilets in the flat.

3 ACTIVITY   My home

a) Draw your house or flat.
Make room labels.

More help p.134

> My flat is nice. It has two bedrooms,
> a living room, ... The bathroom is here
> and this is the garage. In the living room
> there's a big green sofa, a TV and ...

b) 👥 Walk around: Show your picture to
different partners and talk about it.

> It's nice / big / cool.
> What's this room?

Ellie's family

🎧 **1** **Meet the family**

a) Look at the pictures: Who are the people? Guess. Then read and check.

Ellie	Hi, Mum, this is Berry.
Mum	Hi, Berry. Nice to meet you. I'm Jackie.
Berry	Hello.
Ellie	Is Zoe upstairs?
Mum	Yes, she is. And Conor is in the living room.
Ellie	Oh no! Why is he always in the living room? There's no space for Berry and me!
Mum	Oh, here's Conor. This is Berry, Ellie's new friend.
Conor	Hi, Berry. Are you at Eggbuckland?
Berry	Yes, I am. What about you?
Conor	I'm at Plymouth High School.
Mum	And here's Zoe, Ellie's big sister.
Zoe	Hi, welcome to the madhouse!
Mum	Conor, can the girls go into the living room? Is that OK?
Conor	Oh, OK.

Berry and Ellie are in the living room.

Berry	Your family is fun. Is Conor your real brother?
Ellie	No, he isn't. He's my stepbrother. And Zoe is my stepsister.
Berry	They're all nice.
Ellie	They're OK.
Berry	What about your stepdad? Is he nice?
Ellie	He's OK. But I miss my real dad. He lives with his new partner and his baby boy. Look, I have a photo on my mobile.
Berry	Their baby is cute. You're lucky. You have two brothers and a sister.
Ellie	You're lucky because you live with your mum and your dad. I miss that.

b) Complete the sentences with the right endings.

1 Jackie is ...
2 Zoe is ...
3 Conor is ...
4 Ellie's dad has ...
5 Ellie lives with ...
6 Their house is ...

> her mum and stepdad. • Ellie's big sister. •
> her dad. • a new family. • a madhouse. •
> Ellie's mum. • her mum and dad. •
> Ellie's stepbrother.

2 Ellie's family tree

Grandma Martin

Grandma and Grandpa Cole

Aunt Lorna ↔ **Uncle Andrew** **My mum, Jackie** ↔ **My stepdad, Pete** **My dad, Steve** ↔ **My stepmum, Alisha**

My cousin, Owen **My cousin, Lily** **My step-sister, Zoe** **My step-brother, Conor** **Me!** **My half-brother, Finn**

a) Ellie is writing about her family, but she's very messy. Write the smeared words.
This is my crazy family. I have a half- **1** , Finn, a step **2** , Conor, and a step **3** , Zoe.
And I have two **4** too – Owen and Lily. Lily is fun. Her mother is my **5** Lorna. She's
great. And Lily's father is my **6** Andrew. He's mum's **7** . My grandparents are very
special too. Grandma Martin is mum's **8** . She lives in a small flat with five cats. Grandma
and **9** Cole are dad's parents. They swim in the sea every day. People say, "Your
grandmother and grandfather are crazy!" And I say, "That's my family!"

b) Quiz Who is it?

1 I have a new partner. Her name is Jackie. I'm …	6 He has a new family. Alisha is his partner. He's …
2 Zoe and Ellie are his sisters. He's …	7 They live with their dad and their stepmum. They're …
3 Her dad has a new partner and a baby. She's …	8 Ellie is his half-sister. Jackie isn't his mum. He's …
4 She lives with Jackie. Pete is her dad. She's …	
5 Ellie lives with me. Pete is my partner. I'm …	

👥 Check your answers with a partner.

3 ACTIVITY Your family tree

a) Draw your family tree or your
dream family tree. You can put it
in your DOSSIER.   ▶ Wordbank 4, p. 186

c) 🔘 Write sentences about
your family – as many as you can.
For help see 2a.

b) 👥 Talk to a partner about your
family tree.

Who's that boy / girl?...

This is my …

Is that your …?

And that's …

What's his / her name?

Problems at home

1 **What's your problem?**

a) **Is Zoe happy? Why (not)? Read and find out.** Zoe ... happy because ...

Ellie shares a bedroom with her stepsister, Zoe.

Zoe ___ Ellie, look at the room!

Ellie ___ What's your problem? It's OK!

Zoe ___ OK? What about the pullover? Is it yours?

Ellie ___ Yes, it is.

Zoe ___ And the shoes? Are they yours too?

Ellie ___ Yes, they are. What's your problem?

Zoe ___ The room is messy! That's my problem!

Ellie ___ Is it your room? No, it isn't. It's my room too!

b) **Now Ellie is in the kitchen. Is she happy? Why (not)?** Ellie ... happy because ...

Mum ___ Are you OK, Ellie?

Ellie ___ No, I'm not.

Mum ___ Why not? What is it?

Ellie ___ It's Zoe. She's bossy, Mum.

Mum ___ Oh, Ellie!

Ellie ___ And there's no space in our room. I can't do my homework.

Mum ___ What about the kitchen?

Ellie ___ It's too busy!

Mum ___ You can work in the living room.

Ellie ___ How can I? It's too noisy!

Mum ___ Oh, Ellie!

2 **Ellie's problems**

Look at the dialogues in 1 again. Pick A, B, C or D.

1 Zoe is ...   A busy.   B noisy.   C bossy.   D messy.
2 The room is ...   A OK.   B messy.   C big.   D busy.
3 Ellie has no ...   A shoes.   B space.   C bedroom.   D pullover.
4 The kitchen is too ...   A small.   B new.   C busy.   D noisy.
5 The living room is too ...   A big.   B pink.   C messy.   D noisy.

3 **Zoe is bossy!**

a) **Look at the picture. Act the dialogue with Ellie and Zoe.**

b) **Make groups of four. Each student puts four things on the desk. Now ask questions.**

A: What about the ruler? Is it yours, Till?

B: No, it isn't. Is it yours, Anna?

C: Yes, it is. What about the ...?

What about the ...? Is it yours?
What about the ...? Are they yours?
– Yes, it is.
– Yes, they are.

4 Ellie's dream room

a) Ellie is talking to her friends. Listen. What's her dream room – 1 or 2?

b) Listen again. What's in Ellie's dream room? Write the numbers.

1	2	3	4	5	6	7	8	9	10	11	12
a rug	a desk	a chair	a lamp	a table	books	a bed	cushions	a mirror	a wardrobe	posters	shelves

c) Write sentences about the things in Ellie's dream room. Use *there is … / there are …* .
In Ellie's dream room there's a … / there are …

More practice 1 p. 135

▸ *Language file 4, p. 178*

5 👥 What's different?

Partner B: Go to page 126.

Partner A: Look at room A. Your partner looks at room B. Talk to your partner about the things in room A. Take turns. Find four different things or more. Make notes about the different things.

Partner A __ There's a bed in room A.
Partner B __ There's a bed in room B too.
  OK. There are three cushions in room B.
Partner A __ There are no cushions in room A. That's different!

Room A	Room B
no cushions	3 cushions
…	…

🎧 **1 Are you OK?**

Right or wrong? Read and check.

1 Ellie's dad is happy in the new flat.
2 Ellie is happy in her mum's house.

Dad ___	Hi, Ellie. This is a nice surprise.
Ellie ___	Hi, Dad. Is Finn OK?
Dad ___	Yes, he is. He's fine.
Ellie ___	And Alisha? Is she OK?
Dad ___	Yes, she is. She's fine too, but she's tired.
Ellie ___	And the new flat? Is it OK?
Dad ___	Yes, it is. It's really nice.
Ellie ___	Are you and Alisha happy in the flat?
Dad ___	Yes, we are. We love it. – Ellie, are you OK?

Ellie ___	Yes, I am. I'm fine.
Dad ___	Are you sure? Are you really OK?
Ellie ___	... No, I'm not. I'm not happy.
Dad ___	Oh! What's the problem? Is your stepdad too strict?
Ellie ___	No, he isn't. Pete is OK.
Dad ___	And what about Zoe and Conor? Are they mean to you?
Ellie ___	No, they aren't. They're OK. But I share a room with Zoe and she's really bossy. And Conor is really noisy. There's no space for me. Dad, I'm not happy in this house.
Dad ___	Oh, Ellie. Listen. I have an idea.

2 Questions and answers

a) Complete the questions and answers. Look at the sentences in 1 for help.
Check with a partner.

1 *Is* Finn OK? – Yes, *he is*.
2 And the new flat? ... it OK? – Yes, ...
3 ... you and Alisha happy in the flat? – Yes, ...
4 Ellie, ... you OK? – Yes, ...
5 ... you really OK? – No, ...
6 ... your stepdad too strict? – No, ...
7 ... Zoe and Conor mean to you? – No, ...

> Im Englischen antwortet man auf eine Frage oft nicht nur mit *Yes* oder *No*, sondern mit Kurzantworten. Das ist höflicher.

b) Make the rules for questions.

FOCUS

... I OK?
... you OK?
... he / she / it OK?
... we / you / they OK?

c) Make the rules for short answers.

FOCUS

Yes, I ... – No, I ...
Yes, you ... – No, you ...
Yes, he / she / it ... – No, he / she / it ...
Yes, we / you / they ... – No, we / you / they ...

▸ *Language file 3, p. 177*

3  **NOW YOU** ⏩● p.135

a) Write the answers. Choose your answers from the box.

1 Are you noisy?
2 Are your friends fun?
3 Is your grandmother from Germany?
4 Is your dad bossy?
5 Are your parents strict?
6 Is your room messy?

> Yes, I am. / No, I'm not.
> Yes, he is. / No, he isn't.
> Yes, she is. / No, she isn't.
> Yes, it is. / No, it isn't.
> Yes, they are. / No, they aren't.

b) 👥 Ask your partner the same questions.

4 👥 ⭕ **Who am I?**

Play this game with a partner. You're one of the people in the house. Can your partner guess who you are?

> Are you a girl / boy?
> Are you upstairs / downstairs?
> Are you in the kitchen / ...?
> Are you big / small?
> Are you Ben / Liz / ...?

Yes, I am.   No, I'm not.

5 **QUIZ** **Who is who?**

Partner B: Go to page 126.
Partner A: a) Write the complete questions and answers (✓ = yes, ✗ = no).

1 ... Finn Ellie's half-brother? (✓)
2 ... Pete Ellie's uncle? (✗)
3 ... Conor and Zoe Pete's children? (✓)
4 ... grandpa Cole Zoe's grandfather? (✗)
5 ... Andrew and Lorna Ellie's parents? (✗)
6 ... Andrew Jackie's brother? (✓)

b) 👥 Ask Partner B your questions. One point for each right answer.
Then answer B's questions (for help, look at Ellie's family tree on p. 37). Who has more points?

More practice 2 p.135

6 **What do you think?**

a) Copy the table and think of two more questions. Then answer the questions with ✓ or ✗.

b) 👥 Walk around: Ask as many partners as you can.

c) ⏺ Pick one interesting answer. Tell the class.

Meike says she isn't bossy!   Jan says school is fun!

	Me	Partner 1	Partner 2	...
1 Is English easy?	✓			
2 Is school fun?	✗			
3 Are you bossy?				
4 ...				
5 ...				

1 👥 Before you read about Ellie's week

Choose one or two pictures (1–7). Answer the questions about your pictures. Then tell the class.

1 Where is Ellie? (at her mum's house / at her dad's flat / in the kitchen / in the ...)

2 Is Ellie happy / sad / lonely / ...?

Example:

In picture 1 Ellie is at her mum's house. She's in the kitchen. She's happy.

🎧 The best of both worlds

MONDAY
Dear Diary
Great news! I can live with dad, Alisha and the baby, Finn. Tuesday is the big day! Zoe is happy. But mum isn't happy.

TUESDAY

Ellie ___ ... and I love my new bedroom. I have a desk and a lamp and lots of space. I can do my homework here. No noise and no bossy Zoe. And I have a red rug!

Berry ___ Wow, it's your dream room!

Ellie ___ You're right! ... OK, it's pink, but it's great!

WEDNESDAY
Dear Diary
Finn is very cute. And Alisha is really nice. Dad and Alisha are at the cinema now. Finn is with me. I like babysitting. No Conor! Now I can watch all my favourite TV programmes.

THURSDAY

Ellie ___ ... please, Finn, eat! ... Sorry, Berry. I'm in the kitchen with Finn.

Berry ___ Where are your dad and stepmum?

Ellie ___ What? Oh, dad is at work and Alisha is tired. She's in the bedroom. But dad's home soon – I hope ...

Berry ___ Finn isn't very happy. Are you OK?

Ellie ___ What? Can you say that again?

FRIDAY
Dear Diary
Dad and Alisha are at a restaurant. It's Alisha's birthday. Finn is with me – again! And he isn't very happy – again! What can I do? Be quiet, Finn!

SATURDAY
Ellie _____ ... Pony riding with your dad? That's great. You're really lucky, Berry.
Berry _____ And what about you?
Ellie _____ Finn is here with me, again. Dad and Alisha are in town. My dad has no time for me. He's in love ... I'm lonely, Berry. I miss my mum. And I miss Conor and Pete and my cats – and Zoe!

SUNDAY
Dear Diary
A difficult first week at dad's flat.
But I have a new idea!
From Monday to Friday I'm with mum, and on Saturday and Sunday I'm with dad.
The best of both worlds! I'm happy again.

2   Ellie's week

Read the text. Find the right heading for each day (Monday–Sunday).
Example: Monday: Good news for Ellie   Tuesday: ...

Lots of TV now   A new idea   Good news for Ellie   Alisha's birthday

Day one in a new home   Dad at work   Ellie misses her mum

Pony riding with Finn   Lots of time with dad

3   //○ Is Ellie happy? //● p.136

Complete the sentences with the right endings.

1 On Monday Ellie is happy because ...	she can watch her favourite TV programmes.
2 On Tuesday Ellie is happy because ...	she's lonely.
3 On Wednesday Ellie is happy because ...	Finn isn't happy.
4 On Thursday Ellie isn't happy because ...	she has a new idea.
5 On Friday Ellie isn't happy because ...	she can live with her dad.
6 On Saturday Ellie isn't happy because ...	dad and Alisha are at a restaurant.
7 On Sunday Ellie is happy again because ...	she has a nice room.

4   ● A week later

Write Ellie's diary.
Dear Diary
happy again / mum's house - home / in - bedroom -
Zoe / nice / I - ~~messy~~ - Zoe - ~~bossy~~ / mum - here /
she - happy / cats - happy / homework - living room /
Conor - quiet / Finn - ~~here~~ / OK

More help p.136

More practice 3 p.136

1 Cyril's house

A mind map can help you organize your ideas for a text.
Look at Cyril's mind map and finish his text in your exercise book.

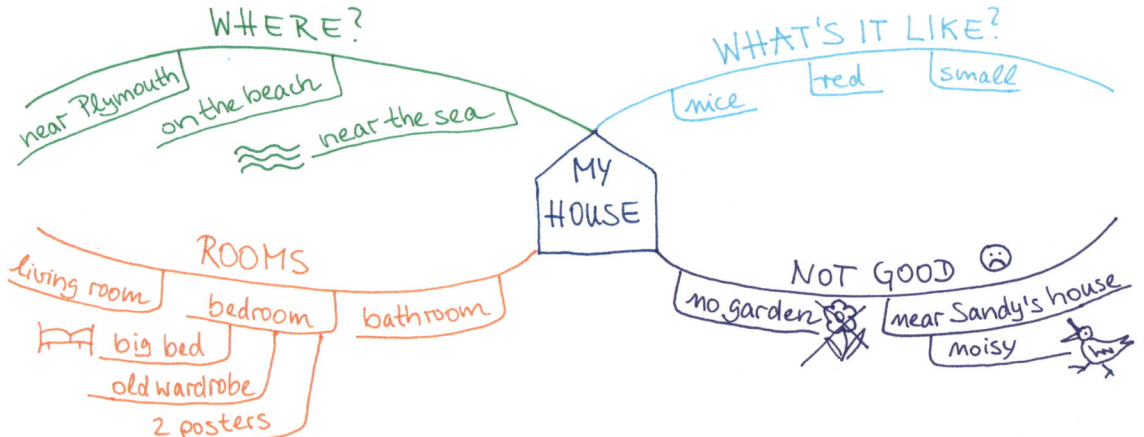

WHERE?
near Plymouth
on the beach
near the sea

WHAT'S IT LIKE?
nice   red   small

MY HOUSE

ROOMS
living room
bedroom
bathroom
big bed
old wardrobe
2 posters

NOT GOOD
no garden
near Sandy's house
noisy

My house

Hi. This is my ... It's near
Plymouth. It's on the ...,
near the ...
It's nice. It's ... and it's ...
There are three rooms in
my house. There's a ...,
a ... and a ...
My favourite room is my
bedroom. There's a big ...
and an old ... in my bedroom.
There are two ... too.
What isn't good about my
house? – There's ... garden
and it's near Sandy's ...
She's very noisy!

2 NOW YOU

a) Make a mind map for your dream
house or dream flat. Use ideas from Cyril's
mind map. Then draw your dream home.

▶ *Wordbank 5, p. 186*

b) Write about your dream house or
dream flat. Use your mind map. You can
put your text in your DOSSIER.

More help p. 136

Mind maps

Bevor du einen Text schreibst, ist es immer gut,
deine Ideen zu sammeln und zu ordnen. Eine
mind map kann dir dabei helfen.

▶ *Skills file 2, p. 172*

1 Classroom phrases

a) Match the phrases (A–L) with the pictures (1–12) in the game.

Example: 'What's that in English?' goes with picture 7.

A What's that in English?
B It's your turn.
C Work with a partner.
D Close the door, please.

E Quiet, please!
F Can I go to the toilet, please?
G What's for homework?
H Can you say that again, please?

I Listen, please!
J What page is it, please?
K Please look at the board.
L Sorry, I forgot my homework.

b) Listen. When you hear the classroom phrases from 1a, point at the pictures 1–12.

More practice 4   p.137

WAS? Ein Würfel und drei oder vier Spielsteine. **WIE?** Landest du auf einem Nummernfeld, nenne die *classroom phrase*. War sie korrekt, bleibe auf dem Feld. Hast du einen Fehler gemacht, gehe zwei Felder zurück. Dann ist der/die Nächste an der Reihe.

2 👥 GAME The banana skin game

Play this game in groups of three or four.

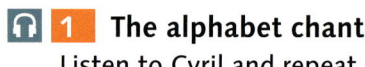

1 The alphabet chant
Listen to Cyril and repeat.

> AB–CDE   We're a happy family.
> FG–HIJ   Come and visit us today.
> KL–MNO   Plymouth is the place to go.
> PQ–RST   Lots of fun for you and me.
> UVW–XYZ Now we're tired and off to bed!

More practice 5   p. 137

2 Addresses and phone numbers

What's your address?

What's your phone number?

Can you say that again, please?

Is that one word?

Can you spell that, please?

Is that right?

a) Listen. What are the right answers?
1 Ellie talks to her friends about …
   A her mum's house.   B her dad's flat.   C her new room.
2 What's the right address?
   A 11 Great Field Street.   B 10 Gratefeld Street.   C 11 Greatfield Street.
3 Three numbers are wrong in Ellie's phone number.
   What's her phone number?

> Bei Telefonnummern sagt man *oh* oder *zero* für die 0.

01792 803 3647

b) Listen and repeat the questions.

c) Listen and write Berry's address.   More help   p. 137

3 What's your address?
a) How can you say your address and phone number in English? Think about it.

b) Double circle:
Talk to different partners.
Write their address or their phone number.

> What's your address?
> What's your phone number?
> Can you spell that, please?

> Im Englischen gibt es kein **ä**, **ö**, **ü** und **ß**.
> Du kannst sie ersetzen durch:
> **ä → ae**
> **ö → oe**
> **ü → ue**
> **ß → ss**

1 The kids from Harbour Road:
Homework time

a) Watch the film. Then put the photos (A–F) in the right order.

First we see … Then / Next we see …

Sarah   Paul   Anna

A

B

C

D

E

F

b) Before you watch again: What's the right answer? Then watch and check.

1 The three friends are at
  Sarah's / Anna's house.
2 They have / don't have lots of homework.
3 They talk about shopping / football.
4 Then they go upstairs into
  Sarah's / Tom's room.

5 Tom is Sarah's big / little[1] brother.
6 Tom is / isn't happy because Sarah, Paul and
  Anna are in his room.
7 Anna and Paul say Tom is mean / OK.
8 Later Tom and Sarah are / aren't friends again.

2 People and places: A tour of my room

a) Before you watch: What are your five favourite things in your room? Write a list.

My favourite things are my …

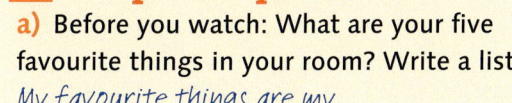

b) Now watch Joe's film. Name his favourite things – as many as you can. Make a list.
👥 Compare your list with a partner.

c) Watch the film again. Pick the right words:
1 Joe's favourite lesson is English / history.
2 Joe's pet is a dog / cat.
3 Joe's tie / guitar isn't his favourite thing.
4 Joe has a baby brother / sister.
5 Joe is good at music / sport.
6 Joe's most favourite thing is his
  computer / football.

d) Copy and complete this diagram:

My favourite things   *Joe's favourite things*

👥 Compare your diagram with a partner.

[1] little *klein*

STOP! CHECK! GO!

Ein Lösungsblatt für die Aufgaben 1 bis 6 kannst du von deiner Lehrerin / deinem Lehrer erhalten.
Die Audio-Dateien (S.49) findest du online bei den Dateien zum Workbook.

1 WORDS Can you remember Ellie's family?

a) Find the right family word and write the sentences.

I'm Pete. I'm Ellie's ... (1).

I'm Jackie. I'm Ellie's ... (2).

I'm Conor. I'm Ellie's ... (3).

I'm Zoe. I'm Ellie's ... (4).

I'm Steve. I'm Ellie's ... (5).

I'm Alisha. I'm Steve's ... (6).

And this is my big ... (8).

This is Finn. He's Ellie's ... (7).

b) Think of five more family words. Write six sentences about Ellie's family tree (see p. 37).
Andrew is Ellie's ... Owen and Lily are Andrew's ...
Check with a partner.

2 WORDS Sandy's house

a) O Match the labels (A–H) with the places (1–8) in the picture.

A kitchen   B hall

C living room

D bedroom

E bathroom

F toilet   G garden

H garage

b) Sandy is all wrong. But what's right? Correct the mistakes.

Hi! Welcome to my ~~madhouse~~ *house*. The ~~hall~~ is yellow. And the ~~bathroom~~ is pink. This is my ~~toilet~~ – it has a red sofa. My ~~bedroom~~ is red – cool! And look at my ~~kitchen~~ – there's a bike. But the ~~garage~~ is my favourite room because I love eating!

c) House quiz: What room is it?
1 It's a very small, white room!
2 I make lunch here.
3 My bed and wardrobe are here.
4 My bike is here.
5 I watch TV here.

3 REVISION Sandy's family

Complete the text for Sandy.

My family ... (1) big. This ... (2) my father.
Dad ... (3) very strict, but he... (4) fun too.
This ... (5) my mum. She... (6) cool, but she... (7)
strict too.

My brothers and sisters ... (8) OK. But they... (9)
very messy. We... (10) all very noisy. I... (11)
happy because I... (12) in my new house.
It... (13) great!

4 Questions for Sandy  p.138

Cyril has questions for Sandy. Choose the right answers.

1 Hey, Sandy. Are you happy?
2 Is your family small?
3 Are your parents strict?
4 Is your mum cool?
5 Are your brothers and sisters mean?
6 Are you and your family noisy?
7 Is your new house messy?

Yes, they are.
No, she isn't.
Yes, I am.
No, it isn't.
Yes, it is.
No, I'm not.
Yes, she is.
Yes, we are.
No, they aren't.

5 LISTENING Numbers and addresses

a) Numbers: The mobile numbers are wrong. Listen. Write the right numbers.

12.44
Adam
07821 443 1931
OPTIONS VIEW BACK

12.45
Berry
07794 191 5515
OPTIONS VIEW BACK

12.46
Luca
077951 819 632
OPTIONS VIEW BACK

b) Addresses: Listen. Which address (1, 2 or 3) is Luca's address?

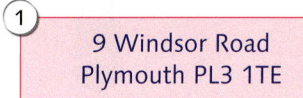

1 9 Windsor Road
Plymouth PL3 1TE

2 9 Windsor Street
Plymouth PL3 2ET

3 19 Winsbury Road
Plymouth PL6 7NN

c) Listen. Write Adam's address.

 6 WRITING   An email to a new e-pal

> Hi! I'm Tom, your new e-pal.
> I live in England, but I'm from America. My family is small.
> My parents aren't together. I live with my mum and my sister.
> Our house is in Plymouth. Plymouth is nice. It's a big city in England.
> My room is OK. I have a computer. I play games with my friends.
> My school is in Plymouth too. It's very big. I have lots of friends.
> They're very cool. My teachers are OK too. I have lots of questions for you.

a) ◯ Read Tom's email. Complete his questions and write your short answers.

1 *Are* you from England? *No, I'm not.*
2 ... your family small?
3 ... your house in a city?
4 ... your room nice?
5 ... your school big?
6 ... your friends cool?
7 ... your teachers OK?

b) ● Write Tom an email about yourself. Tom's email can help you. You can write about your ...

> city • family • friends • home • school •
> ...

 7   SPEAKING   Good shops

PARTNER B: Go to page 127.

a) PARTNER A:

You're in Plymouth and you want to find a good mobile shop. Ask partner B these questions.
Write: – the name of the shop
         – the address
         – the phone number.

b) Partner B wants to find a good sports shop. Answer his or her questions.

> Do you know a good mobile shop in Plymouth?

> What's the name of the shop, please?

> What's the address?

> Can you spell that, please?

> Do you know the phone number?

> Can you say that again, please?

8 READING   A new hobby

a) Read the story.

What's the problem, Zoe?

I'm bored! I have no hobby!

What about tae kwon do? It's great fun.

1 In Ellie and Zoe's room

Is tae kwon do fun?

Yes, it is.

Is it for boys too?

Yes, of course!

2 Conor is in the room

Hey. We don't have tae kwon do clothes.

That's OK. I have lots of old clothes.

But for me too?

No problem. Tae kwon do clothes are for girls *and* boys.

3 But there's a problem

You're new. Welcome to our club. Are you ready to start?

Yes, we are!

Thanks!

4 Now they're at the club

You're very good!

Thanks.

This is easy!

5 Later

Are you tired?

Well, erm … Yes, now I am. Football is better!

I think it's great. I have a new hobby!

6 Zoe is happy now

b) Answer the questions with complete sentences. *1 Zoe is bored.   2 She's bored because …*

1 Who's bored?
2 Why is she bored?
3 Is tae kwon do fun?

4 Who has no tae kwon do clothes?
5 Is Zoe good at tae kwon do?
6 Who thinks tae kwon do is easy?

7 Who's tired?
8 Who has a new hobby?

9   My learner log

Write your learner log for Unit 2.
Put it in your DOSSIER.

My learner log

My favourite picture in Unit 2 is … You can see… I like it because …
My favourite character in Unit 2 is …   He/she is…   I like him/her because …
My favourite text in Unit 2 is … because …
Ten words about my house / flat: …
Ten family words: …
Difficult words in Unit 2 are: …
My progress in English is: GREAT! 👍 / OK ✊ / NOT VERY GOOD 👎

My Plymouth

1 This is my town

a) Before you listen to Luca, match the sentences (A–F) with the photos (1–6).

> A My favourite shop is a mobile shop.
> B I often go to the cinema with my friends.
> C At the weekend I ride my BMX bike in the park.
> D We live in a nice road.
> E We go to a swimming pool in the summer.
> F My dad works at a fire station.

b) Listen and check.

c) Listen again and pick the right names.

Luca's street:	**A** Windy	**B** Windsor	**C** Winfield
Park:	**A** Centre	**B** Royal	**C** Central
Fire station:	**A** Greenside	**B** Greenbank	**C** Freebank
Swimming pool:	**A** Tinside Lido	**B** Tinbank Lido	**C** Greenside Lido
Cinema:	**A** Royal	**B** Reel	**C** Wheel
Mobile shop:	**A** Phones 4U	**B** Phones for Me	**C** Phones R Us

d) Check your notes with a partner.

2 Places in Plymouth

a) These places are in Plymouth too. Find them on the map.

theatre

museum

church

police station

b) Talk about the places with a partner. Swap roles.

A: Where's the theatre?
B: The theatre is in … (name of street)

A: Is that near …?
B: Yes, it is. / No. it isn't. It's near …

3 Your town or village

a) What places can you find in your town or village? Make a list – as many as you can.

▶ Wordbank 6, p. 187

b) Make sentences about your town or village.

I live in … / In my town we have …   I often / … go to …   My favourite place is … It's in / near …

c) Talk to your class about your town or village.

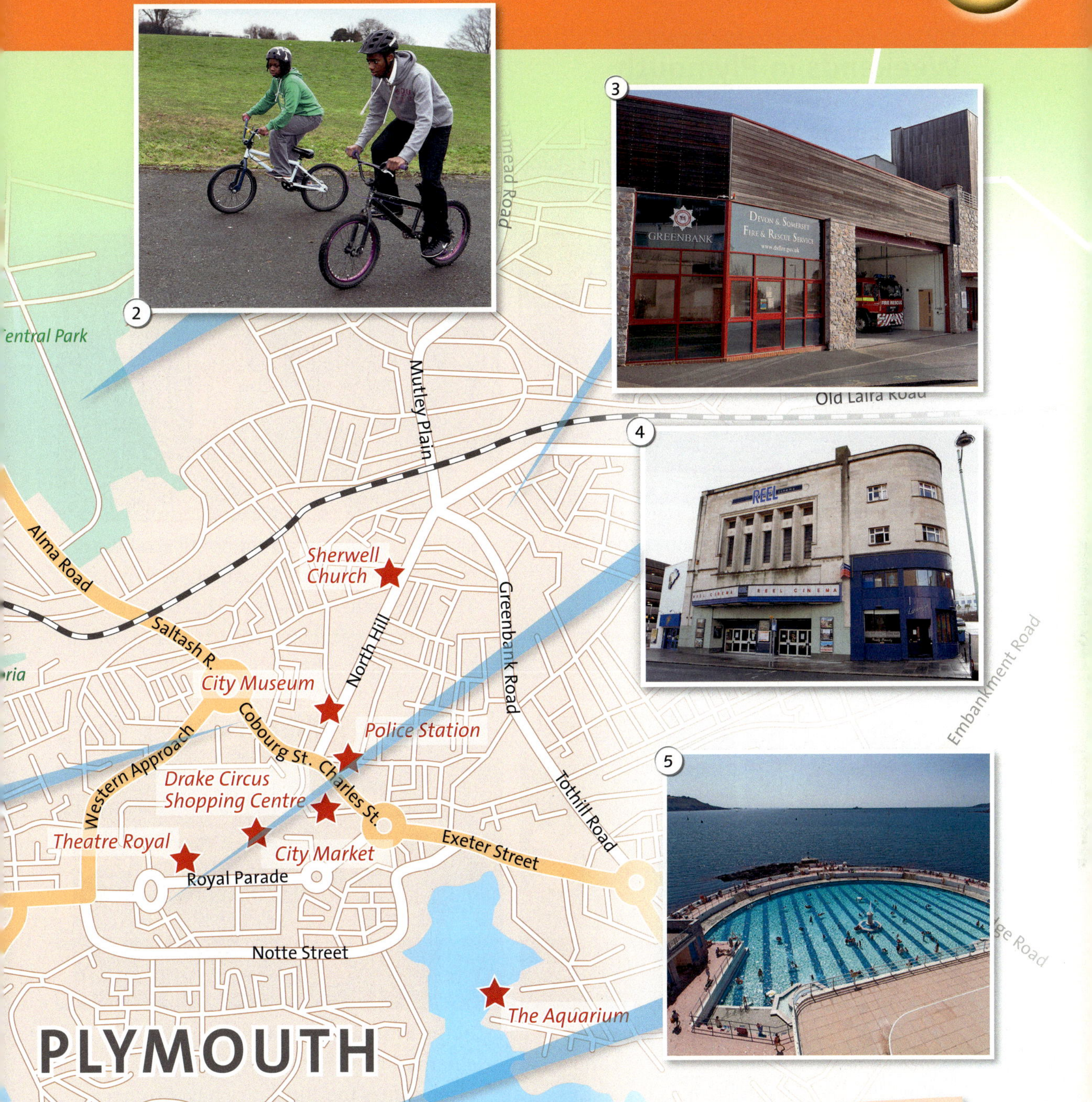

Old Laira Road

Central Park

Mutley Plain

Alma Road

Saltash R.

Sherwell
Church ★

North Hill

Greenbank Road

Embankment Road

City Museum ★

Western Approach

Cobourg St.

Charles St.

Police Station ★

Drake Circus
Shopping Centre ★

Theatre Royal ★

Exeter Street

Tothill Road

City Market ★

Royal Parade

Notte Street

★ The Aquarium

PLYMOUTH

This is my city

This is my town, this is my city.
Through my eyes it looks so pretty.
This is my town, this is my city now.

These are my people, this is my song.
Dirty streets, where I belong.
This is my town, this is my city now.
This is my city now.
                                    Timothy Victor

🎧 **4** **SONG** **This is my city**
Listen to the song and sing along.

Weekends in Plymouth

🎧 **1** **Saturdays are great**

a) Before you read, look at the pictures: Where is Luca?

In picture … Luca is …

Saturdays are great. I have no school. Mum always works on Saturdays. But dad stays at home. I often make a big breakfast for everybody. It's really easy. Grace sometimes helps me.

In the morning we go shopping. First we go to the supermarket. It's usually very full. Then we go to the market. That's more fun. Dad buys vegetables. Jack, Grace and I often buy sweets or other things.

In the afternoon Dad and Grace usually play games in the living room. Jack and I don't like their games. We usually go to Central Park. We ride our BMX bikes there.

In the evening I sometimes go to the cinema. I meet my friends there. Jack often comes too. But Grace never comes. Mum doesn't like the idea.

b) Right (✓), wrong (✗) or not in the text? Correct the wrong sentences.

1 On Saturdays Luca has no school.
2 Mum never works on Saturdays.
3 In the morning Jack goes swimming.
4 At the market Luca often sees his Eggy friends.
5 Dad and Grace like playing games in the afternoon.
6 Jack and Luca ride their bikes in Central Park.
7 In the evening Luca sometimes goes to the theatre.
8 Grace often comes.

2 NOW YOU

a) ⬜ Make a table about your Saturdays.
Use ideas from the box. ⫽ ● p.138

I always	I sometimes	I never
go shopping	...	...

buy sweets • go shopping •
go to the park • have a big breakfast •
meet friends • play football • play music •
ride my bike • stay at home •
watch TV • ...

I always go shopping on Saturdays. What about you?

Me too!

b) 👥 Who does the same things?
Find people in your class.

c) Write about your Saturdays. Use ideas from 1 and 2.
In the morning I ... / First we ... / Then I ...

🎧 3 Shopping for a birthday present

a) Can Jack and his dad find a present for Luca? Find out.
It's Luca's birthday soon. Jack and his dad are in a sports shop.

Dad ___ Look, Jack. What about the black trainers?

Jack ___ Oh no, Dad! I know what Luca likes. He doesn't like black
trainers. What about the red trainers? They're cool.

Dad ___ Red? Oh no! And they're too expensive – £99!

Jack ___ What about a hoodie then? Luca wants a hoodie. And he
loves green. Look at this.

Dad ___ A hoodie – nice idea. I think brown is a good colour for Luca.

Jack ___ A brown hoodie? Oh dad! You don't know Luca. He hates
brown. ... Hey, what about this yellow BMX shirt?

Dad ___ Yellow? ...

b) Finish the sentences.

1 Dad likes ..., but he doesn't like ....   2 Jack likes the ... and the ...   3 Luca hates ..., but he loves ...

4 I love the hoodie!

a) What's in the picture?
There's a green ... and
there are blue ...

I love the hoodie! What about you?

b) 👥 What do you love or hate?
What's OK / nice / boring / ...?
Talk to different partners –
as many as you can.

Really? I hate the hoodie!

c) ● Tell the class.
– Matteo loves / hates the ...
– He thinks the ... is boring / cool / ...
– Lots of girls hate the ...

Birthdays

1 👥 You and your birthday

What do you do on your birthday?
Tell your partner five things.

On my birthday I	always usually often sometimes never	go swimming. stay at home. get presents. go shopping. visit my aunt. have a party. go to a restaurant. go to the cinema. …

On my birthday I usually go to the beach, then I eat a fish or two …

But you do that every day, stupid bird!

2 Birthday ideas

🎧 **a)** Listen. Which picture (1–4) is Luca's birthday, Ellie's birthday, Adam's birthday or Berry's birthday? **Example:** Picture … is Luca's birthday.

b) Listen again. Match the names with the birthdays.

Luca
Ellie
Berry
Adam

A 9th September
B 14th February
C 1st August
D 25th December

c) Listen again. Complete the sentences.
1 *Luca* ____ I … go to the aquarium.
2 *Ellie* ____ We sometimes … on my birthday.
3 *Adam* ____ I … have a party with my friends.
4 *Berry* ____ I always … with my parents.

👥 Check your answers with a partner.

3 Months and dates

a) Say the months in the right order.
Then write them in your exercise book.

February August November
October July March May
April September
January December
June

🎧 **b)** Listen and repeat the dates.

🎧 **c)** 🔘 **Listen. What dates do you hear?**

1 Ⓐ 15th January   Ⓑ 30th January
2 Ⓐ 1st May   Ⓑ 5th May
3 Ⓐ 2nd December   Ⓑ 22nd December
4 Ⓐ 7th October   Ⓑ 11th October
5 Ⓐ 16th July – 3rd September
   Ⓑ 17th July – 23rd September

d) 👥 Check 3c with a partner.
Say the dates. Take turns.
A: What's number one? B: It's the ... of ...

4 🔘 When's your birthday?

a) Write your birthday. How do you say it?
My birthday is on ...

You write:

1st March
2nd July
3rd September
4th November
5th December

You say:

the first of March
the second of July
the third of September
the fourth of November
the fifth of December

▶ *More dates, p. 243*

b) This is how you say the dates.
Now write them.

1 the third of June
2 the nineteenth of April
3 the sixth of February
4 the twenty-second of August
5 the tenth of December
6 the eleventh of October

5 Talking about birthdays

a) Copy the table. Complete the 'Me' column for you.

Questions	Me	1 o'clock Tina	2 o'clock ...	3 o'clock ...
When's your birthday?	6th March	...	...	
When's your best friend's birthday?	10th July	...		
When's your mum's/dad's birthday?	mum 29th April			
When's your brother's/sister's birthday?	...			

b) Appointments: Make appointments for 1, 2 and 3 o'clock with three students.
Write the names in the table.

 Are you free at 1 o'clock?
 Yes, I am.
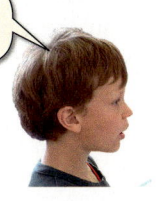 Are you free at 2 o'clock?
 No, I'm not. But I'm free at 3 o'clock.

c) Go to your appointments. Your teacher says when it is 1, 2 or 3 o'clock. Talk to your partners. Ask three questions, or more. Write the birthdays in your table. More practice 1 p. 138

d) Report to your class.
My mum's birthday is on ... / Simon's birthday is on ... / His brother's birthday is on ...

1   A day in Luca's family

Match the sentences (A–I) with the pictures (1–9). Example: *1D, 2 …*

A I get up early and make breakfast for Grace. Jack stays in bed. He always says, "I don't like mornings".

B I usually have lunch in the school canteen. Jack brings his lunch to school.

C Dad often says: "You get up late and you never have breakfast. You don't make our life easy, Jack!"

D Dad's a firefighter, so he doesn't have a normal workday. He often works at night and comes home in the morning.

E After dinner we watch TV. Mum and dad often talk. I say, "Quiet, please!", but it doesn't help. They don't listen to me! Later dad goes to work.

F Mum often comes home late. We always have dinner together and we talk about the day.

G In the afternoon dad sleeps and we do our homework.

H Jack and I usually go to school by bus. It stops near our house. But we don't always go to school together because I sometimes ride my bike.

I In the evening Dad usually makes dinner. Grace helps him. They always have fun.

> Zeit- und Ortsangaben wie *at night* oder *in the school canteen* stellst du meist ans Satzende. Eine Zeitangabe kann auch am Satzanfang stehen.

2 The simple present – positive statements

a) There are lots of verbs in Luca's text,
for example *get* and *stays*. Make two lists:

Verb ohne s	Verb mit s
I get up early.	Jack stays in bed.

b) Choose the two correct answers from A–C.
Then make the rules for positive statements.

FOCUS

Mit dem *simple present* sprichst du darüber, …	I, you, we, they → mit oder ohne 's' am Verb?
A was jeden Tag, oft, manchmal oder nie passiert.	he, she, it → mit oder ohne 's' am Verb?
B was schon passiert ist.	
C was sich nicht ändert oder was immer so ist.	

▸ *Language file 6, p. 179*

3 Luca's day

Complete Luca's sentences.

1 I ... (get up) early and ... (make) breakfast
  for Grace.
2 Jack ... (stay) in bed in the morning.
3 "You always ... (get up) late," dad says to Jack.

4 At dinner we ... (talk) about the day.
5 Dad ... (sleep) in the afternoon,
  so we ... (stay) quiet.
6 The bus ... (stop) near our house.

🎧 4 Who is he?

Listen to the poem. Then repeat it. Who is 'he'?

He lives on the beach.
He walks on the sand.
He swims in the sea.
He pinches my hand.

He chats and he sings.
He sits in the sun.
He watches the fishermen.
Then he jumps up and runs!

Vorsicht bei diesen Verben:
watch – watches
go – goes
have – has

5 Cyril and Sandy's day

Write about Cyril and Sandy. Put in the correct forms of the verbs: get • go • have • watch.

1 In the morning I ... up early. 2 Sandy is lazy. She ... up late. 3 I ... breakfast on the beach.

4 Sandy ... the kids on the
  beach.
5 We ... swimming together.
6 Sandy often ... to Plymouth
  with her friends.

More practice 2 | p. 139

3

6 The simple present – negative statements

Look again at the text on p. 58.

a) Put in *don't* or *doesn't*.

1 I ... like mornings.
2 You ... make my life easy, Jack!
3 He ... have a normal workday.
4 It ... help.
5 They ... listen to me!
6 We ... always go together.

b) Complete the rules for negative statements with *don't* and *doesn't*.

> **FOCUS**
>
> *I, you, we, they* + ... + Verb
> *he, she, it*   + ... + Verb

▶ *Language file 7, p. 179*

7 That's not right!

a) ⊙ Complete the sentences. Use *don't* or *doesn't*. // ● p.139

1 Jack gets up early. – That's not right! He doesn't get up early.
2 Luca and Jack do their homework in the morning. – That's not right! They ...
3 Dad and Grace make breakfast together. – That's not right! They ...
4 Dad works in the afternoon. – That's not right! He ...
5 Mum comes home from work early. – That's not right! She ...
6 After dinner they all sing songs. – That's not right! They ...

b) 👥 ● Write five wrong sentences about Ellie, Berry and Adam. Swap your sentences with other students.
Can you correct all the sentences?

8 ⊙ Working parents // ● p.139

Write the sentences about Luca's mum and dad with the correct form – positive or negative.

1 Luca's mum ... (work) in a mobile phone shop.
2 Luca's dad ... (work) in a museum.
3 He ... (have) a normal workday.
4 She ... (often come) home late.
5 He ... (get up) late in the afternoon.
6 Luca, Jack and Grace ... (see) their parents after school.
7 She ... (go) to work on Saturdays.
8 On Saturdays they ... (have) breakfast together.

More practice 3 p.139

9 NOW YOU

a) Copy the table. Put a tick (✓) or a cross (✗) to make a positive or negative sentence about your day.

b) 👥 Walk around: Talk to two or more partners. Make notes.

A: I have breakfast before school. What about you?
B: I don't have breakfast before school.

	Me	Partner 1	Partner 2	Partner 3
have breakfast before school	✓	...	...	...
go to school by bus	✗	...	...	
do my homework in the afternoon	...	...		
watch TV in the evening	...	...		
help in the kitchen				
go to bed early				

c) 👥 ● Tell the class.

Cem has breakfast before school. Nina watches TV in the evening, but Arne doesn't watch TV. ...

10 A great place for a holiday

This is a new tourist brochure for Plymouth. Pick the right linking words *(and, or, but, because)*.

Come to **Plymouth!**

You want to be in a great place in your holidays,
__1__ (but / or) you don't want to be with lots of people?
Come to Plymouth! People love Plymouth __2__ (because / and)
it's never boring __3__ (or / and) it's never too busy. There's art, music
and theatre __4__ (and / but) there are lots of fun things outdoors.
Come and see! You can visit a museum __5__ (or / but) you can go
swimming at the beach. You can have an evening at the theatre
__6__ (or / because) you can ride bikes at the Hoe. People always
come back to Plymouth __7__ (but / because) it's special. Come to
Plymouth in your next holidays. It's the best!

11 🔵 Plymouth days and nights

Match the sentence parts. Use the right linking word *(and, or, but)*.

1 In the afternoon Adam plays football	he doesn't like working at night.
2 Ellie doesn't see her dad every day	it has a nice swimming pool too.
3 At Eggy the kids have lunch in the canteen	she often visits Ellie, Adam and Luca.
4 Luca's dad likes his job	in the evening he listens to music.
5 Plymouth has a great beach	he goes to the cinema with his friends.
6 Berry doesn't live near her school friends	she goes to his flat at the weekend.
7 In the evening Luca stays at home	they bring their lunch from home.

(and, or, but)

More help p. 140

👥 Check with a partner.

12 🔵 My day

a) Make notes about you and your family. You can use a mind map.  More help p. 140

b) Use your notes and write a text about you and your family. Write positive and negative sentences – as many as you can. Use linking words. More help p. 140

Examples:
In the morning mum makes breakfast and …
We often go to school by bus or we …
I don't often have lunch at school, but …
In the evening we …

1 **Before you read**

Look at the photos. Is Luca's birthday fun?

👥 Talk to a partner.

- I think / don't think Luca's birthday is fun.
- Look at photo … He looks / doesn't look happy.

🎧 Happy birthday, Luca!

Francis and the Drakes LIVE

Plymouth Pavilions 14–15 February

Tickets: Go to our website
www.plymouthpavilions.com

I want to do something different this year – with Adam, Berry and Ellie.

Oh, Luca loves Berry and Ellie!

Shut up, Jack!

Let's make plans for your birthday, Luca.

What about a concert? Your favourite band is in town.

Great idea, Mum. That's different!

1 It's Thursday. Luca's birthday is on Saturday. He wants to do something different with his friends.

Happy birthday to you. You live in a zoo …

Shut up, Jack!

Happy birthday, Luca!

This is great! I love the colour. Thanks!

2 It's Saturday morning and Luca is excited. He opens his birthday presents and gets a nice surprise.

I don't want to go to the park today. Let's do something different!

TO THE HOE ➡

My friends usually ride their bikes at the Hoe. Let's go there.

3 Mum is at work. Grace and dad are at the shops. Luca and Jack are on their bikes.

It doesn't look hard. Let's go!

But …

We always go down this hill!

Come on, birthday boy!

I don't like this idea.

4 Jack and Luca go to the Hoe. Jack meets his friends. They have great BMX bikes and they go down the hill fast.

5 Jack goes down the hill first. He's OK. Now it's Luca's turn.

Luca, are you OK?

No I'm not! Oh, my leg!

I'm really sorry!

Me too!

This is something different for your birthday, Luca!

6 Luca goes down the hill, but he loses control and falls. Jack helps him.

7 Luca and Jack are back from the hospital. Luca has a sore leg. His mum doesn't look very happy!

2 ⃝ Right or wrong? Correct the wrong sentences.

1 Luca wants to do something with his family.
   He doesn't want to … He wants …
2 Luca likes mum's idea.
3 Luca gets a brown hoodie for his birthday.
4 Luca and Jack go shopping with dad.
5 Jack meets his friends at the Hoe.
6 Luca goes down the hill first.
7 Luca falls.
8 Luca and Jack go to the police station.

3 ⬤ Luca's birthday

Write the story.

> On Thursday Luca has no ideas for …
> But his mum …
> On Saturday morning Luca gets …
> Later with Jack, Luca doesn't …
> The boys meet Jack's friends at …
> Jack goes …
> Then Luca …, but …
> Jack and Luca …
> Luca has …
>
> More help p. 141

🎧 4 The end of the story

a) Listen to the end of the story. Who comes to Luca's house? Why is Luca happy in the end?

b) Listen again. What presents does Luca get from his friends?

1 Luca's garage sale

a) Luca needs money for a new bike. Look at the picture. What's in Luca's garage sale? Make two lists:

There's ...	There are
a bike	2 footballs
a ...	3 ...

▶ Language file 5, p. 178

b) Look at your lists. Listen and tick (✓) in your list what you hear.

c) Listen again. How much are the things in the garage sale? ▶ p. 141

1 The calculator is ...
2 The mobile is ...
3 The crab is ...
4 The posters are ...

5 The computer is ...
6 The school bag is ...
7 The blazer is ...
8 The footballs are ...

£5
£20

£9.50 £10 £1 50 p
£4 £5.50

You write:	You say:
£1.50	One pound fifty
50 p	Fifty p

2 British money

a) Write labels for a sale: *A: £1.50, B: ...*

A: One pound fifty
B: Ninety-nine p
C: Seventeen pounds
D: Four pounds twenty-five
E: Five pounds thirty

b) 👥 What do you say? Practise with a partner.

① £3.99 ② 20 p ③ £8.50 ④ £11.25

⑤ £24.90 ⑥ £15

More practice 4   p. 141

▶ Workbook 19–20, p. 42

1 In a bike shop

Can Luca buy his dream bike? Read and find out.

Luca — Mum, it's the Montana. It's my dream bike.

Mum — It looks nice. Is it expensive?

Luca — Excuse me, please. How much is this bike?

Man — It's £279.

Luca — That's too expensive. How much is the 5 Star?

Man — It's £159. It's a special offer.

Mum — That's OK. It looks nice too.

Luca — Yeah, and it's good value. Jack has the same bike. Can I buy it, Mum?

Mum — It's your money.

Luca — Can I try it?

Man — Sure.

Luca — ... Wow, it's really great. I'll take it.

Man — Good. That's £159, please.

2 A new helmet

a) Copy and complete the dialogue. Look at 1 for help.

Luca — This helmet looks ... (1). I like it. Excuse me, ... (2). How ... (3) is the red helmet?

Man — ... (4) £24.99.

Luca — That's too ... (5)! ... (6) much is the white helmet?

Man — It's a ... (7) offer. It's £16.99.

Luca — That's OK. I'll ... (8) it.

b) Listen to the dialogue and check.

3 👥 ROLE-PLAY

A garage sale

Partner B: Go to page 127.

Partner A: You're at a garage sale in Plymouth. You have £15. Buy some things.

> Excuse me, please.
> How much is the ...?
> That's too expensive / OK!
> I'll take it.
> Here you are.

Swap roles.

▶ *Workbook 21–22, p. 43*

1 Plymouth adverts

Match the sentences with the adverts: A, B or C.
Sometimes there are two answers.

1 You can go there in February. — *Adverts A, C.*
2 You like music.
3 You like fish and the sea.
4 It's summer in Plymouth.
5 You can go there in July.
6 You can go there in March.
7 You don't need money.
8 You can watch a film there.

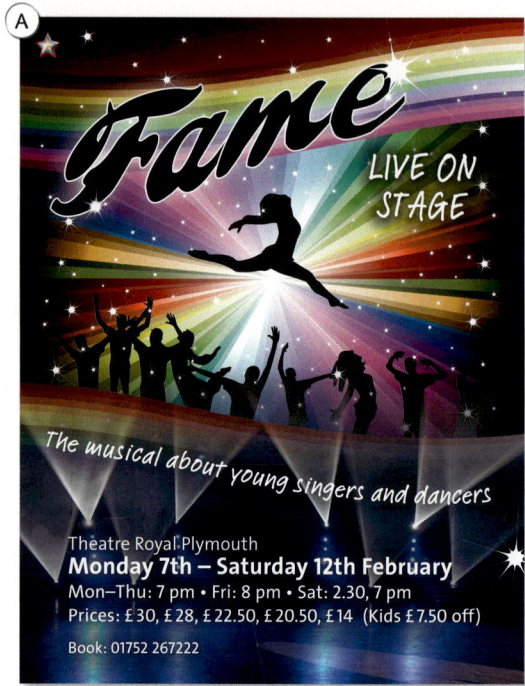

2 Guessing new words

What are these words in German?

1 on stage (advert A), fireworks (advert B)
2 theatre (advert A), festival (advert B)
3 opening times (advert C), adults (advert C)
4 singers (advert A), dancers (advert A)

> **So kannst du manche neue Wörter verstehen:**
> 1. Schau auf die Bilder.
> 2. Gibt es ein ähnliches Wort im Deutschen?
> 3. Schau auf die Wörter vor oder nach dem Wort.
> 4. Steckt im unbekannten Wort ein Wort, das du kennst?

 More help p. 141   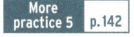 More practice 5 p. 142

▶ *Skills file 3, p. 173*

▶ *Workbook 23, p. 44*

1   The kids from Harbour Road:
Sarah isn't happy!

a) Watch part 1 of the film. Why isn't Sarah with Anna and Paul at the shops?

1 Because Paul and Anna don't like Sarah.
2 Because Sarah hates shopping.
3 Because they want to buy Sarah a present.

b) Watch part 2 of the film. Then match the photos (1–4) with the sentences (A–D).

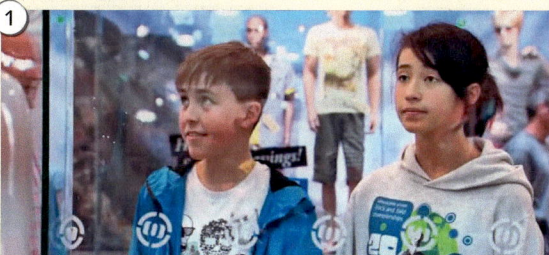

A It's £5.99.
B I'll take this hat[1], please.

C This is Sarah's favourite shop.
D What about this one[2]?

c) Watch part 3. Describe Sarah's feelings.
First she's … Then she's … Then … In the end she's …

angry[3] • happy • surprised[4] • unhappy

2   People and places: Plymouth, England

a) Watch the film about Plymouth. Which places can you see in the film?

The Reel Cinema

The Hoe

The Lido

The aquarium

The shopping centre

The market

b) 👥 What do you think about Plymouth? What place do you want to visit?

Plymouth looks big / nice / great / boring / …

I want to visit / see the … because it's …
What about you?

---

[1] hat [hæt] *Hut*   [2] this one *der / die / das da*   [3] angry ['æŋgri] *wütend*   [4] surprised [sə'praɪzd] *überrascht*

STOP! CHECK! GO!

Ein Lösungsblatt für die Aufgaben 1 bis 5 kannst du von deiner Lehrerin/deinem Lehrer erhalten.
Die Audio-Dateien (S.68) findest du online bei den Dateien zum Workbook.

1 WORDS In a town

a) ⊙ What are the places? Write the names in your exercise book.

b) Finish the sentences.
1 You can watch a film in a ...   2 You can buy vegetables in a ... or a ...
3 You can look at interesting things in a ...   4 You can buy trainers in a ...

c) ⦿ Make sentences.
1 ... in a park. → *You can play games in a park.*   4 ... in a swimming pool.
2 ... in a restaurant. → *You can ...*   5 ... in a mobile phone shop.
3 ... in a shopping centre.   6 ... in a bike shop.

🎧 2 LISTENING In a sports shop
Listen to Ellie. She's in a sports shop. Pick the right answer – Ⓐ, Ⓑ or Ⓒ.
1 Ellie wants ... Ⓐ a T-shirt. Ⓑ a hoodie. Ⓒ a sweatshirt.
2 The hoodie is ... Ⓐ £14.99. Ⓑ £40.19. Ⓒ £40.99.
3 The T-shirts are ... Ⓐ good value. Ⓑ expensive. Ⓒ a special offer.
4 The red trainers are ... Ⓐ £58. Ⓑ £85. Ⓒ £18.50.
5 The white trainers are ... Ⓐ expensive. Ⓑ boring. Ⓒ good value.
6 Ellie buys ... Ⓐ a T-shirt. Ⓑ trainers. Ⓒ a hoodie.

3 WORDS Days, months and dates
a) ⊙ Write correct questions.
1 month / what / it / is ?
2 your / when's / birthday ?
3 date / the / what's / today ?
4 best friend's / when's / your / birthday ?
5 day / what / today / is / it ?

b) How do you write the date?
1 3.1. – *3rd January*   4 18.7. – ...
2 9.3. – ...   5 20.10. – ...
3 12.5. – ...   6 25.12. – ...

🎧 **c)** ⦿ Listen. Write the six dates.

4 REVISION Stupid Cyril!

a)  Complete Cyril's questions for Sandy.

1 … Eggbuckland school busy?
  Is Eggbuckland school busy?
2 … the students at school ?
3 … Luca on his bike ?
4 … the town quiet?
5 … Grace and Mr Boateng at the market?
6 … Mrs Boateng at work?
7 … you tired of my questions?
8 … I your friend?

b) Write Sandy's answers.

1 No, …
  No, it isn't.
2 No, …
3 Yes, …
4 Yes, …
5 No, …
6 No, … It's Sunday, Cyril! You stupid crab!
7 Yes, …
8 Yes, … But you're sometimes difficult!

5 LANGUAGE Cyril's birthdays

a)  Complete the text with the words in the box. Use the *simple present.*

> get up • go • have • love • meet •
> play • talk

Cyril and Sandy usually … (1) early. After breakfast they … (2) to the beach and they … (3) about the day.
Cyril ___ It's my birthday today. I want to … (4) a party again and … (5) all my friends.
Sandy ___ Great! I … (6) your parties. We always … (7) lots of games.

b) Complete the sentences with the right positive or negative verb forms.

1 Sandy always … (get) a birthday present for Cyril, but he … (know) about it. 2 Cyril … (see) his present before the party. 3 He … (have) time to play with Sandy. 4 He always … (work) in the kitchen and … (make) a big birthday lunch for his friends. 5 Sandy … (help) Cyril plan the party games because Cyril … (remember) games very well.

c) ⬤ Complete the sentences about Cyril's parties with the verbs in brackets.
For each sentence, make one verb positive and one negative.

1 Cyril … (do) boring things at his party, he always … (do) fun things!
2 Cyril and his friends … (like) swimming after their big lunch, but they … (love) playing games.
3 Sandy often … (say) "Come on, let's dance!", but Cyril's friends… (like) dancing.
4 Sandy: "You … (have) great parties, Cyril. Your friends … (want) to go home at the end!"

6 SPEAKING At the weekend

a) What about your weekends?
Copy the table and fill it in for you.
Write: always • usually •
often • sometimes • never.

At the weekend	Me	Partner 1	Partner 2
I ... go shopping.	often	...	...
I ... play football.	...		
I ... watch TV			
I ... go to the cinema.			
I ... meet friends.			
I ...			

b) Appointments: Talk to two partners and fill in the table.

I **sometimes** go shopping at the weekend.
What about you?

I **usually** go shopping at the weekend. And I ...

c) Use your table. Tell the class about one of your partners. Don't say the name.
Can the class guess?

This girl **usually** goes shopping at the weekend.
She **never** plays football.
She **sometimes** watches TV.

Is it Abida?

7 WRITING My favourite day

Write about your favourite day. Use: always • usually • often • sometimes • never.
Use linking words: and • or • but • because.

► *Language file 6, p. 179*

My favourite day is
– Friday.
– Saturday.
– ...

I (don't) get up
– early.
– late.
– ...

Then I have breakfast
– in the kitchen.
– with ...
– ...

After breakfast I
– play ...
– meet friends ...
– go to ...
– ...

I (don't) have lunch
– at home with ...
– in town with ...
– ...

In the afternoon I
– go shopping.
– ride my bike ...
– ...

In the evening I
– visit ...
– watch ...
– ...

I love	Friday Saturday ...	because	– I (don't) go to school. – I stay at home. – I do something different. – I meet my friends. – ...

8 READING Casper the cat

a) ⊙ Look at the text. Is it from a book, a comic or a newspaper? What do you think?

THE PLYMOUTH NEWS Saturday, 16th January 2010

A cat story from Plymouth

1 Casper is a cat. He's twelve. He lives in Plymouth with Susan Finden.

Every morning Casper leaves the house at the same time. He walks to the bus stop and he waits there for the number 3 bus.

5 When it comes, Casper doesn't run away. He sits on a seat and looks out of the window. The bus goes to the centre. Then it goes to the harbour. Casper doesn't move. He watches everything. He watches the people, the cars, the buses, the houses. The bus travels 11 miles. When the bus comes to Casper's house again, the bus driver opens the doors
10 and Casper gets out.

Everybody on the bus knows Casper. Everybody loves Casper. And Casper loves the number 3 bus. But he never buys a ticket.

b) Read the text. Finish the sentences and tell Casper's story.
Casper is a … (1). He's from … (2). Every day he travels … (3). He watches … (4). When the bus … (5), the bus driver … (6) and Casper … (7). Everybody on the bus … (8). Casper never … (9).

c) ⦿ Find these words in the text. Guess what they mean in German and write the words.

1 leaves (line 3)	4 sits (l. 5)	7 bus driver (l. 9)
2 bus stop (l. 4)	5 window (l. 6)	8 gets out (l. 10)
3 waits (l. 4)	6 travels (l. 8)	

More help p. 142

Was hat dir geholfen, unbekannte Wörter zu verstehen?
– Das Bild zum Text?
– Ein ähnliches deutsches Wort?
– Andere Wörter im Text?

👥 Check with a partner.

9 My learner log

Copy and complete your learner log.

You can put it in your DOSSIER.

My learner log

I can …	Examples	😄	😐	😞
– say the names of places in a town:	cinema, …	…	…	…
– say what I do at the weekend:	I often go shopping.	…	…	
– say what I do every day:		…	…	…
– say what I like and don't like:		…	…	…
– say the numbers 1–100:		…	…	…
– say the months:		…	…	…
– say today's date:		…	…	…
– say what I do on my birthday:		…	…	…
– buy things in a shop:		…	…	…

My progress in English is: GREAT! 👍 / Ok 🤜 / NOT VERY GOOD 👎

1 On Merryweather Farm

Look at the brochure. Match the pictures (A – F) with the activities in the text.
Picture A: *Stroke the …* Picture B: …
Check with a partner.

Lots of visitors come to Merryweather Farm.

Merryweather Farm – Kids love it!

Why do kids love Merryweather? Because it's a real farm and it's fun! You can do lots of things here.

- Ride the ponies in the fields.
- Watch the ducks in the pond.
- Meet the animals in Pets Corner.
- Buy nice things in the shop.
- Stroke the donkeys in the barn.
- Play on the trampoline and the zip wire.

Do you have questions? We want to help. Ask at our information desk.

2 Welcome to the farm

a) ⭕ Match the animal names with the pictures.

Picture 1 is a pony, picture 2 is a ...

> cat • chicken • cow • donkey • duck • fish •
> hamster • pig • pony • rabbit • rat • sheep

b) Listen. Which animals are on Berry's farm?

c) Listen again. Pick the right answer.
1 Berry is ... **A** in the field. **B** in the shop. **C** in the barn.
2 The tickets are ... **A** £15.50. **B** £60.00. **C** £59.50.
3 They don't have ... **A** cows. **B** sheep. **C** pigs.
4 The kids don't like ... **A** pets. **B** rats. **C** cats.
5 The toilets are ... **A** near the shop. **B** in the barn.
　　　　　　　　　　　　 C near the barn.

More practice 1 p. 143

3　NOW YOU

a) Think: You're at Merryweather Farm. Where do you want to go? Pick two places. Why do you want to go there? Make notes.

b) 👥 Pair: Talk to a partner. Agree on two places. Make notes.
A: I want to go into the barn /
　　... because I want to ... / like ...
B: I want to / like ... too. I don't
　　want to ... because ...
　　... are boring / great / nice / ...
A: OK. Let's go to ... and ...

We want to go to the ... and ...

c) Share: Tell the class.

Life on the farm

1 From Monday to Friday

A Berry's day starts early on the farm. She doesn't have an alarm clock. She has Sam, her dog. Every morning Sam wakes Berry at 6 o'clock. When Berry gets up, her mum and dad are outside. They usually feed the farm animals before the sun comes up.

B

At about half past five she goes outside again. First she looks after Harry. Then she helps with the other animals. At five to six Berry gets ready for dinner. She sometimes does sport in the evening. She doesn't watch TV. She doesn't have time!

Before breakfast, at about quarter to seven, Berry and Sam go outside. Berry feeds her pony, Harry. Sam always wants to play with Harry, but Harry doesn't like noisy dogs. At about ten past seven Berry goes back inside for breakfast.

D After breakfast Berry gets ready for school. At quarter past eight she goes to school by car with her dad. At school Berry doesn't think about the farm. She's too busy! She usually comes home before 4 o'clock. Then she eats something and does her homework.

 **C**

Right or wrong? Correct the wrong sentences.

1 Sam wakes Berry at 6 o'clock in the morning.
2 At about quarter to eight Berry feeds Harry.
3 Berry goes inside for breakfast at ten past seven.
4 She comes home from school before 3 o'clock.
5 At half past five Berry goes outside again.
6 She gets ready for dinner at ten to six.

2 Watching the clock
Say what the time is.

It's ... o'clock.   It's quarter past ...   It's half past ...

It's quarter to ...   It's ... past ...   It's ... to ...

3 NOW YOU
a) Write sentences.
1 Every morning I get up at / before / after ...
2 I usually have breakfast at (about) ...
3 At ... I go to school.
4 In the afternoon I ...
5 ...

b) 👥 Tell a partner about your day.

4 At the weekend

a) Look at the board. Put photos A–F in the right order.

Today's activities

10.45	Feed the ducks
10.55	Pony grooming
12.45	Animal handling
1.35	Sit on a tractor
3.00–4.15	Pony rides (2–9 years)
4.45	Feed the ponies

b) ☐ Listen to the four dialogues. What activities (A–F) do the visitors want to do?

Dialogue 1 is photo ..., ...

c) Listen again. What's the time?

Dialogue 1: 10.14 / 10.40
Dialogue 2: 10.50 / 11.15
Dialogue 3: 12.00 / 12.45
Dialogue 4: 3.40 / 4.30

5 The time

a) ☐ Listen and repeat.
10.00 • 12.05 • 4.05 • 5.10 • 9.15 • 7.20 •
8.25 • 12.30 • 11.35 • 2.45 • 6.50 • 1.55

b) 👥 Say one of the times in a).
Your partner points at it. Swap roles.

c) Listen and write the times. More practice 2 p. 143

You write:	You say:
2.00	two o'clock *or* two
2.05	two oh five *or* five past two
2.15	two fifteen *or* quarter past two
2.30	two thirty *or* half past two
2.45	two forty-five *or* quarter to three
2.55	two fifty-five *or* five to three

6 What's the time, please?

a) Draw a clock and write a time on it.

b) 👥 Talk to a partner like this:
A: What's the time please? B: It's ...
A: Thanks. B: You're welcome.

Write your partner's name and time. Swap clocks.

c) 👥 Walk around: Find a new partner. Write your new partner's time.
Then swap clocks again. Talk to as many partners as you can.

Feelings

1 A class discussion

a) Ms Lee, the English teacher, has two questions for the students in her class.

1. When do you feel great? 😊

2. When do you feel fed up? 😟

Partner A: Copy table A. Listen and write the names: Adam, Luca, Berry or Ellie.

A 😄 I feel great when …	
… I do sport.	Luca, …
… I'm with my animals.	
… I'm with my friends.	
… I listen to music.	
… I don't have homework.	

Partner B: Copy table B. Listen and write the names: Adam, Luca, Berry or Ellie.

B 😟 I feel fed up when …	
… my sister is bossy.	Ellie
… my mobile doesn't work.	
… my friends don't text me.	
… people don't talk to me.	
… I have lots of homework.	

b) Swap tables with your partner. Listen again and check your partner's answers.

2 NOW YOU

a) When do you feel great? When do you feel fed up? Make notes like this:

More help p. 143

😄 I feel great …	😟 I feel fed up …
when I play football.	when my dad is bossy.
when I ….	…
…	

b) Talk to your partner.
Ask and answer the questions:

When do you feel great?

When …

When do you feel fed up?

When …

c) Write your favourite positive and favourite negative statement from 2a on a piece of paper.

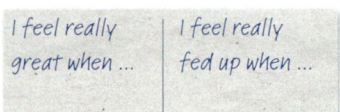

I feel really great when …	I feel really fed up when …

I think it's Jan!

No, it isn't me!

d) Put your pieces of paper together. Each student takes a different person's piece of paper and reads it to the class.
This person feels great when he or she …

Who is it? Make a guess.

🎧 3 Berry's homework

a) Read Berry's homework. Find sentences in the text for the photos.
Photo A – I feel great when I'm ...

My feelings *by Berry Donovan*

I feel great when I'm with the animals at home because I really love animals.

I sometimes feel a bit fed up because I'm the only student at school in a wheelchair. I'm always different.

But I feel great when I'm with my friends. With my friends I'm not 'the girl in the wheelchair'. I'm a normal kid!

I usually feel great when I do sport too. My favourite sport is wheelchair basketball. When I'm in my wheelchair I can go really fast and I'm good with a basketball. I love it when my team wins too.

I feel really fed up when people don't talk to me. They do that because I'm in a wheelchair. They ask my mum: 'Does she want a drink?' They don't ask ME: 'Do YOU want a drink?' At school people ask my friends: 'Does she understand?' But I can speak for myself. My legs don't work well. But my mouth works fine.

b) Finish these sentences for Berry:
– I feel great when ...
– I feel fed up when / because ...

c) Find sentences in Berry's text with these words:
– and, but, because
– always, usually, sometimes
Write one example from the text for each word.

d) 🔵 Write a short text about your feelings. Talk about: at home / at school / with friends / …. Use your notes from 2a and use words from 3c. Write more than one sentence for each feeling. You can put your text in your DOSSIER. | More help p. 144 |

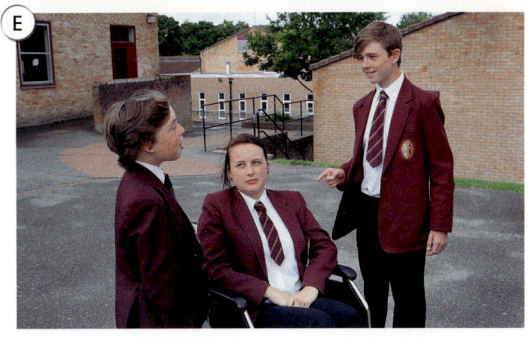

1 A pet or a wild animal?

Berry has lots of pets. But do Ellie, Luca and Adam have pets? Can you remember? Read and check.

A chipmunk

Luca ___ Do you have a cat or a dog, Adam?

Adam _ No, we don't have a pet.

Luca ___ What about you, Ellie?
Do you have a pet?

5 Ellie ___ Yes, I do. I have two cats at mum's house.

Luca ___ What about your dad?
Does he have a pet?

Ellie ___ No. Dad and Alisha don't have a
10 pet. They don't have time.

Berry _ And what about you, Luca?

Luca ___ No, we don't have a pet. Dad is the problem. He doesn't like dogs.

Adam _ And what about your mum?
15 Does she like animals?

Luca ___ She likes dogs, but she doesn't like cats. But I want a pet!

Ellie ___ I have an idea. What about a chipmunk?

Luca ___ A chipmunk? Does it look like a   20
monkey?

Ellie ___ No, it doesn't look like a monkey
– you idiot.

Berry _ We have chipmunks on the farm.
They're small and furry. They're   25
really cute.

Ellie ___ Do they like cats?

Berry ___ No, they don't like other animals.
And they hate cats!

Luca ___ I want a chipmunk.   30

Berry ___ I don't know. A chipmunk is a wild
animal. It isn't really a good pet for
a house.

Luca ___ Oh!

2 The simple present – questions

a) Put *do* or *does* in the questions.

1 … you have a pet? (line 4)
2 … he have a pet? (l. 8)
3 … she like animals? (l. 15)
4 … it look like a monkey? (l. 20)
5 … they like cats? (l. 27)

b) Complete the rules with *do* or *does*.

FOCUS		?
… + I, you, we, they + verb ?		
… + he, she, it + verb ?		

▶ *Language file 8, p. 180*

3 NOW YOU

a) Complete the questions with *do* or *does*.

1 What about you? … you like animals?
2 What about your parents? … they like animals?
3 And your best friend? … he / she have a pet?
4 And your teacher? … he / she have a pet?

b) Listen. Answer the questions.

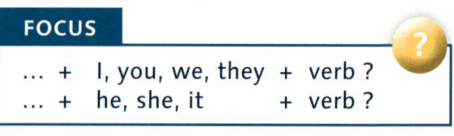

Yes, I do. No, I don't.

Yes, he / she does. No, he / she doesn't.

c) 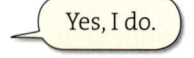 Write four or more questions for your partner with *do* or *does*.
One partner asks questions, the other partner answers. Then swap.

4 A good pet?

Are rats good pets? Read and find out.

Luca __ What pets do you have, Berry?

Berry __ I have a dog – Sam. And we have hamsters, rabbits, chipmunks and rats.

Luca __ Rats? Are they good pets?

Berry __ Yes. I love our rats.

Ellie __ Why do you love rats?

Berry __ Because they're friendly. They play. They sit on my shoulder. They're very cute.

Luca __ Where do they live?

Berry __ They live in a cage in Pets Corner.

Adam __ What do they eat?

Berry __ Lots of things like fruit and nuts and …

Ellie __ When do they sleep?

Berry __ At night. I have an idea. Come to the farm and see our pets.

5 Question words

a) Find five questions in the dialogue with the question words: *what*, *when*, *where*, *why*.

b) Match the English and the German question words.

> **FOCUS**
>
> | English: | German: |
> |---|---|
> | What? | Was? Welche? |
> | When? | Warum? |
> | Where? | Wo? Wohin? |
> | Why? | Wann? |

▶ *Language file 9, p. 180*

6 ● What pet do you have?

Find the right question words for the interview.

1 … pet do you have?
2 … do you like rabbits?
3 … does your rabbit live?
4 … does your rabbit eat?
5 … do you feed your rabbit?
6 … other pets do you have?

– I have a rabbit. His name is Bunny.
– Because they're fun and friendly.
– He lives in a big cage in my room.
– He eats lots of things. He loves vegetables.
– In the morning and in the evening.
– A snake, a monkey, a fish, a duck, a …

> The orange words can help you.

7 Talking about pets

a) 👥 Make a dialogue with a partner.

▶ *Wordbank 7, p. 188*

A: Do you have a pet?

B: Yes, I do.   B: No, I don't.

A: What pet do you have?   A: Do you want a pet?

B: I have a …   B: Yes, I do.   B: No, I don't.

A: Where does your pet live?   A: What pet do you want?   A: Why not?

B: It lives inside / outside / …   B: I want a …   B: Because …

b) Write about your favourite pet or a friend's pet. You can put your text in your DOSSIER.

More help p. 145

More practice 3 p. 144

8 Who is it?

a)  Match the answers (A–F) with the questions (1–6). Who is it?

1 When do you get up?

2 What do you like?

3 Where do you go to school?

4 When do you come home?

5 What do you do after school?

6 Where do you live?

?

A Eggy.

B Before 4 o'clock.

C I like my animals.

D Very early – at 6 o'clock.

E In Woolwell.

F My homework.

b) Make the questions for the answers. Who is it?

1 Where / you / live / do / ?   – In Plymouth.
2 What / like / do / you / ?   – My bike!
3 Where / to school / do / you / go / ?   – In Plymouth too.
4 When / to the cinema / you / go / do / ?   – At the weekend.
5 What / do / on Saturdays / you / do / ?   – I ride my bike.
6 Where / bike / do / ride / you / your / ?   – In Central Park.

c) ⬤ Now make questions for these answers. Who is it?

1 On the beach in Kingsand.   4 I like swimming and games.
2 I don't go to school!   5 I don't go to the cinema!
3 On Saturdays I play with Sandy.   6 I get up late, at 10 o'clock.

9 ⬤ Find a person who …

a) You want to find interesting people in your class. Pick three things in this box – or more.

b) What questions can you ask?   [More help] p. 145

Find a person who …
– has an interesting pet.
– has an interesting hobby.
– gets up very early.
– goes to a nice place in the holidays.
– likes an English football team.
– likes homework.

Do you have a pet?

What pet do you have?

Do you go to a nice place in the holidays?

Where …?

c) 👥 Walk around: Talk to different people. Ask your questions. Take notes.

d) Write about the interesting people in your class.

Dana has an interesting pet – a snake!
Jakob gets up very early – at about 6 o'clock.
Hanna loves homework. She loves maths!
Kenan …

1 Before you read

Look at the pictures. Who is it? / Who are they?

1 ... are on the bus.

2 ... doesn't have his sweets.

3 ... has a problem with a chipmunk.

4 ... doesn't like cows.

5 ... are in the barn.

6 ... isn't nervous.

🎧 Adventures in the country

1 **Scene 1** Berry wants to invite her friends to the farm. This is her email.

> Hi guys
> Do you want to see our chipmunks?
> Do you want to come to the farm
> 5 for a sleepover? What about
> next Saturday? There's a bus at
> 3 o'clock. Bring your sleeping bags.
> Berry

10 **Scene 2** It's 3 o'clock on Saturday. Luca, Ellie and Adam are excited. They're at the bus station and they all have their sleeping bags. Ellie has a bag with fruit, Adam has a bag with sandwiches and Luca has a bag

15 with sweets.

"OK. Let's go!" Ellie says.

"Yeah, let's go to the country!" Adam says.

"I'm ready for lots of adventures!" Luca says.

Scene 3 It's 3.45 and the three friends are now in Woolwell. They're very excited, 20 but Luca is unhappy.

"Oh no!" Luca says. "My sweets are on the bus!"

"Don't worry, Luca," Ellie says.

"Yeah, we have lots of nice things," 25 Adam says.

Scene 4 It's 4.30. Berry gives her friends a tour of the farm. First they visit the donkeys, ponies and sheep in the fields. Then they go to Pets Corner. 30

"I want to stroke a chipmunk," Luca says.

"This is Lulu. Do you want her on your shoulder?" Berry asks Luca.

"Oh, she's very cute!" Ellie says.

"Look!" Adam says. 35

"Oh no! My shoulder is wet!" Luca says. Everybody laughs.

Scene 5 It's 5.30.

"I'm hungry," Luca says.

40 "Yes, let's eat," Ellie says.

"How can we? We don't have sweets," Luca says.

"But we have lots of other nice things," Adam says.

45 "I want to buy sweets," Luca says. "Where's the village?"

"OK, Luca. Do you see that field? Go through there and you come to a shop," Berry says.

Scene 6 It's 6.15. Adam, Berry and Ellie are
50 hungry, but Luca isn't back from the village.

"Where is he?" Adam asks.

"I want to eat," Ellie says.

Then Adam gets a text. It's from Luca: They hurry to the field.

55 "Help! It's a bull! What do I do?" Luca says.

"That isn't a bull, Luca. It's a cow," Berry says.

"Cows aren't dangerous!"

60 Everybody laughs. But not Luca.

"Come on, city boy. Let's eat now. We're hungry," Berry says.

Help! I'm in trouble! I'm in the field!

65 **Scene 7** At 11 o'clock the four friends are in sleeping bags in the barn. It's a normal night on the farm ...

"What's that noise?" Adam asks. He's nervous.

"It's a donkey," Berry says.

"And what's that noise?" Ellie asks. 70

"That's a sheep," Berry says with a laugh.

"Oh no! What's that noise?" Luca asks.

"Oh, Luca! It's only a chicken," Berry says.

"Go to sleep!"

"Good night," everybody says. 75

Later Berry can't sleep. Then she hears something.

"What's that noise?" she thinks.

The barn door opens. Berry sees something big. She's nervous. She wants to wake her 80 friends. And then ...

"Is everybody OK?" Berry's dad says.

"Dad! It's only you!" Berry says. "Erm, we're fine, thanks."

Her dad goes back to the house. Berry is 85 tired and ready to sleep. And there are no more noises.

Scene 8 On Sunday Berry wakes up very early. The barn is quiet. She looks at the others. 90

"Huh? Ellie! Adam! Wake up! Luca isn't here!" Berry says.

"What?" Ellie says. "Where is he?"

"I don't know, but this isn't good. Luca doesn't know the farm very well," Berry says. 95

"Do you think he's really in trouble this time?" Adam asks.

"Oh dear. I hope not," Ellie says.

The three friends are worried. They get up fast. 100

"Come on. Let's look for him!" Berry says.

2 What happens next?

a) Think: Read the questions and make notes about your ideas.

1 Is Luca in trouble?
2 Does he meet other animals?
3 Where do they find Luca?
4 Does Luca need help?

b) 👥 Pair: Talk with a partner.

> I don't think Luca is in trouble. What about you?

> I think you're right.

c) 👥👥 Share: Tell the class about your ideas.

3 The end of the story

🎧 **a)** Now listen. Are your answers to 2 right or wrong?

b) Which of these sentences go with the story?

1 Luca wants to ride the ponies.
2 They don't find Luca at the trampolines.
3 Luca is in the duck pond.
4 Luca thinks he has a new friend.
5 When they find Luca, he isn't happy.

👥 Check with a partner.

| More practice 4 | p. 145 |

4 The scenes

a) Match the headings with the scenes (1–8) in the story.

A cute chipmunk

Morning surprise

Time to eat

Let's go to the country

Come to a sleepover

Noises at night

No sweets!

A dangerous animal?

b) 👥 Check with a partner.

5 Questions about the story

a) Make the questions.

1 friends / do / to Woolwell / how / go / the / three / ?
2 bag / in / Adam's / what's / ?
3 they / do / what / animals / see / on Saturday / ?
4 go / village / why / to / Luca / does / the / ?
5 the / night / why / friends / at / nervous / are / ?
6 does / Sunday / Luca / on / where / morning / go / ?

| More practice 5 | p. 146 |

b) Now answer the questions in 1–5 words.

 1 By …

6 👥👥 THEATRE TIME

Work in groups of five. Pick a scene from the story. Read and act the scene.

| More help | p. 146 |

1 READING Signs in Plymouth

Look at the signs. Then match the sentences (1–5) with the signs (A–E).

1 You can get the bus here. → Sign ...
2 You can find this sign at a restaurant.
3 This sign is on Berry's farm.
4 Only people are welcome here.
5 People in wheelchairs, please go left.

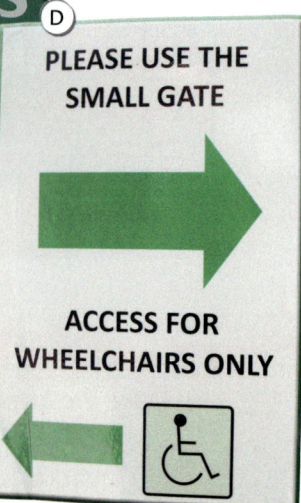

> Du kannst die Schilder verstehen, auch wenn du nicht jedes Wort kennst.

2 👥 MEDIATION Understanding the signs

a) Partner A: Imagine you're in Plymouth. Answer partner B's questions – in German.
Partner B: You can't understand the signs in Plymouth. Ask partner A three questions.
Then swap roles.

1 **Schild A:** Warum steht der Hund hinter Gittern? Ist er im Gefängnis?
2 **Schild A:** Was bedeutet „No smoking"?
3 **Schild B:** Ich habe Hunger. Können wir hier frühstücken?
4 **Schild C:** Es geht um *animals*, also Tiere. Was dürfen wir nicht tun?
5 **Schild D:** Können wir hier hineingehen?
6 **Schild E:** Wie können wir herausfinden, wann der nächste Bus kommt?

b) Pick a sign and talk about it with your partner – in German. Where can you find this sign?
What is it for?

> Ich denke, man findet so ein Schild ...

> Ja, und das Schild ...

1 ◯ An English evening

Match the headings with the boxes (A–E):
Invitation – C, Date – …

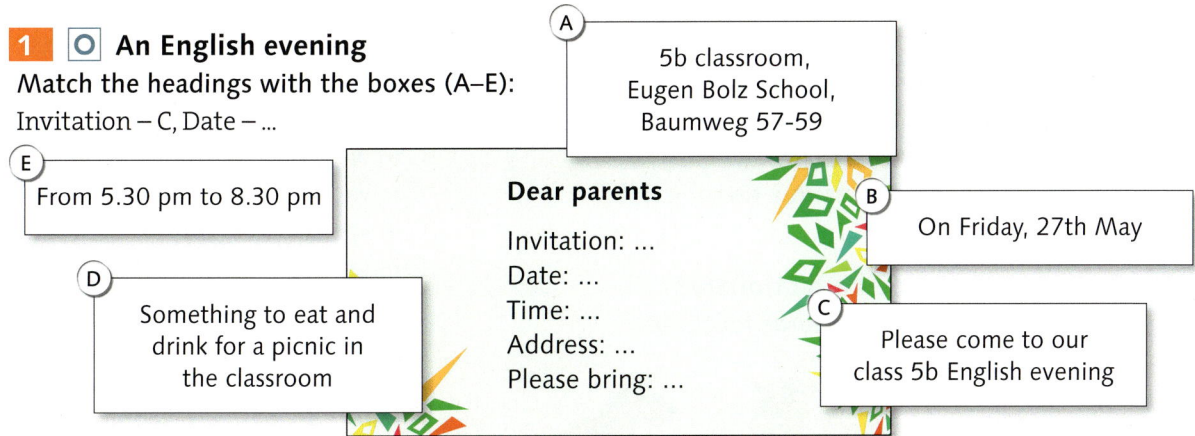

A 5b classroom, Eugen Bolz School, Baumweg 57-59

E From 5.30 pm to 8.30 pm

D Something to eat and drink for a picnic in the classroom

Dear parents

Invitation: …
Date: …
Time: …
Address: …
Please bring: …

B On Friday, 27th May

C Please come to our class 5b English evening

2 An invitation to a sleepover

a) Write an invitation for your partner like this.
You can use colours and pictures on your invitation.

Write your partner's name.

Write the times here.
Example: *From Saturday evening 6.00 pm to Sunday morning*

What can you do together?
Examples: *go swimming, watch a film,…*

INVITATION TO
a sleepover at …'s house
Dear …
Please come to my party.
It's on …
It's at my house: …
It's from … to …
We can …
Please bring …
I hope you can come.
…

Write your name here.

Write the day and the date of your party here.

Write your address here.

What can people bring?
Examples: *a sleeping bag, something to eat, …*

Then give your invitation to your partner.

b) Write an answer to your partner.

Dear …
Thank you for the invitation.
I'd love to come! / Sorry I can't come.
Best wishes
… (your name)

3 ⬤ Other invitations

a) Write an invitation. It can be for:
an English evening, a class party, a birthday party, a Halloween party, a picnic, a DVD evening, a computer game evening, …
Put your invitation on the wall.
You can put it in your DOSSIER later.

b) Reading circle: Look at all the invitations. Which party do you want to go to? Write an answer and put it on the wall.

🎧 **1 A poem**

Read and listen to the poem. Find out:

1 What's the title of the poem? Can you say it?
2 What does the writer want?
3 Who's the writer? A mum, a dad or a child?

2 👥 Do you need a dictionary?

a) ⭕ Find the English words for these animals in the poem.

Du kennst schon viele Tierwörter, andere sind neu, aber du kannst sie erraten.

b) Write these animal words on small cards. Then put them in alphabetical order.

stoat budgie owl guinea pig
parrot kitten horse

Einige Tierwörter musst du im Wörterbuch nachschlagen (ab S. 222). Bringe die Wörter zuerst in eine alphabetische Reihenfolge, dann findest du sie schneller.

c) Now write these animal words on cards too. Put all the words from 2b and 2c in alphabetical order.

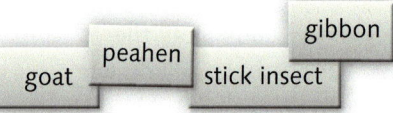

gibbon peahen goat stick insect puppy

d) Which animal words do you need to look up? Find the words in the Dictionary (pp. 222–232). Write the German words on the back of the cards.

▶ *Skills file 4, p. 174*

Muuuuuuummmmmmm

Can we have a kitten
Can we have a dog
Can we call her Frisky
Can we call him Bob?
I can take him out each day
I can brush his fur
I will buy the dog meat
And milk to make her purr
Mum!!

Oh ... no ... well –

Can we have a donkey
Or can we have a horse
A monkey or a parrot
Hamster or a snake?
Can we have a guinea pig
A peahen
Or a stoat
Llama or a budgie
A rabbit or a goat?

Can we have a crocodile
Gibbon or an owl
All the zoos are closing
There's lots and lots around ...
A penguin would be really good
Keep it in the bath
A hyena in the garden
To make the milkman laugh.

No, WE DON'T WANT stick insects
And goldfish aren't much fun ...
Oh can we have a puppy ...
Mum, mum, muuuuuuummmmmmm.

Peter Dixon

Sarah Paul Anna

1 **The kids from Harbour Road:**
A class project
a) Watch the film.
Then complete the captions.

1 The kids need information from the aquarium for their …

2 Paul is busy with his …

3 First they look at the …

4 Then they ask lots of questions about …

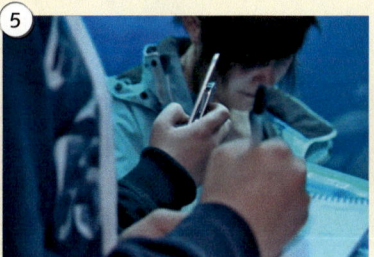

5 Sarah and Anna write notes, but Paul uses his …

6 But now Paul's phone doesn't work. Paul has a big …

b) Watch the film again. Try to remember: Who says it – Anna, Paul, or Sarah?

1 Let's do our project on sharks[1].
2 You're no help!
3 I love my new mobile phone.
4 Do sharks eat other fish in the tank[2]?
5 Do you think we have all the information?
6 Pens and paper are better than[3] mobile phones.

2 **People and places:** **A normal day at school**
a) Watch the film. When does Emily feel fed up / great? Talk about the scences: In scene A / B / …

A Emily feels … when she can't do things alone.

B Emily feels … when people are normal with her.

C Emily feels … when people don't listen to her.

D Emily feels … when Laura invites her.

b) Watch the film again. Is it a good or bad day for Emily? Why?

[1]shark [ʃɑːk] *Haifisch* [2]tank [tæŋk] *Aquarium* [3]better than [ˈbetə ðæn] *besser als*

STOP! CHECK! GO!

Ein Lösungsblatt für die Aufgaben 1 bis 5 kannst du von deiner Lehrerin / deinem Lehrer erhalten.
Die Audio-Datei (S.86) findest du online bei den Audio-Dateien zum Workbook.

1 WORDS On Merryweather Farm

a) Write the names of the things (1–9) in the picture.

b) Now write the names of the animals (A–L) in the picture.

c) 👥 NAME GAME

Close your books. **Partner A:** Think of a thing or animal from the picture. Write the name.
Partner B: Write a second name under partner A's.
Repeat – as many times as you can. The last partner who writes a name wins!

2 WORDS Visitors at the farm

a) Listen to the phrases (1–9). Who's the speaker? Berry or a visitor?
– *1 visitor   2 first a visitor, then ….   3 …*

b) Listen again. Write the sentences.

1 Excuse me, please. We want to …
2 When do you … ?
3 What's the … ?
4 Excuse me, please. … ?
5 What's … ?
6 When can I … ?
7 Look at the hamsters. …
8 When does … ?
9 Come on, Sam. Let's …

c) Listen again. Which times do you hear? Write the times. Example: *10.35*
👥 Check with a partner.

3 REVISION   A day with my family

a) Complete the text with the right positive and negative verb forms.

Every morning I ... (get up) at 6 o'clock. Sam ... (like) it when I sleep late.
After breakfast I ... (go) to school by car with my dad. Sam usually ... (stay)
home – he ... (like) cars. At about 9 o'clock the first visitors ... (come).
Mum and dad ... (have) lunch at 1 o'clock. After lunch dad usually ... (stay) in
the shop and mum ... (work) with the ponies. She ... (work) with Harry when
I'm not there. The animals ... (miss) me when I'm at school, but I ... (miss) them!
I ... (come) home from school with dad before 4 o'clock. Dad often ... (have)
something to eat with me. Then we ... (go) outside. Sam ... (come) with me.

b) ⬤ Make a table like this for a day with your family.
👥 Then tell your partner.

When?	Who?	What?
every morning / before 6 o'clock	mum, dad and I	get up

More help p. 146

4 LANGUAGE   An interview with Cyril and Sandy   // ⬤ p. 147

a) Complete the reporter's questions with *do* or *does*.

1 ... you like Plymouth?
2 ... you have a best friend?
3 ... you and Sandy live on the beach?
4 ... Sandy like Plymouth too?
5 ... Sandy have a best friend?

– Yes, it's great.
– Yes, I do. Her name is Sandy.
– Yes, we live in Kingsand.
– Yes, she loves Plymouth.
– Yes, she does. I'm her best friend!

b) Complete Cyril's short answers.

1 Do you like Mr Johnson?
2 Do you live in a small house?
3 Do you and Sandy go to school?
4 Does Sandy have a bike?
5 Does Sandy eat crabs?

– No, I ... . He isn't nice.
– Yes, I ... . I don't like big houses.
– No, we ...
– Yes, she ...
– No, she ... . I'm a crab!

c) Match the questions with Sandy's answers.

1 Where do you live?
2 When do you get up?
3 Where do you have breakfast?
4 What do you do after breakfast?
5 Why do you like Cyril?

– Very late – after 10 o'clock.
– I always have breakfast on the beach.
– Because he's friendly and he's fun!
– In Kingsand.
– I often go to Plymouth.

STOP! CHECK! GO!

5 WORDS   Useful phrases

at • by • in • through • to (3x) • with

a) Find the right word from the box for these phrases.

1 Help! I'm ... trouble!
2 I want to go ... the toilet!
3 I get up ... 6 o'clock.
4 I go to school ... bus.

5 I listen ... music every evening.
6 I feel great when I'm ... my friends.
7 Go ... that field.
8 Go ... sleep. Good night!

b) ⊙ Match the phrases in a) with the pictures (A–H).

6 WRITING   Luca and you

a) Write the dialogue with Luca in your exercise book. Write as many sentences as you can.

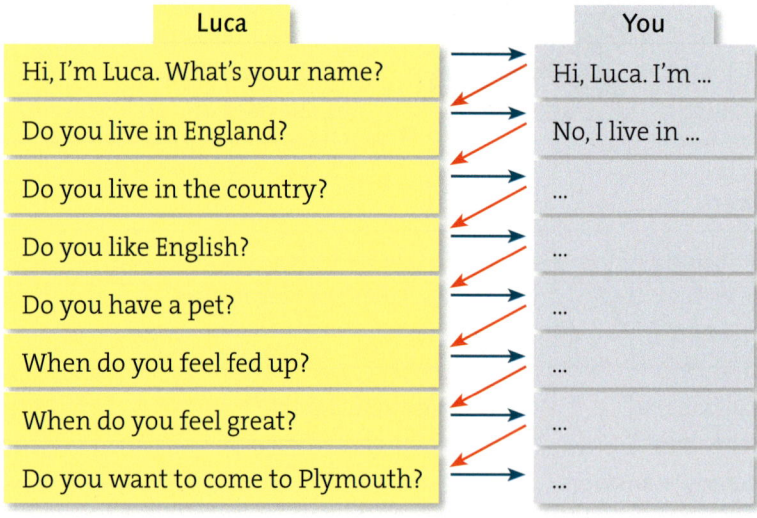

Luca	You
Hi, I'm Luca. What's your name?	Hi, Luca. I'm ...
Do you live in England?	No, I live in ...
Do you live in the country?	...
Do you like English?	...
Do you have a pet?	...
When do you feel fed up?	...
When do you feel great?	...
Do you want to come to Plymouth?	...

b) ⦿ Write a second dialogue with Luca. Now you ask the questions – as many as you can.

7 SPEAKING   An interview with a student in your class

a) Think of good questions for your interview. Write your six best questions on a piece of paper. Example: *What do you ...?   Where do you ...?   When do you ...?*

More help p.147

b) 👥 Walk around: Find a partner. Ask and answer your questions. Then find a new partner.

8 PROJECT Interesting animals

Find out about an interesting animal. You can work alone, with a partner or in a small group.

STEP 1: Pick an animal for your project.

budgie   elephant   guinea pig   tiger   polar bear

STEP 2: Pick five questions – or more – for your project.

> Where do the animals come from (what country)? • What do they look like (colour/furry)? •
> Are they big or small? • How long[1] are they? • Where do they live (cage/nest)? •
> Do they live inside/outside? • What do they eat? • What can they do (run/swim/talk)? •
> How long do they live (one year/two years)? • Are they good pets?

STEP 3: Find the information on the internet. Go to www.cornelsen.de/headlight and put in the webcode Head-1-91.

STEP 4: Make a mind map like this:

STEP 5: Pick a) OR b).
a) ◉ Talk about your animal for one minute.

b) ◉ Write a text about your animal. Find photos for your text. Then put the text on the wall. | More help p.148 |

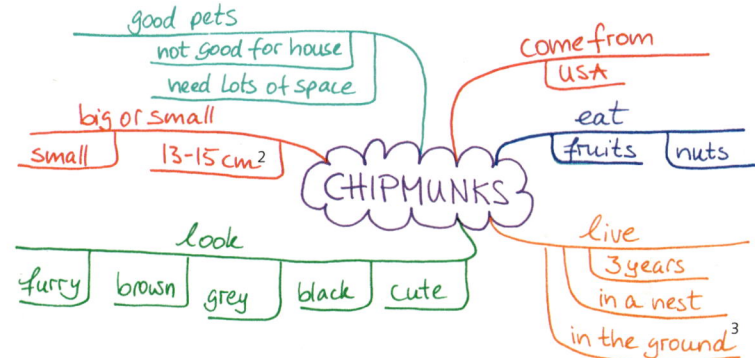

9 My learner log

Copy and complete your learner log. You can put it in your DOSSIER.

My learner log

Now I can ...
– say the names of lots of animals: ...
– say the time: ...
– ask questions in an interview: ...
– say when I feel great or fed up: ...
– write an invitation: 😄 😐 😢
– use a dictionary: 😄 😐 😢

In Unit 4 ...
– my favourite text is on page ...
– my favourite words are ...
– my favourite phrases are ...
– my favourite people are ...
– difficult words are ...

My progress in English is: GREAT! 👍 / Ok 🤚 / NOT VERY GOOD 👎

---

[1] how long? [haʊ ˈlɒŋ] *wie lang? / wie lange?*   [2] cm = centimetre [ˈsentɪmiːtə] *Zentimeter*   [3] ground [ɡraʊnd] *Erde*

Unit 5
All about Adam

1 **The harbour in Plymouth**

a) What can you see on pages 92–93? Group ten words under these themes:
people • places • things

More help p. 148

b) What can you say about the people in photos A–D?
Who are they? Can you guess?
I think the boy is ... / Maybe the woman in photo C is ...

c) Which photo?
Partner A: Describe a photo or a person / thing in a photo.
Partner B: Guess the right photo.
Swap roles.

> In this photo there's a ...
> On the left / On the right /
> In the middle I can see ...

> Is it this photo / photo ...?
> I think it's ...

🎧 2 Adam's family

a) Adam is talking to Ellie. Listen and look at the small photos. Write the letters (A–D) in the right order.

b) Listen again. Choose the right answer.
1 Where is Adam going?
  A To school. B To the cafe. C Home.
2 Where is Adam's dad working now?
  A In the cafe.   B On the ferry.
  C In France.
3 What does Adam want to do?
  A Help in the cafe. B Do his homework.
  C Meet his friends.

c) Answer the questions.
1 Who needs Adam's help?
2 Where is Adam's brother in the afternoons?
3 Who is Alisha?

In the cafe

1 Can I help you?

a) It's 4 pm in the cafe. Adam's mum is busy. Listen. Look at the photos.
What things (A–J) does each customers want? *Customer 1 wants …*

| A a salad | B a cup of coffee | C fish and chips | D a sandwich | E soup |
| F a bottle of water | G a bottle of juice | H omelette and chips | I a cup of tea | J scones |

b) Listen again. Who says this – mum (write M) or a customer (write C)?

1 Can I help you?
2 Here you are.
3 One fish and chips, please.

4 Would you like
  something to drink?
5 I'd like a bottle of
  water, please.

6 That's £10.50, please.
7 Next please.
8 Would you like anything else?
9 No thanks. That's all.

c) Make a dialogue in a cafe. Use words and phrases from a and b. More help p.148

2 How's it going?

a) Does Adam's dad like his new job? Read and find out.

Adam is helping in the cafe. His mobile is ringing.
Adam __ Hey dad, how's it going?
Dad ___ Fine, thanks. How's it going at home?
Adam __ Oh, OK. But I miss you!
  How's your new job on the ferry?
Dad ___ It's great. But I miss you all too.
  Is mum busy now? Is she working?
Adam __ She's cooking. She can't talk to you. The cafe is busy.
Dad ___ Oh, OK. Are you helping mum?
Adam __ Yeah, I'm washing up.
Dad ___ That's great. But you must work hard at school too.
Adam __ Yeah, dad. Sorry, I must go. We're very busy here.
Dad ___ OK. Say hi to everybody. Bye, Adam.
Adam __ Bye, dad. See you at the weekend.

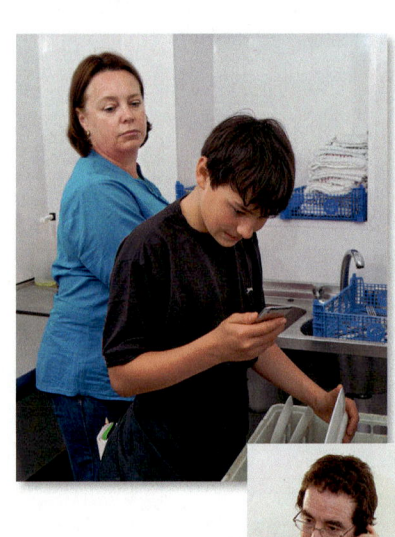

b) What are they doing now? Write five sentences.

1 Dad is …
2 Mum is …
3 Adam is …
4 …
5 …

cooking • talking to Adam • washing up • reading a book •
working on a ferry • helping in the cafe • doing homework

3 What's happening?

🔘 It's a busy afternoon in the cafe.
What's everybody doing? Look at the box
and complete the sentences.

eating something • watching TV •
helping customers • reading a book •
leaving • texting a friend • sitting outside •
cooking • cleaning the tables

1 Mum is ...

2 Luca and Jack are ...

3 Adam is ...

4 A woman is ...

5 Zack and Alisha are ...

6 Two dogs are ...

More practice 1 p.149   More practice 2 p.149

4 A letter from school

a) Read the letter. Why does Adam's teacher write to his parents?

Eggbuckland Community College

A DCSF Designated Technology College • Principal : Katrina Borowski

LEARNING - CARING - ACHIEVING

Dear Mr and Mrs Osmanovic

I'm a bit worried about Adam. I don't think he's very
happy at the moment. He isn't working very hard at
school. He isn't doing his homework and he's often tired.
Please phone me and we can talk about it.

Best wishes
R Lee
Class 7 teacher

b) What do you think Adam's mother says?
1 Ms Lee is ... about you, Adam.
2 She thinks that you aren't very ... at the moment.
3 You aren't working very ...
4 You're often ... at school.
5 I'm ... about this letter, Adam.

More practice 3 p.149

c) 🔵 Adam's mum talks to him about Ms Lee's letter.
Write the dialogue. You can use the phrases from 4b.

More help p.150

It's boring at home!

🎧 **1** **Trouble for Adam**

a) ⭕ Look at the pictures. Where's Adam? Who's with Adam?

It's Tuesday, after school. Adam is helping in his mum's cafe. "Go home now, Adam. You must do your homework. Miss Lee isn't happy with you at school," his mum says.

Adam is walking home. He thinks, "It's so boring at home! Mum and dad aren't there and Zack is with his new baby-sitter." Then he has an idea. Now he's phoning his friends. "Hey, come to the harbour."

Adam isn't thinking about homework now. He and his friends are diving. They're having lots of fun. But diving in the harbour is dangerous. There are lots of big rocks.

Zack and Alisha are walking in the harbour. "Oh no! It's my brother and Alisha. I must hide!" Adam says. But it's too late. Zack is waving, but Adam isn't waving back. He's worried.

Alisha is talking to Adam. "You can't dive here, Adam. It's very dangerous. Go home and do your homework." But Adam isn't listening. "It's boring at home," he says. "Maybe you need a new hobby, Adam," Alisha says.

Alisha has a good idea. Her friend Josie works at the PMZ music club and Adam likes music. Maybe Josie can help Adam. "Hi, Josie. Can you send me a brochure for PMZ, please?"

b) What's happening in the pictures? Read the text and make sentences.

In picture …	Adam is Alisha is Adam and his friends are Zack and Alisha are	phoning his friends. helping in the cafe. talking to Adam. walking in the harbour. phoning Josie. diving in the harbour.

▶ Workbook 6, p. 67

2 Welcome to PMZ

a) Look at the brochure. Find the answers.

1 What does PMZ mean?
2 What can you do there?
3 What instruments can you learn?

4 Where can you go when you want to sing?
5 How old must you be for The Roof Raisers?
6 When can you play the drums?

MAKE MUSIC
EVERY NIGHT OF THE WEEK
AT PLYMOUTH MUSIC ZONE
IT'S FREE!

www.plymouthmusiczone.org.uk

PMZ
plymouth music zone
MUSIC MAKING A DIFFERENCE

MON THE PMZ GUITAR CLUB
4 pm–6.15 pm ¦ Everybody welcome!
Learn to play the guitar.

TUE THE BIG BASH
5 pm–6 pm ¦ 8–18 yrs
Play the drums in a group.

WED JAM BAND
4 pm–5 pm ¦ 8–18 yrs
Bring your instrument. Play in a band.

THUR BEATS PER MINUTE (BPM)
4.30 pm–5.30 pm ¦ 11–25 yrs
Workshop for young disabled musicians.

FRI STREETBEATZ
4 pm–6.15 pm ¦ 12–19 yrs
For young rappers.
Make music in our studio.

SAT THE ROOF RAISERS
10 am–12.30 pm ¦ 11–18 yrs
For young singers. Sing with a real band.

b) ◯ Listen to Adam. Choose A, B, C or D. //● p.150

1 Who is talking to Adam? A Alisha. B Ms Lee. C Josie. D Ellie.
2 What does Adam like? A The drums. B Rapping. C The guitar. D The piano.
3 Where is PMZ? A Near Eggy. B Near the sea.
  C Near the harbour. D Near the city centre.
4 What does Adam want to join? A The Roof Raisers. B Streetbeatz. C Jam Band. D BPM.

c) ● Copy this table. Listen again and take notes.

PMZ address: ...	Times (Sat): ... ...
Bus number: ...	Price: ...
Times (Mon–Fri):	

3 NOW YOU

Find out about music in your class.

a) Appointments: Write the questions from the green box in a table and write your answers.
Then make appointments with two partners. More help p.150 ▶ Wordbank 8, p. 188

b) Ask your partners and take notes.

c) Tell the class about one partner.

d) ● Write a text about you and music.
You can put it in your DOSSIER. More help p.150

– What's your favourite band?
– Who's your favourite singer?
– What's your favourite English song?
– Can you play an instrument? What instrument?
– Can you sing? Can you rap?
– Are you in a band?

1 Photos on Adam's mobile

a) Read the dialogue. Put the photos in the right order.

Ellie ___	Let's see the photos on your mobile then. ... That's your mum. What's she doing?
Adam _	Good question. She's in the cafe. She's making sandwiches, I think. This is me.
Ellie ___	Oh, that's you in the cafe too. Are you setting the tables?
Adam _	Let's see. I'm not sure. No, I'm not setting the tables, I'm cleaning them.
Ellie ___	This must be your little brother Zack. He's with my stepmum, Alisha. What are they doing?
Adam _	They're sitting in a park. I think it's near our house, or maybe it's the Hoe.
Ellie ___	And this must be your dad in the kitchen. Is he washing up?
Adam _	No, he's cooking. He's a great cook. And this is me with my group at PMZ.
Ellie ___	Cool. Let's see. It looks like a concert. Are you singing?
Adam _	No, we aren't singing. We're rapping.
Ellie ___	Really? Can you rap?
Adam _	Well, I'm learning!

b) Find a sentence from the dialogue for each picture.

2 Questions and answers with 'ing'

a) Copy and complete the tables with questions and answers from 1.

Question word	form of `be´	Subject	verb + –ing
What	´s	she	doing?
–	Are	you	...?

Subject	form of `be´	verb + –ing
She	´s	making sandwiches.
I	´m not	setting ...

b) Look at the table with answers again. Complete the rule for positive statements.

FOCUS

Das *present progressive* wird gebildet mit:

I +'m	+	verb + ing
you + ...	+	verb + ing
he / she / it + ...	+	verb + ing
we / you / they + ...	+	verb + ing

Man benutzt die Verlaufsform in der Gegenwart (*present progressive*),
a) um Bilder zu ... und
b) um zu sagen, was ... passiert.

▶ *Language file 10, p. 181*

3 What are you doing?

a) [O] It's Saturday. Ellie is talking to Adam on the phone. Complete the sentences with *'m • is • 's • are • 're.*

1 What am I doing? I'm with my family. My stepdad is making breakfast. He… cooking omelettes. My favourite food! I… making toast.

2 My sister Zoe … feeding the cats. They… making lots of noise. They're hungry!

3 Mum … sitting at the table. She… writing an email.

4 My brother Conor … watching TV. What … you doing now, Adam?

More practice 4 p. 151

b) [●] Adam is talking to Ellie. Complete the sentences with the *present progressive – positive* and *negative statements.*

1 Today is a nice day because dad … (work). Mum … (sit) in the garden. Zack … (ride) his bike there. Mum … (look) after him.

2 I… (look) at them through the window. Zack is unhappy because mum … (play) with him. She… (phone) a friend.

3 Dad and I … (work) in the kitchen. Dad … (make) something special because it's mum's birthday. I… (set) the table.

4 OK Ellie, Dad … (talk) to me. I must go now. See you on Monday.

More practice 5 p. 151

---

4 What's Cyril doing?

a) [O] What's Cyril doing now? [// ●] p. 152
Write the numbers 1–5. Then listen and choose an answer from the box:

1 Cyril is …, 2 He's …

b) 👥 Listen again. Then compare answers with a partner.

> playing football • playing tennis • rapping • reading a story • riding a bike • swimming • talking on the phone • washing up • watching TV • writing a text • writing an email

> I think Cyril is swimming.

> Me too./ No, I think he's …

---

5 NOW YOU

What's your father/mother/sister/ friend/… doing now?
Write sentences about your family and friends – as many as you can.

I think my	mum best friend dog grandparents …	is are	working swimming sleeping …	now.

---

6 👨‍👨‍👦 What are they doing?

a) Look at the photos. Discuss what you think the people are doing. Then write sentences.
A: I think the boy in photo 1 is …
B: Really? I think he's …
C: OK. Let's write: 1 He's …

b) The groups tell the class.
Photo 1: We think …

Check on page 128.

🎧 **1** **Before you read**
Listen to the songs. Do you like them?

> I like / don't like song number …
> – It's great / OK / terrible!
> – I love it! / I don't like it. / I hate it!

🎧 Music makes a difference

It was Friday afternoon. Adam was on the bus, on the way to PMZ. Some other kids were on the bus too.
"Hey you," one boy said to Adam. "You're
5 sitting on my seat!"
The other boys and girls laughed.
"Hey babyface, how old are you? Five?"
a girl asked.
They all laughed again. Adam said nothing.

10 Adam was at PMZ with his rap teacher, Josie.
"Are you feeling OK, Adam?" Josie asked.
"I had a bit of trouble on the bus," Adam said. "Some kids were mean. I'm fed up."
15 "That's terrible," Josie said. "But you can use that feeling in your rap."

In the lesson, Josie said, "When you rap, you must rap about your life." Josie asked, "What's important in your life?"
"Friends … my girlfriend … TV … my family … 20 music." Everybody had different ideas.
"Cool," Josie said. "And you can rap about problems too. Any ideas?"
"Trouble at school … trouble with parents … trouble with other kids …," they said. 25
"OK. We have a rap battle here at PMZ next week. You can write a rap," Josie said.

Come to a
RAP BATTLE
at PMZ on Friday evening
Everybody welcome –
friends and family

On Monday morning Adam was at school.
"How's it going at PMZ?" Luca asked.
"It's great. I'm writing a rap. But it's hard," 30 Adam said.
"Can we listen to it?" Ellie asked.
"Sure. You can all come to the rap battle on Friday," Adam said.
On Friday evening lots of people were at PMZ. 35 Adam was very happy because his dad was there. But Adam was nervous too. His friends

were all there. And the girl from the bus last Friday was there too.

40 "OK, Adam," he thought, "you can be nervous, or you can show these people the real Adam."

"Welcome to PMZ everybody. And welcome to our rap battle," Josie said.

Adam's friends were excited.

45 "Go, Adam, go!" ...

Adam's rap was great. He was second in the rap battle.

"I think you were the best," Luca said to Adam.

50 "Hey, not bad," a girl said. It was the girl from the bus. "Er, sorry about last week," she said.

"It's OK," Adam said.

"Well done, Adam," his mum said.

"I'm very proud of you, Adam," his dad said.

55 "Thanks," Adam said. "Music really makes a difference for me."

Music makes a difference

Chorus
Music makes a difference, a difference, a difference.
Yes, music makes a difference – for me.

Trouble at school, trouble on the bus,
Trouble at home, but I don't make a fuss.
There's one thing that I know
And now I'm telling you,
I need music – and you need it too.

Chorus

Trouble with my mum, and trouble with my dad
Nobody understands, when I'm feeling so bad.
But there's one thing that I know
And now I'm telling you,
I need music – and you need it too.

Chorus

I'm not like you, and you're not like me
Everybody's different – everybody's free.
There's one thing that I know
And now I'm telling you,
I need music – and you need it too.

Chorus

Adam Osmanovic

---

2 Can you remember?

Who said this in the story?

1 "You're sitting on my seat!"
2 "I'm fed up."
3 "What's important in your life?"
4 "How's it going at PMZ?"
5 "Go, Adam, go!"
6 "Sorry about last week."

3 True, false or not in the text?

1 The boys and girls on the bus were nice.
2 Adam's rap teacher is Josie.
3 Josie is from Plymouth.
4 The rap battle was on Friday.
5 Adam's dad wasn't there.
6 Adam was first in the rap battle.
7 Music is important for Adam.

4 RAP Music makes a difference

a) Listen to Adam's rap.
Do you like it? Why (not)?

I like it because I don't like it because	the text the beat the sound	is isn't	good. boring. ...

b) You can have a rap battle in your class.
Pick one verse of Adam's rap. Learn it. Rap for the class. Who's the best rapper?

More practice 6 p. 152

1 In the park

At the top

In the middle

On the left

At the bottom

On the right

| next to | on | between | behind | under | in front of |

a) What can you see? Complete the sentences. Use the words and phrases in the green boxes.

1 On the left I can see a bike.
  It's *behind the tree.*
2 On the right there's a baby. He's …
3 In the middle there are apples. They're …
4 On the right I can see a red ball. It's …
5 At the bottom there are two dogs. …
6 In the middle there's a seagull. …

b) Find more things or people in the picture. Say where they are.

c) ⬤ What are they doing?
Make sentences – as many as you can.

	two dogs …
On the left	a boy …
In the middle	three girls …
On the right	children …
At the top	a girl …
At the bottom	a baby …
	two men …

More help p. 152

d) Look at the picture and listen.
Say what's right or what's wrong.

2 ⬤ 👥 NOW YOU

Partner A: Go to page 157.
Partner B: Go to page 128.

> Wenn du ein Bild beschreibst, nenne die Gegenstände und Personen auf dem Bild nicht einfach, sondern sage, **wo** sie sich befinden.
> Wenn du sagen möchtest, was die Personen auf dem Bild machen bzw. was gerade auf dem Bild passiert, benutze das *present progressive*:
> – The kids **are playing** football. / The baby **is sleeping**.

 ▶ *Skills file 5, p. 175*

1 Four text messages

a) Look at the four text messages. Read each text message aloud.

A Hi Adam. rap was gr8. PMZ is cool. C U at school on Monday.

B Adam where R U? We're rapping at PMZ now. R U coming?

C Mum I'm at home. I'm doing my homework. I can't come 2 the cafe.

D I'm not working in the cafe now. I'm going 2 the market. C U soon. XX

Text message language
+ = and
U = you
C = see
2 = to / too / two
gr8 = great
R U = are you
L8r = later
X = kiss

b) Are they from Adam, Adam's mum, Luca or Josie?
I think text message A is from …

2 👥 MEDIATION What does she mean?

You and your partner get a text from an English friend, Amanda. She's in Germany at the moment. Work with your partner. How do you say it in German?

Amanda fragt, wo …?

Ja, sie schreibt, dass sie …

Hi U 2. Where R U? I'm at a party + it's gr8! What R U doing? U can come 2. C U L8r. X Amanda

3 ⬤ WRITING A text to Amanda

Write a text message to Amanda. **More help** p. 153

1   A recipe for scones

a) Look at the picture in the recipe. Try to explain these words in German: *scone*, *jam*, *cream*.

What's a scone?
A scone is a small round cake. In England people often eat them in the afternoon with tea, coffee or milk.

How do you make scones?
1. Put butter (50g), flour (225g), sugar (50g), baking powder (3 teaspoons) and salt (half a teaspoon) in a bowl.
2. Rub the butter into the flour with your fingers.
3. Add milk (75ml) and one egg.
4. Mix everything together.
5. Make 12 scones with a glass.
6. Put the scones in the oven (230°C) for 8–10 minutes.
7. Cut a scone.
8. Put cream and jam on it – and eat it!

cream   scone   jam

b) Read the recipe for scones and put the pictures (A–H) in the right order (1–8).

A   B   C   D   E   F   G   H

2   New words in the recipe

a) Find these twelve words in the recipe.
What do you think they mean in German?
👥 Then check with a partner.

milk	put	flour	sugar	rub	baking powder
teaspoon	bowl	oven	egg	mix	salt

▸ *Skills file 3–4, pp. 173–174*

b) Check in the Dictionary (pp. 222–232).

> You can often guess the new words.
> Remember:
> Some words are like German words:
> *milk, oven, salt.*
> Look at the pictures in 1b for help:
> – *bowl, rub (picture B)*
> – *teaspoon, flour, baking powder (picture D)*
> – *egg (picture H)*

1 The kids from Harbour Road:
What's your talent[1]?

a) What's your talent? – I can …

Sarah Paul Anna

Watch the film and find out what Anna, Paul and Sarah can do.

b) Look at the picture. Put the sentences in the right order. Then watch part 1 again and check.

A That's four pounds for you, and four pounds for you, please.
B I'm hungry! Can I have a muffin, and … a hot chocolate[2], please.
C Hi!
D Thanks. / Thank you!
E Chocolate or blueberry[3]?
F Hi, Anna!
G I'll have a chocolate muffin, please.
H And yourself?
I A hot chocolate and a blueberry muffin, please.
J We're here!

c) Match the sentence parts. Then watch part 2 and check.

1 In the cafe Anna   cool dance for Anna.
2 She has no idea   wants to sing.
3 Paul wants to   isn't happy.
4 And Sarah   play the guitar.
5 But then Sarah   for the class party.
6 She knows a   has an idea.

d) Watch part 3.
Do Anna's dance.

▶ *Text file 5, p.167*

2 People and places: A visit to PMZ

a) 👥 Watch the film. Talk about PMZ with a partner.
– I think PMZ looks interesting / boring / … What about you?
– I think Jimmy is a good / great / terrible / … rapper.
– I think the Jam Band's music is …

Jimmy

Debbie

Simon

b) Answer these questions. Watch again and check.
1 Who works at PMZ?
2 How many people come to PMZ every week?
3 What instrument does Jimmy play?

---

[1] talent ['tælənt] *Talent*   [2] hot chocolate [hɒt 'tʃɒklət] *heiße Schokolade*   [3] blueberry *Heidelbeere, Blaubeere*

 # STOP! CHECK! GO!

Ein Lösungsblatt für die Aufgaben 1 bis 5 kannst du von deiner Lehrerin / deinem Lehrer erhalten.
Die Audio-Datei (S.107) findest du online bei den Audio-Dateien zum Workbook.

1   REVISION   Questions and answers

a) What do you know about crabs? Do this crab quiz.
Write the answers: *1 No, they don't. 2 Yes, ...*

CRAB QUIZ

1 Do crabs live in towns?
2 Do crabs live on the beach?
3 Do crabs eat fish?
4 Do normal crabs sing?

5 Does Cyril live in a house?
6 Does Cyril talk?
7 Does Cyril walk fast?
8 Does Cyril like people?

b) Now make a seagull quiz. Write the questions.

SEAGULL QUIZ

1 seagulls / live near the sea?
2 seagulls / live in towns?
3 seagulls / eat crabs?
4 seagulls / sing or make a noise?

5 Sandy / live in a house?
6 Sandy / eat crabs?
7 Sandy / talk?
8 Sandy / like pizza?

c) Work with a partner. Ask each other the questions about seagulls and answer them.

d) Make a quiz about another animal. Put it on the board. Who knows the answers?

More help p.153

2   LANGUAGE   Describing pictures

a) Look at the picture. Complete the sentences with the *present progressive*.

1 Cyril ... (sit) on a chair at the beach. 2 He... (listen) to music. 3 He... (watch) three kids.
4 They... (play) football. 5 His mobile ... (ring)
6 "I hope it isn't mum and dad," he... (think).

b) Complete the sentences. Use the verbs in the box with the *present progressive*.

walk • phone • watch • look • feel

Sandy is on the beach too. She... (1) Mr Johnson. He... (2) on the beach. Mrs Johnson is there too. They... (3) at Cyril. They... (4) hungry! Sandy has a mobile. She... (5) Cyril.

c) Look at the pictures. Say what Cyril and Sandy are / aren't doing. Use the verbs.
In picture 1 Cyril is ... . He isn't ...

play football / swim

talk to Cyril / eat lunch

have a party / watch TV

cook dinner / drink tea

3 LANGUAGE People on the ferry

a) Copy the table. Then look at the picture and listen to Adam and his dad. Match the people (A–I) in the picture with the names.

Sam	D	Linda	...	David	...
Anna	...	Toby	...	Uma	...
Rick	...	Gemma	...	Adam's dad	...

b) Look at the picture again. What are the people doing? Write sentences like this:
Sam is eating. Anna ...

clean the table • cook • do nothing • eat • laugh • play a game • talk • talk on the phone • wash up • watch TV

4 READING and SPEAKING A picture

a) Look at the picture and read the text. Are the sentences true (t) or false (f)? Correct the wrong sentences.

1 There are lots of people in the park.
2 On the left I can see a boy and a girl.
3 The boy is talking on the phone.
4 The girl is reading.
5 On the right I can see a family.
6 They're eating lunch.
7 There's a big dog in front of a yellow bag.
8 The animal is looking at the sandwiches.
9 In the middle I can see a red chair.
10 A boy is sitting on the chair.
11 There's a cat under the chair.
12 I can see a big red ball next to the chair.

b) Describe the picture. You can use the ideas in a). On the left a girl is talking on the phone.

5 WORDS Food and drinks

a) ⊙ Find the odd word out.

1 sweets, tea, sandwich, cafe
2 breakfast, soup, lunch, dinner
3 tea, juice, water, chips
4 coffee, chicken, fish, omelette
5 fruit, salad, scones, vegetables

b) Complete the sentences with answers from a.

1 Some people drink ... for breakfast.
2 I often have vegetable ... for lunch.
3 We often have tea and ... in a cafe at the weekend.
4 You can buy food and drinks in a ...
5 My favourite food is fish and ...

6 👥 MEDIATION I'm hungry!

You're in Plymouth with a friend.
Answer his or her questions in German.

1 Ich habe Hunger. Was gibt es hier zu essen?
2 Ich esse weder Fleisch noch Fisch. Gibt es da etwas für mich?
3 Ich habe auch Durst. Was kann ich hier trinken?
4 Gibt es auch etwas Süßes?
5 Wir haben £10 für uns beide. Was schlägst du vor?
6 Müssen wir alles hier essen, oder können wir es auch mitnehmen?

Harbour Cafe

Cup of tea / coffee	£2.55
Cold drinks (small bottle)	£1.50
Juices	£1.99
Sandwiches	£3.50
Fish and chips	£4.25
Omelette and chips	£4.25
Soups	£3.00
Scone and butter	£1.75
Home-made cakes	£2.25
Fruit salad	£2.50
Ice cream — 16 flavours:	
large	£2.00
small	£1.50

Eat in or take away!

7 👥 WRITING and SPEAKING In the Harbour Cafe

a) ⬤ Write a dialogue in your exercise book. Here are some ideas.

> Schau auf die Speisekarte in Aufgabe 6 und bestelle etwas zu essen und zu trinken.

You work in the cafe:
– Hello. Can I ... ?
– OK. Would you like ...?
– ... to drink?
– ... else?
– That's £ ...
– Thanks. ...

> Rufe den nächsten Kunden auf.

You're hungry:
– Hello. Yes, please – ..., please.
– Yes, ..., please.
– Oh, yes, ..., please. And ...
– No, thanks. ...
– OK. Here ...

> Bestelle noch mehr, z.B. etwas Süßes.

> Wenn du genug bestellt hast, sage, dass das alles ist.

> Bezahle alles.

b) Practise your dialogue with a partner.

8 READING and WRITING On Saturday morning …

a) Read the story. Put the phrases (A–G) with the photos (1–7).

1 …

What are you doing, Adam?

2 Hello, Adam. How are you?

…

3 …

Tea and a scone, please.

4 Thank you, Adam.

…

5 Is everything OK at school?

…

6 Listen, Ms Lee. That's my rap.

…

7 The tea was very good. Thanks, Adam.

…

A Can I help you?

B I'm washing up.

C That's a great rap!

D You're welcome. Bye.

E Hello, Ms Lee. I'm fine, thanks.

F Here you are. One tea and a scone.

G Yes, Adam is working very hard at school now.

b) ● Draw a picture for another story in the cafe and write speech bubbles for it.   More help p. 153

9 My learner log

Copy and complete your learner log. You can put it in your DOSSIER.

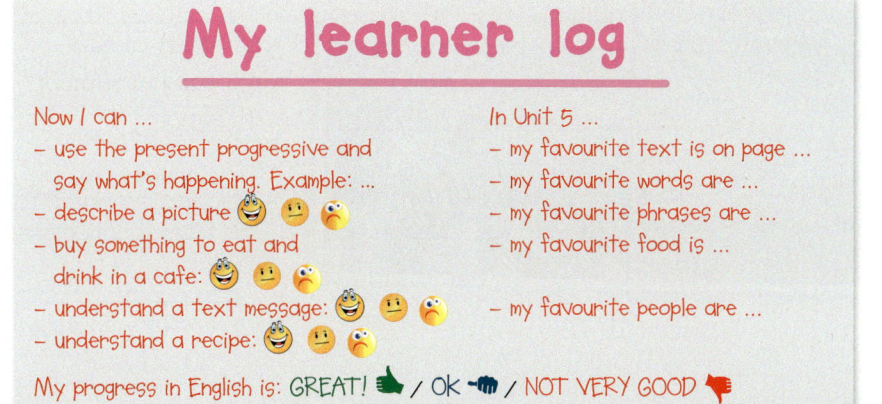

My learner log

Now I can …
– use the present progressive and say what's happening. Example: …
– describe a picture 😄 😐 🙁
– buy something to eat and drink in a cafe: 😄 😐 🙁
– understand a text message: 😄 😐 🙁
– understand a recipe: 😄 😐 🙁

In Unit 5 …
– my favourite text is on page …
– my favourite words are …
– my favourite phrases are …
– my favourite food is …

– my favourite people are …

My progress in English is: GREAT! 👍 / OK ✊ / NOT VERY GOOD 👎

1 Summer sounds

Listen to the summer sounds (1–4) and match them with the brochures (A–D).

Summer sounds 1: Brochure ...
Summer sounds 2: ...
Summer sounds 3: ...
Summer sounds 4: ...

A

The Cawsand Ferry Co.

Visit the smuggler villages of Cawsand and Kingsand. Great beaches, walks, restaurants, shops and cafes.

Smuggler's cave in Cawsand

Ferry times:

Plymouth
10.30 am, 12.00 pm, 2.30 pm, 4.00 pm

Cawsand
9.30 am, 11.00 am, 12.30 pm, 3.00 pm, 4.30 pm

Tickets:
Adults £4 one way
Children £2 one way
Dogs free

B

Canoe Tamar
Experience .... discover .... enjoy ....

Canoe trips: 3–3½ hours with picnic stop

Trips cost: £22 per person

Everybody welcome – dogs too!

2 Four trips

a) Ellie, Luca, Adam and Berry are at school. Listen. Which trip do they pick – A, B, C or D?

b) Listen again. Match the ideas (1–4) with the answers (A–D).

1 What about a trip to Dartmoor?	A Yes, but they're expensive.
2 Well, I'd prefer a canoe trip.	B Oh no! That's boring!
3 I love theme parks.	C I think that's a great idea!
4 I really want to go to the beach!	D But I can't swim very well!

Young Spirit Adventures
Dartmoor Camping

Working together • Cooking together • Having fun

WOODLANDS FAMILY THEME PARK
fun for everybody

Open daily at 9.30 am from 26th March to 7th November. During the winter open weekends and school holidays.

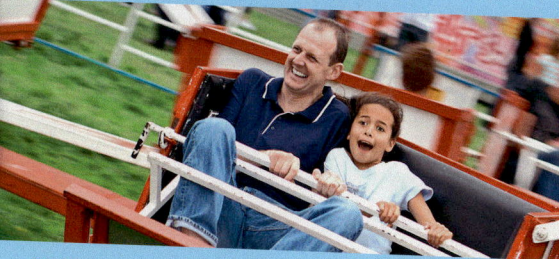

Tickets: £14.45 each / 4 tickets £57.80

3 NOW YOU

a) Think: Look at the brochures.
Pick your favourite trip.
Example: My favourite trip is ...

> the canoe trip • the ferry trip •
> the camping trip • the trip to a theme park

b) Pair: Talk to a partner. Agree on one trip.

> – What about a ...?
> – I'd prefer a ...
> – I really want to do a ...
> – I love ...

> – I think that's a great / terrible idea.
> – Oh no! That's boring / expensive / ...
> – Me too. I really like walking /
>   ferry trips / the beach / ...

KINGSAND IS GREAT!

c) Share: Find another pair that wants to do your trip too.
As a group, talk about why you want to do the trip. Tell the class.

> We want to do the ... because we ...

A trip to the beach

More help p. 154

1 Getting ready

a) What things can you bring to the beach? Start a network.

b) Read the text for more ideas.

It's Friday, the last day of school. The four friends are talking about their trip to Kingsand.

Berry ___ OK, guys! When do we want to go to Kingsand?

Luca ___ What about next Monday – the first day of the summer holidays?

Ellie ___ That's a great idea. What do we need for the beach?

Adam ___ Well, I'm going to bring my swimming trunks, a towel and some suncream.

Ellie ___ Yes, I'm going to bring my swimsuit and my sunglasses ... and a hat ...

Luca ___ We need things for a picnic too – like sandwiches.

Ellie ___ And water – lots of water ...

Berry ___ Yeah. My dad can bring our things in the car. Mum is going to stay on the farm because she's busy.

Adam ___ Are you going to bring Sam?

Berry ___ Maybe. We're going to wait and see. He loves the beach, but he often makes trouble.

Ellie ___ Oh, dear. We don't want a messy picnic!

Luca ___ Now let's talk about food!

c) True or false?

1 The friends are going to go to Kingsand on Monday.

2 Luca is going to bring a hat.

3 Berry's parents are going to come too.

2 Shopping for the picnic

a) 👥 Listen and take notes.

Partner A:
Make shopping lists for Adam and Luca.

Partner B:
Make shopping lists for Ellie and Berry.

b) 👥 Swap lists with your partner. Listen again and check your partner's lists.

c) 👥 Look at the four lists. Agree on more things you can bring to a picnic.

> What about ...?

> Yes, good idea. / No, I don't like ...

d) Add more words to your network from 1a.

Adam ...
Luca ...
Ellie ...
Berry ...

scones · water · crisps · apples · cake · chocolate · biscuits · orange juice · oranges · sandwiches · sausages

3 Things for the beach

a) It's Saturday – two days before the Kingsand trip. Look at the pictures and guess what other things the friends want to bring.

suncream

towels

a camera

shorts

an umbrella

a bodyboard

speakers

a football

a frisbee

a picnic blanket

a swimsuit

a tube

b) Now read the text messages and find out. What do the friends want to bring?

Example: They all want to bring ...   Ellie / Luca / ... wants to bring ...

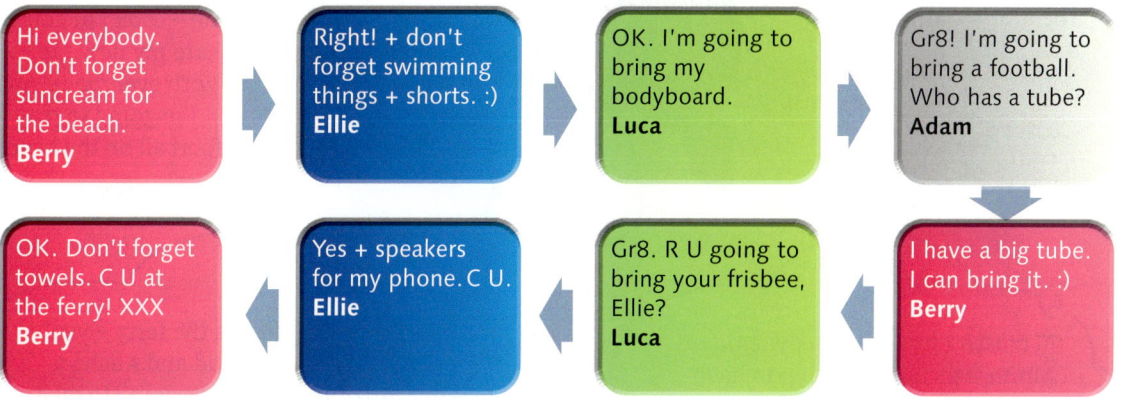

> Hi everybody. Don't forget suncream for the beach.
> **Berry**

> Right! + don't forget swimming things + shorts. :)
> **Ellie**

> OK. I'm going to bring my bodyboard.
> **Luca**

> Gr8! I'm going to bring a football. Who has a tube?
> **Adam**

> OK. Don't forget towels. C U at the ferry! XXX
> **Berry**

> Yes + speakers for my phone. C U.
> **Ellie**

> Gr8. R U going to bring your frisbee, Ellie?
> **Luca**

> I have a big tube. I can bring it. :)
> **Berry**

c) Add more words for the trip to the beach to your network from 1a.

4 👥 Chain game

Imagine that you're going to go to the beach. What do you want to bring?

> I want to bring a tube.

> I want to bring a tube and some sandwiches.

> I want to bring a tube, some sandwiches and a ...

5 A summer song

Listen to Adam's favourite summer song. Do you like it? Why (not)?

> I think it's great! I like it because ...

> It's OK / good / nice / ... . I like the ...

> I think it's boring / stupid / terrible / ... because ...

1 The day before the trip

It's Sunday and everybody is thinking about the big day tomorrow. Match the texts with the characters.

A is Adam / Ellie / ...

A
Mum isn't going to come – that's a pity. But dad's going to be there, and he's going to take me into the water without my wheelchair – great! Later I'm going to give my friends the big news. But before that I want to have some fun!

B
Oh no, the kids are out of school again! They're all going to go to the beach. Well, I'm not going to go there. Hm, what am I going to do?

F
I'm going to visit the ferries tomorrow. The tourists always have some bread or something for me!

C
Mum is going to give us some scones from the cafe – cool! I'm going to share my new rap song with everybody. And I'm going to play football on the beach.

E
I mustn't forget my bodyboard. Mmm, a picnic! I'm going to have some crisps, then I'm going to have some cake, then some chocolate, and then maybe some ...

D
We're going to ride on the ferry – yeah! I'm going to send dad and Alisha a photo. For the beach I'm going to take my new swimsuit. And this time I'm not going to forget suncream.

a) oder b)?
Mit der *going to*-Form kann man über
a) Absichten und Pläne
b) Hoffnungen und Gründe
für die Zukunft reden.

2 Positive and negative statements with 'going to'

Complete the rules for positive and negative statements.

FOCUS

Positive statements		Negative statements		
I + 'm +		I + 'm + not +		
you + ... +	going to + verb	you + aren't +	+ going to + verb	
he / she / it + ... +		he / she / it + ... +	+	
we / you / they + ... +		we / you / they + ... +	+	

▶ *Language file 11, p. 182*

3 What are your plans?

a) 🔘 Adam is telling Ellie about his plans for next weekend. Put in the right verb forms.

1 *Adam* — I don't have any plans, really. I...
going to have fun – that's my plan.
2 *Ellie* — Luca says you... going to have visitors.
3 *Adam* — Yes, my grandma and grandpa ...
going to visit us from Croatia.
They... going to stay for a week.
  Ellie — Oh, that's nice.
4 *Adam* — Zack ... going to meet them for
the first time. And grandma ...
going to cook – yum!

b) 🔘 Now Ellie is talking to Adam. Use the verbs in the box and the right form of *going to*.

> see • take • stay • go • visit

1 *Ellie* — Dad ... me to the theatre. We ... the
musical Starlight Express.
2 *Adam* — Cool! Do you have other plans too?
  Ellie — Dad, Alisha and Finn ... some friends.
3 *Adam* — Ah, and you ... with them.
4 *Ellie* — No! Are you crazy? I... home and watch
TV!

More practice 1 p.154

4 An evening at home

What are they going to do this evening? What aren't they going to do?

1 phone a friend / wash up
2 go to the cinema / play a game
3 practise rapping / do homework

4 watch TV / meet friends
5 write an email / play with Finn
6 listen to music / make pizza

5 This weekend ...

a) Make a table like this example. Write *your* plans for the weekend.

Me	Partner 1	Partner 2	...
meet friends	...	...	
...	...	...	

Here are some ideas:

> clean my room • go shopping •
> go to the cinema • play computer games •
> play football • read • ride my bike • ...

b) 👥 **Walk around:** Talk to two or more partners and take notes.

A — What are you going to do this weekend?
B — I'm going to play football and I'm going to
go to the cinema. What are you going to do?
A — I'm going to meet friends and I'm going to ...

c) 👥 Tell the class. Say what your partners are going to do.

This weekend Arif is going to play football
and he's going to go to the cinema. Julia is
going to ..

1 👥 Before you read

Look at the pictures on this page. Talk to a partner. Who can you see? Where are they?
What are they doing?

A

B

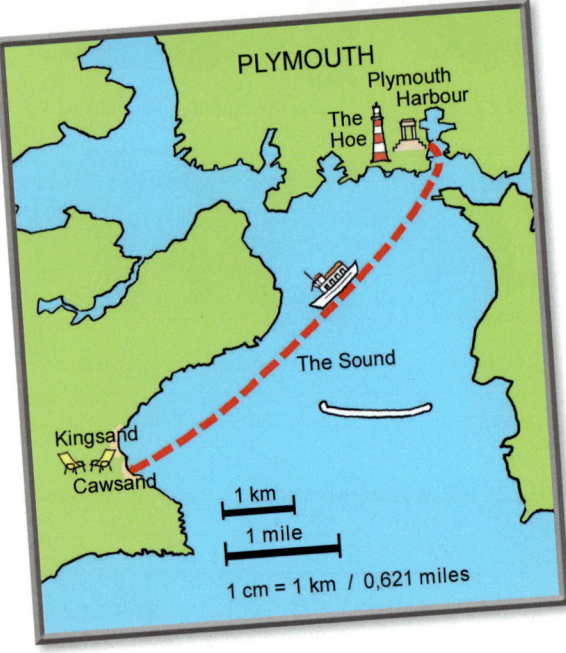

C

2 You're going to go on a ferry trip!

🎧 **a)** Close your eyes. Listen.
Enjoy the ferry trip.

b) 👥 Talk to a partner.
What's the ferry trip like?
What do you see?
What do you hear?
What do you feel?

 More help p. 154

🎧 All aboard!

Scene 1 *A message in a bottle*

Berry	Where's my dad? He's late.
Adam	Don't worry, Berry.
Berry	But he's never late.
5 *Luca*	And he has our picnic!
Ellie	Look at that old woman. She looks like a smuggler from an old story! What's she doing?
Adam	She's putting something in a bottle. I think it's a message!
Luca	A message? Maybe it's for us!
Ellie	She's going away ... Let's go and look!
Luca	The message is for you, Berry.
Berry	For me? What? Oh!

> 15 To Berry and her friends!
>
> **C**awsand is great,
> But Kingsand is better.
> Find the next bottle
> And read the letter!
>
> 20 We have your dad,
> The sea's coming in.
> You have 30 minutes -
> But hurry! He can't swim!
>
> Walk for two minutes
> 25 And then stop.
> You're in a square
> Now find a shop.
>
> From a Kingsand smuggler

Berry	Wow, it's a game. Let's find dad!
30 *Ellie*	But how?
Berry	First we must find a shop.
Luca	This is exciting!
Adam	Look at the big map. There's a shop near here, THE SHOP IN THE SQUARE!
35 *Ellie*	That's it. Let's go.

Scene 2 *We only have 30 minutes!*

Luca	Here's the shop. Can we stop and buy some sweets? I'm hungry.
Adam	Don't be stupid, Luca. We only have 40 30 minutes.
Ellie	Where's the next message?
Berry	Maybe there's another bottle?

Luca	I see one. Look, on that chair.
Ellie	I have it. And here's the message. 45
Adam	Oh, great!

> **S**mugglers are hungry
> They want to eat.
> Find a cafe
> Where smugglers meet. 50

Luca	We must find a cafe. But where?
Adam	Look, there's the old woman.
Ellie	Let's follow her. 55 Come on, Berry!
Berry	I'm coming!

Scene 3 *We only have 20 minutes!*

Luca — There she is again. She's very quick
60 for an old woman. Let's go!

Adam — Are you OK, Berry? You look tired.

Berry — It's hard work!

Ellie — Don't worry, we can push you.

Berry — Yes, please!

65 Ellie — Come on, guys. Push!

Berry — That's great! Thanks!

Adam — Look, a cafe! Maybe that's it.

Ellie — The *Smuggler's Rest*. That must be
it – a cafe where smugglers meet!

70 Adam — Look, on the sign. There's another
bottle. ... Look at this message.

What's the time?
You don't know?
Find a big clock.
Go, go, go!

75

Berry — What's the time? I can look at
my phone.

Luca — No, it says: Find a big clock.

Ellie — I can't see a clock. Do you see
80 the old woman?

Adam — No, she isn't here. She really is
quick. What can we do?

Luca — Come on. We're too slow. We only
have twenty minutes. Look for
85 a big clock.

Scene 4 *We only have 10 minutes!*

Ellie — Look, there's the clock!

Berry — Oh, yes! It's really big! But what
now?

Ellie — There's another bottle – under 90
the clock!

Adam — We must hurry. We only have
ten minutes.

Luca — I have the bottle. And here's the
message. 95

Feeling hot?
Want an ice cream?
Look for the cows
And find your dream.

Berry — Well, I'm feeling very hot – and 100
a bit nervous.

Luca — And I really want an ice cream.

Adam — But what are we looking for?

Ellie — The message says "Look for
the cows". 105

Adam — Cows on the beach?

Berry — Look. I can see cows.

Ellie — Me too. On that poster.

Luca — And there's a bottle.

Berry — Another? Oh dear, we don't have 110
much time!

Scene 5 *We only have one minute!*

Luca ___ There's a message in the bottle.

115
> **O**nly one minute,
> Look near the water.
> A dad is waiting
> For his daughter!

Adam _ Let's look on the beach.

Ellie ___ I can see the old woman.

120 *Luca* ___ But where's Berry's dad?

Adam _ Quick! We only have one minute!

Berry ___ There he is – in the sand! Hey Dad!

Dad ___ Help! I can't get out!

Luca ___ We're coming! Don't worry!

125 *Mum* ___ Hello, everybody.

Berry ___ Mum! You are the Kingsand
smuggler! – Dad, let's get you out
of there.

Ellie ___ That was a great game!

130 *Adam* _ Yeah, it was really good.

Berry ___ But a bit scary too.

Mum ___ Are you OK now? Are you hungry?

Luca ___ Yes!

Dad ___ Your picnic is over there. Sam is

135 looking after it.

Luca ___ I can see Sam.

Adam _ He's eating something.

Berry ___ Oh no! He's eating our
picnic! Sam! Stop!

Scene 6 *Berry's news*

3 **The last scene**

Listen to Scene 6. Answer the questions:

1 Where is Berry going to go in August?
2 Is she happy?
3 Why? Why not?

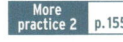 More practice 2 p. 155

4 **THEATRE TIME**

a) Pick a scene. Make groups
of five to six students: Ellie, Berry, Luca,
Adam, Berry's mum and Berry's dad.
Read the scene together.

b) Act your scene for the class.

1 Talking about summer plans

a) The four friends are talking about summer plans.
Listen. Match the names (Luca, Ellie, Adam and Berry) with the tickets (1–4).

1 Wembley 11th Aug
England – Ghana
Kick-off 3pm

2 **London to New York**
12 Aug

3 **Tinside Lido swimming pool**

4 **Exeter to Malaga** 17 August
Malaga to Exeter 24 August
FLIGHT TICKET

b) Listen again. Complete the sentences.

1 We're going to fly from …

2 Nothing … . I'm going to stay at home.

3 When is the game? – It's on … August.

4 Ellie says that she's going to go to Spain for …

5 Luca says that his mum and dad don't have any …

6 Luca says that his granny from Ghana is going to … them.

More practice 3 p.155

▶ *Language file 12, p. 183*

2 What are your summer plans? p.155

Work with a partner. Talk about your summer plans. Use the ideas in the green boxes.

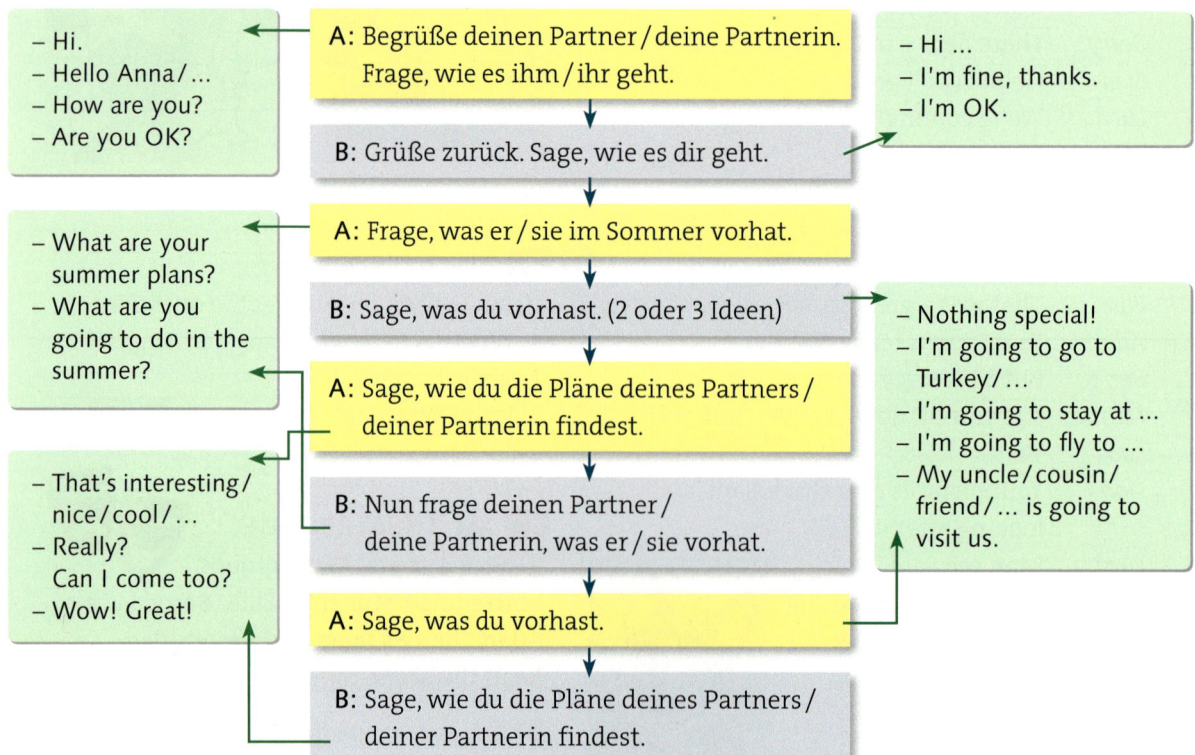

– Hi.
– Hello Anna / …
– How are you?
– Are you OK?

A: Begrüße deinen Partner / deine Partnerin. Frage, wie es ihm / ihr geht.

– Hi …
– I'm fine, thanks.
– I'm OK.

B: Grüße zurück. Sage, wie es dir geht.

– What are your summer plans?
– What are you going to do in the summer?

A: Frage, was er / sie im Sommer vorhat.

B: Sage, was du vorhast. (2 oder 3 Ideen)

– Nothing special!
– I'm going to go to Turkey / …
– I'm going to stay at …
– I'm going to fly to …
– My uncle / cousin / friend / … is going to visit us.

A: Sage, wie du die Pläne deines Partners / deiner Partnerin findest.

– That's interesting / nice / cool / …
– Really? Can I come too?
– Wow! Great!

B: Nun frage deinen Partner / deine Partnerin, was er / sie vorhat.

A: Sage, was du vorhast.

B: Sage, wie du die Pläne deines Partners / deiner Partnerin findest.

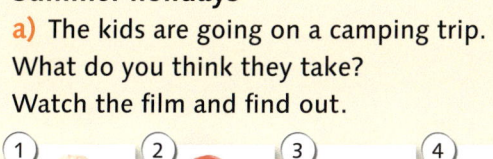

Sarah   Paul   Anna

1 The kids from Harbour Road:
Summer holidays

a) The kids are going on a camping trip.
What do you think they take?
Watch the film and find out.

1 ice cream 2 a tent[1] 3 sandwiches 4 sausages 5 a can of beans[2] 6 a bike 7 matches[3] 8 a can opener[4]

b) Put the photos
in the right order.

A

B

C

D

c) Are these sentences
true or false? Watch
the film again and
check your answers.

1 First the three friends are in a park.
2 They want to sleep in a holiday flat.
3 They want to eat beans and sausages.

4 They need a can opener.
5 They can't find the can of beans.
6 Anna's father helps the kids.

d) Talk to a partner about the kids from Harbour Road.

> I like Paul because …

> Yes, Paul is nice.
> But I prefer … because …

> I think … is fun / cool / …

2 People and places: **A ferry trip to Cawsand**

a) You're going on a ferry trip to Cawsand.
What do you think you can see? Make a list.

More help p. 156

b) Watch the film. What things on your
list do you see?

---

[1] tent [tent] *Zelt*   [2] can of beans [kæn əv ˈbiːnz] *Dose mit Bohnen*   [3] matches [ˈmætʃɪz] *Streichhölzer*
[4] can opener [ˈkæn əʊpnə] *Dosenöffner*

STOP! CHECK! GO!

Ein Lösungsblatt für die Aufgaben 1 bis 4 kannst du von deiner Lehrerin/deinem Lehrer erhalten.

1 WORDS On the beach

a) Look at the picture. Write the names of the things (1–12).

b) Choose five things and make a sentence with each thing.
Example: I always bring a towel to the beach.

c) What other things can you see in the picture? Make a list (five things or more).
👥 Compare with a partner. Who has more things? Add more to your list.

2 REVISION Quiz time

a) Cyril is asking Sandy. Complete his questions with the question words *what*, *where*, *when* and *why*.

Cyril
1 ... do the children go back to school?
2 ... do Cawsand and Kingsand both have?
3 ... do people eat crabs?
4 ... do crabs like for dinner?
5 ... does the Cawsand Ferry go?
6 ... do crabs love going to the beach?

Sandy
– After the summer holidays.

– Erm ... oh! Sand!

– Because they like them.
– Pizza, of course.
– Erm ... to Cawsand!
– Erm ... in the morning?

Cyril
– Right. I can't wait!

– Yes!

– Wrong. Because they're stupid!
– That question is too easy.
– You're clever, Sandy.
– No. After the summer holidays!

b) Book quiz: Answer the quiz questions about Units 1–6 in your book.
1 Why is Ellie in trouble at Eggy? (Unit 1)
2 When is Ellie at her dad's flat? (Unit 2)
3 Where does Luca's dad often go in the evening? (Unit 3)
4 When does Berry wake up in the morning? (Unit 4)
5 Why does Ms Lee write to Adam's parents? (Unit 5)
6 What's Berry going to do in the summer? (Unit 6)
👥 Check with a partner.

c) Make your own book quiz. Write five questions with the question words *what*, *where*, *when* and *why*.
👥 Ask your partner. Then answer your partner's quiz questions. Who has more right answers?

3 LANGUAGE Here's the plan

Ellie and her dad are talking about their trip to Spain.

a) Complete the dialogue. Use *going to* and the right positive and negative forms.

1 *Dad* __ OK, here's the plan: We ... (leave) on Saturday. Alisha and Finn ... (come) with us. They ... (visit) grandma and grandpa.

Ellie ___ Cool! A holiday together – just you and me!

2 *Dad* __ Yes. Now listen. We ... (fly) at 7.30 am from Bristol.

Ellie ___ From Bristol? Oh dear. I hope you ... (wake) me on Saturday morning, Dad.

3 *Dad* __ Don't worry. We ... (leave) here on Saturday. We ... (go) to Bristol the day before.

Ellie ___ Oh, good. What are you going to bring?

4 *Dad* __ It's hot in Malaga, so I ... (bring) lots of things. I ... (have) one small bag. And you?

Ellie ___ Zoe ... (give) me her small rucksack.

5 *Dad* __ That's good. I hope you ... (remember) your swimsuit this time.

Ellie ___ Yes. And this time I ... (forget) my sunglasses and my frisbee, oh and my ...

6 *Dad* __ Don't worry, Ellie. Alisha ... (make) a list for you.

b) Correct the wrong statements. Use the negative form of *going to*.

Example: They aren't going to go on ..., they're going to ...

1 They're going to go to Malaga on Friday.
2 Alisha and Finn are going to come later.
3 Ellie is going to have a holiday with Alisha and Finn.
4 They're going to fly from Plymouth.
5 They're going to go to Bristol on Saturday.
6 Ellie's dad is going to have a big rucksack.
7 Alisha is going to give Ellie her small rucksack.
8 Ellie's dad is going to make a list for her.

4 LANGUAGE Berry's last days

Berry is going to go to America soon. Look at her calendar with her plans.

Saturday, 10th August
10.00 go shopping with Ellie
12.30 meet Adam and Luca for lunch
15.30 get my things ready
18.00 say goodbye to animals

Sunday, 11th August
With Mum and Dad:
– go by bus to London
– meet Mum's friend Helen at bus station
– dinner and sleep at Helen's house

Monday, 12th August
4.30 get up
8.00 fly to New York!

a) Write sentences with *going to*. Use linking words.

On Saturday at 10.00 Berry is going to ...
After that at 12.30 she ...
On Sunday Berry and her parents are going to ...

b) 👥 Talk about Berry's plans. Look at the calendar, not at your sentences.

What are Berry's plans on Saturday? ...

At ... she's going to ..., then at ...

c) Make your own plans for the weekend.
👥 Tell your partner.

STOP! CHECK! GO!

5 READING and MEDIATION   The village tour

You and a friend are on the ferry to Cawsand. You have a brochure about the village tour, but your friend needs help with the text. Answer his or her questions in German.

The Cawsand and Kingsand tour

Welcome! On this tour you're going to see the exciting smugglers' villages. The two villages are very small and because they are next to each other, they look like one village, but they aren't. When people think about Cawsand and Kingsand, they usually think about smugglers. Smuggling is a big part of their history, so you're going to learn about that. First we're going to walk to the big clock in Kingsand. There we're going to visit the Smugglers' Museum. Then you can have lunch in The Smuggler's Rest, a café with a long history. Our tour ends with a visit to the smugglers' caves.

Price: £ 4.00 per person (lunch not included)

1 Was werden wir sehen?
2 Was steht da? Ein Dorf mit zwei Namen?
3 Woran denken die Leute bei den Namen?
4 Wo gehen wir als erstes hin?
5 Was machen wir da?
6 Und was ist mit dem Mittagessen?

6   WRITING and SPEAKING   When I'm older …

a) Make notes about your plans: *When I'm older …*

… I'm going to … I'm not going to	be	lots of children / lots of money / a nice house / …
	live	a teacher / a firefighter / a fisherman / …
	work	lots of countries / England / Portugal / …
	try	riding / cooking / …
	have	in a city / in a small town / in the country / …
	visit	in a shop / in a restaurant / on a ferry / …
	…	…

b) Write complete sentences – as many as you can. Use linking words: *and, but, or, then, later, …*

When I'm older I'm going to live in a big city. I'm going to work in a restaurant and I'm going to have a nice house with a big garden. Later I'm going to … and maybe I'm going to …

c) Present your text to the class.

7 PROJECT Let's have a picnic!

It's the end of the school year.
Plan a picnic for your class.

Step 1:

Think about:

a) when   c) what you need

b) where   d) what activities

Make notes.

Step 2:

 Plan in small groups. Talk about the points from Step 1.
One person makes notes. These words and phrases can help you:

> When / Where do we want to have our picnic?
> What do we need? / What activities do we want to have?
> We can ... / Let's ... / We need ... / I want to ...
> We need things to eat and drink: fruit / sweets / ... (see p. 112)
> We can listen to music / dance / play games / speak English / ...

Step 3:

 Each group presents their notes from Step 2. As a class, decide on these points:

a) date and time

b) place

c) things to bring

d) who brings what

e) party activities

Write them on the board.

> – We think ... is a good time / place.
>   We want to have the picnic ...
>   next Friday / in two weeks / on the 3rd of June / ...
>   in the park / in the classroom / ...
>   Who wants to have the picnic ...?
> – I / we / Sarah / Leon / ... can bring ...
>   Who can bring ...?
> – At the picnic we can listen to music / play games /
>   speak only English / ...
>   Who wants to ...?

8 My learner log

Copy and complete your learner log. You can put it in your DOSSIER.

My learner log

Now I can ...

– say what I want to do or plan to do ...
  • in the next moment.
  • any time in the future. 😄 😐 😟
  Examples: I'm going to ...

– talk about different foods: ...

– talk about things that you can bring to the beach: ...

I know five words about summer holidays: food / picnics / ...

My progress in English is: GREAT! 👍 / OK ✊ / NOT VERY GOOD 👎

In Unit 6 ...
– my favourite pages are ...
– my favourite phrases are ...
– my favourite food is ...

Unit 1 ▸ Stop! Check! Go!

11 👥 **SPEAKING   A timetable**   ▸ *Unit 1, p. 33*

a) Partner A: Copy this timetable into your exercise book. Some lessons are missing.
Answer partner A's questions. Then ask partner B. Complete the timetable.

		Our class timetable			
Lesson	Monday	Tuesday	Wednesday	Thursday	Friday
1	....	music	technology	geography	PE
2	maths	English	history	German	....
3	science	....	PE	....	English
4	art	maths	....	science	German
5	....	German	maths	....	....

> What's lesson two on Monday?

> It's maths. What's lesson one on Monday?

> It's English.

Unit 2

5 👥 **What's different?**   ▸ *Unit 2, p. 39*

Look at room B. Your partner looks at room A.

Talk to your partner about the things in room B. Take turns. Find four different things in your rooms (or more if you can). Make notes about the different things.

Partner A __ There's a bed in room A.
Partner B __ There's a bed in room B too.
      OK. There are three cushions in room B.
Partner A __ There are no cushions in room A. That's different!

Room A	Room B
no cushions	3 cushions
...	...

6 **QUIZ** **Who is who?**   ▸ *Unit 2, p. 41*

a) Partner B: Write the complete questions and answers (✓ = yes, ✗ = no).

1 ... Jackie Ellie's mother? (✓)
2 ... Finn Ellie's stepbrother? (✗)
3 ... Ellie and Lily sisters? (✗)
4 ... Zoe and Ellie stepsisters? (✓)
5 ... Jackie Lily's aunt? (✓)
6 ... Conor and Finn brothers? (✗)

b) 👥 Answer Partner A's questions (for help, look at Ellie's family tree on p. 37).
Now ask A your questions. One point for each right answer. Who has more points?

7 **SPEAKING** **Good shops** ► *Unit 2, p. 50*

a) You're in Plymouth. Partner A wants to find a good mobile shop. Answer his or her questions.

b) You want to find a good sports shop in Plymouth. Ask Partner A these questions.
Write: – the name of a shop
– the address
– the phone number.

Phones 4U

1 Charles Street
Plymouth PL1 1EA

☎ 01752 665 115

Do you know a good sports shop in Plymouth?

What's the name of the shop, please?

What's the address?

Can you spell that, please?

Do you know the phone number?

Can you say that again, please?

Unit 3

3 **ROLE-PLAY** **A garage sale** ► *Unit 3, p. 65*

PARTNER B: You have a garage sale in Plymouth. Listen to your partner's questions. Pick the best answer.

It's £ ...
It's a special offer.
It isn't expensive.
It's good value.
Good. That's £..., please.
Thank you.

Swap roles.

Unit 5

2 👥 ⬤ **NOW YOU** ▶ Unit 5, p. 102
Partner B

a) Listen to your partner. He/She is talking about
picture 1. There are five differences in your picture.
When you hear a difference, tell your partner.
In my picture the car is …
In my picture the girls are ….

b) Now describe *picture 2* to your partner.
Say what you can see, where the things and
people are, and what they're doing.
On the left / In the middle / On the right /
At the top / At the bottom I can see …
It's / They're / There's a … next to / in front of / …
He's / She's / They're playing …

Your partner listens and looks at his or her picture.
Some things are different in your picture.
He or she must find five differences.

Lösung:

Unit 5

6 👥 **What are they doing?** ▶ Unit 5, p. 99
Look at the photos and check your answers.

DIFF BANK

Unit 1

More practice 1 **The first morning** ► *Unit 1, p. 17*

👥 Practise the dialogue with a partner. Practise roles A and B.

> A: Hi, …
> B: Hi, … How are you?
> A: I'm fine, thanks. And you?
> B: OK, thanks.
> A: Hey, I like your …

> B: Thanks. It's new.
> A: It's a nice colour.
> B: Yes, I like it too.
> A: Well, see you later.
> B: OK, see you.

More practice 2 **NOW YOU** ► *Unit 1, p. 19*

b) 👥 Let's talk. Practise the dialogue with a partner.

Partner A	Partner B
Hi. I'm … What's your name?	Hi, … My name is …
I'm in class … And you?	I'm in class … too. How old are you?
I'm … What about you?	I'm … (too).
What's your favourite colour?	I like … What about you?
My favourite colour is …	Nice colour! What's your favourite hobby / sport?
I like … And you?	My favourite … is …
Cool!	

More practice 3 👥 **About me, about you** ► *Unit 1, p. 19*

a) Use your table from 2a. Give this information about you to your partner:

age: … from: … school: … class: … brothers: … sisters: …

b) Then make notes about your partner.

Julius is eleven. He's from Osnabrück. He's at Albert-Einstein-Schule. He has one brother, Ben.

// ● 4 At Eggy ► *Unit 1, p. 23*

Put in: *I'm • You're • He's • She's • It's • We're • You're • They're*

1 Eggy is my new school. … big.
2 Luca is a new student at Eggy. … cool.
3 "My name is Berry. … from Woolwell."
4 "Thanks, Ms Lee. … a great teacher."
5 "Can we have lunch now, Ms Lee? … hungry!"
6 Adam and Berry aren't in class 7X. … in class 7Y.
7 "I like you, Ruby and Charlie. … my best friends!"
8 Mrs Ford is at Eggy too. … the art teacher.

he   she

it   they

Unit 1

More help **5** **Pets and friends** ▶ *Unit 1, p. 23*

b) Write about your friend(s) or pet(s). You can write:

(Name) is my friend.
(Names) are my friends.

He's / She's ten / …
They're ten and … / …

He's / She's from … .
They're (both) from …

He's / She's / They're nice / fun / great / …
My friend is / isn't at my school /
in my class.
My friends are / aren't at my school /
in my class.

(Name) is my pet.
(Names) are my pets.

He's / She's a dog / cat / hamster …
They're dogs / cats / …

He's / She's four / six / …
They're four and six / …

He's / She's / They're big / small / …
He's / She's / They're brown / black / …
He's / She's / They're nice / fun / great / …

More help **6** **People and places in Plymouth** ▶ *Unit 1, p. 23*

b) Match the sentences.

1 Plymouth isn't in Germany.
2 Eggy isn't in London.
3 Cyril isn't a seagull.
4 Sandy isn't a crab.
5 Mr Brown isn't a maths teacher.
6 The four friends aren't from Germany.
7 Ellie and Berry aren't teachers at Eggy.
8 Luca and Adam aren't girls.
9 Ms Lee and Mr Brown aren't students.

A He's a crab.
B They're teachers.
C It's in Plymouth.
D They're boys.
E They're from England.
F It's in England.
G She's a seagull.
H They're students at Eggy.
I He's an ICT teacher.

More help **7** **Make a quiz for the class** ▸ *Unit 1, p. 23*

a) Pick some quiz cards. Complete the cards with the ideas in the green boxes.

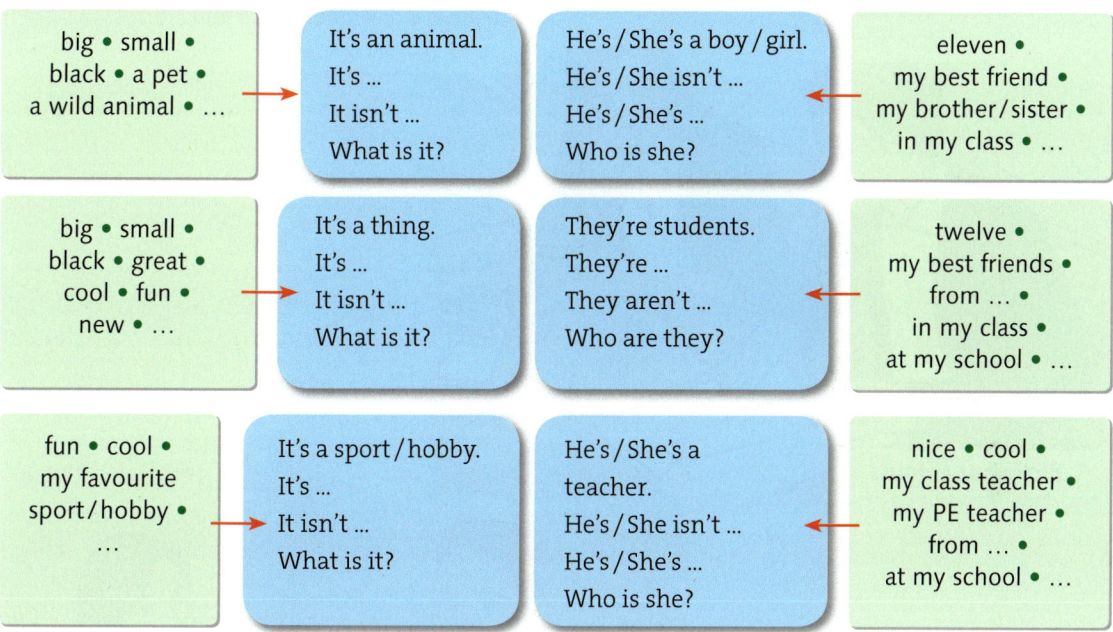

More practice 4 **The story** ▸ *Unit 1, p. 25*

Put the sentences in the right order and tell the story.

Part 1

1 Miss Borowski is in the assembly hall.
2 Ellie knows it's important.
3 It's assembly at Eggy.
4 Miss Borowski says, "The uniform is important!"
5 The students are in the assembly hall too.
6 But Ellie has no tie.

Part 2

1 Now they're in the canteen.
2 Ellie has a new tie.
3 Class 7Y is in the art lesson.
4 They need paper, scissors and colours.
5 It's a very nice tie. But it isn't the school tie.
6 Luca has an idea.

More practice 5 **Clothes** ▸ *Unit 1, p. 25*

👥 Look at your partner's clothes for five seconds. Then look away. Now make sentences.
Jonas has blue trousers, a white shirt and brown shoes.
Swap partners.

Unit 1

More practice 6 **Make a school tie** ▶ *Unit 1, p. 25*

> I like pink and purple. What about you?

> Purple is OK. And are blue and purple OK too?

1 Pick your colours.

> I have colours.

> I have scissors / paper / …

2 Make the tie.

3 Pick the best tie.

> I like the black and white tie!

> I like the red and green tie!

//● **1** **Make networks** ▸ *Unit 1, p. 27*

a) Copy the network. Complete it with words from the box.

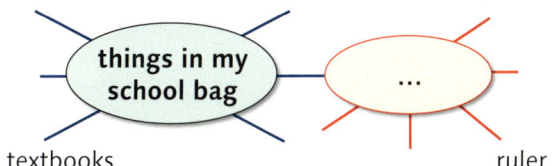

textbooks   ruler

> calculator • diary •
> exercise book • hole punch •
> pen • pencil case •
> pencil sharpener • pencils •
> rubber • …

More help **1** **Make networks** ▸ *Unit 1, p. 27*

b) Copy this school network and add the words from the box to your network.
Can you add more words?

c) 👥 Compare networks. Add to your network.

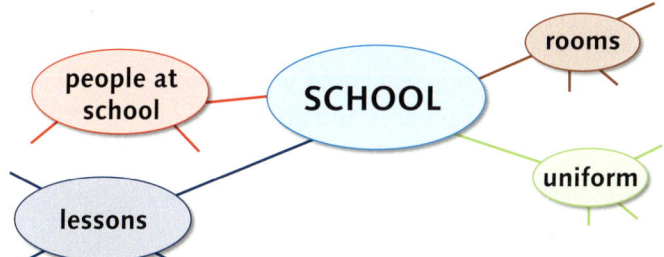

> art room • blazer •
> classroom • class teacher •
> computer room • English •
> French • history • maths •
> PE • skirt • sports hall •
> student • sweatshirt •
> teacher • tie • trousers • …

//● **2** 👥 **NOW YOU** ▸ *Unit 1, p. 28*

Practise the dialogue. Use words and phrases from page 28, exercise 1.

Partner A	Partner B
Say hello to B. Ask B how he/she is.	Say hello and say how you are. Ask A how he/she is.
Say how you are. Ask B: … favourite lesson?	Answer A's question. Ask A: … borrow a pencil?
Say yes and give the pencil to B.	Say thank you. Ask A: … favourite boy/girl in our class?
Say who your favourite boy/girl is.	Say you like him/her too. Say who your favourite boy/girl is.

Unit 1 ▸ Stop! Check! Go!

//● **4** **LANGUAGE** **Remember Ellie?** ▸ *Unit 1, p. 31*

Ellie is with her dad. She has some pictures on her mobile. Complete the sentences.

1 Look, this ... my new school.
2 It... very big.
3 The students in my class ... OK.
4 The teachers ... OK too.
5 This ... my new friend, Berry.
6 She... great.
7 My friends Ruby and Charlie ... at my school too.
8 But they ... No in my class.
9 This ... my new uniform.
10 It ... No very nice.

Unit 2

More help **3** **ACTIVITY** **My home** ▸ *Unit 2, p. 35*

a) Draw your house or flat.
Here's an example.

b) 👥 **Walk around:** Talk about your house
or flat. Use these phrases and add more:

My house / flat is ...	new / old / big / small / ...
My house / flat has ...	a bedroom / three bedrooms / ... a bathroom / two bathrooms / ...
There's ...	a nice garden / a balcony / a garage / ...
The living room is ...	white / red / ...
...	...

More practice 1 **Katie's room** ▶ *Unit 2, p. 39*

Describe Katie's room.
Write sentences – as many as you can:

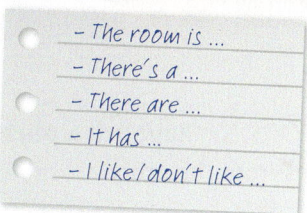

– The room is …
– There's a …
– There are …
– It has …
– I like/don't like …

3 **NOW YOU** ▶ *Unit 2, p. 41*

a) Answer the questions.

1 Are you noisy?
2 Are your friends fun?
3 Is your grandmother from Germany?

4 Is your dad bossy?
5 Are your parents strict?
6 Is your room messy?

b) 👥 Ask your partner the same questions.

More practice 2 **More questions** ▶ *Unit 2, p. 41*

Write the correct questions in your exercise book and answer them.

1 from – you – Are – Germany – ?
2 mum and dad – Germany – Are – from – your – ?
3 a – Is – father – teacher – your – ?
4 your – English – school bag – Is – book – your – in – ?
5 best friend – class – your – Is – your – in – ?
6 strict – your – Are – teachers – ?

3   Is Ellie happy? ▸ *Unit 2, p. 43*

Complete the sentences.

1 On Monday Ellie is happy because …
2 On Tuesday Ellie is happy because …
3 On Wednesday Ellie is happy because …
4 On Thursday Ellie isn't happy because …

5 On Friday Ellie isn't happy because …
6 On Saturday Ellie isn't happy because …
7 On Sunday Ellie is happy again because …

More help 4   A week later ▸ *Unit 2, p. 43*

Write Ellie's diary. Use the words from the box.

are • bedroom • can • happy • in •
is (2x) • isn't (2x) • it's • not • OK • quiet

*Dear Diary
I'm very … ☺ again. Mum's house …
my home. I'm in the … with Zoe and
… really nice. I'm … messy and Zoe …
bossy. Mum … here too. She's happy.
The cats … happy too. And I … do my
homework … the living room. Conor is
really …! Finn … here and that's … !*

More practice 3   WORDS   Favourite phrases ▸ *Unit 2, p. 43*

a) Put the phrases from the story
in two lists: 😄   😦

b) 👥 Check your lists with a partner.

Great news! • I'm lonely. • Finn isn't very happy. •
Tuesday is the big day. • I miss my mum. •
Finn is very cute. • Dad has no time for me. •
The best of both worlds! • Be quiet, Finn!

More help 2   NOW YOU ▸ *Unit 2, p. 44*

b) Write about your dream house or flat. Use your mind map.
You can use sentences like this. Write as much as you can.

*My (dream) house / flat is in Hamburg / Dresden / …
It's near a village / city / …
The colour is nice. It's yellow / red / …
It's small / big / great / cool / …
There are three / four / … rooms in my house / flat.
There's a kitchen, a living room, a … / …
My favourite room is …
There's a table / … in the living room / …
There are lots of chairs / pictures / … too.
It's messy / noisy / …!
There's no TV / I share a room with my brother / sister / …*

More practice 4 **NOW YOU** ▶ *Unit 2, p. 45*

How do you say these things in English?

1 Wie fragst du nach einem englischen Wort?
2 Wie fragst du, ob du auf die Toilette gehen darfst?
3 Wie fragst du, was ihr als Hausaufgaben aufhabt?
4 Wie bittest du jemanden, etwas noch einmal zu wiederholen?

5 Wie fragst du, auf welcher Seite ihr gerade seid?
6 Wie sagst du, dass dir etwas leidtut?
7 Wie bedankst du dich?
8 Wie fragst du, ob du dir einen Radiergummi borgen kannst?
9 Wie fragst du, was ihr in der nächsten Stunde habt?

More practice 5 **Can you spell that?** ▶ *Unit 2, p. 46*

Partner A: Look at the pictures in box A. **Partner B:** Turn the page upside down.

A

garden   homework

pencil   trousers   school bag

a) Choose one of the words from your box. Spell it for partner B. Partner B listens and writes the word. Check the spelling.

b) Swap roles.

Then swap roles again.
writes the word. Check the spelling.
Spell it for partner A. Partner A listens and
b) Choose one of the words from box B.

village   teacher   house   tie   baby

B

a) Partner B: Listen to partner A. Write the word. Then check the spelling.

More help **2** **Addresses and phone numbers** ▶ *Unit 2, p. 46*

🎧 **c)** Copy the notes. Listen to Berry. Add the missing letters.

| M | E | R | | Y | W | | A | | H | E | R | | | | | M |
| W | O | | L | | E | | | | | | | | | | | |

Unit 2 ▶ Stop! Check! Go!

4 Questions for Sandy ▶ Unit 2, p. 49

Answer Cyril's questions for Sandy.

1 Hey, Sandy. Are you happy? — Yes, I am.
2 Is your family small? — NO, …
3 Are your parents strict? — …
4 Is your mum cool?
5 Are your brothers and sisters mean?
6 Are you and your family noisy?
7 Is your new house messy?

Unit 3

2 NOW YOU ▶ Unit 3, p. 55

a) Make a table about your Saturdays.

buy … • go to … • have … • meet … •
play … • ride … • stay … • watch … • …

I always	I sometimes	I never
go shopping	…	…

More practice 1 **ACTIVITY** **A birthday calendar** ▶ Unit 3, p. 57

You can make a birthday calendar for your family and friends too.

Step 1: Make 12 groups. Pick a month for your group. Write it on a piece of paper.

Step 2: Find out who has a birthday in your month – and the date. Write it on your month.

Step 3: Draw a picture for your month.

Step 4: Put the months together. Put the calendar on the wall of your classroom.

More practice 2 **Ellie's weekend** ▸ *Unit 3, p. 59*

Complete the sentences about Ellie.

1 At the weekend I … (go) to my dad's flat.
2 He always … (get up) first.
3 He … (make) breakfast for me and Finn.
4 Alisha, my stepmum, … (stay) in bed.
5 Dad, Finn and I sometimes … (go) shopping at the supermarket.
6 After lunch I … (meet) my friends in town.
7 In the evening dad … (watch) TV with Alisha.
8 I sometimes … (watch) too. I sometimes … (play) with Finn.
9 On Sunday evening I … (go) to my mum's house.

// ● **7** **That's not right!** ▸ *Unit 3, p. 60*

a) Complete the sentences. Use *don't* or *doesn't*. Then write the correct sentence.

1 Jack gets up early. – That's not right! He doesn't get up early. He gets up late.
2 Luca and Jack do their homework in the morning. – That's not right! …
3 Dad and Grace make breakfast together. – That's not right! …
4 Dad works in the afternoon. – That's not right! …
5 Mum comes home from work early. – That's not right! …
6 After dinner they sing songs. – That's not right! …

// ● **8** **Working parents** ▸ *Unit 3, p. 60*

Write the sentences about Luca's mum and dad with the correct form – positive or negative.

1 Luca's mum … (work) in a mobile phone shop.
2 Luca's dad … (work) in a museum.
3 He … (have) a normal workday.
4 She … (often come) home late.
5 He … (get up) late in the afternoon.
6 Luca, Jack and Grace … (see) their parents after school.
7 She … (go) to work on Saturdays.
8 On Saturdays they … (have) breakfast together.

More practice 3 **8** **Luca and Jack** ▸ *Unit 3, p. 60*

Put in the right verb form. Use both positive and negative forms.

Luca and Jack are very different. They … (1 get up) at the same time. Luca is an early bird, but Jack … (2 stay) in bed because he … (3 like) mornings. Luca… (4 have) breakfast before school, but Jack isn't hungry in the morning, so he … (5 have) breakfast. Jack always … (6 go) to school by bus, but Luca sometimes … (7 ride) his bike. He says, "Come on, lazy boy!", but Jack says, "No thanks, I … (8 want) to ride my bike to school." And Jack … (9 bring) his lunch to school, but Luca … (10 bring) his lunch. He says, "The Eggy canteen is OK with me!"

Unit 3

More help **11** **Plymouth days and nights** ▸ Unit 3, p. 61

Match the sentence parts. Pay attention to the linking words *(and, or, but).*

1 In the afternoon Adam plays football
2 Ellie doesn't see her dad every day
3 At Eggy the kids have lunch in the canteen
4 Luca's dad likes his job
5 Plymouth has a great beach
6 Berry doesn't live near her school friends
7 In the evening Luca stays at home

but he doesn't like working at night.
and it has a nice swimming pool too.
but she sometimes visits Ellie, Adam and Luca.
and in the evening he listens to music.
or he goes to the cinema with his friends.
but she goes to his flat at the weekend.
or they bring their lunch from home.

More help **12** **My day** ▸ Unit 3, p. 61

a) Make notes about your day. You can use a mind map like this: ▸ Unit 3, p. 61

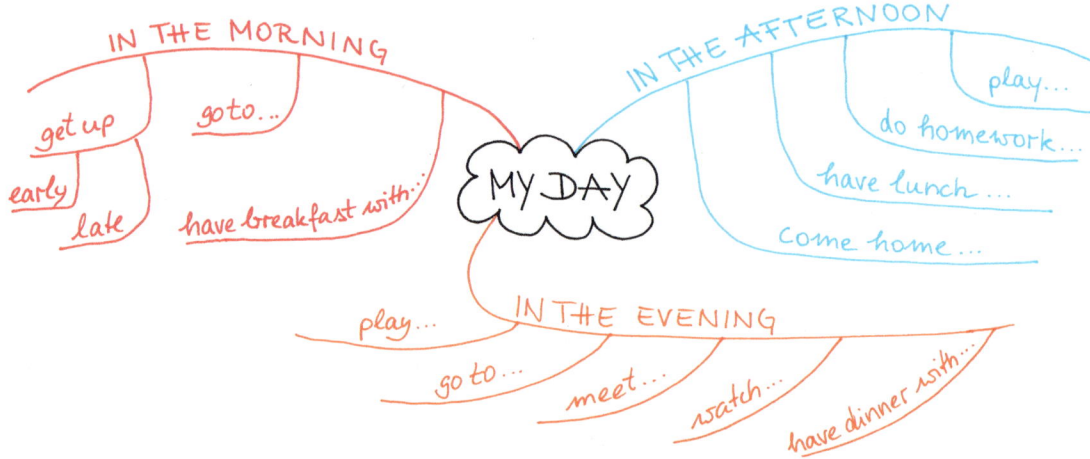

More help **12** **My day** ▸ Unit 3, p. 61

b) Use your notes and write a text about you and your family. Write positive and negative sentences. Choose from the phrases you see here. You can use other words too.

> Use **always • usually • often • sometimes • never**:
> – I usually get up late.
> – I always have lunch at school.
> – She doesn't often go by bus.

> **My day**
> In the morning I always / usually / often / ...get up early / late.
> I have breakfast together with my mum / dad / parents / brother / ... .
> Our mum / dad / ... doesn't have breakfast.
> He / she isn't hungry / doesn't have time / doesn't like to eat in the morning.
> I always / usually / often / ... go to school by bus / car / ... or I walk / ride my bike.
> I don't have lunch at school, but I have a banana / ... at the break.

You can put your text in your DOSSIER.

More help **3** **Luca's birthday** ▸ *Unit 3, p. 63*

Finish the sentences. The sentence parts in the green box can help you.

On Thursday Luca has no ideas for ...
But his mum ...
On Saturday morning Luca gets ...
Later with Jack, Luca doesn't ...
The boys meet Jack's friends ...
Jack goes ...
Then Luca ..., but ...
Jack and Luca go to ...
Luca has ...

... has a great idea – a concert!
... down the hill first.
... his birthday.
... goes down the hill
... the hospital.
... a sore leg.
... at the Hoe.
... he falls.
... great presents.
... want to go to Central Park.

//● **1** **Luca's garage sale** ▸ *Unit 3, p. 64*

c) **Listen again. How much are the things**
in the garage sale? Write the prices.

1 The calculator is £...   5 The computer is ...
2 The mobile is £...   6 The school bag is ...
3 The crab is ...   7 The blazer is ...
4 The posters are ...   8 The footballs are ...

You write:	You say:
£1.50	One pound fifty
50 p	Fifty p

More practice 4 **Jack helps with the prices** ▸ *Unit 3, p. 64*

🎧 **Listen and write the prices in your exercise book.**

More help **2** **Guessing new words** ▸ *Unit 3, p. 66*

a) **What are these words in German? Find the words in the adverts on p. 66.**
Then read the sentences in German here. They can help you.

1	on stage (advert A)	Wo befinden sich bei einer Show die Leute, die singen und tanzen? Schau dir das Bild an.
	fireworks (advert B)	Das Bild hilft dir. Gibt es ein ähnliches deutsches Wort?
2	theatre (advert A)	Das deutsche Wort ist sehr ähnlich, es wird nur etwas anders geschrieben.
	festival (advert B)	Das Wort gibt es auch im Deutschen. Schau auf das Wort davor. Gibt es auch ein *summer festival* bei euch?
3	opening times (advert C)	Was kommt nach diesem Wort im Text? Es sieht aus wie Uhrzeiten, oder? Du hörst oft im Unterricht: *Open your book*. Und dann öffnest du dein Buch. Was könnte *opening times* heißen?

4	adult (advert C)	*Adults* müssen £11 Eintritt zahlen. *Children* zahlen nur £6.50. Sind *adults* älter oder jünger als Kinder? Was könnte das Wort heißen?
	singers (advert A)	Es steckt ein Wort in *singers*, das du kennst. Anhand dieses Wortes kannst du den Sinn erschließen.
	dancers (advert A)	Es steckt ein Wort in *dancers*, das du kennst. Anhand dieses Wortes kannst du den Sinn erschließen.

More practice 5 👥 **More words from the adverts** ▶ *Unit 3, p. 66*

a) Work with a partner. One partner opens the book at p. 66.
Try to guess these words in the adverts:

In advert A: live, price, book
In advert B: championships, free
In advert C: fantastic, dive show, tiger sharks, tickets

b) What helps you to guess the words?

Unit 3 ▶ **Stop! Check! Go!**

More help **8** **READING** **Casper the cat** ▶ *Unit 3, p. 71*

Find these words in the text. Guess what they mean in German.
The sentences in German can help you.

1 leaves (line 3)	Schau dir die Wörter davor und danach an. Was macht Casper jeden Morgen?
2 bus stop (l. 4)	Du kennst beide Wörter aus dem Deutschen. Das erste Wort ist klar, aber das zweite Wort musst du etwas anders übersetzen. Dort stoppt der Bus.
3 waits (l. 4)	Casper ist an der Bushaltestelle. Was macht er dort zunächst?
4 sits (l. 5)	Das Wort ist auch einem deutschen Wort sehr ähnlich.
5 window (l. 6)	Schau dir das Foto an. Was ist neben Casper? Er kann dadurch nach draußen schauen.
6 travels (l. 8)	Es geht um den Bus. Was macht er? Achte auf die Zahl nach dem Wort.
7 bus driver (l. 9)	Schau dir die Wörter danach an. Könnte das eine Person sein? Was hat er/sie mit dem Bus zu tun?
8 gets out (l. 10)	Schau auf die Wörter davor. Was macht Casper? Er ist wieder an seinem Haus.

Unit 4

More practice 1 **Animal words** ▶ *Unit 4, p. 73*

Collect as many animal words as you can.
Copy this diagram and complete it.

Or write two lists, like this:

Pets *Farm animals*

cat donkey cow

Pets	Farm animals
...	...

More practice 2 **On school days** ▶ *Unit 4, p. 75*

a) Copy and complete the table for you.

b) Appointments: Make appointments
with two partners. Then talk to your
partners like this:

> I get up at 6 o'clock.
> What about you?

Listen to their answers and
complete the table.

c) Tell the class about your partners.

	Me	1 o'clock ...	2 o'clock ...
get up	6.00	...	...
have breakfast	6.15	...	...
go to school	...		
come home			
have lunch			
do my homework			
have dinner			
go to bed			

More help **2** **NOW YOU** ▶ *Unit 4, p. 76*

a) Find more ideas when you feel great or when you feel fed up. Look at the box for help.
Make notes like this:

😎 I feel great ...	😖 I feel fed up ...
when I play football	when my dad is bossy.
when I ...	...
...	

- when I'm with my family/...
- when I (don't) have school.
- when my best friend/... doesn't text me.
- when my parents/teachers are strict.
- when my brother/... borrows my things.
- when my mum/... doesn't have time for me.
- when I write a good/bad test.

Unit 4

More help **3** **Berry's homework** ▶ *Unit 4, p. 77*

d) Write a short text about your feelings. Talk about: at home / at school / with friends / … .
Use your notes from exercise 2a and use words from exercise 3c.
Write more than one sentence. Here are some ideas:

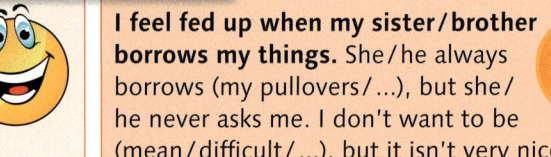

My feelings

At school I feel great when I do sport.
My favourite sport is … I often play with … and I love to run fast.

And I feel really great when I'm with my animals. It's always lots of fun. My (dog / cat / …) makes me very happy. We play every evening. She's / he's my best friend.

I feel fed up when my sister / brother borrows my things. She / he always borrows (my pullovers / …), but she / he never asks me. I don't want to be (mean / difficult / …), but it isn't very nice when she / he does that.

At home I feel really fed up when my parents are strict. They often say:
Do your homework!
Go to bed early!
You can't … (watch TV / go to the cinema with your friends / …)!
But I'm not a little child!

More practice 3 **More questions about pets** ▶ *Unit 4, p. 79*

👥 With your partner think of three more questions for your dialogues on page 79.
Use the ideas in the boxes or your own ideas.

Questions for partners with a pet:
Do you …   play with your pet?
             talk to your pet?
             go outside with your pet?

Where does your pet sleep?
Does your pet …   sleep in your room?
                  have a cage?
                  like other animals?
                  …

Questions for partners with no pet:
Does your mum / dad / …   like animals?
                            want a pet?
Does   your grandmother /
       your friend / …   have a pet?

Do you play with the pet?

…

More help 7 Talking about pets ▸ Unit 4, p. 79

b) Write about your favourite pet or a friend's pet. Use the ideas in the boxes.

<u>My favourite pet</u>
I like / don't like ….
I have / don't have …
My aunt / friend has a dog / …
It lives inside / in the garden /
It eats …

<u>Martin's pet</u>
Martin has a dog / cat / ….
It lives in the house / a cage / …
It eats …
It likes games / …
It doesn't like dogs / children / cars / …

<u>Pia's favourite pet</u>
Pia wants a pet.
She doesn't want a cat / crocodile / …
She wants a rabbit / a hamster / …
Hamsters / … are cute / nice.
They eat …
They live in a cage / outside / …

▸ Wordbank 7, p. 188

More help 9 Find a person who … ▸ Unit 4, p. 80

b) Ask questions like this:

Find someone who …	Questions
… has an interesting pet.	Do you have an interesting pet? What pet do you have?
… has an interesting hobby.	Do you have an interesting hobby? What hobby do you have? Why do you like your hobby?
… gets up very early.	Do you get up very early? When do you get up? Do you like to get up early?
… goes to a nice place in the holidays.	Do you go to a nice place in the holiday? Where do you go? What do you like about the place?
… likes an English football team.	Do you like an English football team? What team do you like? Why do you like the team?
… likes homework.	Do you like homework? What homework do you like? Why do you like it?

More practice 4 ● The end of the story ▸ Unit 4, p. 83

Complete the text with the words in the box. Two words in the box don't work.

Berry, Adam and Ellie go looking for Luca. Ellie doesn't find him at the … (1), and he isn't at the duck pond. Berry and Ellie are worried. "Luca, … (2) are you?" First it's quiet, then they … (3) a sound from the … (4). They find Luca there and he isn't in … (5). Or is he? The "…" (6) is hungry. And Luca has her … (7). But there is something Luca doesn't know.

> breakfast • hear •
> field • cow •
> trouble • bull •
> trampolines •
> where • barn

Unit 4

More practice 5   ● **More questions about the story**   ▶ *Unit 4, p. 83*

Answer the questions in complete sentences.

1	Why do the three friends go to Woolwell?	–	They go to Woolwell because …
2	Why is Luca unhappy?	–	He's unhappy because …
3	Why does Luca go to the village?	–	He goes to the village …
4	Is Luca really in trouble? Why / Why not?	–	Luca …
5	What do the friends do on Saturday evening?	–	…
6	Why is there trouble in the field on Sunday?	–	…

More help   **6**   👥👥 **THEATRE TIME**   ▶ *Unit 4, p. 83*

Here are some ideas to help you to act the story:

1	Damit die Geschichte spannend klingt, solltet ihr die Sätze mit Betonung sprechen.	→ For ideas, listen to the story on the CD.
2	Lest nicht alles vor. Anweisungen und Beschreibungen wie "Ellie says" oder "Adam says" könnt ihr weglassen.	→ In your group read through your scene. Which words can you leave out?
3	Andere Dinge könnt ihr weglassen, weil ihr schauspielert. Im Text steht z.B. "Everybody laughs. But not Luca." Also lachen hier alle außer Luca!	→ Are there more parts in your scene like this?

Unit 4   Stop! Check! Go!

More help   **3**   REVISION   **A day with my family**   ▶ *Unit 4, p. 89*

b) Make a table like this for a day with your family. Make both positive and negative statements. You can use some ideas from the boxes.

👥 Then tell your partner.

When?	Who?	What?
every morning / before 6 o'clock	mum, dad and I	get up

When?
- Every day / morning / afternoon / evening
- Before breakfast / lunch / dinner / school
- After breakfast / lunch / dinner / school
- In the morning / afternoon / evening
- At 10 o'clock / 11.15 / 12.30 / 1.45

Who?
- I
- my mum
- my dad
- my brother
- my sister
- my aunt
- …

What?
- get up / have breakfast / feed my hamster / …
- go to school / go to work
- stay at home / work at home
- go shopping / have lunch
- come home from work / from school
- do homework / do sport / play a game
- watch TV / meet friends / read a book
- make / have dinner with …
- go to bed

4 LANGUAGE An interview with Cyril and Sandy ▶ *Unit 4, p. 89*

a) Make the questions for the reporter.

1 Plymouth / you / ... / like / ?
2 you / ... / a best friend / have / ?
3 you and Sandy / live / ... / on the beach / ?
4 like / ... / Sandy / Plymouth too / ?
5 Sandy / have / a best friend / ... / ?

– Yes, it's great.
– Yes, I do. Her name is Sandy.
– Yes, we live in Kingsand.
– Yes, she loves Plymouth.
– Yes, she does. I'm her best friend!

b) Complete Cyril's short answers.

1 Do you like Mr Johnson?
2 Do you live in a small house?
3 Do you and Sandy go to school?
4 Does Sandy have a bike?
5 Does Sandy eat crabs?

– No, ... He isn't nice.
– Yes, ... I don't like big houses.
– No, ...
– Yes, ...
– No, ... I'm a crab!

c) Complete the questions for Sandy.

1 ... do you live?
2 ... do you get up?
3 ... do you have breakfast?
4 ... do you do after breakfast?
5 ... do you like Cyril?

– In Kingsand.
– Very late – after 10 o'clock.
– I always have breakfast on the beach.
– I often go to Plymouth.
– Because he's friendly and he's fun!

More help 7 SPEAKING An interview with a student in your class ▶ *Unit 4, p. 90*

a) Here are some more ideas for your interview questions:

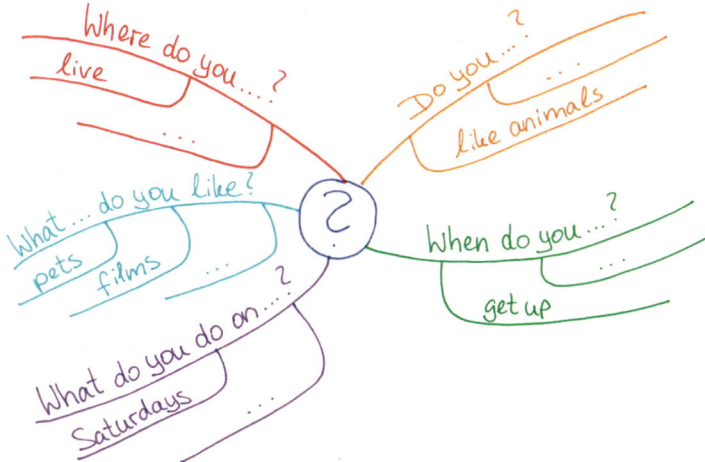

Where do you ...?
live
...

Do you ...?
like animals
...

What ... do you like?
pets
films
...

When do you ...?
get up
...

What do you do on ...?
Saturdays
...

4–5 DIFF BANK

Unit 4 **Stop! Check! Go!**

More help **8** PROJECT **Interesting animals** ▸ Unit 4, p. 91

b) You can write a text like this about your animal.

> My project is about chipmunks.
> Chipmunks come from the USA. They're brown, grey
> and black. They're furry and very cute.
> They're small – 13 to 15 cm long.
> They live in a nest, in the ground.
> They eat fruit and nuts. They usually live for three years[1].
> Chipmunks are fun, but they aren't good pets.

Unit 5

More help **1** **The harbour in Plymouth** ▸ Unit 5, p. 92

b) How many of the things in the box can you find on pages 92–93?
Group the words under these themes: people • places • things

baby • beach • bike • blazer • bus • car • chair • child/children • city • dog • garden • helmet •
house • kid • man • park • people • phone • restaurant • road • sea • seagull • shop • sign •
swimming pool • table • teenagers • tree • visitors • woman • …

More help **Can I help you?** ▸ Unit 5, p. 94

c) 👥 Make a dialogue in a cafe. Here are some useful words and phrases.

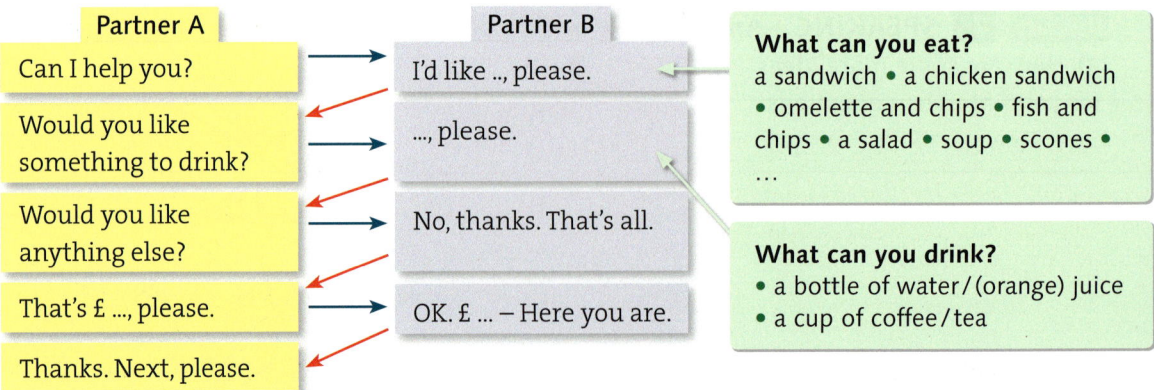

Partner A	Partner B
Can I help you?	I'd like .., please.
Would you like something to drink?	…, please.
Would you like anything else?	No, thanks. That's all.
That's £ …, please.	OK. £ … – Here you are.
Thanks. Next, please.	

What can you eat?
a sandwich • a chicken sandwich • omelette and chips • fish and chips • a salad • soup • scones • …

What can you drink?
• a bottle of water/(orange) juice
• a cup of coffee/tea

---

[1] for three years *drei Jahre lang*

148 one hundred and forty-eight

More practice 1 **Who is doing what?** ▶ *Unit 5, p. 95*

It's 7 pm. Look at Adam's family and friends. What are they doing? Look at the box and complete the sentences.

1 Mum ... 2 The boys ... 3 Dad ...
4 Berry ... 5 Luca ... 6 Ellie and Zoe ...

More practice 2 **GAME** **What am I doing?** ▶ *Unit 5, p. 95*

One student mimes one of the activities in the green box. The other students guess. Then swap roles.

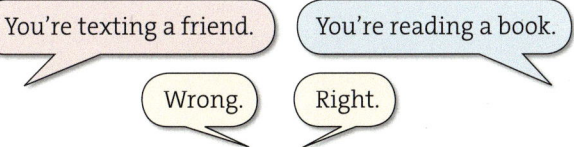

You're texting a friend. Wrong. You're reading a book. Right.

eating something • watching TV • helping customers • reading a book • leaving • texting a friend • sitting outside • cooking • cleaning the tables

More practice 3 **Adam and his family** ▶ *Unit 5, p. 95*

Finish the sentences about Adam and his family. You can use the ideas in the box.

1 Adam's dad works on ...
2 Adam's dad likes ...
3 But Adam misses ...
4 The cafe is often ...
5 Adam's mum works ...
6 Adam sometimes helps in ...
7 At school Adam isn't very ...
8 And he isn't doing ... at the moment.

a ferry • happy • his dad • his homework • his new job • the cafe • very busy • very hard

Unit 5

More help **4** **A letter from school** ▶ *Unit 5, p. 95*

c) Adam's mum talks to him about Ms Lee's letter. Write the dialogue.
Use the phrases from 4b. You can use the ideas here too.

Mum

– I want to talk (to you) about .../
  Let's talk about .../We must talk about ...
– What's wrong?
– Are you tired/unhappy/bored/...?
– You aren't working hard/doing your
  homework/...
– Why?/Is it because ...?
– You must work hard/do your homework/
  talk to me when you have problems/...

Adam

– Yes, Mum./What do you want
  to know, Mum?
– I don't know, Mum.
– No/Yes, I feel ... (because ...)
– I don't know why./I think it's because ...
– I want to help in the cafe./I miss dad./
  My homework is too hard./I'm bored./
  I don't have time for myself./I don't like
  working./...
– I'm sorry.
– Can I go/go outside/... now?

🎧 ⫽● **2** **Welcome to PMZ** ▶ *Unit 5, p. 97*

b) Listen to Adam. Answer the questions.

1 Who is talking to Adam?
2 What does Adam like?
3 Where is PMZ?
4 What does Adam want to join?

More help

3 **NOW YOU** ▶ *Unit 5, p. 97*

a) Appointments:
Copy this table and
write your answers.
Then make appointments
with two partners.

	Me	1 o'clock ...	2 o'clock ...
What's your favourite band?			
Who's your favourite singer?			
What's your favourite English song?			
Can you play an instrument?			
What instrument?			
Can you sing? Can you rap?			
Are you in a band?			

▶ *Wordbank 8, p. 188*

More help

3 **NOW YOU** ▶ *Unit 5, p. 97*

d) Write a text about you and
music. Here are some ideas.
You can put your text in your
DOSSIER.

I love pop/rap/... music.
My favourite band/singer is ...
My favourite English song is ...
I (can't) play an instrument.
My favourite instrument is the guitar/drums/...
I play the guitar/piano/...
I can sing/rap/...
I'm in a band./My friend is in a band. The name of the band is ...

More practice 4 **Reading – riding – rapping** ▶ *Unit 5, p. 99*

1 ⃝ Just add *-ing*.

read – reading
clean – …
eat – …
do – …

2 There's no 'e' with *-ing*!

rid**e** – riding
mak**e** – …
com**e** – …
writ**e** – …

3 Double the last letter.

rap – rap**p**ing
get – …
swim – …
sit – …

More practice 5 **What are they saying?** ▶ *Unit 5, p. 99*

Finish the sentences A–F. Use the *present progressive*.

A

Berry __ It's 2 o'clock.
We're late, Ellie!
Ellie ___ OK, I… (come)!

B

Mum __ Are you helping
your dad?
Luca ___ Yes, mum. But Jack
is lazy. He … (help).

C

Ms Lee _ What are you doing,
Ellie?
Ellie ___ Sorry, Miss.
I… (eat) a sweet.

D

Ms Lee _ Is Ellie OK?
Berry __ No, she … (feel) well.

E

Adam _ Are they looking
at me?
Luca ___ No, they… (look)
at me!

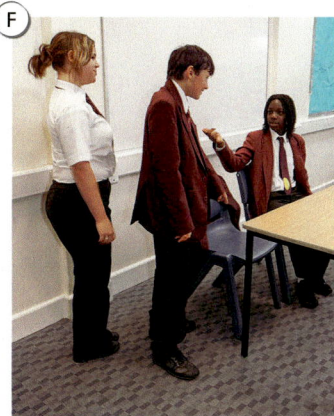

F

Adam _ Who… (sit) here?
Luca ___ Ellie. Look, she's there.

Unit 5

🎧 ▮▮ ● **4** **What's Cyril doing?** ▶ *Unit 5, p. 99*

a) What's Cyril doing now? Write the numbers 1–5. Then listen and write what you think.

1 Cyril is ..., 2 ...

More practice 6 **An email to Adam** ▶ *Unit 5, p. 101*

Write an email to Adam about the story. Here are some ideas.

Dear Adam

I think the story about you at PMZ is ...

Best wishes
(Your name)

You can tell Adam something about you too:
– Do you like rap?
– Who's your favourite rapper?
– Can you rap?
– ...

I think	the girls and boys on the bus were you were Josie was your rap is PMZ is your parents are	bad · boring · bossy · cool · different · friendly · fun · great · good · happy · important · interesting · mean · nervous · nice · stupid · terrible · ...

More help **1** **In the park** ▶ *Unit 5, p. 102*

c) What are they doing? Make sentences.

On the left In the middle On the right At the top At the bottom	two dogs a boy three girls children a girl a baby two men	is are	working. eating. riding a bike. sleeping playing football. talking and laughing. reading a book.

More help **3** WRITING **A text to Amanda** ▸ *Unit 5, p. 103*

Write a text message to Amanda. Here are some ideas for your text.

- I'm sitting at home / …
- I'm (not) working hard / …
- I'm learning English / doing my homework / …
- My friend / mum / brother / … is here.
- He's / She's listening 2 music / …
- I'm feeling gr8 / happy / terrible / …
- How R U?
- Yes, I can come 2 the party.
- Sorry. I can't come 2 the party.

Unit 5 ▸ **Stop! Check! Go!**

More help **1** REVISION **Questions and answers** ▸ *Unit 5, p. 106*

d) Make a quiz about another animal. Use these ideas:

- Do tigers / penguins / … live in Germany?
- Do … live in fields / on farms / in the sea / …?
- Do … live in cages / in zoos / …?
- Do … eat fruit / nuts / special food / other animals / …?
- Do … like people?
- Do … walk fast?

More help **8** READING and WRITING **On Saturday morning** ▸ *Unit 5, p. 109*

b) Here are some ideas for another story in the cafe.

I'm hungry. • A big chicken sandwich, please. •
Would you like anything else? •
Can I help you? • …

Hi, Dad. • You're early. • That's great. •
This is a surprise. • I'm really happy. •
How's it going? • How are you? • …

More help **1** **Getting ready** ▸ *Unit 6, p. 112*

a) What things can you bring to the beach? Start a network like this.
Then read the text for more ideas.

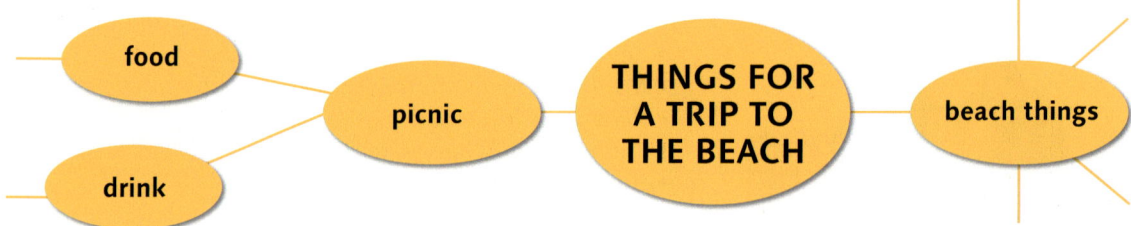

food

drink

picnic

THINGS FOR A TRIP TO THE BEACH

beach things

More practice 1 **That's not right!** ▸ *Unit 6, p. 115*

Complete the sentences with the negative form of *going to*.

1 Ellie *isn't going to send* Zoe and Conor a photo from the ferry.
2 Adam ... (play) frisbee on the beach.
3 The four friends ... (go) to Dartmoor.
4 Luca ... (bring) his skateboard.
5 Cyril and Sandy ... (play) on the beach together.
6 Adam's mum ... (give) the kids fish and chips for their picnic.
7 Berry's mum ... (come) to the picnic.

More help **2** **You're going to go on a ferry trip!** ▸ *Unit 6, p. 116*

b) 👥 Talk to a partner.

What's the ferry trip like? – It's fun / nice / ...
What do you see? – The harbour / ...
What do you hear? – The noisy ferry / ...
What do you feel? – The cool water / ...

> the sea • seagulls • the harbour • buses •
> fun • the cool water • the city • a beach •
> the noisy ferry • an old woman •
> boring • a cafe • lots of kids • great •
> the swimming pool • cars • nice • a village •
> nice houses • cool • a man / ...

More practice 2 **Right or wrong?** ▶ *Unit 6, p. 119*

Correct the wrong sentences.

1 In scene 1 the friends find the first message from the old woman.
2 In scene 2 they must look for a sweet shop.
3 The old woman is very slow.
4 In scene 3 they find out where smugglers meet.
5 One message tells the friends to look for some cows.
6 In scene 4 they only have 20 minutes.
7 The friends find Berry's dad in the water.

More practice 3 **Summer plans** ▶ *Unit 6, p. 120*

The four friends are talking about summer plans.
Put their sentences into *indirect speech*.

1 Berry says: "We're going to fly to New York." *Berry says that they're ...*
2 Adam says: "I'm going to stay at home all summer."
3 And he says: "I'm going to go to a big football game."
4 Ellie says: "I'm going to stay at home in July."
5 And she says: "I want to stay in bed late every day."
6 Luca says: "My grandma is fun."

// ● 👥 2 **What are your summer plans?** ▶ *Unit 6, p. 120*

Work with a partner. Talk about your summer plans.

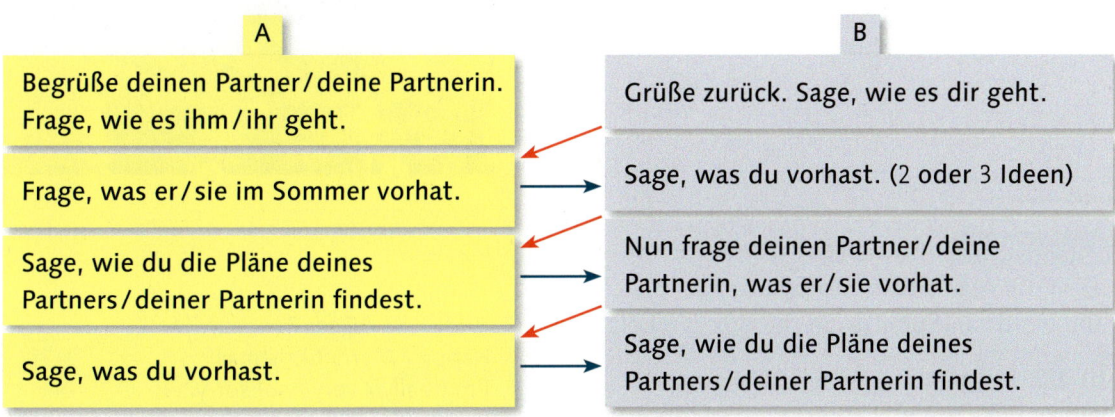

A	B
Begrüße deinen Partner / deine Partnerin. Frage, wie es ihm / ihr geht.	Grüße zurück. Sage, wie es dir geht.
Frage, was er / sie im Sommer vorhat.	Sage, was du vorhast. (2 oder 3 Ideen)
Sage, wie du die Pläne deines Partners / deiner Partnerin findest.	Nun frage deinen Partner / deine Partnerin, was er / sie vorhat.
Sage, was du vorhast.	Sage, wie du die Pläne deines Partners / deiner Partnerin findest.

Unit 6

More help **2 People and places:** **A ferry trip to Cawsand** ► *Unit 6, p. 121*

a) You're going on a ferry trip to Cawsand.
What do you think you can see? Make a list.

> buses • people • bags • food • shops •
> dogs • seagulls • bikes • cars • crabs •
> a ferry • boats • a harbour • houses •
> books • a beach • the sea • tents •
> picnics • smugglers • sunglasses • kids •
> tickets • a map • ...

TF 1

More practice **You stupid boy!** ► *Text file 1, p. 159*

Act a scene between Cyril and Sandy. The ideas in the boxes can help you.

> – Thanks Sandy!
> – Yes, we're good friends!
> – Toby is a stupid boy.
> – I'm OK.
> – Is the picnic good?
> – Oh, thanks, Johnsons!
> – ...

> – That's OK, Cyril.
> – Are you OK now?
> – We're friends.
> – The Johnsons are stupid.
> – This is good!
> – Yeah, thanks, Toby!
> – ...

TF 2

1 ⬤ **Christmas in Britain** ► *Text file 2, p. 162*

What are the Christmas things (1–5)
in the photo? Find the things in the text.

More practice **Alan's text message** ► *Text file 2, p. 162*

a) Write Alan's text message to Zoe.
The words and phrases in the box can help you.

b) 👥 Read your messages in class.
Which message is the best?

> Hi Zoe, ... / Dear Zoe, ... / Zoe ...
> Happy / Merry Christmas!
> I'm (really / very / so) sorry.
> I miss you. / I really like you. / ...
> Can I see you today / tomorrow / ... ?
> When can I see you?
> Love, ... / Yours, ... / See you!

2 👥 ● NOW YOU ▸ Unit 5, p. 102
Partner A

a) Describe *picture 1* to your partner. Say what you can see, where the things and people are, and what they're doing:

On the left / In the middle / On the right I can see …
There's a … next to / in front of …
He's / She's playing …

Your partner listens and looks at his / her picture. Some things are different in your picture.
He / She must find five differences.

b) Then listen to your partner. He / She is talking about *picture 2*. There are five differences in your picture. When you hear a difference, tell your partner.

In my picture there's a seagull on the …
In my picture the boy is …

Lösung:
Unit 1

1 The unit quiz ▸ Unit 1, p. 22
Check your anwers:

1 Plymouth	5 Harry / Berry's pet	9 Grace / Luca's sister
2 Ellie and Berry	6 Ms Lee	10 Ellie
3 Luca	7 Berry	11 PE
4 Luca and Jack	8 (your names)	12 (your name)

TF 1 You stupid boy!

This is great!

It's Sunday morning at Kingsand. Cyril is on the beach. No people. No children. Cyril is happy!

This isn't very good!

Sandy is near the beach. There are no people and no children. No lunch for Sandy! She isn't very happy!

The beach is great!

Look! It's Mr Johnson, Mrs Johnson and Toby Johnson! They're very happy – a nice day on the beach!

Cyril! The Johnsons are here!

Oh no! The Johnsons! Help!

Sandy is on the beach now. She's with Cyril. Cyril isn't happy now.

I like the beach.

I like crabs.

I like fish.

No crabs here?

Can Toby Johnson see Cyril?
Can he see Benny and Babe?

Oh, a crab!

Toby can see Cyril!

Oh no!

Go, Cyril, go!

Hello, crab.

Toby has Cyril!

10 Now I have a pet crab. Hee, hee, hee!

Cyril isn't very happy. But Toby is happy.

11 Two crabs! Great!

Benny and Babe are Cyril's friends. They're next!

12 It's Super Sandy! Yeeeehaaaaa!

13 You stupid seagull!

Toby isn't very happy now.

14 Help!

Where's Toby?

15 Thanks, Sandy.

Cyril is OK now!

16 Are you OK, Toby? Toby?!

Mrs Johnson can't[1] see Toby.

17 I don't like crabs.

Toby is wet[2] and he's cold. He isn't happy.

18 You stupid boy!

No people and no children. But lots of food[3]!
Now it's a nice day on the beach!

More practice p. 156

---

[1] can't [kɑːnt] *kann nicht* [2] wet *nass* [3] lots of food [lɒts əv ˈfuːd] *viel zu Essen*

🎧 TF 2 The best Christmas present[1]

24th December: Christmas Eve[2]

It's Christmas Eve and there are lots of people in Plymouth. They all need things for Christmas. Ellie and her mum are in Plymouth too. First they go to the big supermarket. It's very busy. They
5 need icing[3] for the Christmas cake. Then they go to *Whoopee*, a nice toy shop. Ellie buys a present for Finn – a small red crab.
Now Ellie and her mum are at home. Pete and Conor are there too. But Zoe isn't at home. She's
10 with her boyfriend, Alan.

There are lots of jobs for Christmas Day. Ellie helps her mum with the Christmas cake.

The living room is very nice. There are lots of Christmas cards and decorations. Conor and Ellie put decorations on the Christmas tree. 15
"It's great!" Pete says.
"It's really nice!" mum says.

"Ding-dong." Carol singers are at the door.
"We wish you a Merry Christmas,
We wish you a Merry Christmas, 20
We wish you a Merry Christmas
And a Happy New Year."

"Ding-dong." Now Zoe is at the door too. But she isn't happy.
"Hi, Zoe," mum says. "What's the problem?" 25
"I think it's over with Alan and me," Zoe says and she goes to her room.

Christmas cake

---

[1] Christmas present ['krɪsməs preznt] *Weihnachtsgeschenk*   [2] Christmas Eve [krɪsməs 'iːv] *Heiligabend*
[3] icing ['aɪsɪŋ] *Zuckerguss*

25th December: Christmas Day

It's Christmas morning – 6 o'clock. Ellie is in bed.
"Zoe! Zoe!" she says.

30 "What?" Zoe says.

"Thanks dad," Conor says. "Oh, speakers – great!"
"And here's a present for you Zoe – from Alan," mum says. 50
"I don't want it![2]" Zoe says and she goes to her room. She isn't very happy.

It's time for Christmas lunch. There are lots of nice things – a big turkey[3], potatoes[4], vegetables[5]. And then there's Christmas 55 pudding. And they all have Christmas crackers.
"Conor, pull[6] a cracker with me," Ellie says.

BANG! In the cracker there's a 60 small present – a pen. There's a paper hat[7] and a joke[8] too.
"Why is it always cold at Christmas?" Ellie reads. 65

cracker

"Our Christmas stockings are here!" Ellie says.
She looks into her stocking.
"Oh, look Zoe. A computer game
35 – *Let's Dance!* Great!"
"Ellie, please be quiet," Zoe says.
"And a book ... and a new hoodie ... and chocolate ...
Thank you, Father Christmas,"
40 Ellie says and she laughs[1].
Ellie is happy. But Zoe isn't very happy.

stocking

Later the family has a big Christmas breakfast. Then they go to the living room.
It's present time.
45 "Here's a present for you, Conor. It's from Pete," mum says.

"Er ... no idea! What's the answer?" Pete says.
"Because it's Decemberrrrrrrr!" Ellie says and they all laugh.
"Zoe, pull a cracker with me," Pete says.
"No, thanks," Zoe says. 70

Christmas dinner

Christmas pudding

---

[1] laugh [lɑːf] *lachen* [2] I don't want it! [dəʊnt ˈwɒnt] *Ich will es nicht!* [3] turkey [ˈtɜːki] *Truthahn*
[4] potatoes [pəˈteɪtəʊz] *Kartoffeln* [5] vegetable [ˈvedʒtəbl] *Gemüse* [6] pull *ziehen* [7] hat *Hut*
[8] joke [dʒəʊk] *Witz*

Later on Christmas Day

"Ellie, it's your dad," Conor says. "He's at the door."

"Happy Christmas, dad," Ellie says.

75 "Happy Christmas, Ellie. Let's go to our flat, to Finn and Alisha," her dad says.

It's Finn's first Christmas.

He's very happy.

And his present from Ellie is great.

80 At 3 o'clock the Queen is on TV. She's always on TV on Christmas Day.

"At Christmas, family and friends are very important ...," the Queen says.

85 Ellie has an idea. She writes a text message on her mobile phone to Alan, Zoe's boyfriend:

Happy Christmas Alan. Please text Zoe! Love Ellie

The Queen's Christmas Message[1]

90 Later Ellie is in the kitchen with her dad, Finn and Alisha. It's time for tea and Christmas cake. Ellie has a text message from Zoe:

95 Hi Ellie. Great news. Nice text from Alan! That's my best Christmas present! Zoe

---

1 ⃝ **Christmas in Britain** //⬤ p.156

What are the Christmas things (1–5) in the photo?

> a paper hat • a turkey • a Christmas cracker •
> a Christmas tree • a Christmas card

---

2 **Be a Christmas detective: Right or wrong?** **Correct the wrong sentences.**

1 On Christmas Eve lots of people go shopping.
2 In Britain people get presents on Christmas Eve.
3 Carol singers go from door to door and sing Christmas songs.
4 The presents in the Christmas stockings are from Father Christmas.
5 There are no presents under the Christmas tree.
6 There's fish for lunch on Christmas Day.
7 In a Christmas cracker there's a small present, a paper hat and a joke.
8 The Queen is on TV on Christmas Eve.

  More practice p.156

---

[1] Christmas Message ['krɪsməs mesɪdʒ] *Weihnachtsansprache*

TF 3 A world champion

You're in a dream: *You're on your bike at the start of a BMX race[1]. It's a big race – you can be the world champion of bicycle[2] motocross! The riders[3] are all very good. Lots of people are there. You're nervous*
5 *and excited. Then the race starts and everybody waves and shouts. You ride as fast as you can. The race is difficult – everybody wants to win. The other riders are fast. But at the end you're faster and you win the race.*
10 *Everybody congratulates[4] you. You're tired, but you're so happy. You're the world champion!*

Shanaze Reade

For Shanaze Reade this isn't a dream – it's real. Shanaze is from England. She races BMX all around the world for a British team. And she wins. She's the world champion of 2007, 2008 and 2010.
15 Shanaze was[5] like lots of kids. She had[6] her first BMX bike when she was 10. It was a fun hobby. Today she's different. She's a professional rider, and her name and her picture are often in the news and on TV. But Shanaze is a normal girl too. Her family is important to her. She has a brother and sister and a dog, Alfie. She loves music and often listens to her
20 MP3 player when she rides her bike. She likes to have fun. But she works hard too. Her sport isn't easy. Sometimes she falls off her bike and goes to the hospital. And sometimes she doesn't win. "I'm a person like everybody else," Shanaze says. "I don't like losing. But when I lose, I don't give up[7]." That's why she's a winner.

What's bicycle motocross?
Bicycle motocross (BMX) is a popular bicycle sport. With a BMX bike you can ride:

On a track[8] – You can ride your bike on a special BMX track. BMX is a new Olympic sport. It's very fast.

In a special park – You can do tricks on your bike in BMX parks or skateboard parks. There are special jumps[9].

In the street – You can ride in the street or in a sports hall. You can do tricks there too. You don't need jumps.

1 What is BMX?   **2** Why is Shanaze Reade different?   **3** What do you like about Shanaze?

---

[1] race [reɪs] *Rennen*   [2] bicycle [ˈbaɪsɪkl] *Fahrrad*   [3] rider [ˈraɪdə] *Radfahrer/in*   [4] congratulate [kənˈgrætʃuleɪt] *gratulieren*
[5] was *war*   [6] had *bekam*   [7] I don't give up. [dəʊnt gɪv ˈʌp] *Ich gebe nicht auf.*   [8] track *Piste*   [9] jump [dʒʌmp] *Schanze, Rampe (zum Springen)*

TEXT FILE

TF 4 The new boy in class

It's 9 o'clock in the morning. All the students are happy because it's Friday. Ms Lee comes in. "Good morning," she says. "We have a new student today."

5 All the students look at the new boy, who sits alone at a table.

"This is Ben," Ms Lee says.

"Hello," Ben says. He's very quiet and doesn't look happy.

10 "Please help Ben feel welcome in our class," Ms Lee says.

"Do you live in Plymouth, Ben?" Ellie asks.

"No. We're only here for two weeks," Ben says.

"We go to different towns and I go to different schools." 15

"Different towns? Why?" Berry asks.

"You can all talk to Ben later," Ms Lee says. "Now let's open our books at page 61."

1 How does Ben feel in the classroom?

It's 1 o'clock and time for lunch. Ellie, Adam, 20 Luca and Berry are in the canteen. They see Ben.

"Hi, Ben. Do you want to sit with us?" Berry asks.

"Sure, thanks," Ben says.

"Is it fun going to different schools?" Adam 25 asks.

"No, not really. You're lucky. You see your friends every day at school. I don't," Ben says.

"Where do you live?" Ellie asks.

"Live? Erm ... in a caravan[1]," Ben says.

30 "A caravan? Cool – it's like camping!" Luca says.

"I don't know anybody who[2] lives in a caravan. What's it like?" Adam asks.

"It's OK. There are always things to do," Ben says.

"Things to do?" Berry is surprised. "Like what?" 35

"Oh, you know, things ... Sorry, I must[3] go now. I can tell you more later," Ben says. "See you."

"OK – Bye – See you," the others say.

After Ben goes, Berry says: "Hm. He's nice, but he's a bit strange[4]." 40

"Yeah. It's like he doesn't want to tell us something," Luca says.

"Maybe[5] he needs help," Ellie says.

2 Where does Ben live?

3 What does Berry say about Ben?

---

[1] caravan ['kærəvæn] *Wohnwagen* [2] I don't know anybody who ... ['enibɒdi] *Ich kennen niemanden, der ...*
[3] must *müssen* [4] strange [streɪndʒ] *merkwürdig* [5] maybe ['meɪbi] *vielleicht*

It's 3.15 in the afternoon and school is out.
45 Luca and Ellie are at the bus stop.
"Hey, there's Ben. Hi Ben!" says Ellie.
Ben sees Ellie and Luca. He waves and hurries away[1].
"Why does he hurry away like that?" Ellie asks.
50 "Maybe he's unhappy about something. Let's see where he goes," Luca says.

Ellie and Luca watch Ben. They wait[2] for a moment and then follow[3]. They walk[4] for a long time. Then they see Ben go into Central Park. He walks fast. 55
"I don't see him. Where is he?" Ellie says.
"Come on. Let's find him!" Luca says.

4 Where does Ben go?

Later in Central Park.
"He's not here, Ellie. Let's go home," Luca says.
60 "You're right. We can't find him," Ellie says.
"Hey, what's that big tent[5] over there[6]?" Luca asks.
"I don't know, but it looks interesting," Ellie says. "Let's go have a look."

65 The tent is big and round. A man in a red circus costume is at the entrance. "Ladies and gentlemen! Russell's Circus starts in 15 minutes! Get your tickets!"
"Cool – a circus!" says Luca.
70 "We don't have money for this, Luca. Come on," Ellie says.

Then the man looks at Ellie and Luca. "What can I do for you two?" he asks.
"Oh, we want to find a school friend," Ellie answers. 75
"But he isn't here," Luca says.
"Maybe I know your friend," the man says with a laugh. "It's a small world! What's his name?"
Ellie and Luca laugh too. He's a funny[7] man. 80
"OK," Luca says. "His name is Ben."
"Well, you see?" the man says with a big smile. "You're in the right place. Come in! Ben's inside."

5 Who's inside the circus tent?

---

[1] hurry away [hʌri ə'weɪ] *forteilen*   [2] wait *warten*   [3] follow ['fɒləʊ] *folgen*   [4] walk [wɔːk] *laufen, gehen*   [5] tent *Zelt*
[6] over there [əʊvə 'ðeə] *da drüben*   [7] funny *lustig*

85 Ellie and Luca are in the tent. There's music and lots of people and a big circus ring[1] in the centre.

"That man was really nice," Ellie says.

"Yeah. Mmm, I smell[2] popcorn," Luca says.

90 "Oh, Luca! This isn't the time for popcorn. We want to find Ben," Ellie says.

Then the music stops and a spotlight[3] goes on in the ring. A man speaks into a microphone. It's the same man from before. He's the
95 ringmaster[4]!

"Ladies and gentlemen, welcome to Russell's Circus!" he says.

"We can't find Ben now, Ellie," Luca says. "Let's watch the circus and then look for him."
100 "Well, OK," Ellie says.

An hour[5] later the last circus act[6] starts. "Here come the clowns again!" Luca laughs. A small clown runs around the ring after two big clowns. They do tricks and the people laugh. They're very funny.   105

"They're my favourites," Ellie says.

The clowns wave to the people. Then the small clown's big red nose falls off. Everybody laughs. Ellie and Luca see the clown's face[7].

"It's Ben!" they both say.   110

Ben sees Ellie and Luca. He laughs and waves.

6 What does Luca want to do?
7 What's Ben's job?

It's 8.30 on Monday morning. Ben, Ellie and Luca are in the hall at Eggy.

"Well, now you know about me," Ben says.
115 "You guys are great," Ellie says. "Who are the other two clowns?"

"That's my mum and dad," Ben says.

"They're your parents?" says Luca. "Wow. You're a family of clowns!"
120 "Yes. I love my parents and it's fun with mum and dad," Ben says. "But we're so different from other families. That's why it's difficult for me to talk about my family. Do you understand?"
125 Ellie and Luca laugh. "Now we understand."

8 Who are the other two clowns?
9 What's difficult for Ben and why?

---

[1] circus ring ['sɜːkəs rɪŋ] *Manege*   [2] smell *riechen*   [3] spotlight ['spɒtlaɪt] *Scheinwerfer*   [4] ringmaster ['rɪŋmɑːstə] *Zirkusdirektor/in*   [5] hour ['aʊə] *Stunde*   [6] act [ækt] *Zirkusnummer*   [7] face [feɪs] *Gesicht*

TF 5 Hip-hop workout[1]

🎧 **1** **Listen and look at the instructions.**

A Step[2]-touch[3]

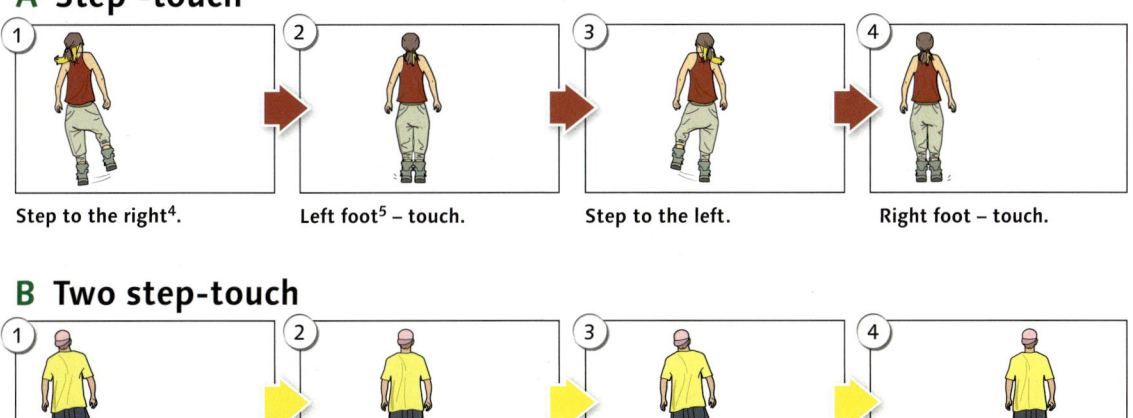

1	2	3	4
Step to the right[4].	Left foot[5] – touch.	Step to the left.	Right foot – touch.

B Two step-touch

    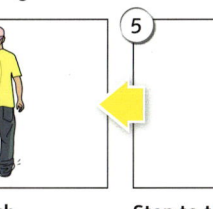 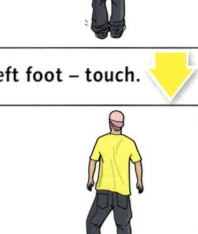

1	2	3	4
Step to the right.	Left foot – touch.	Step to the right again.	And left foot – touch.

8	7	6	5
And right foot – touch.	Step to the left again.	Right foot – touch.	Step to the left.

C Grapevine[6]

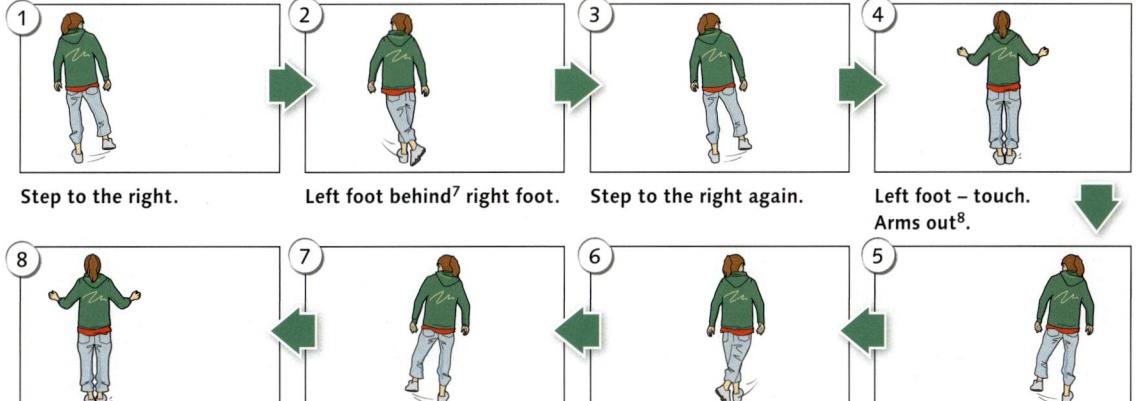

1	2	3	4
Step to the right.	Left foot behind[7] right foot.	Step to the right again.	Left foot – touch. Arms out[8].

8	7	6	5
Right foot – touch. Arms out.	Step to the left again.	Right foot behind left foot.	Step to the left.

2 **Practise the workouts with your class. One student can say the instructions. Play the CD and do the hip-hop workout. Have fun!**

---

[1] workout ['wɜːkaʊt] *Fitnesstraining*   [2] step *einen Schritt machen*   [3] touch [tʌtʃ] *berühren*
[4] to the right [raɪt] *nach rechts*   [5] foot [fʊt] *Fuß*   [6] grapevine ['ɡreɪpvaɪn] *Kreuzschritt*   [7] behind [bɪ'haɪnd] *hinter*
[8] arms out [ɑːmz 'aʊt] *Arme ausstrecken*

TEXT FILE

Bilingual module **BIOLOGY**

TF 6 Seagulls

Seagulls – some people like them, and some people hate them.

People like seagulls because they're intelligent, and they often have pretty **plumage**, so it's fun watching them. Other people hate seagulls because they're noisy, they're very messy, and they're aggressive and dangerous.

Like them or hate them, seagulls are interesting birds!

- Seagulls are usually white with black or grey **wings** and **tail feathers**.
- They have strong **bills** and **webbed feet**.
- Small seagulls can be 120 g and 29 cm. Big seagulls can be 1.75 kg and 76 cm.

A **gull** (the official name for these birds):

bill

wing

plumage

tail feather

webbed feet

Key terms

attack [ə'tæk] *angreifen*

bill *Schnabel*

catch *fangen*

colony (pl. colonies) ['kɒləni] *Kolonie*

landfill site ['lændfɪl saɪt] *Mülldeponie*

nest *sich einnisten; Nest*

plumage ['pluːmɪdʒ] *Gefieder*

rubbish ['rʌbɪʃ] *Müll*

(sea)gull [gʌl] *Möwe*

steal [stiːl] *klauen, stehlen*

tail feather ['teɪl feðə] *Schwanzfeder*

webbed feet [webd 'fiːt] *Füße mit Schwimmhäuten*

wing *Flügel*

More interesting information about seagulls

Seagulls …

- eat small fish or crabs, but they eat lots of other things too.
- eat or try to eat any food or **rubbish** on the beach.
- learn fast and remember. They sometimes use other things to get more food. For example, they use bread to **catch** fish.
- often take food away from other seabirds. They **steal** food from people too.
- don't fly out to sea very often. Many seagulls live inland and find food at **landfill sites**, on farms and in other places.
- are good parents. They have one partner all their lives, and both parents look after the eggs and baby gulls.
- **nest** in big noisy **colonies**, and together they **attack** people or animals that go near the baby gulls.
- are good swimmers and can walk and run on land too.
- can drink seawater. Most animals can't do this.
- can live a long time – some live 25 years!

 **1** **O** Make a fact file about seagulls using short facts and photos. Display your fact file in class. Then you can put it in your DOSSIER.

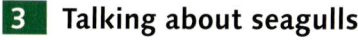 **2** **●** Make another fact file about …
a) a different seabird (pelican, albatross, or penguin)
   or
b) crabs.
The information on this website can help you:
www.cornelsen.de/headlight. Put in the webcode Head-1-169.

3 **Talking about seagulls**
What do you think? Do you like seagulls? Say why or why not.
You can use the phrases in the green box.

Seagulls
- are interesting birds
- have pretty plumage
- are intelligent

- eat small fish, crabs or other things

Activate your English	
I think I like them because I don't like them because	they're interesting / intelligent / noisy / messy / aggressive / … they have pretty / ugly / big / small / … plumage / wings / feet / … they can fly really well / learn things fast / … they make lots of noise / trouble / … they eat rubbish / they steal food from … / …

SF 1   Learning words – Vokabellernen leicht gemacht ▸ *Unit 1, p. 27*

Woran muss ich **immer** denken?

– Lerne nur 5 bis 10 Vokabeln auf einmal.

– Lerne und wiederhole regelmäßig. Zehn Minuten am Tag sind sinnvoller als einmal zwei Stunden pro Woche. Wiederhole direkt am nächsten Tag.

– Lerne mit jemandem zusammen. Es macht mehr Spaß und ihr könnt euch gegenseitig abfragen.

– Beim Wiederholen solltest du die Vokabeln abwechselnd lesen, laut aussprechen und vor allem auch schreiben. Beginne mal mit dem deutschen Wort und mal mit dem englischen Wort.

What's *Lieblingstier* in English?

Fluffy, my cat. No, sorry. Favourite animal.

1   Vokabeln lernen mit dem *Vocabulary*

Vokabellernen beginnt mit dem *Vocabulary* in deinem Englischbuch (S. 189–221). Auf S. 189 kannst du sehen, wie es aufgebaut ist.
– Lies das englische Wort laut.
– Lies dann die deutsche Übersetzung und den Beispielsatz.

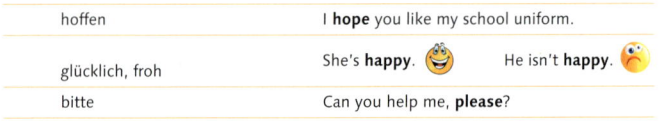

hoffen	I **hope** you like my school uniform.
glücklich, froh	She's **happy**. 😄 He isn't **happy**. 😟
bitte	Can you help me, **please**?

Wenn du testen möchtest, ob du die Wörter weißt, gehe eine Seite Zeile für Zeile durch:
– Decke die beiden rechten Spalten ab und sage die deutsche Übersetzung / den Beispielsatz.

– Gehe die Seite erneut durch und decke mit zwei Blatt Papier die linke Spalte und die rechte Spalte ab und sage die englischen Wörter.

Schreibe Vokabeln, mit denen du Probleme hast, auf selbstklebende Zettel. Die klebst du dann zu Hause an Gegenstände im Zimmer, die du immer wieder ansiehst.

2   Vokabelheft

– Du kannst neue Wörter in ein Vokabelheft oder -ringbuch schreiben. Benutze ein **dreispaltiges** Vokabelverzeichnis.
– Trage in die linke Spalte das englische Wort ein und daneben die deutsche Übersetzung.
– In die rechte Spalte kannst du ein Bild einfügen oder einen Beispielsatz schreiben. Manchmal findest du gute Beispiele im *Vocabulary* deines Buches.
– Lies die geschriebenen englischen Wörter dabei immer laut vor.

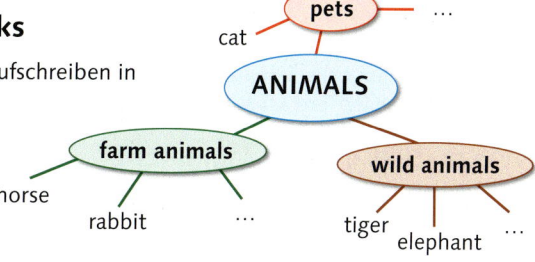

3 Sammeln und ordnen – Make networks

Du behältst neue Vokabeln leichter, wenn du sie beim Aufschreiben in Gruppen ordnest, z.B. in einem Wörternetz.

4 Vokabeln lernen mit Karteikarten

1. Du kannst neue Vokabeln auch auf Karteikarten schreiben.
   Dazu benötigst du:
   – viele kleine Kärtchen (oder gleich große Zettel)
   – einen passenden Kasten (oder einfach zwei Gummibänder)
   – eine **OK**- und eine **?**-Karte.

2. Auf die Vorderseite der Kärtchen schreibst du die englischen Wörter mit einem Beispielsatz und, wenn du magst, einem Bild. Auf die Rückseite schreibst du das deutsche Wort.
   Dann sortierst du die Kärtchen. Wie? Wie du willst!
   Am Anfang stehen alle Kärtchen im **?**-Fach.

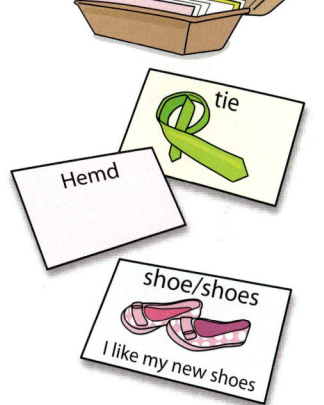

3. Schau dir die Rückseite jeder Karte an:
   Du weißt das englische Wort?
   ▸ Die Karte wandert in das **OK**-Fach (oder auf den **OK**-Stapel).

   Du weißt es nicht?
   ▸ Die Karte kommt zurück in das **?**-Fach (oder auf den **?**-Stapel).

   Beim nächsten Mal beginnst du mit diesen Karten.

Wiederhole auch regelmäßig die Vokabeln aus dem **OK**-Fach. Wenn du sie nach zwei bis drei Wochen noch weißt, kannst du sie aussortieren.

5 ⌨ Vokabellernen am Computer

Vielleicht fällt dir das Vokabellernen auch leichter, wenn du am Computer übst – mit dem e-Workbook oder mit der elektronischen Vokabelkartei.

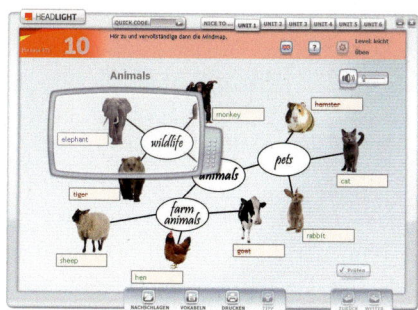

SF 2 Mindmaps ▶ *Unit 2, p. 44*

Wozu sind Mindmaps gut?
Mindmaps helfen beim Sammeln und Ordnen von Ideen, z.B. bevor du einen Text schreibst oder etwas vorträgst.

Wie machst du eine Mindmap?
Stell dir vor, du sollst einen Text über deine Familie schreiben. Dazu fertigst du zunächst eine Mindmap an.

Was benötigst du?
– ein leeres, unliniertes Blatt Papier im Querformat
– Stifte in verschiedenen Farben

Wie erstellst du eine Mindmap?

1. Schreibe in die **Mitte** des Blattes das **Thema** und male z.B. einen **Kreis** oder eine **Wolke** darum.

2. Überlege, über welche Hauptthemen du schreiben oder sprechen willst. Zeichne für jedes Hauptthema einen **Hauptast** in unterschiedlichen Farben und schreibe das Thema darauf. Verwende nur Schlüsselwörter.

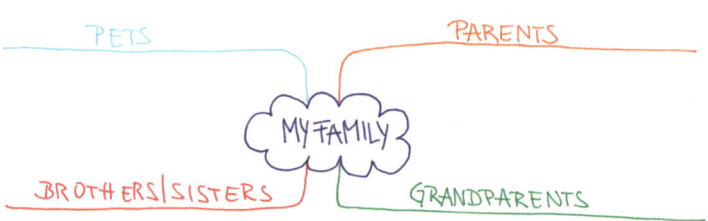

3. Wenn dir zu den Hauptthemen noch Unterthemen einfallen, dann ergänze Nebenäste in der gleichen Farbe. Schreibe die Unterthemen auf die Nebenäste. Verwende auch hier nur Schlüsselwörter.

   An die Nebenäste kannst du noch mehr Ideen „anhängen".

4. Du kannst statt Wörtern auch **Zahlen, Bilder oder Symbole** verwenden.

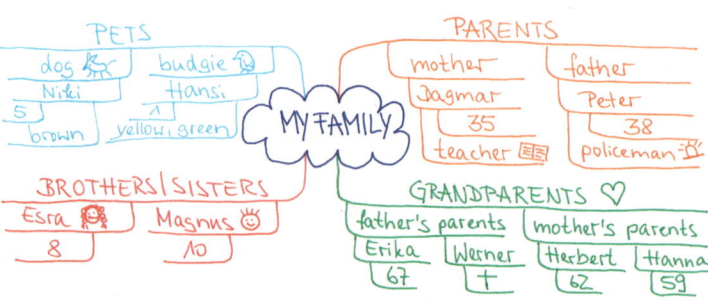

> Es gibt auch Computerprogramme, mit denen du Mindmaps erstellen kannst.

SF 3 Unbekannte Wörter verstehen? – Kein Problem! ▸ *Unit 3, p. 66*

Englische Texte enthalten oft Wörter, die du noch nicht kennst oder gelernt hast. Aber du kannst viele Texte verstehen, wenn du folgende Dinge beachtest.

Was hilft dir, unbekannte Wörter zu verstehen?

1 Schau auf die Bilder

Häufig gibt es zu Texten auch Bilder. Sie zeigen oft die Dinge, die du im Text nicht verstehst.

Was bedeuten *forefinger* und *wrist* im folgenden Text?

> How to check your pulse:
>
> Put your forefinger and your middle finger on your wrist.
> Count your pulse for 60 seconds.

2 Denke an ähnliche Wörter im Deutschen

Viele englische Wörter werden ähnlich wie im Deutschen geschrieben oder klingen ähnlich wie deutsche Wörter, z.B. in dem kleinen Text oben:

– *pulse* hat Ähnlichkeit mit dem deutschen Wort "Puls"

– *middle finger* ist natürlich im Deutschen der "Mittelfinger"

Was bedeuten wohl die folgenden Wörter auf Deutsch?

> brilliant • camera • cost • Danish • fresh • half • price • hang •
> loudspeaker • nervous • ocean • penguin • plan • round • study •
> suncream • tomato sauce

Hmm, *nervous* sieht so aus wie das deutsche Wort „nervös", oder?

Ja, das ist es!

3 Schau auf die Wörter vor und nach dem unbekannten Wort

Häufig kannst du ein unbekanntes Wort aus dem Satzzusammenhang erschließen. Dabei helfen dir die Wörter, die vor oder nach dem unbekannten Wort stehen.

Was könnten *building* und *stay* bedeuten?

> 1. Our school is new. It's a very nice building with lots of big classrooms.
> 2. You can't see your friend this afternoon. Stay at home and do your homework!

Also, es geht um die Schule und es wird gesagt, dass es …

Ich hab's!

4 Steckt im unbekannten Wort ein Wort, das du kennst?

Manchmal versteckt sich im unbekannten Wort auch ein Wort, das du bereits gelernt hast. Anhand dieses Wortes kannst du oft den Sinn erschließen.

Was könnten die folgenden Wörter auf Deutsch bedeuten?

> actor • player • reader • swimmer • visitor • worker • writer

play**er**

visit**or**

writer

SF 4 Im Wörterbuch nachschlagen ▸ *Unit 4, p. 86*

Wenn du in einem englischen Text ein Wort noch nicht kennst oder vergessen hast (z.B. *donkey*), dann hilft dir das *English-German Dictionary* weiter (S. 222–232). Du kannst Wörter natürlich auch in einem umfangreicheren Wörterbuch nachschlagen.

> *Uncle Ernie's farm*
>
> *Uncle Ernie has a farm near Plymouth. On his farm there are lots of animals. He has 20 pigs and 85 cows. But his favourite animal is his donkey.*

Wie kannst du englische Wörter im *Dictionary* finden?

1. Die **blau** und **fett** gedruckten Stichwörter (z.B. **family**, **farm**, **fast**) sind alphabetisch angeordnet, also **f** vor **g**, **fa** vor **fe**, **fam** vor **far**.

   Ordne die folgenden *farm animals* alphabetisch:

   > horse • cat • bull • donkey • chicken • pig • duck • sheep • dog • rabbit

   > Wo findest du **donkey** im *Dictionary*? Zwischen *dinner* und *dog* oder zwischen *do* und *door*?
   > Überprüfe dich selbst (*Dictionary* S. 224)!

Welche Informationen liefert dir das *Dictionary*?

2. Beachte die Wörter und Wendungen, die **schwarz** und **fett** gedruckt sind. Es sind
   – zusammengesetzte Wörter, z.B. **family name**
   – Redewendungen oder längere Ausdrücke, z.B. **I'm fine**, **thanks** oder **in the field**.

3. Zusammengesetzte Wörter und längere Ausdrücke findest du oft unter mehr als einem Stichwort, z.B. **feel fed up** unter **fed** und **feel** oder **in the field** unter **in** und **field**.

4. In den eckigen Klammern hinter den Stichwörtern steht, wie das Wort ausgesprochen und betont wird.
   (Lautschriftzeichen → S. 242; Betonungszeichen → S. 205).

   > Wie wird das ‚a' in *family* und *father* ausgesprochen?
   > Wie das ‚o' in *donkey* oder in *home*?

5. Die Ziffern **1.**, **2.** usw. zeigen, dass das englische Wort mehrere unterschiedliche Bedeutungen hat. Welche Bedeutung die richtige ist, kannst du meist aus dem Satzzusammenhang erkennen.

   Welche Mehrfachbedeutungen kannst du für folgende Wörter finden?

   > text • before • phone • too • right • drink

F

face [feɪs] Gesicht 5 (98)
fall [fɔːl] fallen; hinfallen 3 (61)
family [ˈfæməli] Familie 2 (36)
family name Familienname, Nachname 3 (52) **family tree** (Familien-)Stammbaum 2 (37)
farm [fɑːm] Bauernhof, Farm 4 (70)
fast [fɑːst] schnell 3 (61)
father [ˈfɑːðə] Vater 2 (34)
favourite [ˈfeɪvərɪt] Lieblings- (10)
favourite colour Lieblingsfarbe (10)
February [ˈfebruəri] Februar 3 (56)
fed up [fed ˈʌp]: **feel fed up** genervt sein, sauer sein; die Nase voll haben 4 (74)
feed [fiːd] füttern 4 (72)
feel [fiːl] sich fühlen; fühlen 4 (74)
  feel fed up genervt sein, sauer sein; die Nase voll haben 4 (74)
feeling [ˈfiːlɪŋ] Gefühl 4 (74)
ferry [ˈferi] Fähre 5 (91)
field [fiːld] Feld; Weide 4 (70)
  in the field auf dem Feld 4 (70)
fill sth. in [fɪl ˈɪn] etwas ausfüllen
film [fɪlm] Film 3 (64)
find [faɪnd] finden 4 (79)
  °**find out** herausfinden
fine [faɪn] gut; in Ordnung 1 (17)
  I'm fine, thanks. Danke, (es geht mir) gut. 1 (17)
finish [ˈfɪnɪʃ] beenden
fire station [ˈfaɪə steɪʃn] Feuerwache 3 (52)
first [fɜːst]:
  1. erste(r, s) 1 (17)
  2. zuerst, als Erstes 3 (54)
  the first morning der erste Morgen 1 (17)
fish [fɪʃ] Fisch; Fische (12)
fisherman, *pl* **-men** [ˈfɪʃəmən] Fischer/in, Angler/in
five [faɪv] fünf (8)
flat [flæt] Wohnung 2 (34)

SF 5 Über Bilder und Fotos sprechen

▶ Unit 5, p. 102

Häufig ist es notwendig, jemandem ein Bild oder ein Foto genau zu beschreiben. Das geht besonders gut, wenn du die folgenden Schritte beachtest.

1 Beginne allgemein

Sage zunächst, was du allgemein im Bild oder Foto siehst.
Welcher Ort, welcher Gegenstand oder welche Personen sind zu sehen?

In the picture I can see a classroom with a teacher and his students.

2 Gehe in einer bestimmten Reihenfolge vor

Sage dann, **wen** oder **was** du siehst und wo sich die Personen oder Gegenstände im Bild oder Foto befinden.
Gehe dabei in einer bestimmten **Reihenfolge** vor: Sage z.B. zunächst, was du links siehst, gehe dann zur Mitte und zum Schluss beschreibst du, was du rechts im Bild oder Foto siehst.
Benutze dabei **allgemeine Ortsangaben** wie:

On the left I can see …
In the middle there are …
On the right there's …
At the top there's …
At the bottom there are …

3 Beschreibe alle Teile genauer

Beschreibe genauer, **wo** sich eine Person oder ein Gegenstand befindet:

There's a student under the table.
A student with a green T-shirt is behind the teacher.
There's a girl with a mobile phone next to the boy.
The teacher is in front of the class.

4 Beschreibe, was die Personen machen

Wenn du sagen willst, was gerade im Bild oder Foto passiert oder **was die Personen gerade tun**, benutze das ***present progressive***.

On the right there's a girl in a purple T-shirt. She's eating an apple.
A girl in an orange T-shirt is sitting next to her. She's reading a comic.

▶ Language file 10, p. 181

LF 1 Personalpronomen (Personal pronouns) ▶ *Unit 1, p. 22–23*

| I | you | he | she | it |
| we | you | they |

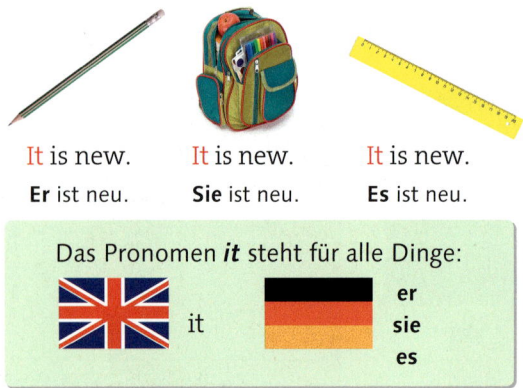

It is new.   It is new.   It is new.

Er ist neu.   **Sie** ist neu.   **Es** ist neu.

You're nice.   You're nice.   You're nice, Ms Lee.

Du bist nett.   **Ihr** seid nett.   **Sie** sind nett, Frau Lee.

> Das Pronomen *it* steht für alle Dinge:
>
> it   er / sie / es

> Das Pronomen *you* steht für:
>
> you   du / ihr / Sie

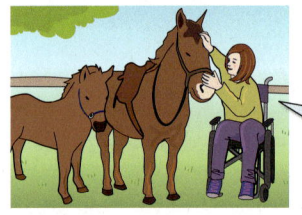

> This is my pony Harry. He's big. My pony Connie is old. She's seventeen.

> Über Haustiere, die einen Namen haben, sprichst du mit **he** oder **she**, nicht mit **it**.

LF 2 'm – 's – 're: das Verb be („sein") in der Gegenwart

a) Aussagen (Statements)   ▶ *Unit 1, p. 22*

> I'm from Plymouth and I'm twelve.
> This is Berry. She's my friend.
> We're at Eggy in class 7Y.
> Luca and Adam **are** in class 7Y too.

Das Verb *be* hat in der Gegenwart *(present)* drei Formen: *'m*, *'s* und *'re*.
Das sind die Kurzformen.
Es gibt auch Langformen, das sind:
am, **is** und **are**.

Bejahte Aussagen — Yes

I'm (= I am)	
You're (= You are)	
He's (= He is)	
She's (= She is)	new.
It's (= It is)	
We're (= We are)	
You're (= You are)	
They're (= They are)	

Kurzformen sind sehr häufig. Sie werden besonders in der gesprochenen Sprache verwendet.

Ellie / Luca / The bike	**is**	new.
The teacher**s** / The book**s**	**are**	

Die Langformen benutzt du meistens nach Eigennamen (*Ellie, Luca*) oder Nomen (*bike, teachers*).

Verneinte Aussagen — No

I'm not (= I am not)	
You aren't (= You are not)	
He isn't (= He is not)	
She isn't (= She is not)	
It isn't (= It is not)	from Plymouth.
We aren't (= We are not)	
You aren't (= You are not)	
They aren't (= They are not)	

Bei der Verneinung werden fast immer die Kurzformen benutzt.

Die englische **Wortstellung** ist genau festgelegt. In Aussagesätzen ist sie immer:

Subjekt	Verb	Objekt
Berry	is	at Eggy.
The kids	aren't	from London.
They'	re	very cool.

LF 3 b) Fragen und Kurzantworten (Questions and short answers)

▶ Unit 2, p. 40

Are you my friend?
Who are you?

Fragen

Am I …?
Are you …?
Is he / she / it …?

Are we …?
Are you …?
Are they …?

What's this?
Who are they?
Where are your books?

Du kannst Fragen stellen

– **ohne Fragewort** (*Are you …?*), auf die du Antworten mit Ja oder Nein bekommst oder

– **mit Fragewort** (*Who …? / Where …?*). Nach einem Fragewort kannst du *is* verkürzen:
  What's your name?
  Where's your tie, Ellie?

Are you my friend?

No, I'm not. Uhh … Yes, I am.

Kurzantworten — Yes / No

Yes	No
Yes, I am.	No, I'm not.
Yes, you are.	No, you aren't.
Yes, he / she / it is.	No, he / she / it isn't.
Yes, you / we / they are.	No, you / we / they aren't.

Eine kurze Antwort nur mit **yes** oder **no** kann unhöflich klingen. Antworte besser: *Yes, I am. / No, she isn't. / …*

LANGUAGE FILE

LF 4   There's … / There are …   ▸ *Unit 2, p. 39*

Mit **There's … / There are …** drückst du aus, dass irgendwo etwas vorhanden ist:

— In meinem Zimmer steht ein Tisch.   →   **There's** a table in my room.

— Auf dem Tisch liegen Bücher.   →   **There are** books on the table.

— Es gibt / sind drei Stühle in …   →   **There are** three chairs in …

   Nie: It ~~gives~~ …, sondern immer: **There's … / There are …**

>  Im Deutschen beginnst du oft mit einer Ortsangabe:
> In meinem Zimmer **steht ein Tisch**.
>
>  Im Englischen steht die Ortsangabe meist am Ende und die Sätze beginnen mit **There's … / There are …**
> There's a table in my room.

In Fragen stehen **is** und **are** vor dem **there**:

— Gibt es auch einen Kleiderschrank?   →   **Is there** a wardrobe too?

— Sind Jungen in deiner Klasse?   →   **Are there** boys in your class?

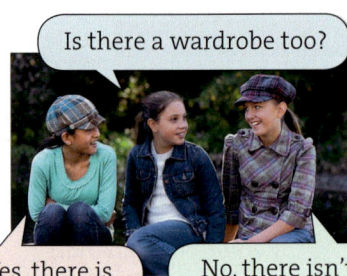

> Is there a wardrobe too?

> Yes, there is.

> No, there isn't.

LF 5   Der Plural der Nomen (The plural of nouns)   ▸ *Unit 3, p. 64*

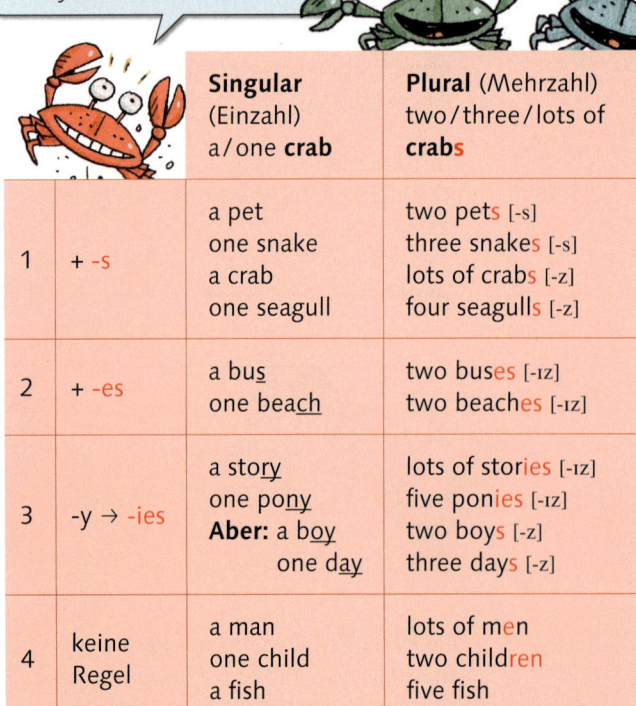

> Hi! It's me again, Cyril the crab.
> My friend**s** are crab**s** too.

		Singular (Einzahl) a / one **crab**	Plural (Mehrzahl) two / three / lots of **crabs**
1	+ -s	a pet one snake a crab one seagull	two pet**s** [-s] three snake**s** [-s] lots of crab**s** [-z] four seagull**s** [-z]
2	+ -es	a bu**s** one bea**ch**	two bus**es** [-ɪz] two beach**es** [-ɪz]
3	-y → -ies	a stor**y** one pon**y** **Aber:** a b**oy** one d**ay**	lots of stor**ies** [-ɪz] five pon**ies** [-ɪz] two boy**s** [-z] three day**s** [-z]
4	keine Regel	a man one child a fish	lots of m**e**n two child**ren** five fish

1 Die meisten Nomen (Hauptwörter) haben im Plural die Endung **-s**. Beachte die unterschiedliche Aussprache!

2 Nach **-s, -x, -sh** oder **-ch** wird **-es** angehängt.

3 Nach einem Konsonanten (Mitlaut) **+ y** (z.B. **-ry, -ny, -ly, -ty**) wird **-y** zu **-ies**.

4 Ein paar Nomen haben unregelmäßige Pluralformen. Diese musst du auswendig lernen.

LF 6 Die einfache Form der Gegenwart (The simple present)

a) Bejahte Aussagen (Positive statements)

> I like Saturdays. Dad likes Saturdays too.
> In the morning we go shopping. Dad always goes to the market.
> In the afternoon he plays games with Grace or he sometimes watches sport on TV.

▶ Unit 3, pp. 58–59

Mit dem **simple present** sprichst du darüber:
– was sich **nicht ändert** oder **immer** so ist.
– was **wiederholt** (oder auch **nie**) passiert, oft mit *always* (immer), *sometimes* (manchmal), *often* (oft), *never* (niemals), in the *morning/afternoon* (vormittags/nachmittags).

> I like the beach and Sandy likes the fish.

Das **simple present** hat zwei Formen:
1 *I/you/we/they* + verb
2 *he/she/it* + verb + **s**

Yes

I	like	
You	like	
He	likes	
She	likes	
It	likes	the beach.
We	like	
You	like	
They	like	

He, she, it – ein *-s* muss mit!

Wenn das Verb auf **-ss**, **-x**, **-sh**, **-ch** (z.B. *watch*) oder auf **-o** (z.B. *go*) endet, fügst du bei *he/she/it* **-es** hinzu:

– *watch:* he/she/it *watches* [-ɪz]
– *go:* he/she/it *goes* [gəʊz]
– *do:* he/she/it *does* [dʌz]
(siehe auch LF 5: Plural der Nomen)

LF 7 b) Verneinte Aussagen (Negative statements)

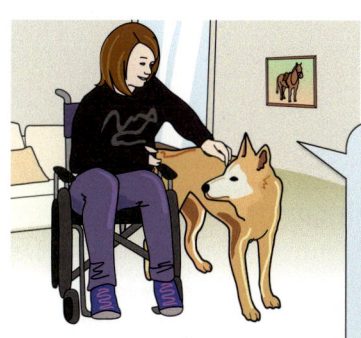

▶ Unit 3, p. 60

Das **simple present** verneinst du mit **don't** oder **doesn't** + verb:

– *I/you/we/they* **don't** + verb
– *he/she/it* **doesn't** + verb

Die Langformen sind: **do not** und **does not**.

> I don't need an alarm clock. Sam lives in the house and he always wakes me. Harry, my pony, is a pet too – but he doesn't live in the house!

No

I don't like	
You don't like	
He/She/It doesn't like	dogs.
We/You/They don't like	

> I don't like dogs and Sandy doesn't like cats ... Oh, no! Help!

LF 8 Fragen mit do/does und Kurzantworten ▸ *Unit 4, p. 78*
(Do-/Does-questions and short answers)

a) Fragen

Do you **have** ponies on the farm?

Yes, we do.

Does the farm **have** a shop?

Yes, it does.

Do I like …?	Do we like …?
Do you like …?	Do you like …?
Does he/she/it like …?	Do they like …?

Wenn du im **simple present** auf eine Frage die Antwort „Ja" oder „Nein" erwartest, fängst du die Frage mit **Do** oder **Does** an:

– **Do** + I/you/we/they + verb ?
  Do you **have** ponies?
– **Does** + he/she/it + verb ?
  Does the farm **have** a shop?

b) Kurzantworten

Do you like seagulls, Cyril?

Stupid question! No, I don't.
Erm … OK. Yes, I do – sometimes.

Es ist oft unhöflich, nur mit *Yes* oder *No* zu antworten. Besser ist eine Kurzantwort:

– nach *Yes* mit *do* oder *does*, z.B.
  Yes, I do. / Yes, she does.
– nach *No* mit *don't* oder *doesn't*, z.B.
  No, I don't. / No, he doesn't.

Yes	**No**
Yes, I do.	No, I don't.
Yes, he/she/it does.	No, he/she/it doesn't.
Yes, you/we/they do.	No, you/we/they don't.

LF 9 Fragen mit Fragewörtern (Questions with question words)

▸ *Unit 4, p. 79*

1 When do you feed Harry?

2 Where does Harry sleep?

3 What do hamsters eat?

4 Why do chipmunks hate cats?

Wenn du eine Frage mit Fragewort (*When, Where, What, Why, How*) bilden willst, setzt du das Fragewort vor *do* bzw. *does*:

> **Do** you **like** rabbits?
> *Why* **do** you **like** rabbits?

> **Does** Berry **feed** the donkeys?
> *When* **does** she **feed** the donkeys?

1 Wann fütterst du Harry?   2 Wo schläft Harry?
3 Was fressen Hamster?   4 Warum hassen Streifenhörnchen Katzen?

LF 10 Die Verlaufsform der Gegenwart (The present progressive)

▶ Unit 5, p. 98

In the photo mum and I are working in the cafe.
I'm setting the tables and mum is talking to a customer.
We aren't making sandwiches.

Im Gegensatz zum Deutschen gibt es im Englischen zwei Formen der Gegenwart: die einfache Form und die Verlaufsform.

Mit der einfachen Form (**simple present**) sprichst du über Dinge, die wiederholt passieren (siehe LF 6, S. 179).

Wenn du aber über etwas sprichst, das **gerade jetzt** passiert, benutzt du die Verlaufsform der Gegenwart (**present progressive**), oft mit *now* (jetzt) oder *at the moment* (im Moment).

Diese Form benutzt du auch, um Bilder zu beschreiben.

Im Deutschen gibt es keine Verlaufsform.

 Adam is setting the tables.

   – Adam deckt gerade die Tische.
– Adam ist gerade dabei, die Tische zu decken.

Yes

I'm helping.	We're helping.
You're helping.	You're helping.
He's/She's/It's helping.	They're helping.

Du bildest das **present progressive** mit
'm/'re/'s + verb + -ing
z.B. *she's*   + **talking**

No

I'm not helping.	We aren't helping.
You aren't helping.	You aren't helping.
He/She/It isn't helping.	They aren't helping.

Achtung Schreibung:
– Ein nicht mitgesprochenes *e* fällt weg:
  make → making   *write → writing*
– Nach einem Vokal (a, e, i, o, u) wird der Konsonant (meist p, b, m, n, d, t) verdoppelt:
  rap + *-ing* → *rapping*
  swim + *-ing* → *swimming*
  set + *-ing* → *setting*

?

Am I helping?	Are we helping?
Are you helping?	Are you helping?
Is he/she/it helping?	Are they helping?

What are you doing?	
Are you helping?	– Yes, I am. /
	No, I'm not.

What's Adam doing?	
Is he making sandwiches?	– Yes, he is. /
	No, he isn't.

Die Kurzantworten sind wie beim Verb *be* (siehe LF 3, S. 177).
Nach einem Fragewort kannst du *is* verkürzen: **What's ... / When's ...**

LF 11 Das Futur mit *going to* (The *going to*-future) ▶ Unit 6, p. 114

I'm going to help with the sandwiches for the picnic and mum is going to make us some scones.

Cool! We're going to have fun – and we aren't going to talk about school.

Wenn du sagen willst, was jemand in der Zukunft **plant**, **vorhat** oder **beabsichtigt**, verwendest du das Futur mit *going to*. Es wird mit einer Form von *be (am/are/is)* gebildet, oft mit den Kurzformen:

> **'m/'re/'s + going to + verb:**
>
> | I'm | going to | help. |
> | We're | going to | have fun. |

In der Verneinung steht **not** vor **going to**:

> I'm **not going to** make the scones.
> We are**n't going to** talk about school.

Merke: *going to* hat hier nichts mit dem deutschen Wort „gehen" zu tun. Es heißt hier *werden / wollen / vorhaben / beabsichtigen*.

 The friends are going to have a picnic on the beach.

 Die Freunde werden / wollen am Strand ein Picknick machen.
Die Freunde haben vor / beabsichtigen, am Strand ein Picknick zu machen.

I'm going to help with the food too!

Yes

I'm going to		
You're going to		
He's/She's/It's going to	help.	
We're going to		
You're going to		
They're going to		

No

I'm not going to		
You aren't going to		
He/She/It isn't going to	help.	
We aren't going to		
You aren't going to		
They aren't going to		

?

Am I going to		
Are you going to		
Is he/she/it going to	help?	
Are we going to		
Are you going to		
Are they going to		

Are you going to stay at home, Cyril?
– Yes, I am. / No, I'm not.

What are you going to do, Cyril?
Where is Cyril going to be in the holidays?

Are you going to stay at home, Cyril?

Yes, I am!

What are you going to do, Cyril?

I'm going to have lots of fun!

LF 12 *Indirekte Rede (Indirect speech) ▸ *Unit 6, p. 120*

a) *Direct speech* (direkte Rede)

I love my animals.

Berry says, "I love my animals."

Mit der **direkten Rede** gibst du **wörtlich** wieder, was jemand sagt, schreibt oder denkt. Direkte Rede steht meist in Anführungszeichen.

b) *Indirect speech* (indirekte Rede)

Berry says _ (that) she loves her animals.

> **Merke:** Im Englischen steht vor der indirekten Rede **kein** Komma, und *that* („dass") wird oft weggelassen.

Mit der **indirekten Rede** berichtest du, was jemand sagt, schreibt, denkt. Einleitende Verben sind z.B. *say*, *answer*, *think*.

❗ Bei der **indirekten Rede** achte darauf, **wer** spricht bzw. schreibt. Entsprechend musst du Personen und Pronomen ändern:
"I love my animals." → *... she loves her animals.*

Grammatische Fachbegriffe (Grammatical terms)

answer	[ˈɑːnsə]	Antwort(satz)
future	[ˈfjuːtʃə]	Zukunft, Future
going to-**future**	[ˈɡəʊɪŋ tu fjuːtʃə]	Futur mit *going to*
infinitive	[ɪnˈfɪnətɪv]	Infinitiv (Grundform des Verbs)
linking word	[ˈlɪŋkɪŋ wɜːd]	Bindewort
negative statement	[neɡətɪv ˈsteɪtmənt]	verneinte Aussage
noun	[naʊn]	Nomen, Hauptwort, Substantiv
persononal pronoun	[pɜːsnl ˈprəʊnaʊn]	Personalpronomen (persönliches Fürwort)
plural	[ˈplʊərəl]	Plural, Mehrzahl
positive statement	[pɒzətɪv ˈsteɪtmənt]	bejahte Aussage
present	[ˈpreznt]	Gegenwart
present progressive	[preznt prəˈɡresɪv]	Verlaufsform der Gegenwart
pronoun	[ˈprəʊnaʊn]	Pronomen, Fürwort
question	[ˈkwestʃən]	Frage(satz)
question word	[ˈkwestʃən wɜːd]	Fragewort
short answer	[ʃɔːt ˈɑːnsə]	Kurzantwort
simple present	[sɪmpl ˈpreznt]	einfache Form der Gegenwart
singular	[ˈsɪŋɡjələ]	Singular, Einzahl
statement	[ˈsteɪtmənt]	Aussage(satz)
subject	[ˈsʌbdʒɪkt]	Subjekt
verb	[vɜːb]	Verb

*Diese Struktur ist nur in Baden-Württemberg in Klasse 5 oder 6 Pflichtstoff.

Wordbank 1: Sports and hobbies

▶ *Nice to meet you!, p. 11*

I like	dancing. football. playing games. reading books. riding. skateboarding. swimming. watching TV.

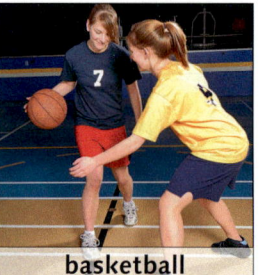
basketball

boxing

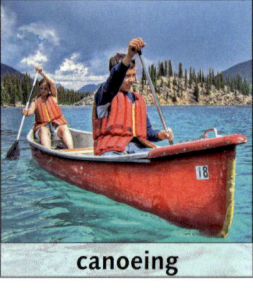
canoeing

climbing

collecting stamps

cycling

doing athletics

drawing

ice hockey

ice skating

inline skating

listening to music

making models

skiing

snowboarding

surfing the internet

table tennis

taking photos

Wordbank 2: My favourite thing ▶ *Nice to meet you!, p. 13*

bag	card collection	books	football	game console	guitar	keyring

laptop	mobile phone	remote-control car	TV	watch

game console [ˈɡeɪm kɒnsəʊl] *Spielkonsole*   remote-control car [rɪˈməʊt kəntrəʊl ˈkɑː] *ferngesteuertes Auto*

Wordbank 3: Timetable ▶ *Unit 1, p. 33*

I have art, drama, English, French, geography, German, history, ICT, maths, music, PE, science, technology, …

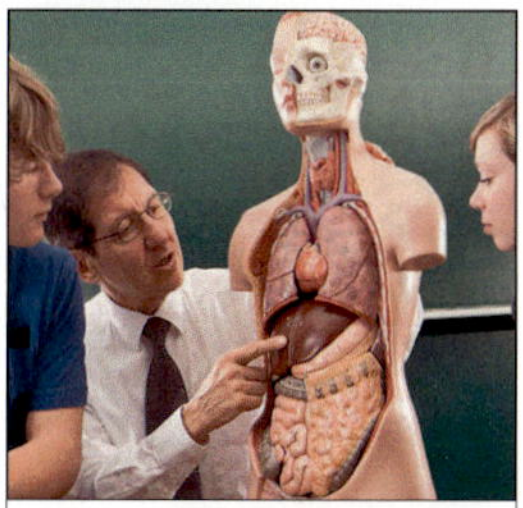

biology	 chemistry	 class assembly	ethics
 home economics	 physics	 projects	 RE
 social studies	 Spanish	 special needs training	 woodwork

class assembly *Klassenlehrerstunde*   RE = religious education *Religionslehre*   social studies *Gesellschaftslehre*
special needs training *Förderunterricht*

Wordbank 4: My family ▶ *Unit 2, p. 37*

My uncle Peter. He's my dad's brother. He's Silke's husband. and I'm his nephew.

My aunt Silke. She's married to Peter. She's Peter's wife.

My uncle Holger. He's single. He and Theresa's mum are divorced.

My aunt Anja. She's my mum's sister. Lisa is her niece.

My mum

Me

My dad

My grandma and her grandson Tim

My sister Lisa

Charly

My cousin Tim. He's Peter and Silke's son.

My grandpa and his granddaughter Anna. Her parents are dead.

My cousin Theresa. She's Holger's daughter.

nephew ['nefjuː] *Neffe*   niece [niːs] *Nichte*   grandson *Enkel*   granddaughter *Enkelin*   husband *Ehemann*
wife [waɪf] *Ehefrau*   single *alleinstehend*   married to *verheiratet mit*   divorced *geschieden*   dead *tot*

Wordbank 5: My house ▶ *Unit 2, p. 44*

bedroom

window

bedside table

bathroom

shower

washing machine

bath

living room

curtains

stairs

armchair

kitchen

sink

fridge

cooker

dishwasher

cupboard

Wordbank 6: My town ▶ *Unit 3, p. 52*

a factory

a bus station

a train station

a bank

a museum

a fire station

a police station

In my town we have …

a mosque

a library

a church

a cinema

a school

a hospital

a market

an airport

a town hall

my town

the swimming pool

the park

the fast food restaurant

the video shop

the zoo

the football stadium

My favourite places are …

the shopping centre

the sports club

the skate park

the department store

the youth centre

department store [dɪˈpɑːtmənt stɔː] *Kaufhaus*   library [ˈlaɪbrəri] *Bücherei, Bibliothek*   mosque [mɒsk] *Moschee*

Wordbank 7: Talking about pets ▶ Unit 4, p. 79

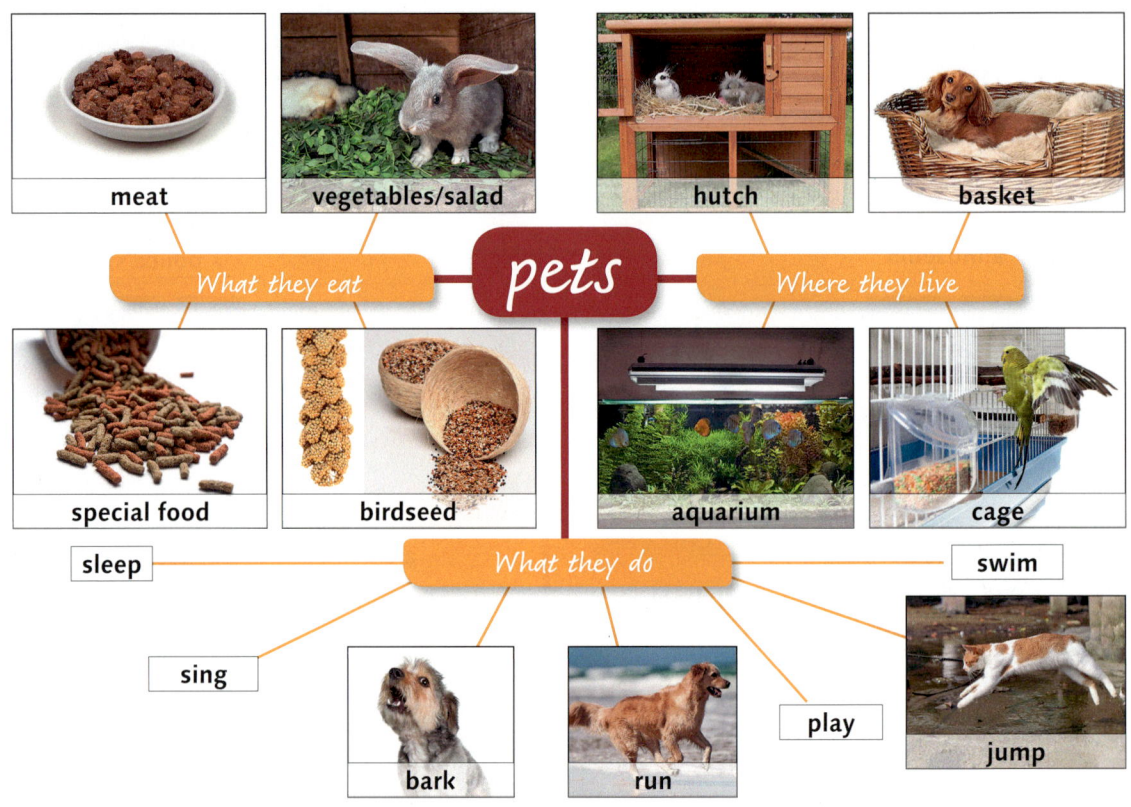

bark [bɑːk] *bellen*   birdseed ['bɜːdsiːd] *Körnerfutter, Vogelfutter*   hutch [hʌtʃ] *Hütte, kleiner Stall*
jump [dʒʌmp] *springen*   meat [miːt] *Fleisch*   run [rʌn] *rennen*

Wordbank 8: Instruments ▶ Unit 5, p. 97

I play the drums, the guitar, the piano, the ...   **I don't play an instrument. I like the ...**

flute [fluːt] *(Quer-)Flöte*   violin [vaɪə'lɪn] *Violine, Geige*

VOCABULARY

Das **Vocabulary** (S. 189–221) enthält alle neuen Wörter und Wendungen des Buches, die du **lernen** musst. Sie stehen in der Reihenfolge, in der sie im Buch zum ersten Mal vorkommen.

Hier siehst du, wie das **Vocabulary** aufgebaut ist:

> Diese Zahl gibt die **Seite** an, auf der die Wörter zum ersten Mal vorkommen. p. 17 = Seite 17

> Die **Lautschrift** zeigt dir, wie ein Wort ausgesprochen wird. Eine Übersicht über die **Lautschriftzeichen** findest du auf S. 242.

> Das **rote Ausrufe- zeichen** bedeutet: Vorsicht, hier macht man leicht Fehler!

girl [gɜːl]	Mädchen	[ɜː] ist das Zeichen für den Lau...
teacher [ˈtiːtʃə]	Lehrer/in	
car [kɑː]	Auto	
mobile (phone) [ˈməʊbaɪl ˈfəʊn]	Handy	! Deutsch: **Handy** Englisch: **mobile phone** oder **mobile**
p. 17 **the first morning** [fɜːst ˈmɔːnɪŋ]	der erste Morgen	[ŋ] ist wie „ng" in „Ding" oder „n" in „pink".
here [hɪə]	hier; hierher	 Linda, where are you?
Well, … [wel]	Nun, …/ Also, …/ Na ja, …	
Have a good day.	Ich wünsche dir einen schönen Tag. / Schönen Tag (noch).	I'm here.

> **Blau** gedruckte Wörter kennst du wahrscheinlich schon aus dem Englischunterricht in der Grundschule.

> Dies ist das „Gegenteil"- Zeichen. **Hello.** ◄► **Bye. / Good- bye** bedeutet: „**Hello** ist das Gegenteil von **Bye**".

good [gʊd]	gut	a **good** school/teacher...
thanks, thank you [θæŋks, ˈθæŋk juː]	danke (schön)	[θ] gibt es im Deutsche... klingt etwa so, als ob m... „besser" lispelt.
Bye. [baɪ]	Tschüs.	**Hello.** ◄► **Bye. / Goodbye.**
p. 18 **Good morning.**	Guten Morgen.	**what?** was?
Ms Lee [mɪz, məz]	Frau Lee	**who?** wer?
English [ˈɪŋglɪʃ]	Englisch; englisch	**where?** wo?
Who are you? [huː]	Wer bist du? / Wer seid ihr? →	**how?** wie?
village [ˈvɪlɪdʒ]	Dorf	
near [nɪə]	nahe (bei), in der Nähe von	Woolwell is **near** Plymouth.

> Der **blaue Pfeil** heißt: Zu diesem Eintrag gibt es in der rechten Spalte einen blauen Kasten.

> Die **blauen Kästen** solltest du dir immer besonders gut ansehen. Dort stehen wichtige Hinweise zu den neuen Wörtern.

Tipps zum Wörterlernen findest du im **Skills file** auf den Seiten 170 und 171.

Im **Vocabulary** werden folgende **Abkürzungen** verwendet:

p. = page (Seite)
sth. = something (etwas)
pl = *plural* (Mehrzahl)
infml = *informal* (umgangssprachlich)

Wenn du **nachschlagen** möchtest, was ein englisches Wort bedeutet oder wie man es ausspricht, dann solltest du das **Dictionary English – German** auf den Seiten 222–232 verwenden.

Und wenn du vergessen hast, wie etwas auf Englisch heißt, dann kann dir das **Dictionary German – English** auf den Seiten 233–241 eine erste Hilfe sein.

Nice to meet you!

p.8 **Nice to meet you.** — Freut mich, dich/euch/Sie kennenzulernen.

nice [naɪs] — nett, schön

meet [miːt] — kennenlernen; treffen

you [ju, juː] — du; dich; dir; ihr; euch; Sie; Ihnen

Hi. [haɪ] — Hallo.

I'm (= I am) [aɪm, aɪ ˈæm] — ich bin

> ❗ „I" wird immer großgeschrieben – auch wenn es nicht am Satzanfang steht.

the crab [ðə ˈkræb] — der Krebs →

the	
the computer	**der** Computer
the show	**die** Show
the baby	**das** Baby

What's your name? [wɒts jɔː ˈneɪm] — Wie heißt du? (*wörtlich*: Was ist dein Name?)

what? [wɒt] — was?

> Der Laut [ɒ] klingt wie das „o" in „do**ch**".

your [jɔː, jə] — dein/e; euer/eure; Ihr/e

> [ɔː] ist der „o"-Laut aus dem englischen Wort „Bas**e**ball".

name [neɪm] — Name

> one **name** – two **name**s

1 **one** [wʌn]	5 **five** [faɪv]	9 **nine** [naɪn]	13 **thirteen** [θɜːˈtiːn]
2 **two** [tuː]	6 **six** [sɪks]	10 **ten** [ten]	14 **fourteen** [fɔːˈtiːn]
3 **three** [θriː]	7 **seven** [ˈsevn]	11 **eleven** [ɪˈlevn]	
4 **four** [fɔː]	8 **eight** [eɪt]	12 **twelve** [twelv]	(▶ *Numbers*, p.243)

How old are you? [haʊ ˈəʊld ɑː juː] — Wie alt bist du?

you're [jʊə] **(= you are)** [ju ˈɑː] — du bist; ihr seid; Sie sind

> [ɑː] ist ein langes „a" wie in „Kram".

from Plymouth [frɒm] — aus Plymouth

in England [ɪn ˈɪŋglənd] — in England

Where are you from? [weər ə juː ˈfrɒm] — Wo kommst du her?

where? [weə] — wo? / wohin?

> [eə] kennst du aus „fair".

Germany [ˈdʒɜːməni] — Deutschland

> ❗ Ländernamen werden immer großgeschrieben: in **E**ngland; in **G**ermany

class [klɑːs] — Klasse

> ❗ one **class** – two **class**es

p.9 **game** [geɪm] — Spiel

I can see ... [siː] — ich kann ... sehen

can [kæn, kən] — können

and [ænd, ənd] — und

a beach [ə ˈbiːtʃ] — ein Strand →

a	
a computer	**ein** Computer
a show	**eine** Show
a baby	**ein** Baby

Cyril's song [sɒŋ] — Cyrils Lied

p.10	**my** [maɪ]	mein/e	**my** name (**mein** Name)
			my class (**meine** Klasse)
			[aɪ] klingt wie das „ei" in „Kl**ei**d".

favourite colour [feɪvərɪt 'kʌlə]	Lieblingsfarbe	
colour ['kʌlə]	Farbe	
place [pleɪs]	Ort, Platz	[eɪ] kennst du aus „Hey!".
love [lʌv]	lieben, sehr mögen	
aquarium [ə'kweəriəm]	Aquarium	
fish, *pl* **fish** [fɪʃ]	Fisch; Fische	! one fish – two **fish**
great [greɪt]	toll, großartig	
Look at the sweets! ['lʊk ət]	Sieh/Schau dir die Süßig-keiten an!	
all [ɔːl]	alle(s)	
sweets *(pl)* [swiːts]	Bonbons, Süßigkeiten	
Welcome to Plymouth. ['welkəm]	Willkommen in Plymouth.	[ə] ist ein „e" wie am Ende von „bitt**e**" oder „Aff**e**".

red [red]	rot	**brown** [braʊn]	braun	**purple** ['pɜːpl]	violett, lila
yellow ['jeləʊ]	gelb	**orange** ['ɒrɪndʒ]	orange	**white** [waɪt]	weiß
blue [bluː]	blau	**grey** [greɪ]	grau	**black** [blæk]	schwarz
green [griːn]	grün	**pink** [pɪŋk]	pink, rosa		

like [laɪk]	mögen
I don't like ... [aɪ 'dəʊnt laɪk]	ich mag ... nicht
My favourite colour **is** ... [ɪz]	Meine Lieblingsfarbe ist ...

My favourite colour is red. What's your favourite colour?

I don't like red. I like green.

p.11	**sport** [spɔːt]	Sport; Sportart

hobby ['hɒbi]	Hobby	! Englisch: one **hobby** – two **hobbies**
		Deutsch: ein **Hobby** – zwei **Hobbys**
football ['fʊtbɔːl]	Fußball	
music ['mjuːzɪk]	Musik	[z] ist ein „s" wie in „Musik".
I like watching TV. [wɒtʃɪŋ tiː'viː]	Ich sehe gern fern.	[tʃ] klingt wie „tsch" in „Quatsch".
TV [tiː'viː]	Fernseher	[v] klingt wie „Vampir" – nicht wie „Vater"!
too [tuː]	auch	! I'm from Berlin. – I'm from Berlin **too**.
		– Ich bin **auch** aus Berlin.

dance [dɑːns]	tanzen		
play [pleɪ]	spielen		
read [riːd]	lesen		
book [bʊk]	Buch		
ride [raɪd]	reiten		
skateboard [ˈskeɪtbɔːd]	Skateboard fahren		
swim [swɪm]	schwimmen		
What are …? [ˈwɒt ɑː]	Was sind …?	➡	
number [ˈnʌmbə]	Zahl, Ziffer, Nummer		

> I like dancing and playing games. And you?
>
> My hobby is skateboarding.

> **What's …?** (= What is) • **What are …?**
> • **What's** your favourite song?
>   (Was **ist** dein Lieblingslied?)
> • **What are** your hobbies?
>   (Was **sind** deine Hobbys?)

What about you? [wɒt əbaʊt ˈjuː]	Und du? / Was ist mit dir?
but [bʌt, bət]	aber
our [ˈaʊə]	unser/e

Luca is ten, **but** Jack is fourteen.

our poster   (**unser** Poster)
our class   (**unsere** Klasse)

p.12 **animal** [ˈænɪml]	Tier		
have [hæv]	haben		
pony [ˈpəʊni]	Pony		
cat [kæt]	Katze		
bear [beə]	Bär		
rat [ræt]	Ratte		
monkey [ˈmʌŋki]	Affe	➡	
bird [bɜːd]	Vogel		
an elephant [ən ˈelɪfənt]	ein Elefant	➡	

❗ [ˈpəʊni] klingt anders als „Pony" im Deutschen.

> Plural von Wörtern mit -y am Wortende:
> Konsonant+-y: one po**ny** – two po**nies**
>   Vokal+-y: one monk**ey** – two monk**eys**

> **a – an**
> **a d**og   **an e**lephant

snake [sneɪk]	Schlange
dog [dɒg]	Hund
crocodile [ˈkrɒkədaɪl]	Krokodil
rabbit [ˈræbɪt]	Kaninchen
hamster [ˈhæmstə]	Hamster
tiger [ˈtaɪgə]	Tiger

> I have a hamster, and I like dogs. What about you?
>
> I don't like dogs – I like cats. And I love rabbits.

remember [rɪˈmembə]	sich erinnern (an)

❗ Englisch: Can you **remember** my name?
Deutsch: Kannst du **dich an** meinen Namen
     erinnern?

pet [pet]	(Haus-)Tier
wild [waɪld]	wild

❗ [waɪld] klingt anders als „wild" im Deutschen.

p.13	**thing** [θɪŋ]	Ding, Sache	

a **fish** – **it's** yellow (**er** ist gelb)

a **snake** – **it's** brown (**sie** ist braun)

a **rabbit** – **it's** white (**es** ist weiß)

it's [ɪts] (= it is)	es ist (*bei Dingen und Tieren auch:* er ist, sie ist)	
it has [hæz, həz]	es (er, sie) hat	→
wheel [wiːl]	Rad	

I	**have**	he	**has**
you	**have**	she	**has**
we	**have**	it	**has**
they	**have**		

small [smɔːl]	klein	
go [gəʊ]	gehen; fahren	
to [tu, tə]	zu, nach	
on [ɒn]	auf	
it's fun [ɪts ˈfʌn]	es macht Spaß	
fun	Spaß	
bike [baɪk]	Fahrrad	

My bike is great.

Riding is fun.

a girl on a bike   a boy on a pony

new [njuː]	neu	
big [bɪg]	groß	
camera [ˈkæmərə]	Fotoapparat; Kamera	
with [wɪð]	mit	
listen (to) [ˈlɪsn]	(sich etwas) anhören; zuhören	→
talk (to) [tɔːk]	sprechen, reden (mit)	

new ◄► old

big ◄► small

Listen.	Hört zu.
Listen to Ellie.	Hört Ellie zu.
Listen to the song.	Hört euch das Lied an.

Talk to your friends about your favourite songs.

p.14	**the last day** [lɑːst ˈdeɪ]	der letzte Tag	
	holiday(s) [ˈhɒlədeɪ]	Urlaub; Ferien	
	the last day of the holidays [ɒv, əv]	der letzte Tag der Ferien / der letzte Ferientag	→
	story [ˈstɔːri]	Geschichte	
	Hello. [həˈləʊ]	Hallo.	
	It's me. [ɪts ˈmiː]	Ich bin's.	→
	no [nəʊ]	nein	
	yes [jes]	ja	

of
- the colour **of** my bike
  (die Farbe meines Rades)
- the last day **of** the holidays
  (der letzte Tag der Ferien)

„ich": me statt I
- Hello, Ellie. It's **me**, Luca.
  (Hallo, Ellie. Ich bin's, Luca.)
- I'm twelve. – **Me** too.
  (Ich bin zwölf. – Ich auch.)

away [əˈweɪ]	weg, fort
stupid [ˈstjuːpɪd]	dumm, blöd
seagull [ˈsiːgʌl]	Möwe
This is ... [ˈðɪs ɪz]	Dies ist ... / Das ist ...
help [help]	Hilfe

This is Cyril the crab.

Oh go away, you stupid seagull.

help [help]	helfen
Goodbye. [gʊdˈbaɪ]	Auf Wiedersehen!

| p.15 | **Yippee!** [jɪˈpiː] | Hurra! | |
| | **chant** [tʃɑːnt] | Sprechgesang | |

Unit 1: Welcome to our school

p.16	**school** [skuːl]	Schule	
	sight [saɪt]	Anblick, Bild	[s] ist ein scharfes „s" wie in „lassen".
	in the picture [ˈpɪktʃə]	auf dem Bild	
	student [ˈstjuːdnt]	Schüler/in; Student/in	
	sound [saʊnd]	Geräusch; Klang, Laut	[aʊ] klingt ähnlich wie das „au" in „blau".
	boy [bɔɪ]	Junge	[ɔɪ] klingt ähnlich wie das „eu" in „treu".
	girl [gɜːl]	Mädchen	[ɜː] ist das Zeichen für den Laut in „T-Shirt".
	teacher [ˈtiːtʃə]	Lehrer/in	
	car [kɑː]	Auto	
	mobile (phone) [məʊbaɪl ˈfəʊn]	Handy	❗ Deutsch: **Handy** Englisch: **mobile phone** oder **mobile**
p.17	**the first morning** [fɜːst ˈmɔːnɪŋ]	der erste Morgen	[ŋ] ist wie „ng" in „Ding" oder „n" in „pink".
	here [hɪə]	hier; hierher	Linda, where are you? I'm here.
	Well, … [wel]	Nun, …/ Also, …/ Na ja, …	
	Have a good day.	Ich wünsche dir einen schönen Tag. / Schönen Tag (noch).	
	good [gʊd]	gut	a **good** school/teacher/story/…
	thanks, thank you [θæŋks, ˈθæŋk juː]	danke (schön)	[θ] gibt es im Deutschen nicht. Der Laut klingt etwa so, als ob man das „s" in „besser" lispelt.
	Bye. [baɪ]	Tschüs.	**Hello.** ◄► **Bye. / Goodbye.**

Theme 1

p.18	**Good morning.**	Guten Morgen.	
	Ms Lee [mɪz, məz]	Frau Lee	
	English [ˈɪŋglɪʃ]	Englisch; englisch	
	Who are you? [huː]	Wer bist du? / Wer seid ihr? ➡	**what?** was? **who?** wer? **where?** wo? **how?** wie?
	village [ˈvɪlɪdʒ]	Dorf	
	near [nɪə]	nahe (bei), in der Nähe von	Woolwell is **near** Plymouth.
	no [nəʊ]	kein, keine	I have a bike, but I have **no** car.
	brother [ˈbrʌðə]	Bruder	[ð] klingt wie ein gelispeltes „Wiese".
	sister [ˈsɪstə]	Schwester	

we're (= we are) [wɪə, wi ˈɑː]	wir sind	
best [best]	beste(r, s); am besten	
friend [frend]	Freund/in	
they're (= they are) [ðeə, ðeɪ ˈɑː]	sie sind	→

're (are)	
you**'re** (you are)	du **bist**; ihr **seid**
we**'re** (we are)	wir **sind**
they**'re** (they are)	sie **sind**

at this school [æt, ət]	auf/an dieser Schule	
they aren't … (= they are not) [ðeɪ ˈɑːnt, ðeɪ ɑː ˈnɒt]	sie sind nicht …; sie sind keine …	They **aren't** in the park. They **aren't** brothers. Sie sind **nicht** im Park. Sie sind **keine** Brüder.
I'm not … [nɒt]	ich bin nicht …; ich bin kein/e …	I'm **not** ten. And I'm **not** a boy. Ich bin **nicht** zehn. Und ich bin **kein** Junge.
he's (= he is) [hiːz, hi ˈɪz]	er ist	→

's (is)	
he**'s** (he is)	– He**'s** my brother.
she**'s** (she is)	– She**'s** my sister.
it**'s** (it is)	– It**'s** fun.
what**'s** (what is)	– What**'s** your name?
who**'s** (who is)	– Who**'s** in class 7Y?

she's (= she is) [ʃiːz, ʃi ˈɪz]	sie ist	→
he/she/it isn't … ['ɪznt] **(= is not)**	er/sie/es ist nicht … er/sie/es ist kein/e …	→

n't	
isn't (is not)	**aren't** (are not)

ride a bike/a BMX [raɪd ə ˈbaɪk, raɪd ə biː em ˈeks]	mit dem Fahrrad/dem BMX-Rad fahren	
age [eɪdʒ]	Alter	
p.19 **yourself** [jə'self]	du/dir/dich selbst	
about me [ə'baʊt]	über mich	
me [miː]	mich; mir	→

me	
Meet **me** in the park.	**mich**
Help **me**.	**mir**

Theme 2

p.20 **at school**	in der Schule	**!** Englisch: they're **at school** Deutsch: sie sind **in der Schule**
a **tour of** the school [tʊə]	ein Rundgang durch die Schule	
canteen [kæn'tiːn]	Kantine, (Schul-)Mensa	
science ['saɪəns]	Naturwissenschaft	
lab [læb]	Labor	
room [ruːm, rʊm]	Raum, Zimmer	

a **science lab**

art [ɑːt]	Kunst	
sports hall ['spɔːts hɔːl]	Sporthalle	
PE (physical education) [piː ˈiː, fɪzɪkl edʒuˈkeɪʃn]	(Schul-)Sport	
lesson ['lesn]	(Unterrichts-)Stunde	
now [naʊ]	nun, jetzt	

ICT (Information and Communication technology) [aɪ siː ˈtiː, ɪnfəmeɪʃn ənd kəmjuːnɪˈkeɪʃn teknɒlədʒi]	Informations- und Kommunikationstechnologie	
I'm not lost. [lɒst]	Ich habe mich nicht verlaufen/ verirrt.	

p.21	**German** [ˈdʒɜːmən]	deutsch; Deutsch	
	timetable [ˈtaɪmteɪbl]	Stundenplan	
	community college [kəˈmjuːnəti kɒlɪdʒ]	(GB) weiterführende Schule mit gymnasialer Oberstufe	
	time [taɪm]	Zeit; Uhrzeit	

Monday [ˈmʌndeɪ], [ˈmʌndi]	Montag	**Friday** [ˈfraɪdeɪ], [ˈfraɪdi]	Freitag
Tuesday [ˈtjuːzdeɪ], [ˈtjuːzdi]	Dienstag	**Saturday** [ˈsætədeɪ], [ˈsætədi]	Samstag
Wednesday [ˈwenzdeɪ], [ˈwenzdi]	Mittwoch	**Sunday** [ˈsʌndeɪ], [ˈsʌndi]	Sonntag
Thursday [ˈθɜːzdeɪ], [ˈθɜːzdi]	Donnerstag	❗ Die Wochentage werden immer großgeschrieben.	

assembly [əˈsembli]	Schulversammlung	
registration [redʒɪˈstreɪʃn]	(etwa) Anwesenheitskontrolle und Ankündigung aktueller Ereignisse vor dem Unterricht	
technology [tekˈnɒlədʒi]	Technik(unterricht); Technologie	
geography [dʒiˈɒɡrəfi]	Geografie, Erdkunde	
maths [mæθs]	Mathe(matik)	
history [ˈhɪstri]	Geschichte	
French [frentʃ]	Französisch; französisch	
break [breɪk]	Pause	
lunch [lʌntʃ]	Mittagessen	[ʌ] klingt ähnlich wie das kurze „a" in „Kamm".
drama [ˈdrɑːmə]	Schauspiel, darstellende Kunst	
every [ˈevri]	jede(r, s)	We go to school **every** morning.
on Monday	am Montag	What's lesson one **on Monday**?
right [raɪt]	richtig	
wrong [rɒŋ]	falsch	❗ Das **w** am Anfang wird nicht ausgesprochen. **right** ◄► **wrong**

Focus on language

p.22	**unit quiz** [ˈjuːnɪt kwɪz]	Unit-Quiz	❗ one **quiz** – two **quizzes**
	city [ˈsɪti]	(Groß-)Stadt	
	it starts	er/sie/es beginnt, er/sie/es fängt an	
	start [stɑːt]	beginnen, anfangen	
	classroom [ˈklɑːsruːm]	Klassenzimmer	
	positive [ˈpɒzətɪv]	positiv	

negative [ˈnegətɪv]	negativ	negative ◄► positive
p.23 **We're hungry.** [wɪə ˈhʌŋgri]	Wir haben Hunger.	
Mrs Ford [ˈmɪsɪz]	Frau Ford	**!** **Ms** = allgemeine Anrede für Frauen **Mrs** = Anrede für verheiratete Frauen

15 **fifteen** [fɪfˈtiːn]	20 **twenty** [ˈtwenti]	30 **thirty** [ˈθɜːti]
16 **sixteen** [sɪksˈtiːn]	21 **twenty-one** [twentiˈwʌn]	31 **thirty-one** [θɜːtiˈwʌn]
17 **seventeen** [sevnˈtiːn]	22 **twenty-two** [twentiˈtuː]	32 **thirty-two** [θɜːtiˈtuː]
18 **eighteen** [eɪˈtiːn]	…	…
19 **nineteen** [naɪnˈtiːn]		(► *Numbers*, p.243)

say [seɪ]	sagen	
people [ˈpiːpl]	Leute, Menschen	
Mr Brown [ˈmɪstə]	Herr Brown	

five people

Story

p.24 **before** [bɪˈfɔː]	bevor; vor (zeitlich)	**before** the lesson **before** you read **vor** der Stunde **bevor** du liest
blazer [ˈbleɪzə]	Blazer *(Jackett, oft Teil der Schuluniform)*	
pullover [ˈpʊləʊvə]	Pullover	
shirt [ʃɜːt]	Hemd	
shoe [ʃuː]	Schuh	
skirt [skɜːt]	Rock	
sock [sɒk]	Socke	
tie [taɪ]	Krawatte	

blazer — skirt
shirt — tights
tie — shoes

tights *(pl)* [taɪts]	*(eine)* Strumpfhose →	**tights** und **trousers** sind immer Plural:
trousers *(pl)* [ˈtraʊzəz]	*(eine)* Hose →	• My **tights** are blue. **They're** new. (Meine **Strumpfhose** ist blau. Sie ist neu.)
Ellie is **in trouble.**	Ellie hat Ärger. / Ellie ist in Schwierigkeiten.	• **Are** your **trousers** new? **They're** cool. (Ist deine **Hose** neu? Sie ist cool.)
trouble [ˈtrʌbl]	Ärger, Schwierigkeiten	
Miss Borowski [mɪs]	Frau Borowski	**!** **Miss** = Anrede für unverheiratete Frauen
principal [ˈprɪnsəpl]	Rektor/in, Schulleiter/in	
hope [həʊp]	hoffen	I **hope** you like my school uniform.
happy [ˈhæpi]	glücklich, froh	She's **happy**. 🙂 He isn't **happy**. 🙁
uniform [ˈjuːnɪfɔːm]	Uniform	**!** Am Wortanfang sprichst du ein [j].
please [pliːz]	bitte	Can you help me, **please**?

	remember [rɪˈmembə]	daran denken, nicht vergessen	**!** **1. Remember**, this is important! *(Denk dran!)* **2.** Can you **remember** my name? *(dich erinnern an)*
	important [ɪmˈpɔːtnt]	wichtig	
	be over [ˈəʊvə]	vorbei sein, zu Ende sein	Olivia isn't at school. School is **over**.
	Sorry. / I'm sorry. [ˈsɒri]	Tut mir leid. / Entschuldigung.	
	at home [ət ˈhəʊm]	zu Hause	School is over. Luca is **at home**.
	home [həʊm]	Heim, Zuhause	
	That isn't good. [ðæt]	Das ist nicht gut.	**That** isn't right. **That's** wrong.
	homework [ˈhəʊmwɜːk]	Hausaufgabe(n)	➜ **homework** hat keinen Plural: **Homework is** important. **Hausaufgaben sind** wichtig.
	write [raɪt]	schreiben	
	know [nəʊ]	wissen; kennen	**!** Die ersten Buchstaben von „write" und „know" werden nicht ausgesprochen: [raɪt], [nəʊ].
p.25	**Look, Adam.** [lʊk]	Sieh mal, Adam. / Schau mal, Adam.	
	bad [bæd]	schlecht; schlimm	**bad ◄► good**
	idea [aɪˈdɪə]	Idee	[ɪə] klingt wie das „ier" in „hier".
	need [niːd]	brauchen, benötigen	
	paper [ˈpeɪpə]	Papier	
	scissors (pl) [ˈsɪzəz]	*(eine)* Schere	➜ **scissors** ist immer Plural: Where **are** my **scissors**? Wo **ist** meine **Schere**?
	guys [gaɪz]	Leute *(als Anrede verwendet)*	
	guy [gaɪ]	Typ, Kerl	a nice **guy** Hello, **guys!** ein netter **Typ** Hallo, **Leute!**
	very [ˈveri]	sehr	
	word [wɜːd]	Wort	
	for [fɔː, fə]	für	
	What do you think? [wɒt du ju ˈθɪŋk]	Was meinst du? / Was denkst du?	Are uniforms a good idea? **What do you think?**
	think [θɪŋk]	denken, meinen, glauben	I **think** uniforms are cool.
	ugly [ˈʌgli]	hässlich	
	boring [ˈbɔːrɪŋ]	langweilig	
	theatre [ˈθɪətə]	Theater	

Skills training

p.26	**brochure** [ˈbrəʊʃə]	Broschüre, Prospekt	[ʃ] klingt wie das „sch" in „schön".
	shop [ʃɒp]	Laden, Geschäft	

back [bæk]	zurück	
pound (£) [paʊnd]	Pfund *(britische Währung)*	**!** you write: **£5** – you say: five **pounds**
(pencil) sharpener [ˈpensl ʃɑːpnə]	(Bleistift-)Anspitzer	
rubber [ˈrʌbə]	Radiergummi	
ruler [ˈruːlə]	Lineal	
special offer [speʃl ˈɒfə]	Sonderangebot	
special [ˈspeʃl]	besondere(r, s)	
exercise book [ˈeksəsaɪz bʊk]	(Schul-)Heft	
exercise [ˈeksəsaɪz]	Übung, Aufgabe	an **exercise book** a **diary**
diary [ˈdaɪəri]	Tagebuch; Kalender	a **book**
hole punch [ˈhəʊl pʌntʃ]	Locher	
half [hɑːf]	halbe(r, s)	
price [praɪs]	(Kauf-)Preis	
pen [pen]	Kugelschreiber, Stift; Füller	
pencil [ˈpensl]	Bleistift	
pencil case [ˈpensl keɪs]	Federmäppchen	
calculator [ˈkælkjuleɪtə]	Taschenrechner	
child, *pl* **children** [tʃaɪld, ˈtʃɪldrən]	Kind, Kinder	
Africa [ˈæfrɪkə]	Afrika	
give [gɪv]	geben	
send [send]	senden, schicken	
when [wen]	wenn	I'm happy **when** it's Friday and school is over.
buy [baɪ]	kaufen	
at MARTINS	bei MARTINS	
p.27 **network** [ˈnetwɜːk]	Netz; Wortnetz	
(school) bag [ˈskuːl bæg]	(Schul-)Tasche	
textbook [ˈtekstbʊk]	Schulbuch, Lehrbuch	
phrase [freɪz]	Ausdruck, (Rede-)Wendung	
card [kɑːd]	Karte	
See you later. [siː ju ˈleɪtə]	Bis später.	
box [bɒks]	Kasten, Kiste, Kästchen	
in English	auf Englisch	What's 'Schultasche' **in English**, please?

p.28	**How are you?** [haʊ]	Wie geht's? / Wie geht es dir/euch/Ihnen?			
	I'm fine. [aɪm ˈfaɪn]	Mir geht es gut.	I'm **fine**. Mir geht's **gut**.	Let's go. – **Fine**. **In Ordnung**.	a **fine** day ein **schöner** Tag
	fine [faɪn]	gut, in Ordnung; schön			
	borrow [ˈbɒrəʊ]	(aus)leihen, sich borgen			
	next [nekst]	nächste(r, s) ➡	**last** weekend — letztes Wochenende **this** weekend — dieses Wochenende **next** weekend — nächstes Wochenende		
	sure [ʃʊə, ʃɔː]	sicher	The next lesson is art. – Are you **sure**? Can you help me? – **Sure**. (Sicher! / Na klar!)		
	Here you are. [hɪə ju ˈɑː]	Bitte schön. / Hier, bitte.			

Two pencils, please.

Here you are.

Unit 2: At home with Ellie

p.34	**with Ellie** [wɪð]	bei Ellie	Where's Cyril? – He's **with** Sandy.	
	road [rəʊd]	Straße (Landstraße zwischen Orten; Straße in Orten) ➡	**in Hill Road** — in der Hill Road **in Park Street** — in der Park Street	
	street [striːt]	Straße (in Ortschaften) ➡		
	in the photo [ˈfəʊtəʊ]	auf dem Foto		
	there's [ðeəz] **(= there is)** **there are** [ˈðeər ɑː, ˈðər ə]	es ist … / es gibt … es sind … / es gibt …	**There's** a ruler in the pencil case, but **there are** no pencils.	

	modern [ˈmɒdn]	modern	
	house [haʊs]	Haus	
	flat [flæt]	Wohnung	
	block of flats [blɒk əv ˈflæts]	Mehrfamilienhaus, Wohnblock	
	kitchen [ˈkɪtʃɪn]	Küche	
	bedroom [ˈbedruːm]	Schlafzimmer	
	living room [ˈlɪvɪŋ ruːm]	Wohnzimmer	
	garden [ˈgɑːdn]	Garten	
	balcony [ˈbælkəni]	Balkon	
	hall [hɔːl]	Flur, Diele	
	table [ˈteɪbl]	Tisch	
	chair [tʃeə]	Stuhl	
	bed [bed]	Bett	
	sofa [ˈsəʊfə]	Sofa	

a **block of flats** with **balconies**

a **table**

live [lɪv]	leben, wohnen	Ellie **lives** in Plymouth.
her father [hɜː ˈfɑːðə]	ihr Vater	**Her** friends live in Plymouth too.
mother [ˈmʌðə]	Mutter	
partner [ˈpɑːtnə]	Partner/in	

p.35

dad [dæd]	Papa, Vati
bathroom [ˈbɑːθruːm]	Bad(ezimmer)
end [end]	Ende
toilet [ˈtɔɪlət]	Toilette
garage [ˈɡærɑːʒ]	Garage

toilet   bathroom   bedroom

kitchen

living room

Theme 1

p.36

family [ˈfæməli]	Familie
Ellie's family	Ellies Familie

Apostroph + s: etwas gehört (zu) jemandem. Aber beachte **die Stellung** des Apostrophs!
Singular + Apostroph + s: **eine** Person   Plural -s + Apostroph: **mehrere** Personen

the **girl's** bike
das Fahrrad des Mädchens

the **girls'** bikes
die Fahrräder der Mädchen

mum [mʌm]	Mama, Mutti
upstairs [ʌpˈsteəz]	(nach) oben (*die Treppe hoch*)
downstairs [daʊnˈsteəz]	(nach) unten (*die Treppe hinunter*)

upstairs

downstairs

why [waɪ]	warum	→

what?	was?	**where?**	wo(hin)?
who?	wer?	**why?**	warum?

always [ˈɔːlweɪz]	immer
space [speɪs]	Platz
high school [ˈhaɪ skuːl]	(GB etwa:) Gesamtschule
madhouse [ˈmædhaʊs]	Irrenhaus
into the living room [ˈɪntʊ, ˈɪntə]	in das Wohnzimmer (hinein)
OK [əʊˈkeɪ]	okay, gut, in Ordnung
real [rɪəl]	echt, wirklich
stepdad [ˈstepdæd]	Stiefvater	→
miss [mɪs]	vermissen

step- („Stief-")
stepdad, stepfather
stepmum, stepmother
stepsister
stepbrother

their [ðeə]	ihr/e *(Plural)*	→
cute [kjuːt]	niedlich, süß	
you're lucky ['lʌki]	du hast Glück	
because [bɪ'kɒz]	weil	You're lucky **because** you have a cute baby brother!

> I – **my** bike   **we** – **our** bikes
> **you** – **your** bike   **you** – **your** bikes
> **he** – **his** bike   **they** – **their** bikes
> **she** – **her** bike

p.37 **family tree** [fæməli 'triː]	Familienstammbaum	
tree [triː]	Baum	
aunt [ɑːnt]	Tante	
uncle ['ʌŋkl]	Onkel	
cousin ['kʌzn]	Cousin, Cousine	
half-brother ['hɑːf brʌðə]	Halbbruder	**half-brother** ◄► **half-sister**
crazy ['kreɪzi]	verrückt	Is this a madhouse? Are you all **crazy**?
she's fun [fʌn]	es macht Spaß, mit ihr zusammenzusein	
grandparents ['grænpeərənts]	Großeltern	→
parents ['peərənts]	Eltern	
sea [siː]	Meer, *(die)* See	

> **grand-** („Groß-")
> grandparents
> grandfather   grandpa
> grandmother   grandma

Theme 2

p.38 **problem** ['prɒbləm]	Problem	
share a room with ... [ʃeə]	sich ein Zimmer mit ... teilen	
yours [jɔːz]	deine, deiner, deins	
messy ['mesi]	unordentlich	
What is it?	Was ist los?	

Are they yours?

bossy ['bɒsi]	herrisch, rechthaberisch	
I can't (= cannot) do my homework. [kɑːnt, 'kænɒt]	Ich kann meine Hausaufgaben nicht machen.	→
do [duː]	machen, tun	
too old/big/... [tuː]	zu alt/groß/...	This shirt is **too** big.
The kitchen is too **busy.** ['bɪzi]	In der Küche ist zu viel los.	
work [wɜːk]	arbeiten	
noisy ['nɔɪzi]	laut, voller Lärm	
p.39 **dream** [driːm]	Traum	

> **can – can't**
> I/you/he/she/it/we/you/they **can** swim
> I/you/he/she/it/we/you/they **can't** dance

rug [rʌg]	Teppich, Läufer	
desk [desk]	Schreibtisch	

a desk

shelf, *pl* **shelves** [ʃelf, ʃelvz]	Regal, Regale	❗ one **shelf** − two **shelves**
lamp [læmp]	Lampe	
cushion [ˈkʊʃn]	Kissen	
mirror [ˈmɪrə]	Spiegel	
wardrobe [ˈwɔːdrəʊb]	Kleiderschrank	

different [ˈdɪfrənt]	verschieden; anders	You can buy the shirt in three **different** colours. That's a **different** photo.

Focus on language

p.40	**surprise** [səˈpraɪz]	Überraschung	
	tired [ˈtaɪəd]	müde	
	really [ˈriːəli, ˈrɪəli]	wirklich	Our teachers are **really** nice.
	strict [strɪkt]	streng	But our maths teacher is too **strict**.
	mean [miːn]	gemein, fies	
p.41	**easy** [ˈiːzi]	einfach, leicht	

Story

p.42	**at her mum's house**	bei ihrer Mutter zu Hause, bei ihrer Mutter daheim	
	sad [sæd]	traurig	
	lonely [ˈləʊnli]	einsam	
	the best of both worlds	das Beste von beidem	
	both [bəʊθ]	beide	
	world [wɜːld]	Welt	
	Dear ... [dɪə]	Liebe/r ...	*Dear Paul* *Plymouth is great.*
	news [njuːz]	Nachrichten	❗ Englisch: That**'s** good **news**. Deutsch: Das **sind** gute **Nachrichten**.
	noise [nɔɪz]	Geräusch; Lärm	Listen! What's that **noise** in the garden? All that **noise**! I can't do my homework.

at the cinema ['sɪnəmə]	im Kino	
babysitting ['beɪbisɪtɪŋ]	Babysitten	
watch [wɒtʃ]	*sich etwas* anschauen; beobachten	➡

> **look • see • watch**
> • **Look!** There's Cyril.
> • I can **see** Sandy.
> • I always **watch** the news on TV. Can we **watch** the monkeys?

programme ['prəʊgræm]	(Fernseh-)Sendung	
eat [iːt]	essen; fressen	
at work [ət 'wɜːk]	bei der Arbeit, am Arbeitsplatz	
soon [suːn]	bald	
again [ə'gen]	wieder, noch einmal	
at a restaurant ['restrɒnt]	in einem Restaurant	➡
It's her birthday. ['bɜːθdeɪ]	Sie hat Geburtstag.	
Be quiet. [bi 'kwaɪət]	Sei still. / Sei leise. / Sei ruhig.	

> **at**
> **at** the cinema   **im** Kino
> **at** a restaurant **in** einem Restaurant
> **at** school   **in** der Schule
> **at** work   **bei** der Arbeit
> **at** Ellie's house **bei** Ellie daheim

p.43	**in town** [taʊn]	in der Stadt	
in love (with) [lʌv]	verliebt (in)	Steve is **in love with** Alisha.
difficult ['dɪfɪkəlt]	schwierig	**difficult ◄► easy**
week [wiːk]	Woche	
from Monday **to** Friday	von Montag bis Freitag	
lots of ['lɒts əv]	viel/e	There are **lots of** books on the desk.

Skills training

p.44	**mind map** ['maɪnd mæp]	Gedankenkarte, Wörternetz, Mindmap	
on the beach [ɒn]	am Strand	
What's it like?	Wie ist es? / Wie sieht es aus?	Our house is near Plymouth. – **What's it like?** – It's small and blue and very nice.
good about my house [ə'baʊt]	gut an meinem Haus	What's **good about** your house? – It's big and it has a nice garden.
p.45	**go with** ['gəʊ wɪð]	passen zu, gehören zu	Picture 4 **goes with** text 2.
It's your turn. [tɜːn]	Du bist dran. / Du bist an der Reihe.	
close [kləʊz]	schließen, zumachen	
door [dɔː]	Tür	Can you close the **door**, please?
What's for homework?	Was haben wir als Hausaufgabe(n) auf?	
What page is it?	Auf welcher Seite sind wir? / Auf welcher Seite steht das?	
board [bɔːd]	Tafel	
I forgot my homework. [fə'gɒt]	Ich habe meine Hausaufgaben vergessen.	
p.46	**alphabet** ['ælfəbet]	Alphabet	

address [ə'dres]	Adresse	What's your **address**? – 11 Greatfield Street.
phone number ['fəʊn nʌmbə]	Telefonnummer	
spell [spel]	buchstabieren	

Unit 3: My Plymouth

p.52	**often** ['ɒfn, 'ɒftən]	oft	I **often** ride my bike to school.
	to the cinema	ins Kino	➜
	at the weekend [wiːk'end]	am Wochenende	

go **to** the cinema	**ins** Kino gehen
go **to** the beach	**an** den Strand gehen
go **to** school	**zur** Schule gehen
go **to** work	**zur** Arbeit gehen
go **to** bed	**ins** Bett gehen

	swimming pool ['swɪmɪŋ puːl]	Schwimmbad	
	summer ['sʌmə]	Sommer	
	fire station ['faɪə steɪʃn]	Feuerwache	Luca's dad works at a **fire station**.
	museum [mjuˈziːəm]	Museum	
	church [tʃɜːtʃ]	Kirche	
	police station [pəˈliːs steɪʃn]	Polizeiwache	
p.53	**market** ['mɑːkɪt]	Markt	at a **market**
	shopping centre ['ʃɒpɪŋ sentə]	Einkaufszentrum	

Theme 1

p.54	**stay** [steɪ]	bleiben	Can't we **stay** at home? Can't I **stay** in bed?
	make [meɪk]	machen, herstellen	
	breakfast ['brekfəst]	Frühstück	

our **breakfast**

	everybody ['evribɒdi]	jeder, alle	**Everybody** likes the beach.
	sometimes ['sʌmtaɪmz]	manchmal	
	go shopping [gəʊ 'ʃɒpɪŋ]	einkaufen gehen	On Saturdays we **go shopping** at the market.
	first [fɜːst]	zuerst, als Erstes	
	supermarket ['suːpəmɑːkɪt]	Supermarkt	

usually [ˈjuːʒuəli]	normalerweise, meistens	
full [fʊl]	voll	
then [ðen]	dann, danach	First we go shopping, **then** we play games.
more [mɔː]	mehr, weitere	
vegetables (pl) [ˈvedʒtəblz]	Gemüse	**!** Englisch: **Vegetables are** good for you. Deutsch: **Gemüse ist** gut für dich.
or [ɔː]	oder; sonst	Are you a boy **or** a girl?
other [ˈʌðə]	andere(r, s)	The dog is in the garden. Where are the **other** animals?
in the afternoon [ɑːftəˈnuːn]	am Nachmittag	I always do my homework **in the afternoon**.
there [ðeə]	da, dort; dahin, dorthin	I often go to the park. I usually meet my friends **there**.
evening [ˈiːvnɪŋ]	Abend	

• **in** the morning	morgens, am Morgen	• **on** Monday	am Montag
in the afternoon	nachmittags, am Nachmittag	**on** Tuesdays	dienstags, an Dienstagen
in the evening	abends, am Abend	**on** Friday morning	freitagmorgens, am Freitagmorgen

come [kʌm]	(mit)kommen	
never [ˈnevə]	nie, niemals	➡
she doesn't like ... [ˈdʌznt]	sie mag ... nicht	never — sometimes — often — usually — always
p.55 **have breakfast; have lunch**	frühstücken; (zu) Mittag essen	
present [ˈpreznt]	Geschenk	a **present**
trainers (pl) [ˈtreɪnəz]	Sportschuhe	
expensive [ɪkˈspensɪv]	teuer	
hoodie [ˈhʊdi]	Kapuzenpullover	

The red **trainers** are great, but the **hoodie** is too **expensive**.

want [wɒnt]	wollen	
hate [heɪt]	hassen	hate ◄► love

40	**forty** [ˈfɔːti]	80	**eighty** [ˈeɪti]	101	a/one hundred and one
50	**fifty** [ˈfɪfti]	90	**ninety** [ˈnaɪnti]	102	a/one hundred and two
60	**sixty** [ˈsɪksti]	100	**a hundred / one hundred**	103	a/one hundred and three
70	**seventy** [ˈsevnti]		[əˈhʌndrəd], [wʌnˈhʌndrəd]	...	(► Numbers, p.243)

Theme 2

p.56 **go swimming**	schwimmen gehen	
get [get]	bekommen	I usually **get** nice presents on my birthday.
visit [ˈvɪzɪt]	besuchen	Can we **visit** Sophie on Sunday?
have a party [ˈpɑːti]	eine Party feiern	

Einzahl (Singular)	Mehrzahl (Plural)	Einzahl (Singular)	Mehrzahl (Plural)	! Aber:	
baby	babies	hobby	hobbies	day	days
city	cities	party	parties	boy	boys
diary	diaries	pony	ponies	monkey	monkeys
family	families	story	stories		

1 **January** ['dʒænjuəri]
Januar

2 **February** ['februəri]
Februar

3 **March** [mɑːtʃ]
März

4 **April** ['eɪprəl]
April

5 **May** [meɪ]
Mai

6 **June** [dʒuːn]
Juni

7 **July** [dʒuˈlaɪ]
Juli

8 **August** ['ɔːgəst]
August

9 **September** [sepˈtembə]
September

10 **October** [ɒkˈtəʊbə]
Oktober

11 **November** [nəʊˈvembə]
November

12 **December** [dɪˈsembə]
Dezember

The months [mʌnθs]
(Die Monate)

Monatsnamen werden immer großgeschrieben.

p.57 **date** [deɪt] — Datum

when? [wen] — wann? ➡

what?	was?	where?	wo(hin)?
who?	wer?	when?	wann?
how?	wie?	why?	warum?

When's (= when is) your birthday? — Wann hast du Geburtstag?

! Englisch: **When is** your birthday?
Deutsch: **Wann hast** du Geburtstag?

on 1st March [ɒn] — am 1. März

! • you write: **on 1st March** –
  you say: **on the first of March**
• mit Datum: My birthday is **on 1st March**.
  ohne Datum: My birthday is **in March**.

second ['sekənd] — zweite(r, s) ➡

1	one	eins	1st	first	erste(r, s)
2	two	zwei	2nd	second	zweite(r, s)
3	three	drei	3rd	third	dritte(r, s)
4	four	vier	4th	fourth	vierte(r, s)
5	five	fünf	5th	fifth	fünfte(r, s)
					(▶ *Numbers*, p. 243)

free [friː] — frei — Can we meet in the afternoon? Are you **free**?

at 1 o'clock [əˈklɒk] — um 1 Uhr / um 13 Uhr — It's **1 o'clock** now.

Focus on language

p.58 **get up** [get ˈʌp] — aufstehen — My sister **gets up** at 6 o'clock every morning.

early ['ɜːli] — früh — I get up **early** too.

bring [brɪŋ]	bringen, mitbringen	Max, bring me the shoe!

late [leɪt]	spät	**late ◄► early**
life, *pl* **lives** [laɪf, laɪvz]	*(das)* Leben, *(die)* Leben	❗ one **life** – nine **lives**
firefighter [ˈfaɪəfaɪtə]	Feuerwehrmann, Feuerwehrfrau	
so [səʊ]	also, daher	It's Sunday, **so** I can get up late.
normal [ˈnɔːml]	normal	
workday [ˈwɜːkdeɪ]	Arbeitstag	**in** the morning ❗ **at** night
at night [naɪt]	nachts, in der Nacht ➡	**in** the afternoon
		in the evening
home [həʊm]	nach Hause	
after dinner [ɑːftə ˈdɪnə]	nach dem Abendessen	**After dinner** we sometimes watch TV.
later [ˈleɪtə]	später	
together [təˈɡeðə]	zusammen	
sleep [sliːp]	schlafen	
go by bus [baɪ ˈbʌs]	mit dem Bus fahren	I often **go** to school **by bus**.
		My brother always **goes by bike**.
stop [stɒp]	(an)halten; aufhören (mit)	
him [hɪm]	ihm, ihn	Tom is in trouble. Can you see **him**? Please help **him**!
p.59 **lazy** [ˈleɪzi]	faul	My brother is **lazy** – he often gets up late.
p.60 **sing** [sɪŋ]	singen	
p.61 **want to be** [wɒnt]	*etwas* sein wollen	❗ • **want sth.** I **want** a new bike.
		etwas (haben) wollen
		• **want to do sth.** I **want to buy** it now.
		etwas tun wollen
outdoors [aʊtˈdɔːz]	im Freien, draußen	

Story

p.62 **Happy birthday!** [hæpi ˈbɜːθdeɪ]	Herzlichen Glückwunsch zum Geburtstag!	
let's (= let us) [lets]	lass uns / lasst uns	It's late. **Let's** go home.
us [ʌs, əs]	uns	We're here. Can you see **us**?
plan [plæn]	Plan	
year [jɪə]	Jahr(gang)	Our dog is two **years** old.
		I'm in **year** six at Eggy.
Shut up! *(infml)* [ʃʌt ˈʌp]	Halt den Mund!	❗ Vorsicht! Viele Erwachsene finden **Shut up!** sehr unhöflich.
concert [ˈkɒnsət]	Konzert	

zoo [zuː]	Zoo	❗ Aussprache: **zoo** [zuː] – Der Anfangslaut ist wie im deutschen Namen „**S**usie".
excited [ɪkˈsaɪtɪd]	aufgeregt, gespannt	❗ Beachte die Schreibweise: **ex**c**it**ed.
open [ˈəʊpən]	öffnen; aufschlagen *(Buch)*	
today [təˈdeɪ]	heute	

<table>
<tr><td>p.63</td><td>look [lʊk]</td><td>aussehen</td></tr>
</table>

➡️

> **look**
> - **Look at** the pictures.
>   (Sieh dir die Bilder an.)
> - **Look**, Adam. There's a crab.
>   (Schau mal, Adam. Da ist ein Krebs.)
> - My new bike **looks** great.
>   (Mein neues Rad sieht toll aus.)

hard [hɑːd]	schwer, schwierig; hart	This exercise isn't **hard**. You can do it. School is **hard** work sometimes!
hill [hɪl]	Hügel	
down the hill [daʊn]	den Hügel hinunter	❗ Englisch: **down** this hill Deutsch: **diesen Hügel hinunter**
fast [fɑːst]	schnell	They always go down the hill very **fast**.
Come on! [kʌm ˈɒn]	Na los! / Komm(t) (schon)!	
leg [leg]	Bein	
lose control [luːz kənˈtrəʊl]	die Kontrolle verlieren	
fall [fɔːl]	fallen; hinfallen	
hospital [ˈhɒspɪtl]	Krankenhaus	
I have a sore leg. [sɔː]	Mein Bein tut weh.	Luca can't walk. He **has a sore leg**.
something [ˈsʌmθɪŋ]	etwas	Can I ask you **something**?

Skills training

p.64 **garage sale** [ˈgærɑːʒ seɪl]	Garagenflohmarkt *(privater Flohmarkt)*	
sale [seɪl]	Verkauf; Schlussverkauf	
The calculator is £ 1.	Der Taschenrechner kostet 1 Pfund.	
The posters are £ 2.50.	Die Poster kosten 2 Pfund fünfzig.	
50p [fɪfti ˈpiː]	fünfzig Pence	
British [ˈbrɪtɪʃ]	britisch	
money [ˈmʌni]	Geld	
p.65 **Excuse me, …** [ɪksˈkjuːz miː]	Entschuldigung, … / Entschuldigen Sie, …	
How much is / **How much are …?** [haʊ ˈmʌtʃ]	Was (Wie viel) kostet / Was (Wie viel) kosten …?	**Excuse me**, please, **how much is** the football? And **how much are** the books?
man, *pl* **men** [mæn, men]	Mann, Männer	❗ one **man** – two **men**

yeah (infml) [jeə]	ja	
It's **good value.** [ˈvæljuː]	Es ist sein Geld wert. / Es ist preiswert.	
the same [seɪm]	derselbe/dieselbe/dasselbe; dieselben	Luca and his brother Jack are at **the same** school.
try [traɪ]	probieren, ausprobieren	
I'll take it. [aɪl ˈteɪk ɪt]	Ich nehme es (ihn, sie). (beim Einkaufen)	How much is the football? – £ 12. – OK, **I'll take it**.
That's £ 159.	Das macht 159 Pfund.	
helmet [ˈhelmɪt]	Helm	**helmets**
p.66 **advert** [ˈædvɜːt]	Anzeige, Werbung	
guess [ges]	(er)raten	**Guess** how old I am. – 15? – No, I'm 14.

Unit 4: Berry's world

p.72 **visitor** [ˈvɪzɪtə]	Besucher/in; Gast	
field [fiːld]	Feld; Weide	❗ Englisch: the ponies **in** the field Deutsch: die Ponys **auf** der Weide
duck [dʌk]	Ente	
pond [pɒnd]	Teich	
pets corner [ˈkɔːnə]	Streichelzoo	
corner [ˈkɔːnə]	Ecke	
stroke [strəʊk]	streicheln	
donkey [ˈdɒŋki]	Esel	
barn [bɑːn]	Scheune, Stall	
trampoline [ˈtræmpəliːn]	Trampolin	
zip wire [ˈzɪp waɪə]	Seilrutsche	
question [ˈkwestʃən]	Frage	
ask [ɑːsk]	fragen	Can I feed the pigs? – **Ask** my dad, please. ❗ Englisch: Can I **ask** you a **question**? Deutsch: Kann ich dir eine **Frage stellen**?
information [ɪnfəˈmeɪʃn]	Information(en)	❗ **information** niemals mit „an" oder Plural -s! Englisch: read this **information** Deutsch: lies diese **Information**en
information desk	Informationsstand	
p.73 **chicken** [ˈtʃɪkɪn]	Huhn; (Brat-)Hähnchen	
cow [kaʊ]	Kuh	
pig [pɪg]	Schwein	
sheep, pl **sheep** [ʃiːp]	Schaf, Schafe	❗ one sheep – two **sheep**

Theme 1

p.74	**alarm clock** [əˈlɑːm klɒk]	Wecker	
	wake [weɪk]	wecken	My alarm clock usually **wakes** me at 6.30 in the morning.
	outside [aʊtˈsaɪd]	draußen; nach draußen	
	feed [fiːd]	füttern	Can I **feed** the rabbits?
	sun [sʌn]	Sonne	
	come up [kʌm ˈʌp]	aufgehen *(Sonne)*	
	quarter [ˈkwɔːtə]	Viertel	

What's the time? (Wie spät ist es?)

   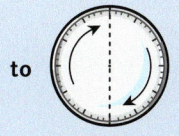

It's quarter past 6. (*oder:* **6.15**)

It's half past 6. (*oder:* **6.30**)

It's quarter to 7. (*oder* **6.45**)

to   past

Englisch: **half past 6**
Deutsch: **halb sieben**

	inside [ɪnˈsaɪd]	drinnen; nach drinnen	**inside ◄► outside**
	get ready (for) [ˈredi]	sich fertig machen (für), sich vorbereiten (auf)	First I have breakfast, then I **get ready for** school.
	be busy [ˈbɪzi]	beschäftigt sein; viel zu tun haben	I can't talk to you now. **I'm busy**!
	about [əˈbaʊt]	ungefähr	We get up at **about** 8.30 on Sundays.
	look after [lʊk ˈɑːftə]	sich kümmern um; aufpassen auf	On Saturday mornings I always **look after** my baby sister.
	do sport	Sport treiben	And on Saturday afternoons I **do sport**.
	clock [klɒk]	(Wand-, Stand-, Turm-)Uhr	
p.75	**dialogue** [ˈdaɪəlɒg]	Dialog	
	You're welcome. [ˈwelkəm]	Bitte, gern geschehen. / Nichts zu danken.	

„bitte"
• in Aufforderungen und Bitten: **please**

Close the door, **please**. / What's the time, **please**?
(Schließ die Tür, bitte. / Wie spät ist es, bitte?)

• wenn sich jemand bedankt hat: **You're welcome.**

It's 9.30. – Thank you. – **You're welcome.**
(9 Uhr 30. – Danke. – Bitte, gern geschehen.)

• wenn du jemandem etwas gibst: **Here you are.**

Can I borrow your pen, please? – **Here you are.**
(Kann ich deinen Stift leihen? – Hier, bitte.)

Theme 2

p.76	**feeling** [ˈfiːlɪŋ]	Gefühl	
	discussion [dɪˈskʌʃn]	Diskussion	

feel [fiːl]	sich fühlen; fühlen	
feel fed up [fed ˈʌp]	genervt sein, sauer sein; die Nase voll haben	
work [wɜːk]	funktionieren	I need your help. My computer doesn't **work**.
text me [tekst]	mir eine SMS schicken	**Text** me when you're back from London, OK?
person [ˈpɜːsn]	Person	❗ Nur selten wird der Plural **persons** benutzt. Normalerweise: one **person** – five **people**.

p.77	**a bit** [ə ˈbɪt]	ein bisschen	5 o'clock in the morning? That's **a bit** early for me.
	the only student [ˈəʊnli]	der einzige Schüler / die einzige Schülerin	Lilly is **the only** English student at our school.
	wheelchair [ˈwiːltʃeə]	Rollstuhl	a **wheelchair**
	win [wɪn]	gewinnen	I feel good when my football team **wins**.

drink [drɪŋk]	Getränk	
drink [drɪŋk]	trinken	
understand [ˌʌndəˈstænd]	verstehen	In English, please. I don't **understand** German.
speak [ˈspiːk]	sprechen	Can you **speak** French?
for myself [maɪˈself]	für mich selbst	
work/speak **well** [wel]	gut funktionieren/sprechen	My computer doesn't work very **well**. My parents speak English very **well**.
mouth [maʊθ]	Mund	

Focus on language

p.78	**chipmunk** [ˈtʃɪpmʌŋk]	Streifenhörnchen
	idiot [ˈɪdiət]	Idiot/in
	furry [ˈfɜːri]	flauschig; pelzig
p.79	**friendly** [ˈfrendli]	freundlich
	sit [sɪt]	sitzen; sich setzen

My cat often **sits** on my desk. *(sitzen)*
You can **sit** on this chair. *(dich setzen)*

shoulder [ˈʃəʊldə]	Schulter
cage [keɪdʒ]	Käfig
fruit [fruːt]	Obst
nut [nʌt]	Nuss

fruit and nuts

p.80	**find** [faɪnd]	finden	

Max, find Nick!

| a person **who …** | eine Person, die … | I know a girl **who** has six cats. |
| **interesting** [ˈɪntrəstɪŋ] | interessant | This book is great. It's very **interesting**. |

Story

p.81 **on the bus**	im Bus	! Englisch: **on the bus** Deutsch: **im Bus**
nervous [ˈnɜːvəs]	nervös, aufgeregt	
adventure [ədˈventʃə]	Abenteuer	
country [ˈkʌntri]	Land	! Englisch: **in** the country Deutsch: **auf** dem Land
scene [siːn]	Szene	
invite (to) [ɪnˈvaɪt]	einladen (zu, nach)	Can I **invite** all my friends to my party?
sleepover [ˈsliːpəʊvə]	Schlafparty	
sleeping bag [ˈsliːpɪŋ bæg]	Schlafsack	
bus station [ˈbʌs steɪʃn]	Busbahnhof	
unhappy [ʌnˈhæpi]	unglücklich	She's **happy**. 😊 He's **unhappy**. 😞

| **Don't worry.** [dəʊnt ˈwʌri] | Mach dir keine Sorgen. | → |

> **Don't …**
> **Don't go** now.   Geh jetzt (noch) nicht.
> **Don't ask**.   Frag nicht.
> **Don't be** stupid. Sei nicht dumm.
> **Don't watch** TV. Sieh nicht fern.

| **worry (about)** [ˈwʌri] | sich Sorgen machen (wegen, um) | Mum always **worries about** me when I come home late. |
| **her** [hɜː] | sie; ihr | → |

> **her**
> • (wessen?) **ihr, ihre**
>   **her** birthday; **her** children
> • (wen?) **sie**
>   Sally? We can meet **her** in the park.
> • (wem?) **ihr**
>   There's Sophie. Let's help **her**.

wet [wet]	nass	
laugh [lɑːf]	lachen	
p.82 **that** field	das Feld (dort), jenes Feld	

> **this – that**
> • Wenn etwas **näher beim Sprecher** ist, verwendet man eher **this** („dies hier").
>
> • Wenn etwas **weiter entfernt** ist, verwendet man eher **that** („das dort").

I like **this top**.   I don't like **that** pullover.

through [θruː]	durch	
hurry [ˈhʌri]	sich beeilen; eilen	
bull [bʊl]	Stier, Bulle	
dangerous [ˈdeɪndʒərəs]	gefährlich	a **dangerous** fish 
with a **laugh** [lɑːf]	mit einem Lachen	
only [ˈəʊnli]	nur, bloß	! it's **only** a chicken es ist **nur** ein Huhn the **only** chicken das **einzige** Huhn

Go to sleep!	Schlaf jetzt!	Be quiet now and **go to sleep**.
hear [hɪə]	hören	**❗ hear** = hören (können) **listen (to)** = zuhören, horchen **Listen!** Can you **hear** that noise?
wake up [weɪk ˈʌp]	aufwachen	
this **time**	dieses Mal	**❗** Do you have **time**? *(Zeit)* the last **time** / this **time** / (the) next **time** *(Mal)*
Oh dear. [əʊ ˈdɪə]	Oje!	
be worried (about) [ˈwʌrid]	beunruhigt sein, besorgt sein (wegen)	**look + Präposition** Let's **look for** Luca. *(suchen)* Can you **look after** Finn? *(sich kümmern um)* **Look at** this! *(anschauen)*
look for	suchen; Ausschau halten nach ➡	
p.83 **happen** [ˈhæpən]	geschehen, passieren	Say what's **happening** in the pictures.
time **to** eat	Zeit zu essen ➡	**to** („zu") It's time **to** eat. Zeit **zu** essen. something **to** drink etwas **zu** trinken Nice **to** meet you. dich kennen**zu**lernen

Skills training

p.84 **sign** [saɪn]	Schild; Zeichen	
left [left]	links; nach links	**left** **right**
right [raɪt]	rechts; nach rechts	
p.85 **invitation (to)** [ɪnvɪˈteɪʃn]	Einladung (zu, nach)	
picnic [ˈpɪknɪk]	Picknick	
5 pm [piːˈem]	5 Uhr nachmittags / abends, 17 Uhr	
9 am [eɪˈem]	9 Uhr morgens / vormittags	
I'd love to come. (= I would love to come.) [wʊd]	Ich komme sehr gern. / Ich würde sehr gern kommen.	
Best wishes [ˈwɪʃɪz]	Viele Grüße … *(Briefschluss)*	
p.86 **use** [juːz]	benutzen, verwenden ➡	**❗** Aussprache: **use** he/she **uses** [ˈjuːzɪz] **close** he/she **closes** [ˈkləʊzɪz] **dance** he/she **dances** [ˈdɑːnsɪz] **guess** he/she **guess**es [ˈgesɪz] **watch** he/she **watch**es [ˈwɒtʃɪz]
dictionary [ˈdɪkʃənri]	Wörterbuch, *(alphabetisches)* Wörterverzeichnis	
poem [ˈpəʊɪm]	Gedicht	

Unit 5: All about Adam

p.92 **harbour** [ˈhɑːbə]	Hafen	
maybe [ˈmeɪbi]	vielleicht	
woman, *pl* **women** [ˈwʊmən, ˈwɪmɪn]	Frau, Frauen	**❗** one **woman**, two **women**

on the left	links, auf der linken Seite
on the right	rechts, auf der rechten Seite
in the middle [ˈmɪdl]	in der Mitte

p.93 **Where is Adam going?** — Wohin geht Adam (gerade)?

Lily   Ben   Ava

**Lily is on the left, Ben is in the middle,
Ava is on the right.**

cafe [ˈkæfeɪ]	Café
ferry [ˈferi]	Fähre
France [frɑːns]	Frankreich

Theme 1

p.94
customer [ˈkʌstəmə]	Kunde, Kundin
salad [ˈsæləd]	Salat *(als Gericht oder Beilage)*
a **cup of …** [kʌp]	eine Tasse …
coffee [ˈkɒfi]	Kaffee
chips *(pl)* [tʃɪps]	Pommes frites
soup [suːp]	Suppe
a **bottle of …** [ˈbɒtl]	eine Flasche …
water [ˈwɔːtə]	Wasser
juice [dʒuːs]	Saft
omelette [ˈɒmlət]	Omelett
tea [tiː]	Tee
scone [skɒn]	*kleines rundes Milchbrötchen, leicht süß, oft mit Rosinen*

**two bottles
of juice**   **a bottle
of water**   **a cup
of coffee**

I'd like … (= I would like) [wʊd]	Ich hätte gern … / Ich möchte …

! **I'd like** a sandwich.
Ich **möchte** ein
Sandwich.   **I'd like to eat** it now.
Ich **möchte** es jetzt
essen.

Next, please.	Der/die Nächste, bitte.
Would you like **anything else?** [eniθɪŋ ˈels]	Möchten Sie sonst noch etwas?

Can I help you?   Four scones, please.

Anything else?   scones

customer

How's it going?	Wie geht's? / Wie läuft's?
ring [rɪŋ]	läuten, klingeln

Adam's mobile
is **ringing**.

cook [kʊk]	kochen, *(Essen)* zubereiten

What are you **cooking**, Dad? – Omelettes.

wash up [wɒʃ ˈʌp]	abwaschen	
must [mʌst]	müssen	❗ kein **-s** bei *he/she/it*: Adam **must** go.
I must go.	*(am Telefon)* Ich muss Schluss machen.	
Say hi to everybody**.**	Grüß alle.	Sorry, I must go now. Say hi to your sister. Bye.
p.95 **leave** [liːv]	*(jemanden)* verlassen; weggehen	
clean [kliːn]	sauber machen, putzen	
letter [ˈletə]	Brief	
at the moment [ˈməʊmənt]	im Moment, gerade	

Theme 2

p.96 **walk** [wɔːk]	wandern, (zu Fuß) gehen	My sister often **walks** to school.
phone [fəʊn]	anrufen	
dive [daɪv]	einen Kopfsprung machen	
rock [rɒk]	Fels(en)	
hide [haɪd]	verstecken; sich verstecken	Let's **hide** in the wardrobe.
wave [weɪv]	winken	➡

❗ Schreibung:

come	coming	make	making
dive	diving	phone	phoning
have	having	ride	riding
hide	hiding	wave	waving

club [klʌb]	Klub	❗ [klʌb] klingt anders als „Klub" im Deutschen.
p.97 **mean** [miːn]	bedeuten	
drums [drʌmz]	Schlagzeug; Trommeln	
It's **free.**	Es ist kostenlos/umsonst.	
guitar [ɡɪˈtɑː]	Gitarre	❗ Englisch: **play the guitar / the drums** Deutsch: **Gitarre / Schlagzeug spielen**
learn [lɜːn]	lernen	
group [ɡruːp]	Gruppe	
instrument [ˈɪnstrəmənt]	Instrument	
young [jʌŋ]	jung	**young ◀▶ old**
disabled [dɪsˈeɪbld]	(körper)behindert	
musician [mjuˈzɪʃn]	Musiker/in	
piano [piˈænəʊ]	Klavier	❗ Englisch: **play the piano** Deutsch: **Klavier spielen**
centre [ˈsentə]	Zentrum, (Stadt-)Mitte	
join a club [dʒɔɪn]	sich einem Klub anschließen; in einen Klub eintreten	I want to **join** the guitar club. What about you?

Focus on language

p.98	**set the table** [set]	den Tisch decken	→

> **!** Schreibung:
>
> | | | | |
> |---|---|---|---|
> | get | ge**tt**ing | sit | si**tt**ing |
> | rap | ra**pp**ing | swim | swi**mm**ing |
> | set | se**tt**ing | | |

them [ðem, ðəm]	sie, ihnen	

Personal pronouns (Personalpronomen)

I (ich)	– **me**	Can you see **me**? (mich)	Help **me**. (mir)
you (du; Sie)	– **you**	Can I phone **you**? (dich; Sie)	Can I help **you**? (dir; Ihnen)
he (er)	– **him**	Can you see **him**? (ihn)	Help **him**. (ihm)
she (sie)	– **her**	Can you see **her**? (sie)	Help **her**. (ihr)
it (es)	– **it**	Can you see **it**? (es)	Help **it**. (ihm)
we (wir)	– **us**	Can you see **us**? (uns)	Help **us**. (uns)
you (ihr; Sie)	– **you**	Can I phone **you**? (euch; Sie)	Can I help **you**? (euch; Ihnen)
they (sie)	– **them**	Can you see **them**? (sie)	Help **them**. (ihnen)

little [ˈlɪtl]	klein	On Saturday mornings I always look after my **little** sister.

cook [kʊk]	Koch, Köchin	**two cooks** 

p.99	**food** [fuːd]	Essen, Lebensmittel; Futter

window [ˈwɪndəʊ]	Fenster	

door   window

Story

p.100	**terrible** [ˈterəbl]	schrecklich, fürchterlich	Dad thinks dogs are **terrible** – he hates dogs.
	difference [ˈdɪfrəns]	Unterschied	
	make a difference	etwas bewirken, etwas ausmachen	
	it **was** Friday [wɒz, wəz]	es war Freitag	→

> | | |
> |---|---|
> | • **I am** (ich bin) | **I was** (ich war) |
> | • **he/she/it is** (er/sie/es ist) | **he/she/it was** (er/sie/es war) |

on the way to … [weɪ]	auf dem Weg zu/nach …	
some [sʌm, səm]	einige, ein paar; etwas, ein wenig	There are **some** sandwiches for you on the table. And there's **some** juice too.

they **were** on the bus [wɜː, wə]	sie waren im Bus	➜
he **said** [sed]	er sagte; er hat gesagt	
seat [siːt]	(Sitz-)Platz	

• **we are** (wir sind)	**we were** (wir waren)
• **you are** (du bist; ihr seid)	**you were** (du warst; ihr wart)
• **they are** (sie sind)	**they were** (sie waren)

they **laughed** [lɑːft]	sie lachten; sie haben gelacht	
face [feɪs]	Gesicht	
she **asked** [ɑːskt]	sie fragte; sie hat gefragt	
nothing [ˈnʌθɪŋ]	nichts	
I **had** [hæd, həd]	ich hatte; ich habe gehabt	
girlfriend [ˈgɜːlfrend]	(feste) Freundin	
boyfriend [ˈbɔɪfrend]	(fester) Freund	
Any ideas? [ˈeni]	Irgendwelche Ideen?	I need help with my text. **Any** ideas?
battle [ˈbætl]	Wettstreit, Battle *(im Rap)*	
p. 101 he **thought** [θɔːt]	er dachte; er hat gedacht	
show [ʃəʊ]	zeigen	
these people [ðiːz]	diese Leute (hier)	❗ Englisch: **this** cup – **these** cups Deutsch: **diese** Tasse – **diese** Tassen
Well done. [wel ˈdʌn]	Gut gemacht!	
proud (of) [praʊd]	stolz (auf)	

> Well done, Max. I'm proud of you.

true [truː]	wahr, richtig	
false [fɔːls]	falsch, unrichtig	
he **wasn't** (= was not) [ˈwɒznt, wəz ˈnɒt]	er war nicht	

Skills training

p. 102 **describe** [dɪˈskraɪb]	beschreiben	❗ Englisch: **Describe** the picture **to him/her**. Deutsch: **Beschreibe ihm/ihr** das Bild.
at the top [tɒp]	oben, am oberen Ende; an der Spitze	
at the bottom [ˈbɒtəm]	unten, am unteren Ende	
in front of [ɪn ˈfrʌnt əv]	vor	

behind the TV	**in front of** the TV	**on** the TV	**under** the TV	**between** the rabbits	**near** the rabbit	**next to** the rabbit

apple [ˈæpl]	Apfel

ball [bɔːl]	Ball		
p.103 **text (message)** ['tekst mesɪdʒ]	SMS		
language ['læŋgwɪdʒ]	Sprache		
kiss [kɪs]	Kuss		
mean [miːn]	meinen *(sagen wollen)*	**!** **mean:** 1. Don't be so **mean**! *(gemein, fies)* 2. What does this word **mean**? *(bedeuten)* 3. What do you **mean**? *(meinen / sagen wollen)*	
p.104 **recipe** ['resəpi]	(Koch-)Rezept		
cake [keɪk]	Kuchen, Torte		
jam [dʒæm]	Marmelade		
cream [kriːm]	Sahne		

Unit 6: School is out – for summer

p.110 **school is out** [aʊt]	die Schule ist aus/vorbei	
I'd prefer ... [prɪˈfɜː]	ich würde ... vorziehen	
canoe [kəˈnuː]	Kanu, Paddelboot	
trip [trɪp]	Ausflug; Reise	What about a **trip** to the beach?
theme park ['θiːm pɑːk]	Themenpark *(Freizeitpark mit Attraktionen zu einem bestimmten Thema)*	

Theme

p.112 **I'm going to bring ...** ['gəʊɪŋ tə]	ich werde ... mitbringen	
swimming trunks *(pl)* ['swɪmɪŋ trʌŋks]	(eine) Badehose →	**swimming trunks** und **(sun)glasses** sind <u>immer Plural</u>: Your **swimming trunks/(sun)glasses** **are** great. **Are they** new? (Deine **Badehose/ Sonnenbrille** <u>ist</u> toll. <u>Ist sie</u> neu?)
towel ['taʊəl]	Handtuch	
suncream ['sʌnkriːm]	Sonnencreme	
swimsuit ['swɪmsuːt]	Badeanzug	
glasses *(pl)* ['glɑːsɪz]	(eine) Brille →	
sunglasses *(pl)* ['sʌnglɑːsɪz]	(eine) Sonnenbrille →	
hat [hæt]	Hut, Mütze	
like [laɪk]	wie	The English word 'supermarket' is **like** the German word *Supermarkt*.
wait (for) [weɪt]	warten (auf)	
wait and see [weɪt]	abwarten	What's going to happen? – **Wait and see!**
crisps *(pl)* [krɪsps]	(Kartoffel-)Chips	**!** Englisch: **crisps** = Deutsch: **Chips** Englisch: **chips** = Deutsch: **Pommes frites**
chocolate ['tʃɒklət]	Schokolade	a **chocolate cake**

biscuit [ˈbɪskɪt]	Keks, Plätzchen	**!** Englisch: **biscuit** = Deutsch: **Keks** Englisch: **cake** = Deutsch: **Kuchen, Torte**
orange [ˈɒrɪndʒ]	Orange, Apfelsine	
sausage [ˈsɒsɪdʒ]	(Brat-, Bock-)Würstchen, Wurst	
p.113 **shorts** *(pl)* [ʃɔːts]	*(eine)* kurze Hose	**!** Englisch: **These shorts are** new. Deutsch: **Diese kurze Hose ist** neu.
umbrella [ʌmˈbrelə]	(Regen-)Schirm	
speaker [ˈspiːkə]	Lautsprecher	
bodyboard [ˈbɒdibɔːd]	Bodyboard *(kurzes Surfbrett, mit dem man auf dem Bauch liegend surft)*	

blanket [ˈblæŋkɪt]	Decke *(zum Zudecken u.Ä.)*	
tube [tjuːb]	Schwimmreifen	
forget [fəˈget]	vergessen	It's dad's birthday tomorrow. Don't **forget** it. **forget** ◄► **remember**
chain [tʃeɪn]	Kette	

a chain

Focus on language

p.114 **That's a pity.** [ˈpɪti]	Das ist schade.	
I mustn't forget ... [ˈmʌsnt]	ich darf ... nicht vergessen ➜	**must – mustn't** • **must – müssen** You **must** do your homework now. • **mustn't – nicht dürfen** You **mustn't** forget suncream.
tourist [ˈtʊərɪst]	Tourist/in	
bread [bred]	Brot	

white **bread**   black **bread**

p.115 **Croatia** [krəʊˈeɪʃə]	Kroatien	
yum *(infml)* [jʌm]	lecker	
take me to the theatre	mit mir ins Theater gehen	
practise [ˈpræktɪs]	üben	I **practise** the piano every day.

Story

p.117 **aboard** [əˈbɔːd]	an Bord	

message in a bottle	Flaschenpost	

a message in a bottle

message ['mesɪdʒ]	Nachricht, Mitteilung	
smuggler ['smʌglə]	Schmuggler/in	
put [pʊt]	(etwas wohin) tun, legen, stellen, stecken	

Put all the photos in the box, please.

better ['betə]	besser	**good – better – best**
the sea's coming in	die Flut kommt; das Wasser steigt	
minute ['mɪnɪt]	Minute	
square [skweə]	Platz (in der Stadt)	
exciting [ɪk'saɪtɪŋ]	aufregend	
map [mæp]	Landkarte, Stadtplan	**maps**
another [ə'nʌðə]	ein/e andere/r/s; noch ein/e	I don't like cats. Can I have **another** pet? Can I have **another** apple? They're very nice.
follow ['fɒləʊ]	folgen; verfolgen	
p.118 **quick** [kwɪk]	schnell	
push [pʊʃ]	schieben	
rest [rest]	Pause, Rast	
fresh [freʃ]	frisch	I love **fresh** scones with jam and cream.
slow [sləʊ]	langsam	**slow ◄► quick**
hot [hɒt]	heiß	
ice cream [aɪs 'kriːm]	(Speise-)Eis	

Ice cream on a **hot** day – great!

p.119 **daughter** ['dɔːtə]	Tochter	
sand [sænd]	Sand	
out of ... ['aʊt əv]	aus ... (heraus/hinaus)	Please take your socks **out of** my room!
scary ['skeəri]	unheimlich, beängstigend, gruselig	
over there [əʊvə 'ðeə]	da drüben, dort drüben	

Skills training

p.120 **fly** [flaɪ]	fliegen	
all summer	den ganzen Sommer	
Spain [speɪn]	Spanien	Yippee! Next week we're going to **fly** to **Spain**!
granny ['græni]	Oma	
Turkey ['tɜːki]	(die) Türkei	

Das **DICTIONARY** besteht aus **zwei alphabetischen Wörterlisten**:
English – German (S. 222–232)   und   **German – English** (S. 233–241)

Im **English – German dictionary** kannst du nachschlagen, wenn du wissen möchtest,
was ein englisches Wort bedeutet, wie man es ausspricht oder wie es geschrieben wird.

Im **Dictionary** werden folgende **Abkürzungen und Symbole** verwendet:

pl = plural (Mehrzahl)

° Mit diesem Kringel sind Wörter markiert, die nicht zum Lernwortschatz gehören.

Die **Fundstellenangaben** zeigen, wo ein Wort zum ersten Mal in *Headlight 1* vorkommt.
Die Ziffern in Klammern bezeichnen Seitenzahlen:

(8)   = Seite 8
1 (19) = Unit 1, Seite 19

Tipps zur Arbeit mit einem Wörterbuch findest du im Skills file auf Seite 170.

A

a [ə] ein/e (9)
aboard [ə'bɔːd] an Bord 6 (117)
about [ə'baʊt]:
  1. über 1 (19) **2.** ungefähr 4 (74)
  about me über mich 1 (19) **good
  about my house** gut an meinem
  Haus 2 (44) **What about you?**
  Und du? / Was ist mit dir? (11)
°**act** [ækt] aufführen, spielen
°**activity** [ək'tɪvəti] Aktivität, Tätig-
  keit
°**add** [æd] hinzufügen, addieren
address [ə'dres] Adresse 2 (46)
°**adult** ['ædʌlt] Erwachsene/r
adventure [əd'ventʃə] Abenteuer
  4 (81)
advert ['ædvɜːt] Anzeige, Werbung
  3 (66)
Africa ['æfrɪkə] Afrika 1 (26)
after ['ɑːftə] nach: nach *(zeitlich)*
  3 (58) **after dinner** nach dem
  Abendessen 3 (58)
afternoon [ɑːftə'nuːn] Nachmittag
  3 (54) **in the afternoon** am Nachmittag 3 (54)
again [ə'gen] wieder, noch einmal
  2 (42)
age [eɪdʒ] Alter 1 (18)
°**agree on** [ə'griː] sich einigen auf
alarm clock [ə'lɑːm klɒk] Wecker
  4 (74)
all [ɔːl] alle(s) (10) **all summer**
  den ganzen Sommer 6 (120)
  °**she is all wrong** sie hat völlig
  Unrecht, sie liegt total falsch
°**alone** [ə'ləʊn] allein
°**aloud** [ə'laʊd]: **read aloud** laut
  (vor)lesen
  alphabet ['ælfəbet] Alphabet 2 (46)

°**alphabetical** [ælfə'betɪkl] alphabetisch
always ['ɔːlweɪz] immer 2 (36)
am [æm]: **I'm (= I am)** ich bin (8)
am [eɪ'em]: **9 am** 9 Uhr morgens/
  vormittags 4 (85/214)
an [ən] ein/e *(vor Vokalen)* (12)
and [ænd], [ənd] und (9)
animal ['ænɪml] Tier (12)
another [ə'nʌðə] ein/e andere/r/s;
  noch ein/e 6 (117)
°**answer** ['ɑːnsə]: **1.** Antwort
  2. antworten (auf), beantworten
Any ideas? ['eni] Irgendwelche
  Ideen? 5 (100)
anything ['eniθɪŋ]: **Would you
  like anything else?** Möchten Sie
  sonst noch etwas? 5 (94)
apple ['æpl] Apfel 5 (102)
°**appointment** [ə'pɔɪntmənt] Ver-
  abredung
April ['eɪprəl] April 3 (56)
aquarium [ə'kweəriəm] Aquarium
  (10)
are [ɑː] bist, sind, seid (8) **The
  posters are £ 2.50.** Die Poster
  kosten 2 Pfund fünfzig. 3 (64)
°**around** [ə'raʊnd] umher- **all
  around me** überall um mich
  herum **there's lots around** es
  gibt viel
art [ɑːt] Kunst 1 (20)
°**as** [æz], [əz]: **as a group** als Gruppe
  as many/much as you can so
  viel/e (wie) du kannst
ask [ɑːsk] fragen 4 (72) **ask questions** Fragen stellen 4 (72) **she
  asked** sie fragte 5 (100) °**ask
  about** fragen nach

assembly [ə'sembli] Schulversammlung 1 (21) °**assembly
  hall** *(etwa)* Aula
at [æt], [ət]: **at MARTINS** bei
  MARTINS 1 (26) **at 1 o'clock**
  um 1 Uhr / um 13 Uhr 3 (57)
  at a restaurant in einem Restaurant 2 (42) **at home** zu Hause 1 (24)
  at night nachts, in der Nacht
  3 (58) **at school** in der Schule
  1 (20) **at the bottom** unten,
  am unteren Ende 5 (102) **at the
  cinema** im Kino 2 (42) **at the
  moment** im Moment, gerade
  5 (95) **at the top** oben, am oberen
  Ende; an der Spitze 5 (102) **at the
  weekend** am Wochenende
  3 (52) **at this school** auf/an dieser
  Schule 1 (18) **at work** bei der
  Arbeit, am Arbeitsplatz 2 (42)
August ['ɔːgəst] August 3 (56)
aunt [ɑːnt] Tante 2 (37)
away [ə'weɪ] weg, fort (14)

B

baby ['beɪbi] Baby 2 (36)
babysitter ['beɪbɪsɪtə] Babysitter
  5 (96)
babysitting ['beɪbɪsɪtɪŋ] Babysitten
  2 (42)
back [bæk]: **1.** zurück 1 (26)
  °**2.** Rückseite
bad [bæd] schlecht; schlimm 1 (25)
°**badminton** ['bædmɪntən] Badminton, Federball
bag [bæg] Tasche 1 (27)
°**baking powder** ['beɪkɪŋ
  paʊdə] Backpulver
balcony ['bælkəni] Balkon 2 (34)
ball [bɔːl] Ball 5 (102)

°**banana** [bəˈnɑːnə] Banane

°**banana skin** [bəˈnɑːnə skɪn] Bananenschale

band [bænd] Band, Musikgruppe 3 (62)

barn [bɑːn] Scheune, Stall 4 (72)

basketball [ˈbɑːskɪtbɔːl] Basketball 4 (77)

°**bath** [bɑːθ] Badewanne

bathroom [ˈbɑːθruːm] Bad(ezimmer) 2 (35)

battle [ˈbætl] Wettstreit, Battle *(im Rap)* 5 (100)

be [biː] sein 1 (24)

beach [biːtʃ] Strand (9) **on the beach** am Strand 2 (44)

bear [beə] Bär (12)

beat [biːt] *(Musik)* Beat, Rhythmus 5 (101) °**beats per minute (BPM)** *(Musik)* Schläge pro Minute

because [bɪˈkɒz] weil 2 (36)

bed [bed] Bett 2 (34)

bedroom [ˈbedruːm] Schlafzimmer 2 (34)

before [bɪˈfɔː] bevor; vor (zeitlich) 1 (24)

behind [bɪˈhaɪnd] hinter 5 (102)

°**belong** [bɪˈlɒŋ] (hin)gehören

best [best] beste(r, s); am besten 1 (18) **Best wishes** Viele Grüße … *(Briefschluss)* 4 (85) **the best of both worlds** das Beste von beidem 2 (42)

better [ˈbetə] besser 6 (117)

between [bɪˈtwiːn] zwischen 5 (102)

big [bɪg] groß (13)

bike [baɪk] Fahrrad (13)

bird [bɜːd] Vogel (12)

birthday [ˈbɜːθdeɪ]: **Happy birthday!** Herzlichen Glückwunsch zum Geburtstag! 3 (62) **It's her birthday.** Sie hat Geburtstag. 2 (42)

biscuit [ˈbɪskɪt] Keks, Plätzchen 6 (112)

bit [bɪt]: **a bit** ein bisschen 4 (77)

black [blæk] schwarz (10)

blanket [ˈblæŋkɪt] Decke *(zum Zudecken u. Ä.)* 6 (113)

blazer [ˈbleɪzə] Blazer *(Jackett, oft Teil der Schuluniform)* 1 (24)

block of flats [blɒk əv ˈflæts] Mehrfamilienhaus, Wohnblock 2 (34)

blue [bluː] blau (10)

BMX [biː em ˈeks] BMX(-Fahrrad) 1 (18)

board [bɔːd] Tafel 2 (45)

°**boat** [bəʊt] Boot

bodyboard [ˈbɒdibɔːd] *kurzes Surfbrett, mit dem man auf dem Bauch liegend surft* 6 (113)

book [bʊk] Buch (11)

°**bored** [bɔːd]: **I'm bored** mir ist langweilig

boring [ˈbɔːrɪŋ] langweilig 1 (25)

borrow [ˈbɒrəʊ] (aus)leihen, sich borgen 1 (28)

bossy [ˈbɒsi] herrisch, rechthaberisch 2 (38)

both [bəʊθ] beide 2 (42) **the best of both worlds** das Beste von beidem 2 (42)

bottle [ˈbɒtl] Flasche 5 (94) **a bottle of …** eine Flasche … 5 (94)

bottom [ˈbɒtəm]: **at the bottom** unten, am unteren Ende 5 (102)

°**bowl** [bəʊl] Schüssel, Schale

box [bɒks] Kasten, Kiste, Kästchen 1 (27)

boy [bɔɪ] Junge 1 (16)

boyfriend [ˈbɔɪfrend] (fester) Freund 5 (100/218)

°**bracket** [ˈbrækɪt] Klammer

bread [bred] Brot 6 (114)

break [breɪk] Pause 1 (21)

breakfast [ˈbrekfəst] Frühstück 3 (54) **have breakfast** frühstücken 3 (55)

bring [brɪŋ] bringen, mitbringen 3 (58)

British [ˈbrɪtɪʃ] britisch 3 (64)

brochure [ˈbrəʊʃə] Broschüre, Prospekt 1 (26)

brother [ˈbrʌðə] Bruder 1 (18)

brown [braʊn] braun (10)

°**brush** [brʌʃ] bürsten

°**budgie** [ˈbʌdʒi] Wellensittich

bull [bʊl] Stier, Bulle 4 (82)

bus [bʌs] Bus 3 (58) **go by bus** mit dem Bus fahren 3 (58) **on the bus** im Bus 4 (81)

bus station [ˈbʌs steɪʃn] Busbahnhof 4 (81)

busy [ˈbɪzi]: **The kitchen is too busy.** In der Küche ist zu viel los. 2 (38) **be busy** beschäftigt sein; viel zu tun haben 4 (74)

but [bʌt], [bət] aber (11)

°**butter** [ˈbʌtə] Butter

buy [baɪ] kaufen 1 (26)

by [baɪ]: **go by bus** mit dem Bus fahren 3 (58)

Bye. [baɪ] Tschüs. 1 (17)

C

cafe [ˈkæfeɪ] Café 5 (93)

cage [keɪdʒ] Käfig 4 (79)

cake [keɪk] Kuchen, Torte 5 (104)

calculator [ˈkælkjuleɪtə] Taschenrechner 1 (26)

°**calendar** [ˈkælɪndə] Kalender

°**call** [kɔːl] nennen

camera [ˈkæmərə] Fotoapparat; Kamera (13)

camping [ˈkæmpɪŋ] Camping 6 (111)

can [kæn], [kən] können (9) **I can't (= cannot) do my homework.** Ich kann meine Hausaufgaben nicht machen. 2 (38)

canoe [kəˈnuː] Kanu, Paddelboot 6 (110)

canteen [kænˈtiːn] Kantine, (Schul-)Mensa 1 (20)

car [kɑː] Auto 1 (16)

card [kɑːd] Karte 1 (27)

cat [kæt] Katze (12)

°**cave** [keɪv] Höhle

CD [siː ˈdiː] CD 4 (85)

centre [ˈsentə] Zentrum, (Stadt-)Mitte 5 (97)

chain [tʃeɪn] Kette 6 (113)

chair [tʃeə] Stuhl 2 (34)

chant [tʃɑːnt] Sprechgesang (15)

°**character** [ˈkærəktə] Figur *(aus einer Geschichte)*

°**chat** [tʃæt] plaudern

°**check** [tʃek] (über)prüfen, kontrollieren

°**chess** [tʃes] Schach

chicken [ˈtʃɪkɪn] Huhn; (Brat-)Hähnchen 4 (73)

child, pl children [tʃaɪld], [ˈtʃɪldrən] Kind, Kinder 1 (26)

chipmunk [ˈtʃɪpmʌŋk] Streifenhörnchen 4 (78)

chips *(pl)* [tʃɪps] Pommes frites 5 (94)

chocolate [ˈtʃɒklət] Schokolade 6 (112)

°**choose** [tʃuːz] (aus)wählen

°**chorus** [ˈkɔːrəs] Refrain *(Lied)*

church [tʃɜːtʃ] Kirche 3 (52)

cinema [ˈsɪnəmə] Kino 2 (42)

°**circle** [ˈsɜːkl] Kreis

city [ˈsɪti] (Groß-)Stadt 1 (22)

class [klɑːs]: **1.** Klasse (8) °**2.** Unterricht

class teacher [ˈklɑːs tiːtʃə] Klassenlehrer/in 1 (19)

classroom [ˈklɑːsruːm] Klassenraum 1 (22)

clean [kliːn] sauber machen, putzen 5 (95)

clock [klɒk] (Wand-, Stand-, Turm-)Uhr 4 (74)

close [kləʊz] schließen, zumachen 2 (45)

°**clothes** [kləʊdz] Kleidung

club [klʌb] Klub 5 (96)

coffee ['kɒfi] Kaffee 5 (94)

°**cold** [kəʊld] kalt

°**collect** [kə'lekt] sammeln

colour ['kʌlə] Farbe (10)

°**column** ['kɒləm] Spalte

come [kʌm] (mit)kommen 3 (54)
Come on! Na los! / Komm(t)
(schon)! 3 (63) **come up** aufgehen
(*Sonne*) 4 (74) **the sea's coming
in** die Flut kommt; das Wasser
steigt 6 (117)

°**comic** ['kɒmɪk] Comic

community college [kə'mjuːnəti
kɒlɪdʒ] weiterführende Schule
(GB) 1 (21)

°**compare** [kəm'peə] vergleichen

°**complete** [kəm'pliːt]: **1.** vervoll-
ständigen **2.** vollständig

computer [kəm'pjuːtə] Computer
1 (20)

concert ['kɒnsət] Konzert 3 (62)

control [kən'trəʊl]: **lose control**
die Kontrolle verlieren 3 (63)

cook [kʊk]: **1.** Koch, Köchin 5 (98)
2. kochen, (*Essen*) zubereiten 5 (94)

cool [kuːl] cool (13)

°**copy** ['kɒpi] kopieren, abschrei-
ben

corner ['kɔːnə] Ecke 4 (72) **pets
corner** Streichelzoo 4 (72)

°**correct** [kə'rekt]: **1.** korrekt
2. korrigieren

°**cost** [kɒst] kosten

country ['kʌntri] Land 4 (81)

cousin ['kʌzn] Cousin/e 2 (37)

cow [kaʊ] Kuh 4 (73)

crab [kræb] Krebs (8)

crazy ['kreɪzi] verrückt 2 (37)

cream [kriːm] Sahne 5 (104)

crisps (*pl*) [krɪsps] (Kartoffel-)
Chips 6 (112)

Croatia [krəʊ'eɪʃə] Kroatien 6 (115)

crocodile ['krɒkədaɪl] Krokodil (12)

°**cross** [krɒs] Kreuz(chen)

cup [kʌp] Tasse 5 (94) **a cup of ...**
eine Tasse ... 5 (94)

cushion ['kʊʃn] Kissen 2 (39)

customer ['kʌstəmə] Kunde,
Kundin 5 (94)

°**cut** [kʌt] schneiden

cute [kjuːt] niedlich, süß 2 (36)

°**cycle** ['saɪkl] Rad fahren

D

dad [dæd] Papa, Vati 2 (35)

°**daily** ['deɪli] täglich

dance [dɑːns] tanzen (11)

dangerous ['deɪndʒərəs] gefährlich 4 (82)

date [deɪt] Datum 3 (57)

daughter ['dɔːtə] Tochter 6 (119)

day [deɪ] Tag (14)

dear [dɪə]: **Dear ...** Liebe/r ...
2 (42) **Oh dear.** Oje! 4 (82)

December [dɪ'sembə] Dezember
3 (56)

°**decide** [dɪ'saɪd] beschließen, sich
entscheiden

°**degu** ['deɪguː] Degu (*Nagetierart*)

describe [dɪ'skraɪb] beschreiben
5 (102)

desk [desk] Schreibtisch 2 (39)

°**diagram** ['daɪəgræm] Diagramm

dialogue ['daɪəlɒg] Dialog 4 (75)

diary ['daɪəri] Tagebuch; Kalender
1 (26)

dictionary ['dɪkʃənri] Wörterbuch,
(*alphabetisches*) Wörterverzeichnis
4 (86)

difference ['dɪfrəns] Unterschied 5 (100) **make a difference** etwas bewirken, etwas
ausmachen 5 (100)

different ['dɪfrənt] verschieden;
anders 2 (39)

difficult ['dɪfɪkəlt] schwierig 2 (43)

dinner ['dɪnə] Abendessen 3 (58)

°**dirty** ['dɜːti] schmutzig

disabled [dɪs'eɪbld] (körper)behin-
dert 5 (97)

°**discover** [dɪ'skʌvə] entdecken

°**discuss** [dɪ'skʌs] diskutieren

discussion [dɪ'skʌʃn] Diskussion 4 (76)

dive [daɪv]: **1.** einen Kopfsprung
machen 5 (96) °**2.** (ein)tauchen

do [duː] machen, tun 2 (38) **do
sport** Sport treiben 4 (74) **she
doesn't like** sie mag nicht 3 (54)
°**what do we see?** was sehen wir?

°**documentary** [dɒkju'mentri]
Dokumentarfilm

dog [dɒg] Hund (12)

done [dʌn]: **Well done.** Gut
gemacht! 5 (101) °**the holidays
are done** die Ferien sind vorbei

donkey ['dɒnki] Esel 4 (72)

door [dɔː] Tür 2 (45)

°**dossier** ['dɒsieɪ] Mappe, Dossier

°**double circle** [dʌbl 'sɜːkl] Doppel-
kreis

down [daʊn]: **down the hill**
den Hügel hinunter 3 (63)

downstairs [daʊn'steəz]
(nach) unten (*die Treppe
hinunter*) 2 (36/201)

drama ['drɑːmə] Schauspiel,
darstellende Kunst 1 (21)

°**draw** [drɔː] zeichnen

dream [driːm] Traum 2 (39)

drink [drɪŋk]: **1.** Getränk 4 (77)
2. trinken 4 (77/212)

drums [drʌmz] Schlagzeug;
Trommeln 5 (97)

duck [dʌk] Ente 4 (72)

°**during the winter** ['djʊərɪŋ]
während des Winters, im Winter

°**DVD** [diː viː 'diː] DVD

E

°**each** [iːtʃ] jede(r, s) (einzel-
ne) **each other** einander, sich
(gegenseitig) **one sentence
each** jeweils ein(en) Satz

early ['ɜːli] früh 3 (58)

easy ['iːzi] einfach, leicht 2 (41)

eat [iːt] essen; fressen 2 (42)
°**eat in** im Restaurant essen
(= *nicht mitnehmen*)

°**egg** [eg] Ei

eight [eɪt] acht (8)

elephant ['elɪfənt] Elefant (12)

eleven [ɪ'levən] elf (8)

else [els]: **Would you like anything else?** Möchten Sie sonst
noch etwas? 5 (94)

email ['iːmeɪl] E-Mail 4 (81)

end [end]: **1.** Ende 2 (35)
°**2.** enden

°**ending** ['endɪŋ] Endung; Ende

England ['ɪŋglənd] England (8)

English ['ɪŋglɪʃ] Englisch;
englisch 1 (18)

°**enjoy** [ɪn'dʒɔɪ] genießen

°**e-pal** [pæl] E-Mail-Freund/in

°**erm** [ɜːm] äh

evening ['iːvnɪŋ] Abend 3 (54)
in the evening abends, am
Abend 3 (54)

every ['evri] jede(r, s) 1 (21)

everybody ['evribɒdi] jeder,
alle 3 (54)

°**everything** ['evriθɪŋ] alles

°**example** [ɪg'zɑːmpl] Beispiel
for example zum Beispiel

excited [ɪk'saɪtɪd] aufgeregt,
gespannt 3 (62)

exciting [ɪk'saɪtɪŋ] aufregend 6 (117)

Excuse me, ... [ɪks'kjuːz miː] Entschuldigung, ... / Entschuldigen
Sie, ... 3 (65)

exercise ['eksəsaɪz] Übung,
Aufgabe 1 (26)

exercise book ['eksəsaɪz
bʊk] (Schul-)Heft 1 (26)

expensive [ɪkˈspensɪv] teuer 3 (55)

°experience [ɪkˈspɪərɪəns] erfahren, erleben

°explain [ɪkˈspleɪn] erklären

°eye [aɪ] Auge

F

face [feɪs] Gesicht 5 (100)

fall [fɔːl] fallen; hinfallen 3 (63)

false [fɔːls] falsch, unrichtig 5 (101)

family [ˈfæməli] Familie 2 (36)

family tree [ˈfæməli ˈtriː] Familienstammbaum 2 (37)

farm [fɑːm] Bauernhof, Farm 4 (72)

fast [fɑːst] schnell 3 (63)

father [ˈfɑːðə] Vater 2 (34)

favourite [ˈfeɪvərɪt] Lieblings- (10) favourite colour Lieblingsfarbe (10)

February [ˈfebruəri] Februar 3 (56)

fed up [fed ˈʌp] **feel fed up** genervt sein, sauer sein; die Nase voll haben 4 (76)

feed [fiːd] füttern 4 (74)

feel [fiːl] sich fühlen; fühlen 4 (76)

feeling [ˈfiːlɪŋ] Gefühl 4 (76)

ferry [ˈferi] Fähre 5 (93)

field [fiːld] Feld; Weide 4 (72) **in the field** auf der Weide 4 (72)

°fill in [fɪl ˈɪn] ausfüllen

film [fɪlm] Film 3 (66)

find [faɪnd] finden 4 (80) °**find out** herausfinden

fine [faɪn] gut, in Ordnung; schön 1 (28) **I'm fine.** Mir geht es gut. 1 (28)

°finger [ˈfɪŋgə] Finger

°finish [ˈfɪnɪʃ]: **1.** beenden, enden **2.** Ende, Ziel

fire station [ˈfaɪə steɪʃn] Feuerwache 3 (52)

firefighter [ˈfaɪəfaɪtə] Feuerwehrmann, Feuerwehrfrau 3 (58)

first [fɜːst]: **1.** erste(r, s) 1 (17) **2.** zuerst, als Erstes 3 (54) **the first morning** der erste Morgen 1 (17)

fish [fɪʃ] Fisch(e) (10)

°fisherman, pl fishermen [ˈfɪʃəmən] Fischer/in, Angler/in

five [faɪv] fünf (8)

flat [flæt] Wohnung 2 (34) **block of flats** Mehrfamilienhaus, Wohnblock 2 (34)

°flavour [ˈfleɪvə] Geschmack, Geschmacksrichtung

°flour [ˈflaʊə] Mehl

fly [flaɪ] fliegen 6 (120)

°focus on language [ˈfəʊkəs ɒn ˈlæŋwɪdʒ] (etwa) Schwerpunkt: Sprache

follow [ˈfɒləʊ] folgen; verfolgen 6 (117)

food [fuːd] Essen, Lebensmittel; Futter 5 (99)

football [ˈfʊtbɔːl] Fußball (11)

for [fɔː], [fə] für 1 (25) **What's for homework?** Was haben wir als Hausaufgabe(n) auf? 2 (45) °**for example** zum Beispiel °**for one minute** eine Minute lang

forget [fəˈget] vergessen 6 (113)

forgot [fəˈgɒt]: **I forgot my homework.** Ich habe meine Hausaufgaben vergessen. 2 (45)

°form [fɔːm] Form

four [fɔː] vier (8)

France [frɑːns] Frankreich 5 (93)

free [friː] frei 3 (57) **It's free.** Es ist kostenlos/umsonst. 5 (97)

French [frentʃ] Französisch; französisch 1 (21)

fresh [freʃ] frisch 6 (118)

Friday [ˈfraɪdeɪ], [ˈfraɪdi] Freitag 1 (21)

friend [frend] Freund/in 1 (18)

friendly [ˈfrendli] freundlich 4 (79)

frisbee [ˈfrɪzbi] Frisbee (13)

from [frɒm] von, aus (8) **from Monday to Friday** von Montag bis Freitag 2 (43) **Where are you from?** Wo kommst du her? (8)

front [frʌnt]: **in front of** vor 5 (102)

fruit [fruːt] Obst 4 (79)

full [fʊl] voll 3 (54)

fun [fʌn] Spaß (13) **she's fun** es macht Spaß, mit ihr zusammenzusein 2 (37) **it's fun** es macht Spaß (13)

°fur [fɜː] Fell (Tiere)

furry [ˈfɜːri] flauschig; pelzig 4 (78)

°fuss [fʌs]: **make a fuss** Theater/Wirbel machen

°future [ˈfjuːtʃə] Zukunft

G

game [geɪm] Spiel (9)

°gap [gæp] Lücke

garage [ˈgærɑːʒ] Garage 2 (35) **garage sale** Garagenflohmarkt (privater Flohmarkt) 3 (64)

garden [ˈgɑːdn] Garten 2 (34)

geography [dʒiˈɒgrəfi] Geografie, Erdkunde 1 (21)

German [ˈdʒɜːmən] deutsch; Deutsch 1 (21)

Germany [ˈdʒɜːməni] Deutschland (8)

get [get] bekommen 3 (56)

get up [get ˈʌp] aufstehen 3 (58)

°gibbon [ˈgɪbən] Gibbon (Affe)

girl [gɜːl] Mädchen 1 (16)

girlfriend [ˈgɜːlfrend] (feste) Freundin 5 (100)

give [gɪv] geben 1 (26)

°glass [glɑːs] Glas

glasses (pl) [ˈglɑːsɪz] (eine) Brille 6 (112)

go [gəʊ] gehen; fahren (13) **Go to sleep!** Schlaf jetzt! 4 (82) **go with** passen zu, gehören zu 2 (45) **How's it going?** Wie geht's? / Wie läuft's? 5 (94) **I must go.** (am Telefon) Ich muss Schluss machen. 5 (94)

°go to gehen/fahren nach

°goat [gəʊt] Ziege

going to [ˈgəʊɪŋ tə]: **I'm going to bring …** ich werde … mitbringen 6 (112)

°goldfish [ˈgəʊldfɪʃ] Goldfisch/e

good [gʊd] gut 1 (17) **Good morning.** Guten Morgen. 1 (18)

good value [ˈvæljuː]: **It's good value.** Es ist sein Geld wert. / Es ist preiswert. 3 (65)

Goodbye. [gʊdˈbaɪ] Auf Wiedersehen! (14)

grandfather [ˈgrænfɑːðə] Großvater 2 (37)

grandma [ˈgrænmɑː] Oma 2 (37)

grandmother [ˈgrænmʌðə] Großmutter 2 (37)

grandpa [ˈgrænpɑː] Opa 2 (37)

grandparents [ˈgrænpeərənts] Großeltern 2 (37)

granny [ˈgræni] Oma 6 (120)

great [greɪt] toll, großartig (10)

green [griːn] grün (10)

grey [greɪ] grau (10)

°groom [gruːm] striegeln

group [gruːp]: **1.** Gruppe 5 (97) °**2.** gruppieren

guess [ges] (er)raten 3 (66)

°guinea pig [ˈgɪni pɪg] Meerschweinchen

guitar [gɪˈtɑː] Gitarre 5 (97)

guy [gaɪ] Typ, Kerl 1 (25) **guys** Leute (Anrede) 1 (25)

H

had [hæd], [həd]: **I had** ich hatte; ich habe gehabt 5 (100)

half [hɑːf] halbe(r, s) 1 (26) **half past 6** halb 7 4 (74) °**half a teaspoon** ein halber Teelöffel

half-brother [ˈhɑːf brʌðə] Halbbruder 2 (37)

half-sister [ˈhɑːf sɪstə] Halbschwester 2 (37/202)

hall [hɔːl] Flur, Diele 2 (34)

°**Halloween** [hæləʊˈiːn] Halloween
(Tag vor Allerheiligen)

hamster [ˈhæmstə] Hamster (12)

°**hand** [hænd] Hand

°**handle sth.** [ˈhændl] mit etwas
umgehen

happen [ˈhæpən] geschehen,
passieren 4 (83)

happy [ˈhæpi] glücklich,
froh 1 (24) **Happy birthday!** Herzlichen Glückwunsch
zum Geburtstag! 3 (62)

harbour [ˈhɑːbə] Hafen 5 (92)

hard [hɑːd] schwer, schwierig;
hart 3 (63) °**work hard** hart
arbeiten

has [hæz], [həz]: **it has** es (er, sie)
hat (13)

hat [hæt] Hut, Mütze 6 (112)

hate [heɪt] hassen 3 (55)

have [hæv] haben (12) **Have a
good day.** Ich wünsche dir einen
schönen Tag. / Schönen Tag
(noch). 1 (17) **have breakfast**
frühstücken 3 (55) **have lunch**
(zu) Mittag essen 3 (55) **I had**
ich hatte; ich habe gehabt 5 (100)

he [hiː] er 1 (18) **he's (= he is)**
er ist 1 (18)

°**heading** [ˈhedɪŋ] Überschrift

°**headlight** [ˈhedlaɪt] Schein-
werfer(licht)

hear [hɪə] hören 4 (82)

Hello. [həˈləʊ] Hallo. (14)

helmet [ˈhelmɪt] Helm 3 (65)

help [help]: **1.** helfen (14/193)
2. Hilfe (14)

her [hɜː], [hə] sie; ihr 4 (81)
°**you like her** du magst sie
(weibliche Person)

her father [hɜː] ihr Vater 2 (34)

here [hɪə] hier; hierher 1 (17)
Here you are. Bitte schön. /
Hier, bitte. 1 (28)

Hi. [haɪ] Hallo. (8) **Say hi to
everybody.** Grüß alle. 5 (94)

hide [haɪd] verstecken; sich
verstecken 5 (96)

high school [ˈhaɪ skuːl] *(GB etwa:)*
Gesamtschule 2 (36)

hill [hɪl] Hügel 3 (63)

him [hɪm] ihm, ihn 3 (58)

his [hɪz] sein/e *(zu „he")* 2 (36)

history [ˈhɪstri] Geschichte 1 (21)

hobby [ˈhɒbi] Hobby (11)

hole punch [ˈhəʊl pʌntʃ]
Locher 1 (26)

holiday [ˈhɒlədeɪ] Urlaub (14)
holidays Ferien (14)

home [həʊm]: **1.** Heim, Zuhause 1 (24) **2.** nach Hause 3 (58)
at home zu Hause 1 (24)

°**home-made** [həʊmˈmeɪd] haus-
gemacht, selbstgemacht

homework [ˈhəʊmwɜːk] Hausauf-
gabe(n) 1 (24) **do your homework** Hausaufgaben machen 2 (38)
I forgot my homework. Ich
habe meine Hausaufgaben
vergessen. 2 (45) **What's for
homework?** Was haben wir
als Hausaufgabe(n) auf? 2 (45)

hoodie [ˈhʊdi] Kapuzenpullover
3 (55)

hope [həʊp] hoffen 1 (24)

°**horse** [hɔːs] Pferd

hospital [ˈhɒspɪtl] Krankenhaus
3 (63)

hot [hɒt] heiß 6 (118)

°**hour** [ˈaʊə] Stunde

house [haʊs] Haus 2 (34)

how [haʊ] wie (8) **How are you?**
Wie geht's? / Wie geht es dir/
euch/Ihnen? 1 (28) **How much
are …?** Was (Wie viel) kosten?
3 (65) **How much is …?** Was
(Wie viel) kostet? 3 (65) **How's
it going?** Wie geht's? / Wie
läuft's? 5 (94) °**how many?**
wie viele?

°**huh?** [hʌ] hm? / was?

hundred [ˈhʌndrəd]: **a hundred,
one hundred** (ein)hundert 3 (55)

hungry [ˈhʌŋgri]: **We're hungry.**
Wir haben Hunger. 1 (23)

hurry [ˈhʌri] sich beeilen; eilen 4 (82)

°**hyena** [haɪˈiːnə] Hyäne

I

I [aɪ] ich (8) **I'm (= I am)** ich bin (8)

ice cream [aɪs ˈkriːm] (Speise-)
Eis 6 (118)

**ICT (Information and Communi-
cation technology)** [aɪ siː ˈtiː],
[ɪnfəmeɪʃn ənd kəmjuːnɪˈkeɪʃn
teknɒlədʒi] Informations- und
Kommunikationstechnologie 1 (20)

idea [aɪˈdɪə] Idee 1 (25)

idiot [ˈɪdiət] Idiot/in 4 (78)

°**I'll** [aɪl] ich werde

°**imagine sth.** [ɪˈmædʒɪn] sich
etwas vorstellen

important [ɪmˈpɔːtnt] wichtig 1 (24)

in [ɪn] in (8) **in English** auf Englisch 1 (27) **in love (with)** verliebt
(in) 2 (43) **in the afternoon** am
Nachmittag 3 (54) **in the country** auf dem Land 4 (81) **in the
evening** abends, am
Abend 3 (54) **in the field** auf der
Weide 4 (72) **in the middle** in
der Mitte 5 (92) **in the morning** morgens, am Morgen 3 (54)
in the photo auf dem Foto 2 (34)
in the picture auf dem Bild 1 (16)
in town in der Stadt 2 (43)

°**included** [ɪnˈkluːdɪd] eingeschlos-
sen, inbegriffen

information [ɪnfəˈmeɪʃn] Informa-
tion(en) 4 (72) **information
desk** Informationsstand 4 (72)

inline skates [ɪnlaɪn ˈskeɪts]
Inlineskates (13)

inside [ɪnˈsaɪd] drinnen; nach
drinnen 4 (74)

instrument [ˈɪnstrəmənt] Instrument
5 (97)

interesting [ˈɪntrəstɪŋ] interessant 4 (80)

interview [ˈɪntəvjuː] Interview 1 (28)

into [ˈɪntu], [ˈɪntə] in: in (… hinein)
2 (36)

invitation (to) [ɪnvɪˈteɪʃn] Einladung
(zu, nach) 4 (85)

invite (to) [ɪnˈvaɪt] einladen (zu,
nach) 4 (81)

is [ɪz] *(er/sie/es)* ist (10) **The
calculator is £ 1.** Der Taschenrechner kostet 1 Pfund. 3 (64)

it [ɪt] er, sie, es (13) **it's (= it
is)** es ist *(bei Dingen und Tieren
auch: er ist, sie ist)* (13)

J

jam [dʒæm] Marmelade 5 (104)

January [ˈdʒænjuəri] Januar 3 (56)

job [dʒɒb] Job, (Arbeits-)stelle 3 (61)

join a club [dʒɔɪn] sich einem
Klub anschließen; in einen Klub
eintreten 5 (97)

juice [dʒuːs] Saft 5 (94)

July [dʒuˈlaɪ] Juli 3 (56)

°**jump up** [dʒʌmp ˈʌp] hochspringen

June [dʒuːn] Juni 3 (56)

°**just** [dʒʌst] nur, bloß

K

°**keep** [kiːp] aufbewahren, (be)halten

°**kick-off** [ˈkɪkɒf] Anstoß *(beim
Fußballspiel)*

kid [kɪd] Kind, Jugendliche/r 3 (59)

kiss [kɪs] Kuss 5 (103)

kitchen ['kɪtʃɪn] Küche 2 (34)
°**kitten** ['kɪtn] Kätzchen, Katzen-
baby
know [nəʊ] wissen; kennen 1 (24)

L

lab [læb] Labor 1 (20)
°**label** ['leɪbl] Etikett, Schild(chen)
lamp [læmp] Lampe 2 (39)
language ['læŋgwɪdʒ] Sprache
5 (103) °**language file** Anhang
zum Thema Sprache
°**large** [lɑːdʒ] groß
last [lɑːst] letzte(r, s) (14)
late [leɪt] spät 3 (58)
later ['leɪtə] später 3 (58) **See you
later.** Bis später. 1 (27)
laugh [lɑːf] lachen 4 (81) **they
laughed** sie lachten; sie haben
gelacht 5 (100) **with a laugh**
mit einem Lachen 4 (82)
lazy ['leɪzi] faul 3 (59)
learn [lɜːn] lernen 5 (97) °**I do
lots and lots of learnin'** (etwa)
ich lerne unheimlich viel
°**learner log** ['lɜːnə lɒg] Lern-Tage-
buch
leave [liːv] (jemanden) verlassen;
weggehen 5 (95) °**leave out**
weglassen
left [left] links; nach links 4 (84)
on the left links, auf der linken
Seite 5 (92)
leg [leg] Bein 3 (63) **I have a sore
leg.** Mein Bein tut weh. 3 (63)
lesson ['lesn] (Unterrichts-)Stun-
de 1 (20)
Let's ... [lets] Lass(t) uns ... 3 (62)
letter ['letə] **1.** Brief 5 (95)
°**2.** Buchstabe
life, pl **lives** [laɪf], [laɪvz] (das)
Leben, (die) Leben 3 (58)
like [laɪk] mögen (10) **I don't
like ...** ich mag ... nicht (10)
I like watching TV. Ich sehe
gern fern. (11) **I'd like ...
(= I would like)** Ich hätte gern
... / Ich möchte ... 5 (94)
like [laɪk] wie 6 (112) **What's it
like?** Wie ist es? / Wie sieht es
aus? 2 (44) °**like this** so, auf diese
Art °**sentences like this** solche
Sätze (wie diese hier)
°**line** [laɪn] Zeile
°**list** [lɪst] Liste
listen (to) ['lɪsn] (sich etwas)
anhören; zuhören (13)
little ['lɪtl] klein 5 (98)
live [lɪv] leben, wohnen 2 (34)

lives [laɪvz] Plural von **life** 3 (58)
°**living room** ['lɪvɪŋ ruːm] Wohnzimmer 2 (34)
°**llama** ['lɑːmə] Lama
lonely ['ləʊnli] einsam 2 (42)
°**long** [lɒŋ] lang
look [lʊk] **1.** aussehen 3 (63)
2. sehen, schauen 1 (25)
look after sich kümmern um;
aufpassen auf 4 (74) **Look at the
sweets!** Sieh/Schau dir die
Süßigkeiten an! (10) **look for**
suchen; Ausschau halten nach
4 (82) °**look up a word** ein Wort
nachschlagen
lose [luːz] verlieren 3 (63) **lose
control** die Kontrolle verlieren
3 (63)
lost [lɒst]: **I'm not lost.** Ich habe
mich nicht verlaufen/verirrt. 1 (20)
lots [lɒts]: **lots of** viel/e 2 (43)
°**there's lots around** es gibt viel
love [lʌv]: **1.** Liebe 2 (43) **2.** lieben,
sehr mögen (10)
**I'd love to come. (= I would
love to come.)** Ich komme sehr
gern. / Ich würde sehr gern
kommen. 4 (85) **in love (with)**
verliebt (in) 2 (43)
lucky ['lʌki]: **you're lucky** du hast
Glück 2 (36)
lunch [lʌntʃ] Mittagessen 1 (21)
have lunch (zu) Mittag essen 3 (55)

M

madhouse ['mædhaʊs] Irrenhaus
2 (36)
make [meɪk] machen, herstellen
3 (54) **make a difference** etwas
bewirken, etwas ausmachen 5 (100)
°**make him laugh** ihn zum Lachen
bringen
°**I make her purr** ich bringe sie
zum Schnurren
man, pl **men** [mæn], [men] Mann,
Männer 3 (65)
°**many** [haʊ 'meni]: **how many?**
wie viele?
map [mæp] Landkarte, Stadtplan 6 (117)
March [mɑːtʃ] März 3 (56)
market ['mɑːkɪt] Markt 3 (53)
°**match with** ['mætʃ wɪð] zuordnen
maths [mæθs] Mathe(matik) 1 (21)
May [meɪ] Mai 3 (56)
maybe ['meɪbi] vielleicht 5 (92)
me [miː] mich; mir 1 (19) **It's me.**
Ich bin's. (14)
mean [miːn] gemein, fies 2 (40)

mean [miːn]: **1.** bedeuten 5 (97)
2. meinen (sagen wollen) 5 (103)
°**meat** [miːt] Fleisch
°**mediation** [miːdi'eɪʃn] Vermitt-
lung,
Sprachmittlung
meet [miːt] kennenlernen; treffen
(8) **Nice to meet you.** Freut mich,
dich/euch/Sie kennenzulernen. (8)
men [men] Plural von **man** 3 (65)
message ['mesɪdʒ] Nachricht,
Mitteilung 6 (117) **message in
a bottle** Flaschenpost 6 (117)
messy ['mesi] unordentlich 2 (38)
middle ['mɪdl] Mitte 5 (92) **in
the middle** in der Mitte 5 (92)
°**milk** [mɪlk] Milch
°**milkman,** pl **milkmen** ['mɪlkmən]
Milchmann, Milchmänner
°**mime** [maɪm] pantomimisch
darstellen
mind map ['maɪnd mæp] Gedankenkarte, Wörternetz, Mindmap 2 (44)
minute ['mɪnɪt] Minute 6 (117)
mirror ['mɪrə] Spiegel 2 (39)
miss [mɪs]: **1.** vermissen 2 (36)
°**2.** fehlen
Miss Borowski [mɪs] Frau Borowski
(Anrede für unverheiratete Frauen)
1 (24)
°**missing** ['mɪsɪŋ]: **the missing letters** die fehlenden Buchstaben
°**mistake** [mɪ'steɪk] Fehler
°**mix** [mɪks] (ver)mischen
mobile (phone) [məʊbaɪl
'fəʊn] Handy 1 (16)
modern ['mɒdn] modern 2 (34)
moment ['məʊmənt] Moment 5 (95)
at the moment im Moment,
gerade 5 (95)
Monday ['mʌndeɪ], ['mʌndi]
Montag 1 (21)
money ['mʌni] Geld 3 (64)
monkey ['mʌŋki] Affe (12)
month [mʌnθ] Monat 3 (56)
more [mɔː] mehr, weitere 3 (54)
morning ['mɔːnɪŋ] Morgen 1 (17)
Good morning. Guten Morgen.
1 (18) **in the morning**
morgens, am Morgen 3 (54)
mother ['mʌðə] Mutter 2 (34)
mouth [maʊθ] Mund 4 (77)
MP3 player [empiː'θriː pleɪə]
MP3-Player (13)
Mr Brown [mɪstə] Herr Brown 1 (23)
Mrs Ford ['mɪsɪz] Frau Ford (Anrede für verheiratete Frauen) 1 (23)

Ms Lee [mɪz], [məz] Frau Lee (all-gemeine Anrede für Frauen) 1 (18)

much [mʌtʃ]: **How much is / How much are …?** Was (Wie viel) kostet / Was (Wie viel) kosten …? 3 (65)

mum [mʌm] Mama, Mutti 2 (36)

museum [mju'ziːəm] Museum 3 (52)

music ['mjuːzɪk] Musik (11)

musical ['mjuːzɪkl] Musical 6 (115)

musician [mju'zɪʃn] Musiker/in 5 (97)

must [mʌst] müssen 5 (94)
I mustn't forget … ich darf … nicht vergessen 6 (114) **I must go.** (am Telefon) Ich muss Schluss machen. 5 (94)

my [maɪ] mein/e (10)

myself [maɪ'self]: **for myself** für mich selbst 4 (77)

N

name [neɪm]: **1.** Name (8) °**2.** (be)nennen
What's your name? Wie heißt du? (8)

°**narrator** [nə'reɪtə] Erzähler/in

near [nɪə] nahe (bei), in der Nähe von 1 (18)

need [niːd] brauchen, benötigen 1 (25)

negative ['negətɪv] negativ 1 (22)

nervous ['nɜːvəs] nervös, aufgeregt 4 (81)

network ['netwɜːk] Netz; Wortnetz 1 (27)

never ['nevə] nie, niemals 3 (54)

new [njuː] neu (13)

news [njuːz] Nachrichten 2 (42)

°**newspaper** ['njuːzpeɪpə] Zeitung

next [nekst] nächste(r, s) 1 (28)
Next, please. Der/Die Nächste, bitte. 5 (94)

next to ['nekst tə] neben 5 (102)

nice [naɪs] nett, schön (8) **Nice to meet you.** Freut mich, dich/euch/Sie kennenzulernen. (8)

night [naɪt] Nacht 3 (58) **at night** nachts, in der Nacht 3 (58)

nine [naɪn] neun (8)

no [nəʊ]: **1.** kein, keine 1 (18)
2. nein (14)

°**nobody** ['nəʊbədi] niemand

noise [nɔɪz] Geräusch; Lärm 2 (42)

noisy ['nɔɪzi] laut, voller Lärm 2 (38)

normal ['nɔːml] normal 3 (58)

not [nɒt]: **I'm not a boy.** Ich bin kein Junge. 1 (18) **I'm not ten.** Ich bin nicht zehn. 1 (18)

°**note** [nəʊt] Notiz **make notes** sich Notizen machen **Take notes.** Mach dir Notizen.

nothing ['nʌθɪŋ] nichts 5 (100)

°**notice board** ['nəʊtɪs bɔːd] Anschlagtafel, Schwarzes Brett

November [nəʊ'vembə] November 3 (56)

now [naʊ] nun, jetzt 1 (20)

number ['nʌmbə] Zahl, Ziffer, Nummer (11)

nut [nʌt] Nuss 4 (79)

O

o'clock [ə'klɒk]: **at 1 o'clock** um 1 Uhr / um 13 Uhr 3 (57)

October [ɒk'təʊbə] Oktober 3 (56)

°**odd word out** [ɒd wɜːd 'aʊt] Wort, das nicht zu den anderen passt

of [ɒv], [əv]: **the last day of the holidays** der letzte Tag der Ferien / der letzte Ferientag (14)

°**of course** [əv 'kɔːs] natürlich, selbstverständlich

°**off to bed** [ɒf] ab ins Bett

often ['ɒfn], ['ɒftən] oft 3 (52)

°**oh** [əʊ] Null

OK [əʊ'keɪ] okay, gut, in Ordnung 2 (36)

old [əʊld] alt (8)

omelette ['ɒmlət] Omelett 5 (94)

on [ɒn] auf (13) **on 1st March** am 1. März 3 (57) **on Monday** am Montag 1 (21) **on the beach** am Strand 2 (44) **on the bus** im Bus 4 (81) **on the phone** am Telefon 5 (99) **on the way to …** auf dem Weg zu/nach … 5 (100)

one [wʌn] eins (8) °**one way** eine Strecke (= ohne Rückfahrt)

only ['əʊnli] nur, bloß 4 (82)

only ['əʊnli]: **the only student** der einzige Schüler / die einzige Schülerin 4 (77)

open ['əʊpən]: **1.** öffnen; aufschlagen (Buch) 3 (62) °**2.** offen, geöffnet

°**option** ['ɒpʃn] Wahl(möglichkeit), Option

or [ɔː] oder; sonst 3 (54)

orange ['ɒrɪndʒ]: **1.** orange (10) **2.** Orange, Apfelsine 6 (112)

°**orange juice** ['ɒrɪndʒ dʒuːs] Orangensaft

°**order** ['ɔːdə] Reihenfolge **put in the right order** in die richtige Reihenfolge bringen

°**organize** ['ɔːgənaɪz] ordnen; organisieren

other ['ʌðə] andere(r, s) 3 (54)

our ['aʊə] unser/e (11)

out [aʊt]: **school is out** die Schule ist aus/vorbei 6 (110)

out of … ['aʊt əv] aus … (heraus/hinaus) 6 (119)

°**outdoors** [aʊt'dɔːz] im Freien, draußen 3 (61)

°**outside** [aʊt'saɪd] draußen; nach draußen 4 (74)

°**oven** ['ʌvn] Backofen

over ['əʊvə]: **be over** vorbei sein, zu Ende sein 1 (24)

over there [əʊvə 'ðeə] da drüben, dort drüben 6 (119)

°**owl** [aʊl] Eule

°**own** [əʊn]: **your own sentences** deine eigenen Sätze

P

p [piː]: **50p** fünfzig Pence 3 (64)

page (= p.) [peɪdʒ] (Buch-, Heft-) Seite 2 (45) **What page is it?** Auf welcher Seite sind wir? / Auf welcher Seite steht das? 2 (45)

°**pair** [peə] Paar

paper ['peɪpə] Papier 1 (25) °**piece of paper** Stück Papier, Zettel

parents ['peərənts] Eltern 2 (37)

park [pɑːk] Park (13)

°**parrot** ['pærət] Papagei

°**part** [pɑːt] Teil

partner ['pɑːtnə] Partner/in 2 (34)

party ['pɑːti] Party 3 (56) **have a party** eine Party feiern 3 (56)

past [pɑːst]: **half past 6** halb 7 4 (74) **quarter past 6** viertel nach 6 4 (74)

PE (physical education) [piː 'iː], [fɪzɪkl edʒu'keɪʃn] (Schul-)Sport 1 (20)

°**peahen** ['piːhen] Pfauhenne, weiblicher Pfau

pen [pen] Kugelschreiber, Stift; Füller 1 (26)

pencil ['pensl] Bleistift 1 (26)

pencil case ['pensl keɪs] Federmäppchen 1 (26)

pencil sharpener ['pensl ʃɑːpnə] Bleistiftanspitzer 1 (26)

°**penguin** ['peŋgwɪn] Pinguin

people ['piːpl] Leute, Menschen 1 (23)

°**per** [pɜː]: **per person** pro Person

person ['pɜːsn] Person 4 (76)

pet [pet] (Haus-)Tier (12)

phone [fəʊn]: **1.** anrufen 5 (96) **2.** Telefon 2 (46)
on the phone am Telefon 5 (99)
phone number ['fəʊn nʌmbə] Telefonnummer 2 (46)
photo ['fəʊtəʊ] Foto 2 (34)
phrase [freɪz] Ausdruck, (Rede-)Wendung 1 (27)
piano [pi'ænəʊ] Klavier 5 (97)
°**pick** [pɪk] (aus)wählen
°**pick up** [pɪk 'ʌp] aufheben
picnic ['pɪknɪk] Picknick 4 (85)
picture ['pɪktʃə] Bild 1 (16)
°**piece of paper** [piːs əv 'peɪpə] Stück Papier
pig [pɪg] Schwein 4 (73)
°**pinch** [pɪntʃ] zwicken
pink [pɪŋk] rosa (10)
pity ['pɪti]: **That's a pity.** Das ist schade. 6 (114)
pizza ['piːtsə] Pizza 6 (115)
place [pleɪs] Ort, Platz (10)
°**the place to go** der Ort, wo man hin muss
plan [plæn]: **1.** Plan 3 (62)
°**2.** planen
play [pleɪ] spielen (11) **play the guitar / the drums** Gitarre / Schlagzeug spielen 5 (97)
please [pliːz] bitte 1 (24)
pm [piː'em]: **5 pm** 5 Uhr nachmittags/abends, 17 Uhr 4 (85)
poem ['pəʊɪm] Gedicht 4 (86)
°**point** [pɔɪnt] Punkt
°**point (at)** [pɔɪnt] zeigen (auf)
°**polar bear** ['pəʊlə beə] Eisbär
police station [pə'liːs steɪʃn] Polizeiwache 3 (52)
pond [pɒnd] Teich 4 (72)
pony ['pəʊni] Pony (12)
°**Portugal** ['pɔːtʃʊgl] Portugal
positive ['pɒzətɪv] positiv 1 (22)
poster ['pəʊstə] Poster (11)
pound (£) [paʊnd] Pfund *(britische Währung)* 1 (26)
°**practice** ['præktɪs] Übung(en)
practise ['præktɪs] üben 6 (115)
prefer [prɪ'fɜː]: **I'd prefer …** ich würde … vorziehen 6 (110)
present ['preznt] Geschenk 3 (55)
°**pretty** ['prɪti] hübsch
price [praɪs] (Kauf-)Preis 1 (26)
principal ['prɪnsəpl] Rektor/in, Schulleiter/in 1 (24)
problem ['prɒbləm] Problem 2 (38)
programme ['prəʊgræm] (Fernseh-)Sendung 2 (42)
°**progress** ['prəʊgres] Fortschritt(e)
°**project** ['prɒdʒekt] Projekt

proud (of) [praʊd] stolz (auf) 5 (101)
pullover ['pʊləʊvə] Pullover 1 (24)
°**puppy** ['pʌpi] (Hunde-)Welpe
purple ['pɜːpl] violett, lila (10)
°**purr** [pɜː] schnurren *(Katze)*
push [pʊʃ] schieben 6 (118)
put [pʊt] *(etwas wohin)* tun, legen, stellen, stecken 6 (117)
°**put in** einsetzen °**put in the right order** in die richtige Reihenfolge bringen

Q

quarter ['kwɔːtə] Viertel 4 (74)
quarter past 6 viertel nach 6 4 (74) **quarter to 7** viertel vor 7 4 (74)
question ['kwestʃən] Frage 4 (72)
ask questions Fragen stellen 4 (72)
quick [kwɪk] schnell 6 (118)
quiet ['kwaɪət] ruhig, still, leise 2 (42) **Be quiet.** Sei still. / Sei leise. / Sei ruhig. 2 (42)
quiz [kwɪz] Quiz 1 (22)

R

rabbit ['ræbɪt] Kaninchen (12)
rap [ræp]: **1.** Rap 1 (21)
2. rappen 5 (97)
rapper ['ræpə] Rapper/in 5 (97)
rat [ræt] Ratte (12)
read [riːd] lesen (11) °**read your sentences to …** lies … deine Sätze vor
°**ready** ['redi] fertig, bereit **get ready (for)** sich fertig machen (für), sich vorbereiten (auf) 4 (74)
real [rɪəl] echt, wirklich 2 (36)
really ['riːəli], ['rɪəli] wirklich 2 (40)
recipe ['resəpi] (Koch-)Rezept 5 (104)
red [red] rot (10)
registration [redʒɪ'streɪʃn] *(etwa)* Anwesenheitskontrolle und Ankündigung aktueller Ereignisse vor dem Unterricht 1 (21)
remember [rɪ'membə]: **1.** daran denken, nicht vergessen 1 (24) **2.** sich erinnern (an) (12)
°**repeat** [rɪ'piːt] wiederholen
°**reporter** [rɪ'pɔːtə] Reporter/in
rest [rest] Pause, Rast 6 (118)
restaurant ['restrɒnt] Restaurant 2 (42)
°**revision** [rɪ'vɪʒn] Wiederholung *(von Lernstoff)*
ride [raɪd]: **1.** reiten (11) °**2.** Ritt, Ausritt
ride a bike/a BMX mit dem

Fahrrad/dem BMX-Rad fahren 1 (18)
right [raɪt] richtig 1 (21)
right [raɪt] rechts; nach rechts 4 (84/214) **on the right** rechts, auf der rechten Seite 5 (92)
ring [rɪŋ] läuten, klingeln 5 (94)
road [rəʊd] Straße *(Landstraße zwischen Orten; Straße in Orten)* 2 (34)
rock [rɒk] Fels(en) 5 (96)
°**role** [rəʊl] Rolle
room [ruːm], [rʊm] Raum, Zimmer 1 (20)
°**rub** [rʌb] (zer)reiben
rubber ['rʌbə] Radiergummi 1 (26)
°**rucksack** ['rʌksæk] Rucksack
rug [rʌg] Teppich, Läufer 2 (39)
°**rule** [ruːl] Regel
ruler ['ruːlə] Lineal 1 (26)
°**run** [rʌn] rennen

S

sad [sæd] traurig 2 (42)
said [sed]: **he said** er sagte; er hat gesagt 5 (100)
salad ['sæləd] Salat *(als Gericht oder Beilage)* 5 (94)
sale [seɪl] Verkauf; Schlussverkauf 3 (64)
°**salt** [sɔːlt] Salz
same [seɪm]: **the same** derselbe/dieselbe/dasselbe; dieselben 3 (65)
sand [sænd] Sand 6 (119)
°**sandcastle** ['sændkɑːsl] Sandburg
sandwich ['sænwɪtʃ], ['sænwɪdʒ] Sandwich 4 (81)
Saturday ['sætədeɪ], ['sætədi] Samstag 1 (21)
sausage ['sɒsɪdʒ] (Brat-, Bock-)Würstchen, Wurst 6 (112)
say [seɪ] sagen 1 (23) **Say hi to everybody.** Grüß alle. 5 (94) **he said** er sagte; er hat gesagt 5 (100)
°**Ellie says** Ellie sagt
scary ['skeəri] unheimlich, beängstigend, gruselig 6 (119)
scene [siːn] Szene 4 (81)
school [skuːl] Schule 1 (16)
school is out die Schule ist aus/vorbei 6 (110) **at school** in der Schule 1 (20)
school bag ['skuːl bæg] Schultasche 1 (27)
science ['saɪəns] Naturwissenschaft 1 (20)
scissors *(pl)* ['sɪzəz] *(eine)* Schere 1 (25)
scone [skɒn] Milchbrötchen *(leicht süß, oft mit Rosinen)* 5 (94)

scooter ['skuːtə] Scooter (kleiner, zusammenfaltbarer Tretroller) (13)

sea [siː] Meer, (die) See 2 (37)

the sea's coming in die Flut kommt; das Wasser steigt 6 (117)

seagull ['siːgʌl] Möwe (14)

seat [siːt] (Sitz-)Platz 5 (100)

second ['sekənd]: **1.** zweite(r, s) 3 (57) °**2.** Sekunde

see [siː] sehen (9) **See you later.** Bis später. 1 (27) °**See you.** Bis dann! Tschüs!

send [send] senden, schicken 1 (26)

°**sentence** ['sentəns] Satz

September [sep'tembə] September 3 (56)

set the table [set] den Tisch decken 5 (98)

seven ['sevn] sieben (8)

share [ʃeə] teilen 2 (38) **share a room with …** sich ein Zimmer mit … teilen 2 (38)

sharpener ['ʃɑːpnə] Anspitzer 1 (26)

she [ʃiː] sie (weibliche Person) 1 (18) **she's (= she is)** sie ist 1 (18)

sheep, pl **sheep** [ʃiːp] Schaf; Schafe 4 (73)

shelf, pl **shelves** [ʃelf], [ʃelvz] Regal, Regale 2 (39)

shirt [ʃɜːt] Hemd 1 (24)

shoe [ʃuː] Schuh 1 (24)

shop [ʃɒp] Laden, Geschäft 1 (26)

°**shop for sth.** ['ʃɒp fə] etwas kaufen (gehen)

shopping ['ʃɒpɪŋ]: **shopping centre** Einkaufszentrum 3 (53) **go shopping** einkaufen gehen 3 (54) °**shopping list** Einkaufsliste

°**short** [ʃɔːt] kurz

shorts (pl) [ʃɔːts] (eine) kurze Hose 6 (113)

shoulder ['ʃəʊldə] Schulter 4 (79)

show [ʃəʊ] zeigen 5 (101)

Shut up! (infml) [ʃʌt 'ʌp] Halt den Mund! 3 (62)

sight [saɪt] Anblick, Bild 1 (16)

sign [saɪn] Schild; Zeichen 4 (84)

sing [sɪŋ] singen 3 (60) °**sing along** mitsingen

singer ['sɪŋə] Sänger/in 5 (97)

sister ['sɪstə] Schwester 1 (18)

sit [sɪt] sitzen; sich setzen 4 (79)

six [sɪks] sechs (8)

skateboard ['skeɪtbɔːd]: **1.** Skateboard (13) **2.** Skateboard fahren (11)

°**skill** [skɪl] Fähigkeit, Fertigkeit; Lern- und Arbeitstechnik

skirt [skɜːt] Rock 1 (24)

sleep [sliːp] schlafen 3 (58) **Go to sleep!** Schlaf jetzt! 4 (82)

sleeping bag ['sliːpɪŋ bæg] Schlafsack 4 (81)

sleepover ['sliːpəʊvə] Schlafparty 4 (81)

slow [sləʊ] langsam 6 (118)

small [smɔːl] klein (13)

°**smeared** [smɪəd] verschmiert

smuggler ['smʌglə] Schmuggler/in 6 (117)

°**smuggling** ['smʌglɪŋ] (das) Schmuggeln

snake [sneɪk] Schlange (12)

so [səʊ] also, daher 3 (58)

°**so pretty** [səʊ] so hübsch

sock [sɒk] Socke 1 (24)

sofa ['səʊfə] Sofa 2 (34)

some [sʌm], [səm] einige, ein paar; etwas, ein wenig 5 (100)

something ['sʌmθɪŋ] etwas 3 (63)

sometimes ['sʌmtaɪmz] manchmal 3 (54)

song [sɒŋ] Lied (9)

soon [suːn] bald 2 (42)

sore [sɔː]: **I have a sore leg.** Mein Bein tut weh. 3 (63)

Sorry. / I'm sorry. ['sɒri] Tut mir leid. / Entschuldigung. 1 (24)

sound [saʊnd]: **1.** Geräusch; Klang, Laut 1 (16) °**2.** Ton (Fernseher, Radio)

soup [suːp] Suppe 5 (94)

space [speɪs] Platz 2 (36)

Spain [speɪn] Spanien 6 (120)

speak [spiːk] sprechen 4 (77)

speaker ['spiːkə]: **1.** Lautsprecher 6 (113) °**2.** Sprecher/in

special ['speʃl] besondere(r, s) 1 (26)

special offer [speʃl 'ɒfə] Sonderangebot 1 (26)

°**speech bubble** ['spiːtʃ bʌbl] Sprechblase

spell [spel] buchstabieren 2 (46)

°**spelling** ['spelɪŋ] Schreibweise, Rechtschreibung

sport [spɔːt] Sport; Sportart (11) **do sport** Sport treiben 4 (74)

sports hall ['spɔːts hɔːl] Sporthalle 1 (20)

square [skweə] Platz (in der Stadt) 6 (117)

start [stɑːt]: **1.** beginnen, anfangen 1 (22) °**2.** Anfang, Start

°**statement** ['steɪtmənt] Aussage(satz)

stay [steɪ] bleiben 3 (54)

°**step** [step] Schritt, Stufe

stepbrother ['stepbrʌðə] Stiefbruder 2 (36)

stepdad ['stepdæd] Stiefvater 2 (36)

stepfather ['stepfɑːðə] Stiefvater 2 (36)

stepmother ['stepmʌðə] Stiefmutter 2 (36)

stepmum ['stepmʌm] Stiefmutter 2 (36)

stepsister ['stepsɪstə] Stiefschwester 2 (36)

°**stick insect** ['stɪk ɪnsekt] Stabheuschrecke

°**stoat** [stəʊt] Hermelin

stop [stɒp]: **1.** (an)halten; aufhören (mit) 3 (58) °**2.** Pause; Unterbrechung

story ['stɔːri] Geschichte (14)

street [striːt] Straße (in Ortschaften) 2 (34)

strict [strɪkt] streng 2 (40)

stroke [strəʊk] streicheln 4 (72)

student ['stjuːdnt] Schüler/in; Student/in 1 (16)

studio ['stjuːdiəʊ] Studio 5 (97)

stupid ['stjuːpɪd] dumm, blöd (14)

°**sugar** ['ʃʊgə] Zucker

summer ['sʌmə] Sommer 3 (52)

sun [sʌn] Sonne 4 (74)

suncream ['sʌnkriːm] Sonnencreme 6 (112)

Sunday ['sʌndeɪ], ['sʌndi] Sonntag 1 (21)

sunglasses (pl) ['sʌnglɑːsɪz] (eine) Sonnenbrille 6 (112)

supermarket ['suːpəmɑːkɪt] Supermarkt 3 (54)

sure [ʃʊə], [ʃɔː] sicher 1 (28)

°**surfboard** ['sɜːfbɔːd] Surfbrett

surprise [sə'praɪz] Überraschung 2 (40)

°**swap** [swɒp] tauschen

sweatshirt ['swetʃɜːt] Sweatshirt 1 (24)

sweets (pl) [swiːts] Bonbons, Süßigkeiten (10)

swim [swɪm] schwimmen (11) **go swimming** schwimmen gehen 3 (56)

swimming pool ['swɪmɪŋ puːl] Schwimmbad 3 (52)

swimming trunks (pl) ['swɪmɪŋ trʌŋks] (eine) Badehose 6 (112)

swimsuit ['swɪmsuːt] Badeanzug 6 (112)

T

table ['teɪbl]: **1.** Tisch 2 (34) °**2.** Tabelle

set the table den Tisch decken 5 (98)

tae kwon do [taɪ kwɒn 'dəʊ] Taekwondo 1 (18)

take [teɪk] nehmen 3 (65) **take me to the theatre** mit mir ins Theater gehen 6 (115) **I'll take it.** Ich nehme es (ihn, sie). *(beim Einkaufen)* 3 (65) °**take the dog out** mit dem Hund rausgehen °**take away** mitnehmen *(Essen aus einem Restaurant)*

talk (to) [tɔːk] sprechen, reden (mit) (13)

tea [tiː] Tee 5 (94)

teacher ['tiːtʃə] Lehrer/in 1 (16)

team [tiːm] Team, Mannschaft 4 (77)

°**teaspoon** ['tiːspuːn] Teelöffel

technology [tek'nɒlədʒi] Technik (unterricht); Technologie 1 (21)

°**tell** [tel] erzählen, sagen

ten [ten] zehn (8)

tennis ['tenɪs] Tennis 5 (99)

terrible ['terəbl] schrecklich, fürchterlich 5 (100)

text [tekst]: **1.** SMS 5 (103) °**2.** Text **text me** mir eine SMS schicken 4 (76)

text message ['tekst mesɪdʒ] *(kurz auch:* **text)** SMS 5 (103)

textbook ['tekstbʊk] Schulbuch, Lehrbuch 1 (27)

°**than** [ðæn]: **more than** mehr als

thank you ['θæŋk juː] danke (schön) 1 (17)

thanks [θæŋks] danke (schön) 1 (17)

that [ðæt]: **1.** das (dort) 1 (24) °**2.** der, die, das *(Relativpronomen)* **that field** das Feld (dort), jenes Feld 4 (82) **That's £ 159.** Das macht 159 Pfund. 3 (65) °**one thing that I know** eine Sache, die ich weiß

°**that** [ðæt]: **imagine that …** stell dir vor, dass …

the [ðə] der, die, das (8)

theatre ['θɪətə] Theater 1 (25)

their [ðeə] ihr/e *(Plural)* 2 (36)

them [ðem], [ðəm] sie, ihnen 5 (98)

°**theme** [θiːm] Thema

theme park ['θiːm pɑːk] Themenpark *(Freizeitpark mit Attraktionen zu einem bestimmten Thema)* 6 (110)

then [ðen] dann, danach 3 (54)

there [ðeə] da, dort; dahin, dorthin 3 (54) **there are** es sind … / es gibt … 2 (34) **there's (= there is)** es ist … / es gibt … 2 (34)

these people [ðiːz] diese Leute (hier) 5 (101)

they [ðeɪ] sie *(Plural)* 1 (18) **they're (= they are)** sie sind 1 (18)

thing [θɪŋ] Ding, Sache (13)

think [θɪŋk] denken, meinen, glauben 1 (25) **he thought** er dachte; er hat gedacht 5 (101) **What do you think?** Was meinst du? / Was denkst du? 1 (25) °**think about** nachdenken über

third [θɜːd] dritte(r, s) 3 (57)

this [ðɪs] dies; diese(r, s) (14) **This is …** Dies ist … / Das ist … (14) **this time** dieses Mal 4 (82)

thought [θɔːt]: **he thought** er dachte; er hat gedacht 5 (101)

three [θriː] drei (8)

through [θruː] durch 4 (82)

Thursday ['θɜːzdeɪ], ['θɜːzdi] Donnerstag 1 (21)

°**tick** [tɪk]: **1.** ankreuzen, abhaken **2.** Häkchen

ticket ['tɪkɪt] Eintrittskarte, Fahrkarte 4 (73)

tie [taɪ] Krawatte 1 (24)

tiger ['taɪgə] Tiger (12)

tights *(pl)* [taɪts] *(eine)* Strumpfhose 1 (24)

time [taɪm] Zeit; Uhrzeit 1 (21) **What's the time?** Wie spät ist es? 4 (74)

time [taɪm]: **this time** dieses Mal 4 (82)

timetable ['taɪmteɪbl] Stundenplan 1 (21)

tired ['taɪəd] müde 2 (40) °**be tired of sth.** die Nase voll haben von etwas

°**title** ['taɪtl] Titel, Überschrift

to [tu], [tə] zu, nach (13) **to the cinema** ins Kino 3 (52) **time to eat** Zeit zu essen 4 (83) **from Monday to Friday** von Montag bis Freitag 2 (43) **quarter to 7** viertel vor 7 4 (74) °**to make her purr** um sie zum Schnurren zu bringen °**the place to go** der Ort, wo man hin muss

toast [təʊst] Toast 5 (99)

today [tə'deɪ] heute 3 (62)

together [tə'geðə] zusammen 3 (58)

toilet ['tɔɪlət] Toilette 2 (35)

°**tomorrow** [tə'mɒrəʊ] morgen

too [tuː] auch (11) **from Berlin too** auch aus Berlin (11)

too old [tuː] zu alt 2 (38)

top [tɒp]: **at the top** oben, am oberen Ende; an der Spitze 5 (102)

tour [tʊə]: **a tour of the school** ein Rundgang durch die Schule 1 (20)

tourist ['tʊərɪst] Tourist/in 6 (114)

towel ['taʊəl] Handtuch 6 (112)

town [taʊn] Stadt 2 (43)

°**tractor** ['træktə] Traktor

trainers *(pl)* ['treɪnəz] Sportschuhe 3 (55)

°**training** ['treɪnɪŋ] Training

trampoline ['træmpəliːn] Trampolin 4 (72)

tree [triː] Baum 2 (37)

trip [trɪp] Ausflug; Reise 6 (110)

trouble ['trʌbl] Ärger, Schwierigkeiten 1 (24) **Ellie is in trouble.** Ellie hat Ärger. / Ellie ist in Schwierigkeiten. 1 (24)

trousers *(pl)* ['traʊzəz] *(eine)* Hose 1 (24)

true [truː] wahr, richtig 5 (101)

try [traɪ] probieren, ausprobieren 3 (65)

°**T-shirt** ['tiː ʃɜːt] T-Shirt

tube [tjuːb] Schwimmreifen 6 (113)

Tuesday ['tjuːzdeɪ], ['tjuːzdi] Dienstag 1 (21)

Turkey ['tɜːki] *(die)* Türkei 6 (120)

turn [tɜːn]: **It's your turn.** Du bist dran. / Du bist an der Reihe. 2 (45) °**take turns** sich abwechseln

TV [tiː'viː] Fernseher (11)

twelve [twelv] zwölf (8)

two [tuː] zwei (8)

U

ugly ['ʌgli] hässlich 1 (25)

umbrella [ʌm'brelə] (Regen-)Schirm 6 (113)

uncle ['ʌŋkl] Onkel 2 (37)

under ['ʌndə] unter 5 (102)

understand [ʌndə'stænd] verstehen 4 (77)

unhappy [ʌn'hæpi] unglücklich 4 (81)

uniform ['juːnɪfɔːm] Uniform 1 (24)

unit ['juːnɪt] Lektion, Kapitel 1 (22) **unit quiz** Unit-Quiz 1 (22)

upstairs [ʌp'steəz] (nach) oben *(die Treppe hoch)* 2 (36)

us [ʌs], [əs] uns 3 (62)

°**USA** [juː es 'eɪ] USA

use [juːz] benutzen, verwenden 4 (86)

°**useful** ['juːsfl] nützlich

usually ['juːʒuəli] normalerweise, meistens 3 (54)

V

value ['vælju:]: **It's good value.** Es ist sein Geld wert. / Es ist preiswert. 3 (65)

vegetables (pl) ['vedʒtəblz] Gemüse 3 (54)

°**verse** [vɜːs] Vers, Strophe (Lied)

very ['veri] sehr 1 (25)

°**view** [vju:] anschauen

village ['vɪlɪdʒ] Dorf 1 (18)

visit ['vɪzɪt] besuchen 3 (56)

visitor ['vɪzɪtə] Besucher/in; Gast 4 (72)

°**vocabulary** [və'kæbjələri] Vokabelverzeichnis

W

wait [weɪt]: **wait (for)** warten (auf) 6 (112) **wait and see** abwarten 6 (112) °**I can't wait!** Ich kann es kaum erwarten!

wake [weɪk] wecken 4 (74)

wake up [weɪk 'ʌp] aufwachen 4 (82)

walk [wɔːk] wandern, (zu Fuß) gehen 5 (96) °**walk around** umhergehen

°**wall** [wɔːl] Wand, Mauer

want [wɒnt] wollen 3 (55) **want to be** etwas sein wollen 3 (61)

wardrobe ['wɔːdrəʊb] Kleiderschrank 2 (39)

was [wɒz], [wəz] war 5 (100) **he wasn't (= was not)** er war nicht 5 (101) **it was Friday** es war Freitag 5 (100)

wash up [wɒʃ 'ʌp] abwaschen 5 (94)

watch [wɒtʃ] sich etwas anschauen; beobachten 2 (42) **watch TV** fernsehen (11) **I like watching TV.** Ich sehe gern fern. (11)

water ['wɔːtə] Wasser 5 (94)

wave [weɪv] winken 5 (96)

way [weɪ]: **on the way to …** auf dem Weg zu/nach … 5 (100)

we [wi], [wiː] wir 1 (18) **we're (= we are)** wir sind 1 (18)

°**website** ['websaɪt] Website

Wednesday ['wenzdeɪ], ['wenzdi] Mittwoch 1 (21)

week [wiːk] Woche 2 (43)

weekend [wiːk'end] Wochenende 3 (52) **at the weekend** am Wochenende 3 (52)

welcome ['welkəm]: **Welcome to Plymouth.** Willkommen in Plymouth. (10)

welcome ['welkəm]: **You're welcome.** Bitte, gern geschehen. / Nichts zu danken. 4 (75)

well [wel]: **Well done.** Gut gemacht! 5 (101) **work/speak well** gut funktionieren/sprechen 4 (77)

Well, … [wel] Nun, …/ Also, …/ Na ja, … 1 (17)

were [wɜː], [wə]: **they were on the bus** sie waren im Bus 5 (100)

wet [wet] nass 4 (81)

what [wɒt]: **1.** was (8) **2.** welche(r, s) 2 (45) **What about you?** Und du? / Was ist mit dir? (11) **What are …?** Was sind …? (11) **What is it?** Was ist los? 2 (38) **What page is it?** Auf welcher Seite sind wir? / Auf welcher Seite steht das? 2 (45) **What's the time?** Wie spät ist es? 4 (74) **What's your name?** Wie heißt du? (8)

wheel [wiːl] Rad (13)

wheelchair ['wiːltʃeə] Rollstuhl 4 (77)

when [wen]: **1.** wann 3 (57) **2.** wenn 1 (26) **When's your birthday?** Wann hast du Geburtstag? 3 (57)

where [weə] wo; wohin (8) **Where are you from?** Wo kommst du her? (8)

°**which** [wɪtʃ] welche(r, s)

white [waɪt] weiß (10)

who [huː]: **1.** der, die (Relativpronomen, Person) 4 (80) **2.** wer 1 (18) °**3.** wem; wen **Who are you?** Wer bist du? / Wer seid ihr? 1 (18) **a person who** eine Person, die … 4 (80)

why [waɪ] warum 2 (36)

wild [waɪld] wild (12)

°**will** [wɪl]: **I will buy** ich werde kaufen

win [wɪn] gewinnen 4 (77)

window ['wɪndəʊ] Fenster 5 (99)

°**winter** ['wɪntə] Winter

wish [wɪʃ]: **Best wishes** Viele Grüße … (Briefschluss) 4 (85)

with [wɪð] mit (13) **with Ellie** bei Ellie 2 (34)

woman, pl **women** ['wʊmən], ['wɪmɪn] Frau, Frauen 5 (92)

word [wɜːd] Wort 1 (25)

°**wordbank** ['wɜːdbæŋk] Wortbank (Sammlung von Wörtern zu einem Thema)

work [wɜːk]: **1.** Arbeit 2 (42) **2.** arbeiten 2 (38) **3.** funktionieren 4 (76) **at work** bei der Arbeit, am Arbeitsplatz 2 (42) °**work hard** hart arbeiten

workday ['wɜːkdeɪ] Arbeitstag 3 (58)

workshop ['wɜːkʃɒp] Workshop (Kurs) 5 (97)

world [wɜːld] Welt 2 (42) **the best of both worlds** das Beste von beidem 2 (42)

worried ['wʌrid]: **be worried (about)** beunruhigt sein, besorgt sein (wegen) 4 (82)

worry ['wʌri]: **worry (about)** sich Sorgen machen (wegen, um) 4 (81) **Don't worry.** Mach dir keine Sorgen. 4 (81)

would [wʊd]: **I'd like … (= I would like)** Ich hätte gern … / Ich möchte … 5 (94) **I'd love to come. (= I would love to come.)** Ich komme sehr gern. / Ich würde sehr gern kommen. 4 (85) °**would be good** wäre gut

°**Wow!** [waʊ] Wow! / Mensch!

write [raɪt] schreiben 1 (24)

°**writer** ['raɪtə] Autor/in, Verfasser/in

wrong [rɒŋ] falsch 1 (21) °**she is wrong** sie hat Unrecht

Y

yeah (infml) [jeə] ja 3 (65)

year [jɪə] Jahr(gang) 3 (62)

yellow ['jeləʊ] gelb (10)

yes [jes] ja (14/193)

Yippee! [jɪ'piː] Hurra! (15)

you [ju], [juː] du; dich; dir; ihr; euch; Sie; Ihnen (8) **you're (= you are)** du bist; ihr seid; Sie sind (8)

young [jʌŋ] jung 5 (97)

your [jɔː], [jə] dein/e; euer/eure; Ihr/e (8)

yours [jɔːz] deine, deiner, deins 2 (38)

yourself [jɔː'self], [jə'self] du/dir/dich selbst 1 (19)

yum (infml) [jʌm] lecker 6 (115)

Z

°**zero** ['zɪərəʊ] Null

zip wire ['zɪp waɪə] Seilrutsche 4 (72)

zoo [zuː] Zoo 3 (62)

Das **German – English dictionary** enthält den **Lernwortschatz** von *Headlight 1*.
Es kann dir eine erste Hilfe sein, wenn du vergessen hast, wie etwas auf Englisch heißt.

Wenn du wissen möchtest, wo das englische Wort zum ersten Mal in *Headlight 1* vorkommt,
dann kannst du im **English – German dictionary** (S. 222–232) nachschlagen.

Es werden folgende **Abkürzungen** und **Symbole** verwendet:

pl = plural (Mehrzahl)

A

Abend evening ['iːvnɪŋ] **am Abend** in the evening
Abendessen dinner ['dɪnə]
abends in the evening ['iːvnɪŋ] **5 Uhr abends** 5 pm [piː'em]
Abenteuer adventure [əd'ventʃə]
aber but [bʌt], [bət]
abwarten wait and see [weɪt]
abwaschen wash up [wɒʃ 'ʌp]
acht eight [eɪt]
Adresse address [ə'dres]
Affe monkey ['mʌŋki]
Afrika Africa ['æfrɪkə]
alle(s) all [ɔːl] alle *(jeder)* everybody ['evrɪbɒdi]
Alphabet alphabet ['ælfəbet]
alphabetisches Wörterverzeichnis dictionary ['dɪkʃənri]
also so [səʊ] **Also, ...** Well, ... [wel]
alt old [əʊld]
Alter age [eɪdʒ]
am: am 1. März on 1st March [ɒn]
  am Arbeitsplatz at work [ət 'wɜːk] **am besten** best [best] **am Montag** on Monday **am Nachmittag** in the afternoon [ɑːftə'nuːn] **am Strand** on the beach **am Telefon** on the phone **am Wochenende** at the weekend [wiːk'end]
an: an Bord aboard [ə'bɔːd] **an dieser Schule** at this school [æt], [ət] **gut an meinem Haus** good about my house [ə'baʊt]
Anblick sight [saɪt]
andere(r, s) other ['ʌðə] **ein(e) andere(r, s)** another [ə'nʌðə]
anders different ['dɪfrənt]
anfangen start [stɑːt]
anhalten *(stoppen)* stop [stɒp]
anhören: (sich etwas) anhören listen to ['lɪsn]
anrufen phone [fəʊn]
anschauen: Schau dir die Süßigkeiten an! Look at the sweets! ['lʊk ət] sich etwas anschauen *(beobachten)* watch [wɒtʃ]

anschließen: sich einem Klub anschließen join a club [dʒɔɪn]
ansehen: Sieh dir die Süßigkeiten an! Look at the sweets! ['lʊk ət]
Anspitzer sharpener ['ʃɑːpnə]
Anwesenheitskontrolle registration [redʒɪ'streɪʃn]
Anzeige *(Werbung)* advert ['ædvɜːt]
Apfel apple ['æpl]
Apfelsine orange ['ɒrɪndʒ]
April April ['eɪprəl]
Aquarium aquarium [ə'kweəriəm]
Arbeit work [wɜːk] **bei der Arbeit** at work [ət 'wɜːk]
arbeiten work [wɜːk]
Arbeitsplatz: am Arbeitsplatz at work [ət 'wɜːk]
Arbeitsstelle job [dʒɒb]
Arbeitstag workday ['wɜːkdeɪ]
Ärger trouble ['trʌbl] **Ellie hat Ärger.** Ellie is in trouble.
auch too [tuː]
auf on [ɒn] **auf dem Bild** in the picture ['pɪktʃə] **auf dem Feld** in the field **auf dem Foto** in the photo ['fəʊtəʊ] **auf dem Land** in the country **auf dem Weg zu/ nach ...** on the way to ... [weɪ] **auf dieser Schule** at this school [æt], [ət] **auf Englisch** in English [ɪn] **Auf Wiedersehen!** Goodbye. [ɡʊd'baɪ]
Aufgabe exercise ['eksəsaɪz]
aufgehen *(Sonne)* come up [kʌm 'ʌp]
aufgeregt excited [ɪk'saɪtɪd]; *(nervös)* nervous ['nɜːvəs]
aufhaben: Was haben wir als Hausaufgabe(n) auf? What's for homework?
aufhören (mit) stop [stɒp]
aufpassen auf look after [lʊk 'ɑːftə]
aufregend exciting [ɪk'saɪtɪŋ]
aufschlagen *(Buch)* open ['əʊpən]
aufstehen get up [ɡet 'ʌp]
aufwachen wake up [weɪk 'ʌp]
August August ['ɔːɡəst]

aus from [frɒm] **aus ... (heraus/ hinaus)** out of ... ['aʊt əv] **die Schule ist aus/vorbei** school is out [aʊt]
Ausdruck phrase [freɪz]
Ausflug trip [trɪp]
ausleihen: sich (aus)leihen borrow ['bɒrəʊ]
ausmachen: etwas ausmachen make a difference [meɪk ə 'dɪfrəns]
ausprobieren try [traɪ]
Ausschau halten nach look for ['lʊk fə]
aussehen look [lʊk] **Wie sieht es aus?** What's it like? [laɪk]
Auto car [kɑː]

B

Baby baby ['beɪbi]
Babysitten babysitting ['beɪbisɪtɪŋ]
Babysitter babysitter ['beɪbisɪtə]
Badeanzug swimsuit ['swɪmsuːt]
Badehose swimming trunks ['swɪmɪŋ trʌŋks]
Bad(ezimmer) bathroom ['bɑːθruːm]
bald soon [suːn]
Balkon balcony ['bælkəni]
Ball ball [bɔːl]
Band *(Musikgruppe)* band [bænd]
Bär bear [beə]
Basketball basketball ['bɑːskɪtbɔːl]
Battle *(im Rap)* battle ['bætl]
Bauernhof farm [fɑːm]
Baum tree [triː]
beängstigend scary ['skeəri]
Beat *(Musik)* beat [biːt]
bedeuten mean [miːn]
beeilen: sich beeilen hurry ['hʌri]
beginnen start [stɑːt]
behindert *(körperbehindert)* disabled [dɪs'eɪbld]
bei with [wɪð] **bei der Arbeit** at work [æt], [ət] **bei ihrer Mutter zu Hause/daheim** at her mum's house **bei MARTINS** at MARTINS
beide both [bəʊθ] **das Beste von beidem** the best of both worlds
Bein leg [leg]

bekommen get [gɛt]
benötigen need [niːd]
benutzen use [juːz]
beobachten watch [wɒtʃ]
beschäftigt sein be busy [ˈbɪzi]
beschreiben describe [dɪˈskraɪb]
besondere(r, s) special [ˈspeʃl]
besorgt sein (wegen) be worried (about) [ˈwʌrid]
besser better [ˈbetə]
beste(r,s) best [best] **das Beste von beidem** the best of both worlds [ðə ˈbest əv bəʊθ wɜːldz]
besuchen visit [ˈvɪzɪt]
Besucher/in visitor [ˈvɪzɪtə]
Bett bed [bed]
beunruhigt sein (wegen) be worried (about) [ˈwʌrid]
bevor before [bɪˈfɔː]
bewirken: etwas bewirken make a difference [meɪk ə ˈdɪfrəns]
Bild picture [ˈpɪktʃə]; *(Anblick)* sight [saɪt]
bis: Bis später. See you later. [si: ju ˈleɪtə] **von Montag bis Freitag** from Monday to Friday
bisschen: ein bisschen a bit [ə ˈbɪt]
bitte *in Fragen und Aufforderungen* please [pliːz] Bitte, gern geschehen. *(Nichts zu danken.)* You're welcome. [ˈwelkəm]
Bitte schön. / Hier, bitte. Here you are. [hɪə ju: ˈɑː]
blau blue [bluː]
Blazer blazer [ˈbleɪzə]
bleiben stay [steɪ]
Bleistift pencil [ˈpensl]
Bleistiftanspitzer pencil sharpener [ˈpensl ʃɑːpnə]
blöd stupid [ˈstjuːpɪd]
bloß *(nur)* only [ˈəʊnli]
BMX(-Fahrrad) BMX [biː em ˈeks]
Bodyboard bodyboard [ˈbɒdɪbɔːd]
Bonbon sweet [swiːt]
Bord: an Bord aboard [əˈbɔːd]
borgen: sich borgen borrow [ˈbɒrəʊ]
Brathähnchen chicken [ˈtʃɪkɪn]
brauchen need [niːd]
braun brown [braʊn]
Brief letter [ˈletə]
Brille glasses [ˈglɑːsɪz]
bringen bring [brɪŋ]
britisch British [ˈbrɪtɪʃ]
Broschüre brochure [ˈbrəʊʃə]
Brot bread [bred]
Bruder brother [ˈbrʌðə]
Buch book [bʊk]
buchstabieren spell [spel]

Bulle bull [bʊl]
Bus bus [bʌs] **im Bus** on the bus **mit dem Bus fahren** go by bus
Busbahnhof bus station [ˈbʌs steɪʃn]

C

Café cafe [ˈkæfeɪ]
Camping camping [ˈkæmpɪŋ]
CD CD [siː ˈdiː]
Chips crisps [krɪsps]
Computer computer [kəmˈpjuːtə]
cool cool [kuːl]
Cousin/e cousin [ˈkʌzn]

D

da: da drüben over there [əʊvə ˈðeə] **da(hin)** there [ðeə]
daheim: bei ihrer Mutter daheim at her mum's house [æt], [ət]
daher so [səʊ]
danach then [ðen]
danke (schön) thank you [ˈθæŋk juː]; thanks [θæŋks]
danken: Nichts zu danken. *(Gern geschehen.)* You're welcome. [ˈwelkəm]
dann then [ðen]
das the [ðə] **das (dort),** ; that [ðæt] **Das ist …** This is … [ˈðɪs ɪz]
dasselbe the same [seɪm]
Datum date [deɪt]
Decke *(zum Zudecken u. Ä.)* blanket [ˈblæŋkɪt]
decken: den Tisch decken set the table [set]
dein/e *(vor Nomen)* your [jɔː], [jə]
deine, deiner, deins yours [jɔːz]
denken think [θɪŋk] **daran denken** remember [rɪˈmembə] **er dachte; er hat gedacht** he thought [θɔːt] **Was denkst du?** What do you think?
der the [ðə]; *(Relativpronomen, Person)* who [huː] **der (dort)** that [ðæt]
derselbe the same [seɪm]
deutsch; Deutsch German [ˈdʒɜːmən]
Deutschland Germany [ˈdʒɜːməni]
Dezember December [dɪˈsembə]
Dialog dialogue [ˈdaɪəlɒg]
dich you [juː], [jʊː] **dich selbst** yourself [jɔːˈself], [jəˈself]
die the [ðə]; *(Relativpronomen, Person)* who [huː] **die (dort)** *(Singular)* that [ðæt]
Diele hall [hɔːl]
Dienstag Tuesday [ˈtjuːzdeɪ], [ˈtjuːzdi]

dies this [ðɪs] **Dies ist …** This is … [ˈðɪs ɪz]
dieselbe(n) the same [seɪm]
diese(r, s) this [ðɪs] diese (hier) *(Plural)* these [ðiːz] **dieses Mal** this time [taɪm]
Ding thing [θɪŋ]
dir you [juː], [juː] **dir selbst** yourself [jəˈself], [jəˈself]
Diskussion discussion [dɪˈskʌʃn]
Donnerstag Thursday [ˈθɜːzdeɪ], [ˈθɜːzdi]
Dorf village [ˈvɪlɪdʒ]
dort: dort drüben over there [əʊvə ˈðeə] **dort(hin)** there [ðeə]
dran: Du bist dran. It's your turn. [tɜːn]
draußen outdoors [aʊtˈdɔːz]; **nach draußen** outside [aʊtˈsaɪd]
drei three [θriː]
drinnen, nach drinnen inside [ɪnˈsaɪd]
dritte(r, s) third [θɜːd]
drüben: da/dort drüben over there [əʊvə ˈðeə]
du you [juː], [juː] **du selbst** yourself [jɔːˈself], [jəˈself]
dumm stupid [ˈstjuːpɪd]
durch through [θruː]
dürfen: ich darf … nicht vergessen I mustn't forget … [ˈmʌsnt]

E

echt real [rɪəl]
Ecke corner [ˈkɔːnə]
eilen hurry [ˈhʌri]
ein/e a [ə]; *(vor Vokalen)* an [ən]
einfach *(leicht)* easy [ˈiːzi]
einhundert a hundred, one hundred [ˈhʌndrəd]
einige some [sʌm], [səm]
einkaufen gehen go shopping [gəʊ ˈʃɒpɪŋ]
Einkaufszentrum shopping centre [ˈʃɒpɪŋ sentə]
einladen (zu, nach) invite (to) [ɪnˈvaɪt]
Einladung (zu, nach) invitation (to) [ɪnvɪˈteɪʃn]
einmal: noch einmal again [əˈgen]
eins one [wʌn]
einsam lonely [ˈləʊnli]
eintreten: in einen Klub eintreten join a club [dʒɔɪn]
Eintrittskarte ticket [ˈtɪkɪt]
einzige(r, s): der/die einzige … the only … [ˈəʊnli]
Eis *(Speiseeis)* ice cream [aɪs ˈkriːm]
Elefant elephant [ˈelɪfənt]

elf eleven [ɪ'levən]
Eltern parents ['peərənts]
E-Mail email ['iːmeɪl]
Ende end [end] **am oberen Ende** at the top [tɒp] **zu Ende sein** be over ['əʊvə]
England England ['ɪŋglənd]
Englisch; englisch English ['ɪŋglɪʃ]
Ente duck [dʌk]
Entschuldigung: Entschuldigung, … / Entschuldigen Sie, … *(Darf ich mal stören?)* Excuse me, … [ɪks'kjuːz mi] Entschuldigung. *(Tut mir leid.)* Sorry. / I'm sorry. ['sɒri]
er he [hiː]; *(Dinge, Tiere)* it [ɪt]
Erdkunde geography [dʒi'ɒgrəfi]
erinnern: sich erinnern (an) remember [rɪ'membə]
erraten guess [ges]
erste(r, s), als Erstes first [fɜːst]
es it [ɪt]
Esel donkey ['dɒŋki]
Essen food [fuːd]
essen eat [iːt]
etwas something ['sʌmθɪŋ]; *(ein bisschen)* some [sʌm], [səm] **Möchten Sie sonst noch etwas?** Would you like anything else? [eniθɪŋ 'els]
euch you [ju], [juː]
euer/eure *(vor Nomen)* your [jɔː], [jə]

F

Fähre ferry ['feri]
fahren go [gəʊ] **mit dem Bus fahren** go by bus **mit dem Fahrrad/dem BMX-Rad fahren** ride a bike/a BMX [raɪd]
Fahrkarte ticket ['tɪkɪt]
Fahrrad bike [baɪk]
fallen fall [fɔːl]
falsch false [fɔːls]; wrong [rɒŋ]
Familie family ['fæməli]
Familienstammbaum family tree ['fæməli 'triː]
Farbe colour ['kʌlə]
Farm farm [fɑːm]
faul *(träge)* lazy ['leɪzi]
Februar February ['februəri]
Federmäppchen pencil case ['pensl keɪs]
feiern: eine Party feiern have a party ['pɑːti]
Feld field [fiːld] **auf dem Feld** in the field
Fels(en) rock [rɒk]
Fenster window ['wɪndəʊ]
Ferien holidays ['hɒlədeɪz]

fernsehen watch TV [wɒtʃ tiː'viː]
Fernseher TV [tiː'viː]
Fernsehsendung programme ['prəʊgræm]
fertig: sich fertig machen (für) get ready (for) ['redi]
Feuerwache fire station ['faɪə steɪʃn]
Feuerwehrmann/-frau firefighter ['faɪəfaɪtə]
fies *(gemein)* mean [miːn]
Film film [fɪlm]
finden find [faɪnd]
Fisch(e) fish [fɪʃ]
Flasche bottle ['bɒtl] **eine Flasche …** a bottle of …
Flaschenpost message in a bottle ['mesɪdʒ]
flauschig *(pelzig)* furry ['fɜːri]
fliegen fly [flaɪ]
Flur *(Diele)* hall [hɔːl]
Flut: die Flut kommt the sea's coming in
folgen follow ['fɒləʊ]
fort away [ə'weɪ]
Foto photo ['fəʊtəʊ]
Fotoapparat camera ['kæmərə]
Frage question ['kwestʃən] **Fragen stellen** ask questions [ɑːsk]
fragen ask [ɑːsk] **sie fragte; sie hat gefragt** she asked [ɑːskt]
Frankreich France [frɑːns]
Französisch; französisch French [frentʃ]
Frau woman, *pl* women ['wʊmən], ['wɪmɪn]; *(allgemeine Anrede für Frauen)* Ms … [mɪz], [məz]; *(Anrede für unverheiratete Frauen)* Miss … [mɪs]; *(Anrede für verheiratete Frauen)* Mrs … ['mɪsɪz]
frei free [friː] **im Freien** outdoors [aʊt'dɔːz]
Freitag Friday ['fraɪdeɪ], ['fraɪdi]
fressen eat [iːt]
Freund/in friend [frend]; *(feste Freundin)* girlfriend ['gɜːlfrend]; *(fester Freund)* boyfriend ['bɔɪfrend]
freundlich friendly ['frendli]
Freut mich, dich/euch/Sie kennenzulernen. Nice to meet you.
Frisbee frisbee ['frɪzbi]
frisch fresh [freʃ]
froh happy ['hæpi]
früh early ['ɜːli]
Frühstück breakfast ['brekfəst]
frühstücken have breakfast
fühlen, sich fühlen feel [fiːl]
Füller pen [pen]
fünf five [faɪv]
funktionieren work [wɜːk]

für for [fɔː], [fə] **für mich selbst** for myself [maɪ'self]
fürchterlich terrible ['terəbl]
Fußball football ['fʊtbɔːl]
Futter food [fuːd]
füttern feed [fiːd]

G

ganz: den ganzen Sommer all summer [ɔːl]
Garage garage ['gærɑːʒ]
Garagenflohmarkt *(privater Flohmarkt)* garage sale ['gærɑːʒ seɪl]
Garten garden ['gɑːdn]
Gast visitor ['vɪzɪtə]
geben give [gɪv] **es gibt** there are ['ðeər ɑː]; there's [ðeəz]
Geburtstag birthday ['bɜːθdeɪ] **Herzlichen Glückwunsch zum Geburtstag!** Happy birthday! **Sie hat Geburtstag.** It's her birthday. **Wann hast du Geburtstag?** When's your birthday?
Gedankenkarte mind map ['maɪnd mæp]
Gedicht poem ['pəʊɪm]
gefährlich dangerous ['deɪndʒərəs]
Gefühl feeling ['fiːlɪŋ]
gehen go [gəʊ] **Mir geht es gut.** I'm fine. [aɪm 'faɪn] **mit mir ins Theater gehen** take me to the theatre **Wie geht's?** How's it going? **Wie geht's (dir/euch/Ihnen)?** How are you? **zu Fuß gehen** walk [wɔːk]
gehören zu go with ['gəʊ wɪð]
gelb yellow ['jeləʊ]
Geld money ['mʌni] **Es ist sein Geld wert.** It's good value. ['væljuː]
gemein *(fies)* mean [miːn]
Gemüse vegetables ['vedʒtəblz]
genervt sein feel fed up [fed 'ʌp]
Geografie geography [dʒi'ɒgrəfi]
gerade *(im Moment)* at the moment ['məʊmənt]
Geräusch sound [saʊnd]; *(Lärm)* noise [nɔɪz]
gern: Ich hätte gern … / Ich möchte … I'd like … **Ich komme sehr gern. / Ich würde sehr gern kommen.** I'd love to come. **Ich sehe gern fern.** I like watching TV.
Gesamtschule (GB) high school ['haɪ skuːl]
Geschäft shop [ʃɒp]

geschehen happen ['hæpən] **Bitte, gern geschehen.** You're welcome. ['welkəm]

Geschenk present ['preznt]

Geschichte *(Erzählung)* story ['stɔːri]; *(vergangene Zeiten)* history ['hɪstri]

Gesicht face [feɪs]

gespannt excited [ɪkˈsaɪtɪd]

Getränk drink [drɪŋk]

gewinnen win [wɪn]

Gitarre guitar [gɪˈtɑː]

glauben think [θɪŋk]

Glück: du hast Glück you're lucky ['lʌki]

glücklich happy ['hæpi]

Glückwunsch: Herzlichen Glückwunsch zum Geburtstag! Happy birthday! ['hæpi 'bɜːθdeɪ]

grau grey [greɪ]

groß big [bɪg]

großartig great [greɪt]

Großeltern grandparents ['grænpeərənts]

Großmutter grandmother ['grænmʌðə]

Großstadt city ['sɪti]

Großvater grandfather ['grænfɑːðə]

grün green [griːn]

Gruppe group [gruːp]

gruselig scary ['skeəri]

Grüße: Viele Grüße … *(Briefschluss)* Best wishes ['wɪʃɪz]

grüßen: Grüß alle. Say hi to everybody.

gut good [gʊd]; *(in Ordnung)* fine [faɪn]; *(okay)* OK [əʊˈkeɪ] **gut an meinem Haus** good about my house **Guten Morgen.** Good morning. **gut funktionieren/sprechen** work/speak well [wel] **Gut gemacht!** Well done. **Mir geht es gut.** I'm fine.

H

haben have [hæv] **die Nase voll haben** feel fed up [fed 'ʌp] **ich hatte** I had [hæd], [həd] **Ich hätte gern …** I'd like … **Sie hat Geburtstag.** It's her birthday. ['bɜːθdeɪ] **viel zu tun haben** be busy ['bɪzi]

Hafen harbour ['hɑːbə]

Hähnchen chicken ['tʃɪkɪn]

Halbbruder half-brother ['hɑːf brʌðə]

halbe(r, s) half [hɑːf] **halb 7** half past 6 [pɑːst]

Halbschwester half-sister ['hɑːf sɪstə]

Hallo. Hello. [həˈləʊ]; Hi. [haɪ]

halten *(stoppen)* stop [stɒp] **Halt den Mund!** Shut up! [ʃʌt 'ʌp]

Hamster hamster ['hæmstə]

Handtuch towel ['taʊəl]

Handy mobile (phone) [məʊbaɪl 'fəʊn]

hart hard [hɑːd]

hassen hate [heɪt]

hässlich ugly ['ʌgli]

Haus house [haʊs] **nach Hause** home [həʊm] **zu Hause** at home

Hausaufgabe(n) homework ['həʊmwɜːk] **Hausaufgaben machen** do your homework **Ich habe meine Hausaufgaben vergessen.** I forgot my homework. [fəˈgɒt] **Was haben wir als Hausaufgabe(n) auf?** What's for homework?

Haustier pet [pet]

Heft exercise book ['eksəsaɪz bʊk]

Heim *(Zuhause)* home [həʊm]

heiß hot [hɒt]

heißen: Wie heißt du? What's your name? [wɒts jɔː 'neɪm]

helfen help [help]

Helm helmet ['helmɪt]

Hemd shirt [ʃɜːt]

Herr Brown Mr Brown ['mɪstə]

herrisch bossy ['bɒsi]

herstellen make [meɪk]

Herzlichen Glückwunsch zum Geburtstag! Happy birthday! ['hæpi 'bɜːθdeɪ]

heute today [təˈdeɪ]

hier(her) here [hɪə]

Hilfe help [help]

hinfallen fall [fɔːl]

hinter behind [bɪˈhaɪnd]

hinunter: den Hügel hinunter down the hill [daʊn]

Hobby hobby ['hɒbi]

hoffen hope [həʊp]

hören hear [hɪə]

Hose trousers ['traʊzəz] **kurze Hose** shorts [ʃɔːts]

Hügel hill [hɪl]

Huhn chicken ['tʃɪkɪn]

Hund dog [dɒg]

hundert *(einhundert)* a hundred, one hundred ['hʌndrəd]

Hunger: Wir haben Hunger. We're hungry. ['hʌŋgri]

Hurra! Yippee! [jɪˈpiː]

Hut hat [hæt]

I

ich I [aɪ] **ich bin** I'm (= I am) [aɪm], [aɪ 'æm] **Ich bin's.** It's me. [ɪts 'miː]

Idee idea [aɪˈdɪə]

Idiot/in idiot ['ɪdɪət]

ihm him [hɪm]

ihn him [hɪm]

ihnen them [ðem], [ðəm]

Ihnen *(höfliche Anrede)* you [juː], [juː]

ihr *(Plural von „du")* you [juː], [juː]

ihr *(zu „she")* her [hɜː], [hə] **Hilf ihr.** Help her.

ihr/e *(besitzanzeigend zu „she")* her [hɜː], [hə]; *(besitzanzeigend zu „they")* their [ðeə]

Ihr/e *(besitzanzeigend zur höflichen Anrede „Sie")* your [jɔː], [jə]

im: im Bus on the bus **im Kino** at the cinema **im Moment** at the moment

immer always ['ɔːlweɪz]

in in [ɪn] **in (… hinein)** into ['ɪntu], ['ɪntə] **in der Nacht** at night **in der Schule** at school **in der Stadt** in town **in einem Restaurant** at a restaurant **ins Kino** to the cinema

Information(en) information [ɪnfəˈmeɪʃn]

Informations- und Kommunikationstechnologie ICT (Information and Communication technology) [aɪ siː 'tiː], [ɪnfəmeɪʃn ənd kəmjuːnɪˈkeɪʃn teknɒlədʒi]

Informationsstand information desk

Inlineskates inline skates [ɪnlaɪn 'skeɪts]

Instrument instrument ['ɪnstrəmənt]

interessant interesting ['ɪntrəstɪŋ]

Interview interview ['ɪntəvjuː]

Irgendwelche Ideen? Any ideas? ['eni]

Irrenhaus madhouse ['mædhaʊs]

J

ja yeah *(infml)* [jeə]; yes [jes]

Jahr(gang) year [jɪə]

Januar January ['dʒænjuəri]

jeder *(alle)* everybody ['evribɒdi]

jede(r, s) *(vor Nomen)* every ['evri]

jene(r, s) that [ðæt]

jetzt now [naʊ]

Job job [dʒɒb]

Jugendliche/r kid [kɪd]

Juli July [dʒuˈlaɪ]

jung young [jʌŋ]

Junge boy [bɔɪ]

Juni June [dʒuːn]

K

Kaffee coffee ['kɒfi]
Käfig cage [keɪdʒ]
Kalender diary ['daɪəri]
Kamera camera ['kæmərə]
Kaninchen rabbit ['ræbɪt]
Kantine canteen [kæn'tiːn]
Kanu canoe [kə'nuː]
Kapuzenpullover hoodie ['hʊdi]
Karte card [kɑːd]
Kartoffelchips crisps [krɪsps]
Kästchen box [bɒks]
Kasten box [bɒks]
Katze cat [kæt]
kaufen buy [baɪ]
Kaufpreis price [praɪs]
kein/e no [nəʊ] **ich bin kein/e …**
I'm not … [nɒt]
Keks biscuit ['bɪskɪt]
kennen know [nəʊ]
kennenlernen meet [miːt] **Freut
mich, dich/euch/Sie kennenzu-
lernen.** Nice to meet you.
Kerl guy [gaɪ]
Kette chain [tʃeɪn]
Kind child, pl children [tʃaɪld],
['tʃɪldrən]; kid [kɪd]
Kino cinema ['sɪnəmə] **im Kino** at
the cinema **ins Kino** to the cinema
Kirche church [tʃɜːtʃ]
Kissen cushion ['kʊʃn]
Kiste box [bɒks]
Klang sound [saʊnd]
Klasse class [klɑːs]
Klassenlehrer/in class teacher
['klɑːs tiːtʃə]
Klassenraum classroom ['klɑːsruːm]
Klavier piano [pi'ænəʊ]
Kleiderschrank wardrobe
['wɔːdrəʊb]
klein little ['lɪtl]; small [smɔːl]
klingeln ring [rɪŋ]
Klub club [klʌb]
Koch, Köchin cook [kʊk]
kochen cook [kʊk]
Kochrezept recipe ['resəpi]
kommen come [kʌm] **die Flut
kommt** the sea's coming in **Ich
komme sehr gern. / Ich würde
sehr gern kommen.** I'd love to
come. **Komm(t) (schon)!** Come
on! **Wo kommst du her?** Where
are you from?
können can [kæn], [kən] **nicht
können** can't (= cannot) [kɑːnt],
['kænɒt]
**Kontrolle: die Kontrolle ver-
lieren** lose control [luːz]
Konzert concert ['kɒnsət]

**Kopfsprung: einen Kopfsprung
machen** dive [daɪv]
körperbehindert disabled [dɪs'eɪbld]
**kosten: Der Taschenrechner kostet
1 Pfund.** The calculator is £ 1.
**Die Poster kosten 2 Pfund fünf-
zig.** The posters are £ 2.50.
Was (Wie viel) kostet / kosten?
How much is / are …?
kostenlos free [friː]
Krankenhaus hospital ['hɒspɪtl]
Krawatte tie [taɪ]
Krebs crab [kræb]
Kroatien Croatia [krəʊ'eɪʃə]
Krokodil crocodile ['krɒkədaɪl]
Küche kitchen ['kɪtʃɪn]
Kuchen cake [keɪk]
Kugelschreiber pen [pen]
Kuh cow [kaʊ]
kümmern: sich kümmern um
look after [lʊk 'ɑːftə]
Kunde, Kundin customer ['kʌstəmə]
Kunst art [ɑːt]
kurze Hose shorts [ʃɔːts]
Kuss kiss [kɪs]

L

Labor lab [læb]
lachen laugh [lɑːf] **mit einem
Lachen** with a laugh **sie lachten**
they laughed [lɑːft]
Laden shop [ʃɒp]
Lampe lamp [læmp]
Land country ['kʌntri] **auf dem
Land** in the country
Landkarte map [mæp]
langsam slow [sləʊ]
langweilig boring ['bɔːrɪŋ]
Lärm noise [nɔɪz]
Lass(t) uns … Let's … [lets]
laufen: Wie läuft's? How's it
going?
Läufer (Teppich) rug [rʌg]
Laut sound [saʊnd]
laut (voller Lärm) noisy ['nɔɪzi]
läuten ring [rɪŋ]
Lautsprecher speaker ['spiːkə]
Leben life, pl lives [laɪf]
leben live [lɪv]
Lebensmittel food [fuːd]
lecker yum (infml) [jʌm]
legen put [pʊt]
Lehrbuch textbook ['tekstbʊk]
Lehrer/in teacher ['tiːtʃə]
leicht (einfach) easy ['iːzi]
leidtun: Tut mir leid. Sorry. / I'm
sorry. ['sɒri]
leihen: sich (aus)leihen borrow
['bɒrəʊ]

leise quiet ['kwaɪət]
Lektion (Schulbuch) unit ['juːnɪt]
lernen learn [lɜːn]
lesen read [riːd]
letzte(r, s) last [lɑːst] **der letzte
Ferientag** the last day of the
holidays
Leute people ['piːpl]; (als Anrede
verwendet) guys [gaɪz]
Liebe/r … Dear … [dɪə]
lieben love [lʌv]
Lieblings- favourite ['feɪvərɪt]
Lieblingsfarbe favourite colour
[feɪvərɪt 'kʌlə]
Lied song [sɒŋ]
lila purple ['pɜːpl]
Lineal ruler ['ruːlə]
links left [left] **auf der linken
Seite** on the left **nach links** left
Locher hole punch ['həʊl pʌntʃ]
los: In der Küche ist zu viel los.
The kitchen is too busy. ['bɪzi]
Na los! Come on! [kʌm 'ɒn]
Was ist los? What is it?

M

machen (herstellen) make [meɪk];
(tun) do [duː] (am Telefon) **Ich
muss Schluss machen.** I must
go. **Das macht 159 Pfund.**
That's £ 159. **Gut gemacht!**
Well done. [dʌn] **Hausauf-
gaben machen** do your home-
work ['həʊmwɜːk] **sich Sorgen
machen (wegen, um)** worry
(about)
Mädchen girl [gɜːl]
Mai May [meɪ]
Mal: dieses Mal this time [taɪm]
Mama mum [mʌm]
manchmal sometimes ['sʌmtaɪmz]
Mann man, pl men [mæn], [men]
Mannschaft team [tiːm]
Markt market ['mɑːkɪt]
Marmelade jam [dʒæm]
März March [mɑːtʃ]
Mathe(matik) maths [mæθs]
Meer sea [siː]
mehr more [mɔː]
Mehrfamilienhaus block of flats
['blɒk əv flæts]
mein/e (vor Nomen) my [maɪ]
meinen (denken, glauben) think
[θɪŋk]; (sagen wollen) mean [miːn]
Was meinst du? What do you
think?
meistens usually ['juːʒuəli]
Mensa canteen [kæn'tiːn]
Menschen people ['piːpl]

mich me [mɪː] **für mich selbst** for myself [maɪˈself]

Mindmap mind map [ˈmaɪnd mæp]

Minute minute [ˈmɪnɪt]

mir me [mɪː]

mit with [wɪð] **mit dem Bus fahren** go by bus [baɪ ˈbʌs] **mit mir ins Theater gehen** take me to the theatre

mitbringen bring [brɪŋ]

mitkommen come [kʌm]

Mittag: (zu) Mittag essen have lunch [lʌntʃ]

Mittagessen lunch [lʌntʃ]

Mitte centre [ˈsentə]; middle [ˈmɪdl] **in der Mitte** in the middle

Mitteilung message [ˈmesɪdʒ]

Mittwoch Wednesday [ˈwenzdeɪ], [ˈwenzdi]

möchten: Möchten Sie sonst noch etwas? Would you like anything else? [eniθɪŋ ˈels] **Ich möchte …** I'd like … (= I would like) [wʊd]

modern modern [ˈmɒdn]

mögen like [laɪk] **ich mag … nicht** I don't like … **sehr mögen** love [lʌv]

Moment moment [ˈməʊmənt] **im Moment** at the moment

Monat month [mʌnθ]

Montag Monday [ˈmʌndeɪ], [ˈmʌndi] **am Montag** on Monday

Morgen morning [ˈmɔːnɪŋ] **am Morgen** in the morning **Guten Morgen.** Good morning.

morgens in the morning [ˈmɔːnɪŋ] **9 Uhr morgens** 9 am [eɪˈem]

Möwe seagull [ˈsiːgʌl]

MP3-Player MP3 player [empiːˈθriː pleɪə]

müde tired [ˈtaɪəd]

Mund mouth [maʊθ] **Halt den Mund!** Shut up! [ʃʌt ˈʌp]

Museum museum [mjuˈziːəm]

Musical musical [ˈmjuːzɪkl]

Musik music [ˈmjuːzɪk]

Musiker/in musician [mjuˈzɪʃn]

Musikgruppe band [bænd]

müssen must [mʌst]

Mutter mother [ˈmʌðə]

Mutti mum [mʌm]

Mütze hat [hæt]

N

Na ja, … Well, … [wel]

nach (örtlich) to [tu], [tə]; (zeitlich) after [ˈɑːftə] **nach dem Abendessen** after dinner **nach Hause**

home [həʊm] **viertel nach 6** quarter past 6 [pɑːst]

Nachmittag afternoon [ɑːftəˈnuːn] **am Nachmittag** in the afternoon

nachmittags: 5 Uhr nachmittags 5 pm [piːˈem]

Nachricht message [ˈmesɪdʒ]

Nachrichten news [njuːz]

nächste(r, s) next [nekst] **Der/Die Nächste, bitte.** Next, please.

Nacht night [naɪt] **in der Nacht** at night

nachts at night [naɪt]

Nähe: in der Nähe von near [nɪə]

nahe (bei) near [nɪə]

Name name [neɪm]

Nase: die Nase voll haben feel fed up [fed ˈʌp]

nass wet [wet]

Naturwissenschaft science [ˈsaɪəns]

neben next to [ˈnekst tə]

negativ negative [ˈnegətɪv]

nehmen take [teɪk] **Ich nehme es (ihn, sie).** (beim Einkaufen) I'll take it.

nein no [nəʊ]

nervös nervous [ˈnɜːvəs]

nett nice [naɪs]

Netz network [ˈnetwɜːk]

neu new [njuː]

neun nine [naɪn]

nicht: ich bin nicht … I'm not … [nɒt]

nichts nothing [ˈnʌθɪŋ] **Nichts zu danken.** You're welcome.

niedlich cute [kjuːt]

nie(mals) never [ˈnevə]

noch: noch ein/e another [əˈnʌðə] **noch einmal** again [əˈgen] **Möchten Sie sonst noch etwas?** Would you like anything else?

normal normal [ˈnɔːml]

normalerweise usually [ˈjuːʒuəli]

November November [nəʊˈvembə]

Nummer number [ˈnʌmbə]

nun now [naʊ] **Nun, …** Well, … [wel]

nur only [ˈəʊnli]

Nuss nut [nʌt]

O

oben (am oberen Ende) at the top [tɒp]; (die Treppe hoch) upstairs [ʌpˈsteəz]

Obst fruit [fruːt]

oder or [ɔː]

öffnen open [ˈəʊpən]

oft often [ˈɒfn], [ˈɒftən]

Oje! Oh dear. [əʊ ˈdɪə]

okay OK [əʊˈkeɪ]

Oktober October [ɒkˈtəʊbə]

Oma grandma [ˈgrænmɑː]; granny [ˈgræni]

Omelett omelette [ˈɒmlət]

Onkel uncle [ˈʌŋkl]

Opa grandpa [ˈgrænpɑː]

Orange orange [ˈɒrɪndʒ]

orange orange [ˈɒrɪndʒ]

Ordnung: in Ordnung fine [faɪn]; OK [əʊˈkeɪ]

Ort place [pleɪs]

P

paar: ein paar some [sʌm], [səm]

Paddelboot canoe [kəˈnuː]

Papa dad [dæd]

Papier paper [ˈpeɪpə]

Park park [pɑːk]

Partner/in partner [ˈpɑːtnə]

Party party [ˈpɑːti] **eine Party feiern** have a party

passen zu go with [ˈgəʊ wɪð]

passieren happen [ˈhæpən]

Pause break [breɪk]; rest [rest]

pelzig (flauschig) furry [ˈfɜːri]

Pence: fünfzig Pence 50p [piː]

Person person [ˈpɜːsn]

Pfund (britische Währung) pound (£) [paʊnd]

Picknick picnic [ˈpɪknɪk]

Pizza pizza [ˈpiːtsə]

Plan plan [plæn]

Platz (freier Raum) space [speɪs]; (in der Stadt) square [skweə]; (Ort) place [pleɪs]; (Sitzplatz) seat [siːt]

Plätzchen (Keks) biscuit [ˈbɪskɪt]

Polizeiwache police station [pəˈliːs steɪʃn]

Pommes frites chips [tʃɪps]

Pony pony [ˈpəʊni]

positiv positive [ˈpɒzətɪv]

Poster poster [ˈpəʊstə]

Preis (Kaufpreis) price [praɪs]

preiswert good value [ˈvæljuː]

probieren try [traɪ]

Problem problem [ˈprɒbləm]

Prospekt brochure [ˈbrəʊʃə]

Pullover pullover [ˈpʊləʊvə]

putzen clean [kliːn]

Q

Quiz quiz [kwɪz]

R

Rad wheel [wiːl]; (Fahrrad) bike [baɪk]

Radiergummi rubber [ˈrʌbə]

Rap rap [ræp]
rappen rap [ræp]
Rapper/in rapper ['ræpə]
Rast rest [rest]
raten (erraten) guess [ges]
Ratte rat [ræt]
Raum room [ruːm], [rʊm]
rechthaberisch bossy ['bɒsi]
rechts, nach rechts right [raɪt]
  auf der rechten Seite on the right
reden (mit) talk (to) [tɔːk]
Redewendung phrase [freɪz]
Regal shelf, pl shelves [ʃelf], [ʃelvz]
Regenschirm umbrella [ʌmˈbrelə]
Reihe: Du bist an der Reihe.
  It's your turn. [tɜːn]
Reise trip [trɪp]
reiten ride [raɪd]
Rektor/in principal ['prɪnsəpl]
Restaurant restaurant ['restrɒnt]
Rezept (Kochrezept) recipe ['resəpi]
Rhythmus (Musik) beat [biːt]
richtig right [raɪt]; true [truː]
Rock skirt [skɜːt]
Rollstuhl wheelchair ['wiːltʃeə]
rosa pink [pɪŋk]
rot red [red]
ruhig quiet ['kwaɪət]
Rundgang: ein Rundgang durch die Schule a tour of the school [tʊə]

S

Sache thing [θɪŋ]
Saft juice [dʒuːs]
sagen say [seɪ] **er sagte** he said [sed]
Sahne cream [kriːm]
Salat (als Gericht oder Beilage) salad ['sæləd]
Samstag Saturday ['sætədeɪ], ['sætədi]
Sand sand [sænd]
Sandwich sandwich ['sænwɪtʃ], ['sænwɪdʒ]
Sänger/in singer ['sɪŋə]
sauber machen clean [kliːn]
sauer sein (genervt sein) feel fed up [fed ˈʌp]
schade: Das ist schade. That's a pity. ['pɪti]
Schaf(e) sheep [ʃiːp]
schauen look [lʊk]
Schauspiel (darstellende Kunst) drama ['drɑːmə]
Schere scissors ['sɪzəz]
Scheune barn [bɑːn]
schicken send [send] **mir eine SMS schicken** text me [tekst]
schieben push [pʊʃ]

Schild sign [saɪn]
Schirm (Regenschirm) umbrella [ʌmˈbrelə]
schlafen sleep [sliːp] **Schlaf jetzt!** Go to sleep!
Schlafparty sleepover ['sliːpəʊvə]
Schlafsack sleeping bag ['sliːpɪŋ bæg]
Schlafzimmer bedroom ['bedruːm]
Schlagzeug drums [drʌmz]
Schlange snake [sneɪk]
schlecht bad [bæd]
schließen (zumachen) close [kləʊz]
schlimm bad [bæd]
Schluss: (am Telefon) **Ich muss Schluss machen.** I must go.
Schlussverkauf sale [seɪl]
Schmuggler/in smuggler ['smʌglə]
schnell fast [fɑːst]; quick [kwɪk]
Schokolade chocolate ['tʃɒklət]
schön fine [faɪn]; nice [naɪs]
  Schönen Tag (noch). Have a good day.
schrecklich terrible ['terəbl]
schreiben write [raɪt]
Schreibtisch desk [desk]
Schuh shoe [ʃuː]
Schulbuch textbook ['tekstbʊk]
Schule school [skuːl] **auf/an dieser Schule** at this school **die Schule ist aus/vorbei** school is out **in der Schule** at school
Schüler/in student ['stjuːdnt]
Schulheft exercise book ['eksəsaɪz bʊk]
Schulleiter/in principal ['prɪnsəpl]
Schulmensa canteen [kænˈtiːn]
Schulsport PE (physical education) [piː ˈiː], [fɪsɪkl edʒuˈkeɪʃn]
Schultasche school bag ['skuːl bæg]
Schulter shoulder ['ʃəʊldə]
Schulversammlung assembly [əˈsembli]
schwarz black [blæk]
Schwein pig [pɪg]
schwer hard [hɑːd]
Schwester sister ['sɪstə]
schwierig difficult ['dɪfɪkəlt]; hard [hɑːd]
Schwierigkeiten trouble ['trʌbl] **Ellie ist in Schwierigkeiten.** Ellie is in trouble.
Schwimmbad swimming pool ['swɪmɪŋ puːl]
schwimmen swim [swɪm] **schwimmen gehen** go swimming
Schwimmreifen tube [tjuːb]
Scooter (kleiner, zusammenfaltbarer Tretroller) scooter ['skuːtə]

sechs six [sɪks]
See: (die) See sea [siː]
sehen look [lʊk]; see [siː]
sehr very ['veri]
Seilrutsche zip wire ['zɪp waɪə]
sein be [biː]
sein/e (zu „he") his [hɪz]
Seite (Buchseite, Heftseite) page [peɪdʒ] **auf der linken/rechten Seite** on the left/right **Auf welcher Seite sind wir? / Auf welcher Seite steht das?** What page is it?
selbst: für mich selbst for myself [maɪˈself]
senden send [send]
Sendung (Radio, Fernsehen) programme ['prəʊgræm]
September September [sepˈtembə]
setzen: sich setzen sit [sɪt]
sicher sure [ʃʊə], [ʃɔː]
sie (bei Dingen und Tieren) it [ɪt]
Sie (höfliche Anrede) you [ju], [juː]
sie (Plural) they [ðeɪ] **für sie** for them [ðem], [ðəm] **mit ihnen** with them
sie (weibliche Person) she [ʃiː] **Frag sie.** Ask her. [hɜː], [hə]
sieben seven ['sevn]
singen sing [sɪŋ]
sitzen sit [sɪt]
Sitzplatz seat [siːt]
Skateboard skateboard ['skeɪtbɔːd]
Skateboard fahren skateboard ['skeɪtbɔːd]
SMS text (message) ['tekst mesɪdʒ] **mir eine SMS schicken** text me
Socke sock [sɒk]
Sofa sofa ['səʊfə]
Sommer summer ['sʌmə]
Sonderangebot special offer [speʃl ˈɒfə]
Sonne sun [sʌn]
Sonnenbrille sunglasses ['sʌnglɑːsɪz]
Sonnencreme suncream ['sʌnkriːm]
Sonntag Sunday ['sʌndeɪ], ['sʌndi]
sonst or [ɔː] **Möchten Sie sonst noch etwas?** Would you like anything else? [eniθɪŋ ˈels]
Sorgen: Mach dir keine Sorgen. Don't worry. [dəʊnt ˈwʌri] **sich Sorgen machen (wegen, um)** worry (about)
Spanien Spain [speɪn]
Spaß fun [fʌn] **es macht Spaß** it's fun **es macht Spaß, mit ihr zusammenzusein** she's fun
spät late [leɪt] **Wie spät ist es?** What's the time?

später later ['leɪtə] **Bis später.** See you later.
Speiseeis ice cream [aɪs 'kriːm]
Spiegel mirror ['mɪrə]
Spiel game [geɪm]
spielen play [pleɪ]
Spitze: an der Spitze at the top [tɒp]
Sport: Sport(art) sport **Sport treiben** do sport [spɔːt] **Sport(unterricht)** PE (physical education) [piː 'iː], [fɪzɪkl edʒuˈkeɪʃn]
Sporthalle sports hall ['spɔːts hɔːl]
Sportschuhe trainers ['treɪnəz]
Sprache language ['læŋgwɪdʒ]
sprechen speak [spiːk] **sprechen (mit)** talk (to) [tɔːk]
Sprechgesang chant [tʃɑːnt]
Stadt (Großstadt) city ['sɪti]; (Kleinstadt) town [taʊn] **in der Stadt** in town
Stadtmitte centre ['sentə]
Stadtplan map [mæp]
Stall barn [bɑːn]
stecken put [pʊt]
stehen: Auf welcher Seite steht das? What page is it?
steigen: das Wasser steigt the sea's coming in
Stelle (Arbeitsstelle) job [dʒɒb]
stellen put [pʊt] **Fragen stellen** ask questions [ɑːsk]
Stiefbruder stepbrother ['stepbrʌðə]
Stiefmutter stepmother ['stepmʌðə]; stepmum ['stepmʌm]
Stiefschwester stepsister ['stepsɪstə]
Stiefvater stepdad ['stepdæd]; stepfather ['stepfɑːðə]
Stier bull [bʊl]
Stift (zum Schreiben) pen [pen]
still quiet ['kwaɪət]
stolz (auf) proud (of) [praʊd]
Strand beach [biːtʃ] **am Strand** on the beach
Straße (in Ortschaften) street [striːt]; (Landstraße zwischen Orten; Straße in Orten) road [rəʊd]
streicheln stroke [strəʊk]
Streichelzoo pets corner ['kɔːnə]
Streifenhörnchen chipmunk ['tʃɪpmʌŋk]
streng strict [strɪkt]
Strumpfhose tights [taɪts]
Student/in student ['stjuːdnt]
Studio studio ['stjuːdiəʊ]
Stuhl chair [tʃeə]
Stunde (Schulstunde) lesson ['lesn]
Stundenplan timetable ['taɪmteɪbl]
suchen look for ['lʊk fə]

Supermarkt supermarket ['suːpəmɑːkɪt]
Suppe soup [suːp]
süß cute [kjuːt]
Süßigkeiten sweets [swiːts]
Sweatshirt sweatshirt ['swetʃɜːt]
Szene scene [siːn]

T

Taekwondo tae kwon do [taɪ kwɒn 'dəʊ]
Tafel (Schule) board [bɔːd]
Tag day [deɪ] **Ich wünsche dir einen schönen Tag. / Schönen Tag (noch).** Have a good day.
Tagebuch diary ['daɪəri]
Tante aunt [ɑːnt]
tanzen dance [dɑːns]
Tasche bag [bæg]
Taschenrechner calculator ['kælkjuleɪtə]
Tasse cup [kʌp] **eine Tasse …** a cup of …
Team team [tiːm]
Technik(unterricht) technology [tekˈnɒlədʒɪ]
Technologie technology [tekˈnɒlədʒɪ]
Tee tea [tiː]
Teich pond [pɒnd]
teilen share [ʃeə] **sich ein Zimmer mit … teilen** share a room with …
Telefon phone [fəʊn] **am Telefon** on the phone
Telefonnummer phone number
Tennis tennis ['tenɪs]
Teppich rug [rʌg]
teuer expensive [ɪkˈspensɪv]
Theater theatre ['θɪətə]
Themenpark theme park ['θiːm pɑːk]
Tier animal ['ænɪml]; (Haustier) pet [pet]
Tiger tiger ['taɪgə]
Tisch table ['teɪbl] **den Tisch decken** set the table [set]
Toast toast [təʊst]
Tochter daughter ['dɔːtə]
Toilette toilet ['tɔɪlət]
toll great [greɪt]
Torte cake [keɪk]
Tourist/in tourist ['tʊərɪst]
Trampolin trampoline ['træmpəliːn]
Traum dream [driːm]
traurig sad [sæd]
treffen, sich treffen meet [miːt]
treiben: Sport treiben do sport
trinken drink [drɪŋk]
Trommel drum [drʌmz]

Tschüs. Bye. [baɪ]
tun do [duː] (etwas wohin) **tun** put [pʊt] **viel zu tun haben** be busy ['bɪzi]
Tür door [dɔː]
Türkei Turkey ['tɜːki]
Typ guy [gaɪ]

U

üben practise ['præktɪs]
über mich about me [əˈbaʊt]
Überraschung surprise [səˈpraɪz]
Übung exercise ['eksəsaɪz]
Uhr (Wanduhr, Standuhr, Turmuhr) clock [klɒk] **5 Uhr nachmittags/abends, 17 Uhr** 5 pm [piː'em] **9 Uhr morgens/vormittags** 9 am [eɪ'em] **um 1 Uhr / um 13 Uhr** at 1 o'clock [əˈklɒk]
Uhrzeit time [taɪm]
um 1 Uhr / 13 Uhr at 1 o'clock
umsonst free [friː]
und and [ænd], [ənd]
ungefähr about [əˈbaʊt]
unglücklich unhappy [ʌnˈhæpi]
unheimlich (beängstigend) scary ['skeəri]
Uniform uniform ['juːnɪfɔːm]
Unit-Quiz unit quiz ['juːnɪt kwɪz]
unordentlich messy ['mesi]
unrichtig false [fɔːls]
uns us [ʌs], [əs]
unser/e our ['aʊə]
unten (am unteren Ende) at the bottom ['bɒtəm]; (die Treppe hinunter) downstairs [daʊnˈsteəz]
unter under ['ʌndə]
Unterrichtsstunde lesson ['lesn]
Unterschied difference ['dɪfrəns]
Urlaub holiday ['hɒlədeɪ]

V

Vater father ['fɑːðə]
Vati dad [dæd]
verfolgen follow ['fɒləʊ]
vergessen forget [fəˈget] **Ich habe meine Hausaufgaben vergessen.** I forgot my homework. [fəˈgɒt] **nicht vergessen** remember [rɪˈmembə]
verirren: Ich habe mich nicht verlaufen/verirrt. I'm not lost. [lɒst]
Verkauf sale [seɪl]
verlassen: (jemanden) **verlassen** leave [liːv]
verlaufen: Ich habe mich nicht verlaufen/verirrt. I'm not lost. [lɒst]
verliebt (in) in love (with) [lʌv]
verlieren lose [luːz]

vermissen miss [mɪs]
verrückt crazy ['kreɪzi]
verschieden different ['dɪfrənt]
verstecken, sich verstecken
  hide [haɪd]
verstehen understand [ʌndə'stænd]
verwenden use [juːz]
viel/e lots of [lɒts] **In der Küche
  ist zu viel los.** The kitchen is
  too busy. ['bɪzi] **Viele Grüße …**
  (Briefschluss) Best wishes ['wɪʃɪz]
vielleicht maybe ['meɪbi]
vier four [fɔː]
Viertel quarter ['kwɔːtə] **viertel
  nach 6** quarter past 6 [pɑːst]
  viertel vor 7 quarter to 7 [tu], [tə]
violett purple ['pɜːpl]
Vogel bird [bɜːd]
voll full [fʊl] **die Nase voll haben**
  feel fed up [fed 'ʌp]
von from [frɒm] **von Montag bis
  Freitag** from Monday to Friday
vor *(örtlich)* in front of [ɪn 'frʌnt
  əv]; *(zeitlich)* before [bɪ'fɔː]
  viertel vor 7 quarter to 7 [tu], [tə]
vorbei: vorbei sein be over ['əʊvə]
  die Schule ist aus/vorbei school
  is out [aʊt]
vorbereiten: sich vorbereiten (auf)
  get ready (for) ['redi]
vormittags: 9 Uhr vormittags
  9 am [eɪ'em]
vorziehen: ich würde … vorziehen
  I'd prefer … [prɪ'fɜː]

W

wahr true [truː]
wandern walk [wɔːk]
wann? when? [wen] **Wann hast
  du Geburtstag?** When's
  (= when is) your birthday?
war: er war nicht he wasn't (= was
  not) **es war Freitag** it was Friday
waren: sie waren im Bus
  they were on the bus [wɜː], [wə]
warten (auf) wait (for) [weɪt]
warum? why? [waɪ]
was? what? [wɒt] **Was ist los?**
  What is it? **Was ist mit dir?**
  What about you? [wɒt əbaʊt 'juː]
  Was (Wie viel) kosten? How
  much are …? [haʊ 'mʌtʃ] **Was
  (Wie viel) kostet?** How much
  is …?
Wasser water ['wɔːtə] **das Wasser steigt** the sea's coming in
wecken wake [weɪk]
Wecker alarm clock [ə'lɑːm klɒk]

Weg way [weɪ] **auf dem Weg zu/
  nach …** on the way to …
weg away [ə'weɪ]
weggehen leave [liːv]
wehtun: Mein Bein tut weh.
  I have a sore leg. [sɔː]
Weide field [fiːld] **auf der
  Weide** in the field
weil because [bɪ'kɒz]
weiß white [waɪt]
weitere more [mɔː]
weiterführende Schule (GB)
  community college [kə'mjuːnəti
  kɒlɪdʒ]
welche(r, s)? what? [wɒt]
  **Auf welcher Seite sind wir? /
  Auf welcher Seite steht das?**
  What page is it?
Welt world [wɜːld]
Wendung *(Redewendung)* phrase
  [freɪz]
wenig: ein wenig some [sʌm], [səm]
wenn when [wen]
wer? who? [huː] **Wer bist du? /
  Wer seid ihr?** Who are you?
Werbung advert ['ædvɜːt]
werden: ich werde … mitbringen
  I'm going to bring … ['gəʊɪŋ tə]
wert: Es ist sein Geld wert. It's
  good value. ['væljuː]
Wettstreit *(im Rap)* battle ['bætl]
wichtig important [ɪm'pɔːtnt]
wie *(ähnlich wie; so wie)* like [laɪk]
wie? how? [haʊ] **Wie alt bist du?**
  How old are you? [haʊ 'əʊld ɑː juː]
  Wie geht es dir/euch/Ihnen?
  How are you? **Wie geht's? / Wie
  läuft's?** How's it going? **Wie ist
  es? / Wie sieht es aus?** What's
  it like? [laɪk] **Wie spät ist es?**
  What's the time?
wieder again [ə'gen]
Wiedersehen: Auf Wiedersehen!
  Goodbye. [gʊd'baɪ]
wild wild [waɪld]
Willkommen in Plymouth.
  Welcome to Plymouth. ['welkəm]
winken wave [weɪv]
wir we [wi], [wiː] **wir sind** we're
  (= we are) [wɪə], [wi 'ɑː]
wirklich really ['riːəli], ['rɪəli];
  real [rɪəl]
wissen know [nəʊ]
wo? where? [weə] **Wo kommst
  du her?** Where are you from?
Woche week [wiːk]
Wochenende weekend [wiːk'end]
wohin? where? [weə]

Wohnblock block of flats
  ['blɒk əv flæts]
wohnen live [lɪv]
Wohnung flat [flæt]
Wohnzimmer living room
  ['lɪvɪŋ ruːm]
wollen want [wɒnt] *etwas
  sein wollen* want to be
Workshop *(Kurs)* workshop
  ['wɜːkʃɒp]
Wort word [wɜːd]
Wörterbuch dictionary ['dɪkʃənri]
Wörternetz mind map ['maɪnd mæp]
Wörterverzeichnis *(alphabetisch)* dictionary ['dɪkʃənri]
Wortnetz network ['netwɜːk]
**wünschen: Ich wünsche dir einen
  schönen Tag.** Have a good day.
**würde: Ich komme sehr gern. /
  Ich würde sehr gern kommen.**
  I'd love to come. (= I would love
  to come.) [wʊd] **ich würde …
  vorziehen** I'd prefer … [prɪ'fɜː]
Wurst sausage ['sɒsɪdʒ]
Würstchen sausage ['sɒsɪdʒ]

Z

Zahl number ['nʌmbə]
zehn ten [ten]
Zeichen sign [saɪn]
zeigen show [ʃəʊ]
Zeit time [taɪm]
Zentrum centre ['sentə]
Ziffer number ['nʌmbə]
Zimmer room [ruːm], [rʊm]
Zoo zoo [zuː]
zu *(örtlich)* to [tu], [tə] **Zeit zu
  essen** time to eat
zu alt too old [tuː]
zu Hause at home [ət 'həʊm]
  bei ihrer Mutter zu Hause
  at her mum's house
zubereiten *(Essen)* cook [kʊk]
zuerst first [fɜːst]
Zuhause home [həʊm]
zuhören listen ['lɪsn]
zumachen close [kləʊz]
zurück back [bæk]
zusammen together [tə'geðə]
zwei two [tuː]
zweite(r, s) second ['sekənd]
zwischen between [bɪ'twiːn]
zwölf twelve [twelv]

English sounds

[iː]	green, he, sea	[b]	bike, table, verb
[ɑː]	ask, class, car, park	[p]	pen, paper, shop
[ɔː]	or, ball, door, four, morning	[d]	day, window, good
[uː]	ruler, blue, too, two, you	[t]	ten, letter, at
[ɜː]	early, her, girl, work, T-shirt	[g]	go, again, bag
[ɪ]	in, big, expensive	[k]	kitchen, car, back
[e]	yes, bed, again, breakfast	[m]	man, remember, mum
[æ]	animal, apple, black, cat	[n]	no, one, ten
[ʌ]	mum, bus, colour	[ŋ]	wrong, young, uncle, thanks
[ɒ]	song, on, dog, what	[l]	like, old, small
[ʊ]	book, good, pullover	[r]	ruler, friend, sorry
[ə]	again, today, a sister	[w]	we, where, one
[i]	happy, monkey	[j]	yes, you, uniform
		[f]	family, after, laugh
[eɪ]	name, eight, play, great	[v]	very, seven, have
[aɪ]	I, time, right, my	[s]	six, poster, yes
[ɔɪ]	boy, toilet, noise	[z]	zoo, quiz, his, music, please
[əʊ]	old, no, road, yellow	[ʃ]	she, station, English
[aʊ]	now, house	[ʒ]	usually, revision, garage
[eə]	where, pair, share, their	[tʃ]	child, teacher, watch
[ɪə]	here, dear	[dʒ]	job, German, project, orange
[ʊə]	tour	[θ]	thing, three, bathroom, both
		[ð]	the, father, with
		[h]	house, who, behind

> Am besten kannst du dir die Aussprache der einzelnen Lautzeichen einprägen, wenn du dir zu jedem Zeichen ein einfaches Wort merkst – das [iː] ist der **green**-Laut, das [eɪ] ist der **name**-Laut usw.

The English alphabet

a	[eɪ]	**h**	[eɪtʃ]	**o**	[əʊ]	**v**	[viː]
b	[biː]	**i**	[aɪ]	**p**	[piː]	**w**	['dʌbljuː]
c	[siː]	**j**	[dʒeɪ]	**q**	[kjuː]	**x**	[eks]
d	[diː]	**k**	[keɪ]	**r**	[ɑː]	**y**	[waɪ]
e	[iː]	**l**	[el]	**s**	[es]	**z**	[zed]
f	[ef]	**m**	[em]	**t**	[tiː]		
g	[dʒiː]	**n**	[en]	**u**	[juː]		

NUMBERS

English numbers

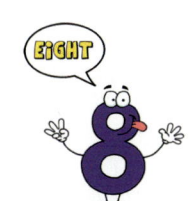

0 **oh, zero, nil** [əʊ, ˈzɪərəʊ, nɪl]
1 **one** [wʌn]
2 **two** [tuː]
3 **three** [θriː]
4 **four** [fɔː]
5 **five** [faɪv]
6 **six** [sɪks]
7 **seven** [ˈsevn]
8 **eight** [eɪt]
9 **nine** [naɪn]
10 **ten** [ten]

11 **eleven** [ɪˈlevn]
12 **twelve** [twelv]
13 **thirteen** [θɜːˈtiːn]
14 **fourteen** [fɔːˈtiːn]
15 **fifteen** [fɪfˈtiːn]
16 **sixteen** [sɪksˈtiːn]
17 **seventeen** [sevnˈtiːn]
18 **eighteen** [eɪˈtiːn]
19 **nineteen** [naɪnˈtiːn]
20 **twenty** [ˈtwenti]

21 **twenty-one** [twentiˈwʌn]
22 **twenty-two** [twentiˈtuː]
23 **twenty-three** [twentiˈθriː]
...

30 **thirty** [ˈθɜːti]
40 **forty** [ˈfɔːti]
50 **fifty** [ˈfɪfti]
60 **sixty** [ˈsɪksti]
70 **seventy** [ˈsevnti]
80 **eighty** [ˈeɪti]
90 **ninety** [ˈnaɪnti]
100 **a / one hundred**
     [ə / wʌn ˈhʌndrəd]

101 **one hundred and one**
102 **one hundred and two**
...

1st **first** [fɜːst]
2nd **second** [ˈsekənd]
3rd **third** [θɜːd]
4th **fourth** [fɔːθ]
5th **fifth** [fɪfθ]
6th **sixth** [sɪksθ]
7th **seventh** [ˈsevnθ]
8th **eighth** [eɪtθ]
9th **ninth** [naɪnθ]
10th **tenth** [tenθ]

11th **eleventh** [ɪˈlevnθ]
12th **twelfth** [twelfθ]
13th **thirteenth** [θɜːˈtiːnθ]
14th **fourteenth** [fɔːˈtiːnθ]
15th **fifteenth** [fɪfˈtiːnθ]
16th **sixteenth** [sɪksˈtiːnθ]
17th **seventeenth** [sevnˈtiːnθ]
18th **eighteenth** [eɪˈtiːnθ]
19th **nineteenth** [naɪnˈtiːnθ]
20th **twentieth** [ˈtwentiəθ]

21st **twenty-first** [twentiˈfɜːst]
22nd **twenty-second** [twentiˈsekənd]
23rd **twenty-third** [twentiˈθɜːd]
...

30th **thirtieth** [ˈθɜːtiəθ]
40th **fortieth** [ˈfɔːtiəθ]
50th **fiftieth** [ˈfɪftiəθ]
60th **sixtieth** [ˈsɪkstiəθ]
70th **seventieth** [ˈsevntiəθ]
80th **eightieth** [ˈeɪtiəθ]
90th **ninetieth** [ˈnaɪntiəθ]
100th **hundredth** [ˈhʌndrədθ]

101st **hundred and first**
102nd **hundred and second**
...

Du und dein Lehrer/deine Lehrerin

Guten Morgen, Herr/Frau …
Guten Tag, Herr …
Entschuldigung, dass ich zu spät komme.
Kann ich bitte das Fenster öffnen/zumachen?
Kann ich bitte zur Toilette gehen?
Auf Wiedersehen!/Bis morgen.

You and your teacher

Good morning, Mr/Mrs/Miss … (bis 12 Uhr)
Good afternoon, Mr … (ab 12 Uhr)
Sorry, I'm late.
Can I open/close the window, please?
Can I go to the toilet, please?
Goodbye./See you tomorrow.

Hausaufgaben und Übungen

Es tut mir leid, ich habe mein Schulheft nicht dabei.
Ich verstehe die Übung nicht.
Ich kann Nummer 3 nicht lösen.
Entschuldigung, ich bin noch nicht fertig.
Ich habe … Ist das auch richtig?
Es tut mir leid, das weiß ich nicht.
Was haben wir (als Hausaufgabe) auf?

Homework and exercises

Sorry, I have no exercise book.
I don't understand this exercise.
I can't do number 3.
Sorry, I haven't finished.
I have … Is that right?
Sorry, I don't know.
What's for homework?

Du brauchst Hilfe

Können Sie mir bitte helfen?
Auf welcher Seite sind wir/steht das?
Was heißt … auf Englisch/Deutsch?
Können Sie das bitte an die Tafel schreiben?
Kann ich das auf Deutsch sagen?
Können Sie/Kannst du bitte lauter sprechen?
Können Sie das bitte noch einmal sagen/abspielen?

You need help

Can you help me, please?
What page is it, please?
What's … in English/German?
Can you write it on the board, please?
Can I say it in German?
Can you speak louder, please?
Can you say/play that again, please?

Partnerarbeit

Kann ich mit Julian arbeiten?
Du bist dran.
Lass uns ein … machen/zeichnen.
Lass uns die Geschichte/den Dialog spielen.

Work with a partner

Can I work with Julian?
It's your turn.
Let's make/draw a …
Let's act the story/dialogue.

What your teacher says

Listen, please./Quiet, please.
Open your books at page 24.
Do exercise 5 for homework, please.
Where's your book, David?
Try again!
That's really good!
That's all for today. You can go.

Was dein Lehrer/deine Lehrerin sagt

Hört bitte zu./Ruhe bitte.
Schlagt bitte Seite 24 auf.
Macht bitte Übung 5 als Hausaufgabe.
Wo ist dein Buch, David?
Versuche es noch einmal.
Das ist wirklich gut!
Das ist alles für heute. Ihr könnt gehen.

Diese Arbeitsanweisungen findest du häufig im Schülerbuch

Act the dialogue / the scenes for the class.	Spiel(t) den Dialog / die Szenen vor der Klasse.
Ask questions. / Ask different partners.	Stelle Fragen. / Frage verschiedene Partner/innen.
Answer the questions (about the story).	Beantworte die Fragen (über die Geschichte).
… as many as you can.	… so viele wie du kannst.
Before you listen / read / …	Bevor du hörst / liest …
Choose a picture / the right answer.	Wähle ein Bild / die richtige Antwort aus.
Compare with a partner.	Vergleiche mit einem Partner / einer Partnerin.
Complete the questions / the rules / the sentences.	Vervollständige die Fragen / die Regeln / die Sätze.
Copy and complete the table / your learner log.	Schreibe die Tabelle / dein Lerntagebuch ab und vervollständige sie / es.
Correct the sentences.	Berichtige die Sätze.
Fill in the table.	Fülle die Tabelle aus.
Find the right answers.	Finde die richtigen Antworten.
Find a heading for each photo.	Finde eine Überschrift für jedes Foto.
Finish the sentences.	Vervollständige die Sätze.
Go to page 25.	Gehe zu Seite 25.
Listen and check / repeat / write.	Hör zu und überprüfe / wiederhole / schreibe auf.
Look at the brochure / photos / pictures.	Sieh die Broschüre / Fotos / Bilder an.
Make a dialogue / a mind map / a table.	Fertige einen Dialog / eine Mindmap / eine Tabelle an.
Match the sentences / headings with the pictures.	Ordne die Sätze / Überschriften den Bildern zu.
Pick a card / words from the box.	Nimm eine Karte / Wörter aus dem Kasten.
Point at the right picture.	Zeige auf des richtige Bild.
Practise with a partner.	Übe mit einem Partner / einer Partnerin.
Put the answers in the right order.	Bringe die Antworten in die richtige Reihenfolge.
Read the text / story.	Lies den Text / die Geschichte.
Right or wrong?	Richtig oder falsch?
Swap partners.	Tausche den Partner / die Partnerin.
Talk about …	Sprich über …
Talk to different partners.	Sprich mit verschiedenen Partnern / Partnerinnen.
Tell the class.	Erzähle das der Klasse.
Use your notes / table.	Benutze deine Notizen / Tabelle.
Walk around.	Gehe herum.
Write a dialogue / sentences about you.	Schreibe einen Dialog / Sätze über dich.
You can put it in your DOSSIER.	Du kannst es in deinem Dossier abheften.

First names (Vornamen)
Boys

Adam ['ædəm]
Alan ['ælən]
Alex ['ælɪks]
Andrew ['ændru:]
Ben [ben]
Benny ['beni]
Bob [bɒb]
Bunny ['bʌni]
Casper ['kæspə]
Charlie ['tʃɑ:li]
Conor ['kɒnə]
Cyril ['sɪrɪl]
Daniel ['dænjəl]
David ['deɪvɪd]
Finn [fɪn]
Grump [grʌmp]
Harry ['hæri]
Jack [dʒæk]
Jimmy ['dʒɪmi]
Joe [dʒəʊ]
Kevin ['kevɪn]
Luca ['lu:kə]
Owen ['əʊɪn]
Paul [pɔ:l]
Pete [pi:t]
Peter ['pi:tə]
Rick [rɪk]
Rob [rɒb]
Sam [sæm]
Simon ['saɪmən]
Steve [sti:v]
Tim [tɪm]
Timothy ['tɪməθi]
Toby ['təʊbi]
Tom [tɒm]
William ['wɪljəm]
Zack [zæk]

First names (Vornamen)
Girls

Alisha [ə'lɪʃə]
Amanda [ə'mændə]
Amy ['eɪmi]
Anna ['ænə]
Babe [beɪb]
Berry ['beri]
Connie ['kɒni]
Daisy ['deɪzi]
Ellie ['eli]
Emily ['eməli]
Emma ['emə]
Frisky ['frɪski]
Gemma ['dʒemə]

Grace [greɪs]
Helen ['helən]
Jackie ['dʒæki]
Janice ['dʒænɪs]
Josie ['dʒəʊsi]
Katie ['keɪti]
Laura ['lɔ:rə]
Lily ['lɪli]
Linda ['lɪndə]
Liz [lɪz]
Lorna ['lɔ:nə]
Lucy ['lu:si]
Lulu ['lu:lu:]
Lynn [lɪn]
Pia ['pi:ə]
Ruby ['ru:bi]
Sandy ['sændi]
Sarah ['seərə]
Shanaze [ʃə'neɪz]
Susan ['su:zən]
Tamara [tə'mɑ:rə]
Tracy ['treɪsi]
Uma ['u:mə]
Zainab ['zeɪnæb]
Zoe ['zəʊi]

Family names / Surnames
(Familiennamen)

Boateng ['bwɑ:teŋ]
Borowski [bə'rɒvski]
Brown [braʊn]
Cole [kəʊl]
Dixon ['dɪksən]
Donovan ['dɒnəvən]
Finden ['fɪndən]
Ford [fɔ:d]
Gray [greɪ]
Hall [hɔ:l]
Johnson ['dʒɒnsn]
Lee [li:]
Martin ['mɑ:tɪn]
Newton ['nju:tən]
Osmanovic [ɒz'mænəvɪtʃ]
Reade [ri:d]
Rooney ['ru:ni]
Victor ['vɪktə]
Young [jʌŋ]

Place names
(Ortsnamen)

America [ə'merɪkə]
Berlin [bɜ:'lɪn]
Bosnia ['bɒzniə]

Boston ['bɒstən]
Bretonside ['bretənsaɪd]
Bristol ['brɪstl]
Cawsand ['kɔ:sænd]
Central Park [sentrəl 'pɑ:k]
Charles Street ['tʃɑ:lz stri:t]
Dartmoor ['dɑ:tmɔ:]
Dartmouth ['dɑ:tməθ]
Drake Circus [dreɪk 'sɜ:kəs]
Exeter ['eksɪtə]
Fore Street ['fɔ: stri:t]
George Street ['dʒɔ:dʒ stri:t]
Ghana ['gɑ:nə]
Gratefeld Street ['greɪtfeld stri:t]
Great Field Road [greɪt fi:ld 'rəʊd]
Greatfield Street ['greɪtfi:ld stri:t]
Greenbank Road [gri:nbæŋk 'rəʊd]
Harbour Road [hɑ:bə 'rəʊd]
Hill Road [hɪl 'rəʊd]
Hoe Lane [həʊ 'leɪn]
Hoe Park [həʊ 'pɑ:k]
Kingsand ['kɪŋsænd]
London ['lʌndən]
Malaga ['mæləgə]
Merryweather Farm [meriweðə 'fɑ:m]
New York [nju: 'jɔ:k]
Plymouth ['plɪməθ]
Plymouth Barbican [plɪməθ 'bɑ:bɪkən]
Plymouth Hoe (the Hoe) [plɪməθ 'həʊ]
Plymouth Pavilions [plɪməθ pə'vɪliənz]
Raglan Road [ræglən 'rəʊd]
Reel Cinema [ri:l 'sɪnəmə]
Sherwell ['ʃɜ:wel]
Tamar ['teɪmɑ:]
Theatre Royal [θɪətə 'rɔɪəl]
Tinside Lido [tɪnsaɪd 'laɪdəʊ]
Wembley ['wembli]
Windsor Road [wɪnzə 'rəʊd]
Windsor Street ['wɪnzə stri:t]
Winsbury Road [wɪnzbəri 'rəʊd]

Woodlands ['wʊdləndz]
Woolwell ['wʊlwel]

Other names
(Andere Namen)

Big Bash [bɪg 'bæʃ]
Digicomp ['dɪdʒikɒmp]
Dreamrooms ['dri:mru:mz]
Eggbuckland Community College [eg'bʌklənd kə'mju:nəti kɒlɪdʒ]
Eggy ['egi]
Francis and the Drakes ['frɑ:nsɪs ənd ðə 'dreɪks]
Jam Band ['dʒæm bænd]
Kaiser Chiefs ['kaɪsə tʃi:fs]
Manchester United ['mæntʃɪstə ju'naɪtɪd]
Phones 4U [fəʊnz fə 'ju:]
Plymouth Argyle [plɪməθ ɑ:'gaɪl]
Plymouth High School [plɪməθ 'haɪ sku:l]
PMZ (Plymouth Music Zone) [pi: əm 'zed], [plɪməθ 'mju:zɪk zəʊn]
Roof Raisers ['ru:f reɪzəz]
Streetbeatz ['stri:tbi:ts]
Travelline ['trævəlaɪn]

Illustrationen

Roland Beier, Berlin (Umschlaginnenseite 1 Edinburgh castle icon (M); S. 201 unten); **Carlos Borrell**, Berlin (Umschlaginnenseite 1 The British Isles (M)); Christian Görke, Berlin (S. 52/53); **Cornelsen Schulverlage** (S. 44 oben: Arnold; S. 75 clocks: Arnold; S. 91 mindmap: Arnold; S. 134: Bensmann; S. 140: Arnold; S. 147 unten: Arnold; S. 153: Bensmann; S. 172 mindmaps: Arnold); **Jeongsook Lee**, Heidelberg (Umschlaginnenseite 1 icons (M); S. 102; S. 107; S. 122; S. 125; S. 128; S. 157; S. 167; S. 170 exercise book; S. 171; S. 172 oben; S. 175; S. 176; S. 178 oben re.; S. 179 Mitte, unten; S. 186; S. 189; S. 190; S. 191; S. 193; S. 194; S. 195; S. 197; S. 198; S. 199; S. 200; S. 201; S. 203; S. 206; S. 207; S. 208; S. 209; S. 210; S. 211; S. 212; S. 213; S. 215; S. 217; S. 218; S. 219; S. 221; S. 244; S. 245); **David Norman**, Meerbusch (S. 72; S. 74 Bild A-D; S. 88; S. 95; S. 115 (u. 154); S. 149; S. 160 oben u. unten; S. 161; S. 162; S. 164-166); **Elwood H. Smith**, Rhinebeck, U.S.A. (S. 9 Cyril; S. 17 Sandy; S. 21; S. 22; S. 26; S. 30 unten Bild A-D; S. 31; S. 44 unten; S. 46; S. 48 unten; S. 49; S. 56 oben; S. 59; S. 69; S. 83 unten; S. 89; S. 106; S. 111; S. 113; S. 114; S. 138 oben; S. 147 oben u. Mitte; S. 158-159; S. 177; S. 178 oben li., unten; S. 179 oben; S. 180; S. 182); **Steffen Wolff**, Brohl-Lützing (S. 8/9 oben; S. 12; S. 14-15; S. 16; S. 18; S. 23 (u. 129); S. 24; S. 30 oben Bild A, B; S. 32; S. 36; S. 38; S. 39; S. 41; S. 42-43 (u. 136); S. 45; S. 48 oben; S. 50 two boys (u. 127); S. 51; S. 54; S. 55; S. 56 Bild 1-4; S. 58; S. 60; S. 64; S. 65; S. 81-84 oben; S. 90; S. 96; S. 100 oben, Mitte li., unten; S. 101 oben li.; S. 116-119; S. 126; S. 127; S. 132; S. 135; S. 138 Bild 1-4)

Bildquellen

Susan Abbey/Frank Donoghue, Nenagh (S. 84 Bild A-D); **Alamy**, Abingdon (S. 8: Picture Partners; S. 11 Bild 5: image100; S. 12 crocodile: moodboard, hamster: Wildlife GmbH; S. 13 games console (u. 185): mediablitzimages (uk) Limited/Martin Lee, car (u. 185): Oleksiy Maksymenko Photography; S. 19 scarf: kris Mercer; S. 34 Bild 5: Elizabeth Whiting & Associates/ ewastock kitchens; S. 35 Bild 3 kitchen (M): Andrew Butterton, Bild 4: Brian Hoffman, Bild 9: Ivan Barta; S. 39 Bild 1: Elizabeth Whiting & Associates/ewastock DIY, Bild 11 re.: Big Cheese Photo LLC/Big Cheese Special; S. 52 Bild 1 dad, Grace (M): Golden Pixels LLC/ Kablonk!; S. 53 Bild 5: Neil Cooper; S. 61 oben: Peter Titmuss; S. 62 Bild 1 dad (M) u. Bild 2 Grace (M): Golden Pixels LLC/ Kablonk!; S. 67 market: Marc Hill; S. 72 Bild C: The Photo-library Wales/Rex Moreton; S. 75 Bild A: Kuttig – People, Bild B: Stephen Bardens, S. 92/93: Marc Hill; S. 92 Bild A ferry (M): Marc Hill; S. 110 A oben: Brian Mitchell, unten re.: Iain Davidson Photographic, unten li.: snappdragon; S. 111 E oben li.: Carpe Diem – France; S. 118 oben re.: ian woolcock; S. 124 unten: moodboard; S. 185 biology: ftStop/Adam Bum, chemistry: Juice Images/Juice Images242, ethics: Eyebyte, home economics li., re. (M) u. woodwork: MBI/Stockbroker, physics: Images Source/IE371; S. 186 dad (M): F1 online digitale Bildagentur GmbH, family (M): Big Cheese Photo LLC; S. 187 bank: flab Istr); **AP Images**, Frankfurt/Main (S. 71: AP Photo/Plymouth Herald/ Amy Standford); **Bank of England** (S. 64 banknote (u. 141) and **The British Royal Mint** S. 64 coins (u. 141), used by permission); **Trevor Burrows Photography**, Plymouth (S. 10 Bild 1-4; S. 11 Bild 1; S. 12 Berry; S. 16 Bild A (M, ohne Hund), Bild B; S. 17 Bild C, D; S. 18; S. 20; S. 23; S. 24; S. 25 Bild 5, 6; S. 28; S. 31 Ellie (M), Berry (M) (u. 134); S. 34 street signs (M); S. 34 Bild 1, 2; S. 37 Zoe, Conor, Ellie; S. 40 Ellie; S. 46; S. 52 Bild 1 mum, Luca, Jack (M), Bild 6; S. 53 Bild 2, 3, 4; S. 62 Bild 1 Luca, Jack, mum (M), Bild 2, 3; S. 63 Bild 4 Jack, Luca (M); Bild 5, 6, 7; S. 65 oben (M), S. 72 Berry; S. 73 Bild D, E, F; S. 76 oben; S. 77 Bild A Berry, pony (M); Bild B-E; S. 78; S. 80; S. 84 Bild E; S. 89; S. 90; S. 92 Bild A dad (M), Bild B; S. 93 Bild D; S. 94 unten; S. 95 unten; S. 98 Bild A-D; S. 99 Ellie, Adam; S. 107; S. 109; S. 112 oben; S. 114; S. 139; S. 151; S. 176 Ellie, Luca, Adam, Ms Lee, Berry; S. 179 oben; S. 180 oben re., unten; S. 181 oben, Adam; S. 182 oben);

Clipdealer.com (S. 190: Feverpitch); **Corbis**, Düsseldorf (S. 68 Bild 8: Corbis Sports/Matthew Ashton/AMA; S. 113 bodyboard: Corbis Yellow/Laurence Manning; S. 163 unten li.: Corbis Sports/ Tim de Waele); **Cornelsen Schulverlage**, Berlin (S. 10 unten: Griebel; S. 11 cycling: Griebel; S. 13 Luca: Zieschang; S. 13 cards: Bensmann; S. 16/17 background: Zieschang; S. 25 Mitte: Bensmann; S. 29 film reel portraits (u. 47 u. 67 u. 87 u. 105 u. 121), Mitte, unten; S. 47; S. 52 theatre, museum, church, police station: Bensmann; S. 61 unten: Bensmann; S. 64 (u. 141): icocat; S. 67 Bild 1-4; S. 67 Hoe, Lido, shopping centre, aquarium; cinema: Bensmann; S. 87; S. 93 Bild C: Bensmann; S. 98 Bild E: Bensmann; S. 104 Bild A-H: Bensmann; S. 105 Mitte cafe, unten; S. 118 oben li.: Bensmann; S. 121 Bild A-D, unten; S. 124 oben: Bensmann; S. 156 oben: Griebel; **Cornwall365.co.uk** (S. 117 Mitte re.); **Eggbuckland Community College**, Plymouth (S. 95 Eggy logo); **Fotolia.com** (S. 13 frisbee: Glenda Powers; S. 184 in-line skating: Kathrin39; S. 191 oben: Michelle Robek, unten: Monkey Business; S. 202 unten: Tamas Vargyasi); **Getty Images**, München (S. 11 Bild 4: Image Source, Bild 7: Sean Justice, Bild 8: Chris Ryan, drawing: Fuse; S. 32: Comstock Images/Thinkstock Images; S. 35 Bild 7: Bob Stevens; S. 163 Mitte: Bryn Lennon; S. 169 oben: Flickr/Sergio Amiti; S. 184 canoeing: Flickr/An Lumatic image, collecting stamps: Photodisc/Vasiliki Varvaki; S. 187 town hall: Photolibrary/Glenn Leblanc); **iStockphoto.com** (S. 11 Bild 2: Michael Braun, Bild 6: Hedda Gjerpen; S. 12 bird: Mr_Jamsey, elephant: Peter Malsbury, snake: VMJones, rabbit: Nikola Spansenoski; S. 13 skateboard: Erdosain, phone (u. 185): Baris Simsek; S. 19 sisters: knape; S. 26 ten pencils: mahesh14, exercise book: Nikolaas Boden, hole punch: Alex Avich, diary: Shebeko; S. 33 oben (u. 126 u. 192): Cliff Parnell; S. 37 Aunt Lorna: ranplett, Jackie: Kelly Cline, Finn: manley099; S. 39 Bild 3: Floortje, Bild 5: David Morgan, Bild 6: Oleg Prikhodko, Bild 12 (2x): paul kline; S. 50 tae kwon do clothes: tarras79; S. 55 hoddie: Fabio Cecconello; S. 68 Bild 2: Barbara Helgason, Bild 3: Vasiliki Varvaki, Bild 4: Jello5700, Bild 7: Mikkel William Nielsen; S. 91 budgie: jeridu; S. 94 Bild I: Gary Radler; S. 97 guitar player (M): Jamie Carrol; S. 103 Bild B, Mitte: Tatiana Popova, Bild D: Amanda Rohde, unten (u. 153 u. 162): 77studio; S. 104 oben: Nikki Bidgood; S. 110 B boats: Marco Maccarini; S. 111 D oben re.: Carmen Martínez Banús; S. 113 suncream: onur kocamaz; S. 137 school bag: Graça Victoria, homework: Photo_Concepts, village: fotoVoyager; S. 160 oben: Richard Hobson; S. 161 unten re.: Edward Shaw; S. 173 oben: LowfatImages; S. 180 oben li.: Steven van Soldt; S. 184 boxing: Chris Schmidt, ice skating: YinYang, mosque: Edward Shaw, sports club: Chris Schmidt; S. 188 clarinet: Christopher Futcher; S. 192 unten girls: Silvia Boratti); **Jason Marker Photography**, Chelmsford (S. 110 A Mitte); **mauritius images**, Mittenwald (S. 187 youth centre: Maskot); **Photolibrary**, London (S. 11 Bild 3: pixtal Images, chess: Fotosearch Premium; S. 19 oben: Imagesource; S. 156 unten (u. 162) (M): Fresh Food Images/Tony Robbins; S. 161 unten li.: Fresh Food Images/Heather Brown; S. 187 town hall: Glenn Leblanc); **Plymouth Music Zone**, Plymouth (S. 97 PMZ logo); **Okapia**, Frankfurt/Main (S. 12 rat: J-L Klein & M-L Hubert/ OKAPIA); **Thomas Schulz**, Teupitz (S. 57; S. 75 unten; S. 76 unten); **Shutterstock.com** (S. 9: wow; S. 12 cat: Irina Bondareva, bear: red-feniks, monkey: Simone van den Berg, dog: Eastimages, fish: Ekaterina V. Borisova, tiger: Tiago Jorge da Silva Estima; S. 13 inline-skates: nito, MP3 player: graja, scooter: Coprid, bike: Attl Tibor, Mädchen unten re.: Andrey-Popov; S. 13 guitar (u. 185): Lebedinski Vladislav, book (u. 185): Vakhrushev Pavel, bag (u. 185): Nokolay Postnikov, laptop (u. 185): Elnur, key ring (u. 184): dean bertonclj, watch (u. 185): Ronen, TV (u. 185): gordana, football (u. 185): Luis Luoro, girl: Andrey_Popov; S. 16 Bild A dog (M): Erik Lam; S. 19 unten li.: Monkey Business Images, Tim: Andrea Slatter, dog: Eric Isselée, unhappy smiley (u. 33 u. 71 u. 76 u. 91 u. 109 u. 125 u. 136 u. 143 u. 144 u. 170): Dawn Hudson, happy smiley (u. 33 u. 71 u. 76 u. 91 u. 109 u. 125 u. 136 u. 143 u. 144 u. 170): In-Finity; S. 21 unten: Syda

Productions; S. 25 unten (u. 83 u. 119 u. 146): Alhovik; S. 26 background pencils: Natticka, pencil sharpener: Gelpi, rubber: Chet, ruler: David Brimm, 10 pens: Volodymyr Krasyuk, pencil case: Brooke Becker, calculator: Fotoline; S. 27 Oleksii Sagitov; S. 33 light bulb: Marish; S. 34 background: Hitdelight; Bild 6: Chertanova; S. 35 background: Ala Alkhouskaya, Bild A bottle, bowl (M): Elena Schweitzer, chair (M): ekipaj, Bild 8: Uroš Medved; S. 37 Grandma Martin, Jackie: Olga Sapegina, Pete: Juriah Mosin, Grandma and Grandpa Cole: Stuart Monk, Uncle Andrew: Ioannis Pantzi, Steve, Lily: Yuri Arcurs, Owen: Elaine Willcock; S. 39 Bild 2: Margo Harrison, Bild 4: Viorel Sima, Bild 7: studiots, Bild 8: karam Miri, Bild 9: italianestro, Bild 10: terekhov igor, Bild 11 li.: Petrafler; S. 40 oben re.: Yuri Arcurs; S. 49 (u. 103 u. 127); S. 50 oben: Blend Images, bike: Paprikakubani, rugby ball: joingate, skateboard: Igorij, snowboard: sabri deniz kizil; S. 55 blazer: Karkas, tie: KULISH VICTORIIA, socks: Alexandr Makarov, shoes: Turumtaev Ildar, trainers: Ronen, pullover, skirt: Karkas, shirt: Boleslaw Kubica; S. 63 Bild 4 boy with red shirt (M): Tomasz Trojanowski; S. 66 Bild A dancer (M): Boobl, stage (M): Patricia Hofmeester, Bild B fireworks: Devmos (M); S. 66 Bild C sea (M): Strejman, 4 D cinema (M): Julien Tromeur, diver (M): Undersea Discoveries; S. 67 smileys: More Trendy Design here; S. 68 Bild 1: HABRDA, Bild 5: s_oleg, Bild 6 OlegD; S. 70 li.: SergiyN, re.: Gelpi; S. 72 Bild A: Graeme Dwes, Bild B: Elena Elisseeva; S. 73 Bild 1: jokerpro, Bild 2: Ivonne Wierink, Bild 3: aleks k, Bild 4: robertimages, Bild 5: Pichugin Dmitry, Bild 6: pgaborphotos, Bild 7: Geanina Bechea, Bild 8: Tom Grundy, Bild 9: Alexruss, Bild 10: nataliia Melnychuk, Bild 11: Maslov Dmitry, Bild 12: gillmar, unten re.: Natalia Sheinkin; S. 74 clock: Slavojub Pantelic; S. 75 Bild C: Michael Ransburg, Bild D: joyfuldesigns, Bild E: cynoclub, Bild F: fpolat69; S. 77 Bild A dog (M): Eric Isselée; S. 79 oben: Grigoryeva Liubov Dmitrievna, unten: Sergii Sergii Figurnyi; S. 82: Oleksiy Mark (u. 103 u. 162); S. 85: tisti; S. 86 hamster, goldfish, snake, monkey, rabbit: Klara Viskova, dog: Louis D. Slyono, donkey, llama: Albert Ziganshin, crocodile: Memo Angeles, penguin: Cory Thoman; S. 91 elephant: Four Oaks, guinea pig: E. Spek, tiger: Kitch Bain, polar bear: VikOl; S. 94 Bild A: Nitr, Bild B: Feng Yu, Bild C: Nayashkova Olga, Bild D: Nitr, Bild EER_09, Bild F: ronstik, Bild G: Vlue, Bild H: Joe Gough, Bild J: jon le-bon; S. 97 (M, ohne guitar player u. Logo): sita ram; S. 99 Bild 1 (u. 128): Tomasz Trojanowski, Bild 2 (u. 128): Monkey Business Images, Bild 3 (u. 128): Fotokostic, Bild 4 (u. 128): Kim Ruoff, Bild 5 (u. 128): qingqing, Bild 6 (u. 128): Monkey Business Images; S. 101 music makes a difference rapper: freelanceartist; S. 105 dancer: sparkdesign, singer: TEA, guitar player: AZ; S. 106 oben: haveseen, unten: Dan Costa; S. 110 B oben: CroMary, B girl canoeing: Elena Elisseeva, dog: Annette Shaff; S. 111 C: Morgan Lane Photo-graphy, D unten: Juriah Mosin; S. 112 scones: Picsfive, water: Nitr, crisps: Ewa Walicka, apples: Smit, cake: Picsfive, chocolate: urfin, biscuits: Aaron Amat, orange juice: Mark Herreid, oranges: rook76, sandwiches: Africa Studio, sausages: Kitch Bain; S. 113 beach: Raia, towels: Arogant, camera: Chiyacat, shorts: Kayros Stuio „Be Happy!", umbrella: Fotocrisis, frisbee: cretolamna, mobile (M): Ungor, speakers (M). Tatiana Popva, blanket: Mazzzur, swimsuit: Ruslan Kudrin, football: Olga Popova, tube: Fotokkden; S. 117 parchment (u. 118 u. 119): Anan Kaewkhammul; S. 120 Bild 1: Roman Sotola, Bild 2: Ghenadie, Bild 3: Renata Novackova, Bild 4: Albina Tiplyashina; S. 121 Bild 1: nicepictures, Bild 2: Ivonne Wierink, Bild 3: Nayashkova Olga, Bild 4: nito, Bild 5: Naturaldigital, Bild 6: vnlit, Bild 7: Roman Sigaev, Bild 8: marco mayer; S. 130 li.: Aivolie, re.: Raisa Kanareva; S. 137 pencil: DenisNata, trousers: Péter Gudella, garden: Sandra Cunningham, teacher: R.legosyn, house: dslaven, tie: Elnur, baby: Vasiliy Koval; S. 160 unten li.: Takra, unten re.: aispl; S. 162 oben li.: Michael C. Gray, oben re.: JCELy; S. 163 oben rechts: Pavel 1964, unten Mitte: Jorg Hackermann, unten re.: Snezana Skundric; S. 168 oben: Mark Winfrey, unten: Dhoxax; S. 169 Mitte: Efiplus, unten: steve estvanik; S. 170 oben: Rene Jansa,

hands: photolinc; S. 171 girl: Blend Images, elephant: Talvi, monkey, bear, cat, sheep, cow: Eric Isselée, guinea pig: vovan, chicken: s_oleg, rabbit: Stefan Petru Andronache; S. 173 oben li.: Ilya Adnriyanov, Mitte exclamation mark, light bulb: i359702, unten: Yayayoyo; S. 176 pencil: R-O-M-A, school bag: Podfoto, ruler: ref34985, flags (u. 178 u. 181 u. 182): Christopher Poliquin; S. 178 girls: PT Images; S. 184 basketball: Lorraine Swanson, climbing: Frances A. Miller, cycling: archana bhartia, doing athletics: max blain, drawing: Jeka, ice hockey: Govorov Pavel, listening to music: Goodluz, making models: Zivica Kerkez, skiing: Gorilla, snowboarding: Konstantin Shishkin, surfing the internet: LUCARELLI TEMISTOCLE, table tennis: JJpixs, taking photos: Jorg Hackermann; S. 185 class assembly: Monkey Business Images, projects: oliveromg, RE: Glam, social studies: Dawn Hudson, Spanish: alpturk33, special needs training: oliveromg; S. 187 factory: Lucschen, bus station: adrian beesley, train station: WH CHOW, bank: flab lstr, library: Stephen Coburn, airport: SBorisov, fast food restaurant: Blend Images, zoo: Glenda M. Powers, video shop: video shop: Pavel L Photo and Video, football stadium: Alexander Chaikin, department store: prim68, Wildscape/Jason Smalley, skate park: ARENA Creative; S. 188 meat: Paul Krugloff, vegetables: missanzi, basket: Hannamariah, special food: Ruben Pinto, birdseed li.: dusan964, birdseed re.: Chepe Nicoli, aquarium: MattJones, cage: Thomas Skjaeveland, bark: Eric Isselée, run: Martin Valigursky, jum: Norman Chan, cello: Fotokostic, saxophone: Anton Albert, recorder: Apollofoto, violin: Brian Chase, flute: Fotokostic, trumpet: Katrina Brown, keyboard: Nicole Gordine; S. 192 hamster: Subbotina Anna, rabbit: Stefan Petru Andronache; S. 198: Sofia; S. 200 Simon Krzic; S. 202 oben: Aksana Yakupava; S. 203: John Kasawa; S. 203: Arkady; S. 205 oben: Guy Erwood, unten: Magone; S. 206: Vasilius; S. 207: Gemenacom; S. 212 oben: Julián Rovagnati, unten: Andrjuss; S. 215 oben: Darrin Henry, unten li.: nito, unten Mitte: R. Gino Santa Maria, unten re.: Tiplyashin Anatoly; S. 216 oben: Suzanne Tucker, Mitte: Igor Dutina, unten: Angelika Smile; S. 217 Wallenrock; S. 219: Pete Saloutos; S. 220 oben: Ramona Heim, Mitte: Koshevnyk, unten li.: Julia Ivantsova, unten re.: Danicek; S. 221 oben: Vibrant Image Studio; S. 242: Laurie Barr; S. 243: HitToon.Com; **ullstein bild**, Berlin (S. 188 hutch: cuveland); **Visit Plymouth**, Plymouth (S. 66 Bild B festival logo (M))

Titelbild
Trevor Burrows Photography, Plymouth

Liedquelle
S. 53 *This is My City*. Text, music and copyright: Timothy Victor www.timothyvictor.com

Textquelle
S.86 *Muuuuuuummmmmmm* © Peter Dixon. Taken from "Read me out loud: Poems to rap, chant, whisper or shout for every day of the year." Chosen by Nick Toczek and Paul Cookson, page 259–260, Macmillan Children's Books 2007

Special thanks to:
The staff and students at **Eggbuckland Community College**, Plymouth and **Canoe Tamar**, Tavistock; **The Cawsand Ferry**, Plymouth/www.cawsandferry.co.uk; **Elvira's Café**, Plymouth; **The Miniature Pony Centre**, Dartmoor/www.miniature-ponycentre.com; **Plymouth Music Zone**, Plymouth, for inspiring and composing 'Music Makes a Difference'/www.plymouthmusiczone.org.uk; **The Strand Tea Rooms**, Plymouth; **The Tuck Shop**, Plymouth; **The National Marine Aquarium**, Plymouth/www.national-aquarium.co.uk; **Visit Plymouth**, Plymouth/www.visitplymouth.co.uk; **Woodlands Family Theme Park**, Totnes/www.woodlandspark.com; **Spirit of Adventure**, Yelverton/www.spirit-of-adventure.com